New St. Joseph

Handbook for Proclaimers of the Word

LITURGICAL YEAR C

2013

By
Rev. Jude Winkler, OFM Conv.

WITH THE "NEW AMERICAN BIBLE" TEXT
FROM THE REVISED SUNDAY LECTIONARY

C.B.   P.C.

CATHOLIC BOOK PUBLISHING CORP.
New Jersey

Published with the approval of the
Committee on Divine Worship
United States Conference of Catholic Bishops

ACKNOWLEDGMENTS

(T-86)

ISBN 978-0-89942-087-5

© 2012 by Catholic Book Publishing Corp., N.J.
Printed in the U.S.A.
www.catholicbookpublishing.com

CONTENTS

CONTENTS

INTRODUCTION

THE WORD OF GOD

"The word of God is living and effective, sharper than any two-edged sword, penetrating even between soul and spirit, joints and marrow, and able to discern reflections and thoughts of the heart" (Hebrews 4:12).

With these words, the author of the Letter to the Hebrews speaks of the power of the word of God. It has a profound effect both upon creation and upon our hearts. It was by the word that God created the heavens and the earth. The word is effective, for in Hebrew theology the word makes present and real the things that it proclaims. Thus, God speaks, and those things come into existence. God even shares the power of the word with us, for he commands Adam to name the animals he had created. By naming the animals, Adam is given dominion over all of creation.

The word is the communication of God's will. He reveals his word to the prophets who then proclaim it to the people of Israel. He gives his law that teaches them how to walk in God's ways. (Remember, the ten commandments are also called the "decalogue," which means the "ten words"). He sends wisdom to reveal his mysteries to his beloved chosen people. Wisdom instructs the foolish and brings them to the path of righteousness.

In the New Testament, we hear that the word of God is Jesus, the Son of God. The word of God existed in the beginning. It was communicated to God's people, Israel, throughout their history. Then, in the fullness of time, it was made flesh and dwelt among us.

Jesus proclaimed the word of God in word and deed to those who would listen and change their hearts. He promised the gift of the Holy Spirit so that the community could remember what he had done and understand what it all meant.

As the community of believers grew and matured, it realized that it needed to preserve their words about Jesus. Members of the community wrote letters, gospels, collections of stories, and even prophetic revelations so that they would know the life and teaching of Jesus and also what those things meant for their daily lives.

MINISTERS OF THE WORD

The Church affirmed that this word (the New Testament) and the word of revelation known as the Hebrew Scriptures (the Old Testament) were inspired by the Holy Spirit. She entrusted that word to the community. Some in the community were called to copy and preserve the word, others to study it, others to proclaim it liturgically, others to preach on how to apply it to their lives, etc.

As lectors, you share in the tradition of proclaiming the word to the community. This is not a responsibility to be taken lightly. God has called you to this mission. The Spirit has given you the gift of being able to present the word to the community and, even more important, the gift of being able to discern its meaning for yourself.

GIFT OF THE SPIRIT

Saint Paul speaks about how the Spirit gives these gifts to members of the community. These gifts are called charisms. Everyone has received gifts from the Lord that were given for the good of that community. Not all the gifts are the same. Not everyone has received the same gift. This is important, for it means that we need everyone and their gifts to make the community complete. If we do not allow certain members of the community to share their gifts, we will be subtly rejecting the gifts that the Spirit of God has given to us, and we will be lacking something of what we need to grow in the Spirit.

Your call to be a lector in the community is not your own choice, nor is it the choice of the pastor or committee that invited you to read at Mass. Rather, it is the Spirit who has called you. The Holy Spirit worked in and through various means (the pastor, the committee, the hunger in your own heart that made you volunteer for service, etc.) to bring you to this ministry.

Now, you must discern how to respond in the best manner possible to that call. It is not enough to say that if the Spirit called you, the Spirit will provide what is needed. As with all gifts of the Spirit, we must work to perform our ministry well. We are, as Saint Paul says in the First Letter to the Thessalonians, God's coworkers. While this is God's work, he has entrusted it to us. It has been said that we must do everything as if it depended upon us, realizing that it all depends upon the Lord.

This preparation involves working on the technique of presentation, but also working on our own hearts so that the things that we proclaim are proclaimed with a profound faith.

PREPARING THE READING

A first logical step in preparing for this service is to read and reread the text that we are going to proclaim. It is not enough to show up in the sacristy a few minutes before the Mass and read over the text once or twice. Preferably, we should have read it early in the week and often during the week.

This text should be read aloud. It might seem a bit embarrassing to read it out loud to ourselves, but it is essential. There are words and phrases that might appear to present no difficulty when we are reading them silently but that end up being much more difficult when we read them out loud.

We must check out the pronunciation of difficult words (especially unusual names). A Pronunciation Guide will be found on pages 419-430 to help you in this task.

If you do not know the meaning of certain words, it is always advisable to do a bit of research in a dictionary or some other source book.

Some of the liturgical texts that you will read are rather short and difficult to understand if you do not know their context. Thus, it might be a good idea to go to the Bible and read at least the entire chapter in which your reading occurs.

A good amount of information has been provided in this handbook so that you might understand better what you are reading (both alongside of the readings and in the appendices at the end of the handbook). If those are not enough, you could check in your parish library or with your liturgy committee or lector coordinator for recommendations for other resources. It might even be a good project to study at least one book of the Bible each year as part of your study preparations for your ministry. Adult education classes are also a good aid to one's own personal growth.

PHYSICAL CONSIDERATIONS

There are also a number of physical considerations in your presentations.

Know when you are supposed to read. Check the schedule and be responsible in either being there when you are assigned or in arranging for a substitute when you cannot be present (each parish has a different way of arranging for substitute readers).

Dress appropriately. You should be drawing attention to the word of God and not to yourself. You should dress in a simple and yet respectful manner, which shows that you recognize the dignity of that which you are doing.

Walk to the lectern with a dignified, deliberate pace. Do not run. Do not walk so slowly that people feel uncomfortable. In theory, only one thing should be happening in the liturgy at a time. Thus, the lector should approach the lectern after the Opening Prayer and not during it (unless you have been instructed by the coordinator of lectors to do otherwise).

Know which year you are reading. If your Sunday Lectionary has A, B, and C readings or your Weekday Lectionary has year 1 and 2 readings, you should know which year it is.

Know your microphone system. Each system is different. Each microphone has an optimal distance and direction from which you should read. Some systems have cut offs that will block the sound if you are too loud. Others are temperamental. Before you ever read for Mass, make sure that you have tried out the system. This should be done at a time when it will not disturb people who are trying to pray in church, e.g., immediately before Mass.

Read questions as questions. Read phrases that end with exclamation points with emphasis. Know the mood of the reading. If the author is being dramatic, the reading should have a bit of drama. Try not to be monotonous in your reading.

Be careful with certain sounds when you read. The letters "S" and "P" can be picked up by the sound system as a hissing or an explosive sound.

Do not make gestures that render you the center of attention. Your hands, in fact, should be placed where they will not distract. If you are nervous, you might hold on to the sides of the lectern.

Read from the Lectionary. There is a certain dignity to that which you are doing. You should not be reading from a missalette or from this handbook. If you have prepared the reading from one of these other sources, check out where the reading is on the page of the Lectionary so that you will not have to search for it when you stand up to read.

Do not read too fast or too slow. Make sure you pause when you reach the end of a phrase (this is much easier now that the Lectionary has divided the reading into sense lines). Read slowly enough that you communicate the dignity of the occasion, without

becoming overly dramatic. If the reading is a hymn, read it as such (i.e., poetry is always read in a more dramatic manner than simple narratives).

Try to look up during the reading. When you first start reading, this might be both difficult and a bit artificial. But it is always good to keep eye contact with the audience.

Know whether you will be reading the Responsorial Psalm or whether it will be sung. It is not a good idea to arrive at the psalm and then glance at the organist with a quizzical look on your face.

A few people have the habit of memorizing the reading and then proclaiming it without reading it. While that is admirable from a certain point of view, it is also very distracting. People almost always are more attentive to the reader's remarkable memory than to what is actually being read.

If you make a mistake, do not become nervous or feel anxious. If you judge it appropriate, simply reread the phrase correctly. If needed, you could make a comment that lets the community know that you have made a mistake (e.g., "I'm sorry, I started the wrong reading").

This ministry is so important to the faith life of the community that it is essential for its ministers to have a sense of humility. Ask your friends or family members to give you an occasional honest critique on your reading style. If you are not reading well, admit it and seek help. If, after having sought help, you still cannot read well, it is important to be humble enough to admit it and suggest to your community that it might be better for you to serve it in some other ministry.

GOD'S WORD AND OUR HEARTS

Having spoken about a number of the physical considerations in reading for the liturgy, we now must speak about some of the questions of the Spirit.

We have to allow God's word to speak to us. If we are not listening to God's word at the deepest part of our heart, then those who are listening to us will perceive that we are reading and not proclaiming. They will understand without our ever saying it that we really do not believe what we are proclaiming.

This means that we must pray God's word. We have to ask ourselves what this word means for us today. We have to allow the Spirit of God to make it real and alive. Just as the Spirit inspired the sacred authors to write these texts in the first place, so now that same Spirit breathes into our hearts so that we can make the word of God alive again for ourselves and our community.

We have to place our own experiences in the context of the word. It is a wonderful thing if we find ourselves asking, "what does God's word say to me in these circumstances?" God's word is not a history book about things long since dead; it is a presentation of salvation history that is still alive and vitally important today.

Every reading and every Gospel should in some way call us to conversion. If after preparing the readings for a Sunday, you cannot say that the readings are calling you to change even one thing in your life, you have probably missed the point. It is not a bad idea to ask what you would preach about the reading if you had the opportunity. (Some parishes, in fact, have preparation meetings in which parishioners suggest to the preachers what might be said that weekend.)

Become that which you read. Your actions on a daily basis will proclaim loud and clear whether what you are proclaiming on Sunday are "just words" or whether they are words that are like a two-edged sword. People do look at what you are doing outside of the church, and they are either edified or scandalized by whether you are living the word of God or in some way denying it.

Finally, if possible, arrive in church well before the beginning of the Mass so that you can pray to the Spirit to guide you in your ministry that day.

May God bless you in your ministry.

Shalom,

Fr. Jude Winkler, OFM Conv.

A LECTOR'S PRAYER

EVERLASTING Father,
in the beginning your Word brought forth life
and called us into being.

In the fullness of time,
Jesus, your Son, the Word became flesh.

In the synagogue at Nazareth
and on the hills of Galilee,
he taught the good news of salvation,
the Gospel of life and of truth.

In an act of everlasting love
he opened his arms on the cross
and by his death destroyed all death,
leading us to everlasting life.

Lord, open my lips,
that my mouth may declare your praise.
Open my heart,
that I may proclaim the Word made flesh.
Strengthen my mind,
that I may live the holy words I speak.

For your Word is all holy and all true
and lives in glory with you and the Holy Spirit,
one God, forever and ever. Amen.

December 2, 2012

FIRST SUNDAY OF ADVENT

Lect. No. 3

FIRST READING: Jeremiah 33:14-16

I will raise up for David a just shoot.

Throughout most of the Book of the Prophet Jeremiah we hear about the devastating punishment that would be inflicted upon the people of Israel for their infidelity. This passage is an exception. It speaks about the restoration that the LORD would visit upon Israel.

She would be favored again not because she deserved it, but rather because the LORD was merciful and he would send an anointed one who would guide the people into the LORD's own way.

A reading from the Book of the Prophet Jeremiah

The days are coming, says the LORD,
  when I will fulfill the promise
I made to the house of Israel and Judah.
In those days, in that time,
  I will raise up for David a just shoot;
  he shall do what is right and just in the land.
In those days Judah shall be safe
  and Jerusalem shall dwell secure;
  this is what they shall call her:
  "The LORD our justice."

The word of the Lord.

Lect. No. 3

RESPONSORIAL PSALM: Ps 25:4-5, 8-9, 10, 14 (℞.: 1b)

We cannot hope to be pleasing to God unless we open our hearts to his instruction. On our own, we are bound to fall into sinful and selfish habits. We fool ourselves, believing that what we are doing is what God wants, but it is really what we wanted to do.

On the other hand, if we humble our heart, we will be able to hear what God is trying to tell us. He wants us to choose justice for that is the only real path to a life filled with peace and joy.

℞. **To you, O Lord, I lift my soul.**

Your ways, O LORD, make known to me;
  teach me your paths,
guide me in your truth and teach me,
  for you are God my savior,
  and for you I wait all the day.

℞. **To you, O Lord, I lift my soul.**

Good and upright is the LORD;
  thus he shows sinners the way.
He guides the humble to justice,
  and teaches the humble his way.

℞. **To you, O Lord, I lift my soul.**

The phrase "fear the LORD" does not mean to be frightened by him. Rather, it is to recognize that God is our creator and we are his creatures. He calls us to obedience, not as a tyrant might, but rather with the concern that one would find in a loving parent.

All the paths of the LORD are kindness and constancy toward those who keep his covenant and his decrees.

The friendship of the LORD is with those who fear him,

and his covenant, for their instruction.

℞. **To you, O Lord, I lift my soul.**

Lect. No. 3

SECOND READING: 1 Thessalonians 3:12—4:2

May the Lord strengthen your hearts at the coming of our Lord Jesus.

This passage from Saint Paul's first Letter to the Thessalonians speaks of two of the main elements of the Christian life: to serve and love the Lord with one's heart, soul and strength, and to love one's brothers and sisters as one loves oneself.

Paul also speaks of his own love for the members of this community. He did not share his faith in an impersonal manner. He lived the things about which he spoke.

One will also notice Paul's mention of the coming of our Lord Jesus in glory. This is a theme we remember on this First Sunday of Advent (which is dedicated to Jesus' coming in glory at the end of time). It appears as if Paul believed that the end of the world would occur within his own lifetime.

A reading from the first Letter of Saint Paul to the Thessalonians

Brothers and sisters:
May the Lord make you increase and abound in love
for one another and for all,
just as we have for you,
so as to strengthen your hearts,
to be blameless in holiness before our God and Father
at the coming of our Lord Jesus with all his holy ones. Amen.

Finally, brothers and sisters,
we earnestly ask and exhort you in the Lord Jesus that,
as you received from us
how you should conduct yourselves to please God
—and as you are conducting yourselves—
you do so even more.
For you know what instructions we gave you through the Lord Jesus.

The word of the Lord.

Lect. No. 3

The Alleluia Verse speaks of the love of God and our salvation. In the Gospel of Luke, salvation is experienced when we realize how much God loves us.

ALLELUIA: Psalm 85:8

℟. **Alleluia, alleluia.**

Show us, Lord, your love;
and grant us your salvation.

℟. **Alleluia, alleluia.**

Lect. No. 3

GOSPEL: Luke 21:25-28, 34-36

Your redemption is at hand.

A reading from the holy Gospel according to Luke

Jesus said to his disciples:
"There will be signs in the sun, the moon, and the stars,
    and on earth nations will be in dismay,
    perplexed by the roaring of the sea and the waves.
People will die of fright
    in anticipation of what is coming upon the world,
    for the powers of the heavens will be shaken.
And then they will see the Son of Man
    coming in a cloud with power and great glory.
But when these signs begin to happen,
    stand erect and raise your heads
    because your redemption is at hand.

"Beware that your hearts do not become drowsy
    from carousing and drunkenness
    and the anxieties of daily life,
    and that day catch you by surprise like a trap.
For that day will assault everyone
    who lives on the face of the earth.
Be vigilant at all times
    and pray that you have the strength
    to escape the tribulations that are imminent
    and to stand before the Son of Man."

The Gospel of the Lord.

We hear Jesus describe the end of the world in Apocalyptic terms (e.g., the great signs that would be seen in the heavens, the Son of Man coming in glory upon the cloud, etc.). This was a common way of speaking about the last days in the time of Jesus. It does not necessarily mean that the description should be understood in a literal manner. Jesus might have been speaking symbolically so that those listening to him could understand.

There is an eternal truth no matter how the world will come to an end: that we should be vigilant. We do not know how much time we have to live, so we should treat each moment of our lives as precious. We cannot afford to put our conversion off until tomorrow.

We should dedicate ourselves to virtue and prayer (especially in this holy season). The goal is that we be ready to greet the Lord whenever he calls us to himself (whether it be at the end of the world or at the end of our earthly lives).

December 8, 2012

THE IMMACULATE CONCEPTION OF THE BLESSED VIRGIN MARY

Lect. No. 689 **FIRST READING: Genesis 3:9-15, 20**

I will put enmity between your offspring and hers.

On this feast of the Immaculate Conception, we read about the entrance of sin into the world and the punishment that we received because of it.

The first effect of sin is alienation: from God, from each other, and even from nature.

Before they sinned, Adam and Eve were naked, but they felt no shame. They had been living in a state of pure innocence. After their sin they felt only shame. They hid themselves and ran away from God, the one who loved them most. They blamed each other and even the snake for their fall.

God punished the man, the woman, and the snake. The man's punishment, which we do not hear in this passage, was to work hard for a living but never receive a just recompense. The woman suffers childbirth pains. The snake loses its legs and crawls on its belly.

We also hear that the woman and her offspring will live in perpetual enmity with the serpent and his offspring. Satan would torment humanity, but Jesus,

A reading from the Book of Genesis

After the man, Adam, had eaten of the tree,
the Lord God called to the man and asked him,
"Where are you?"
He answered, "I heard you in the garden;
but I was afraid, because I was naked,
so I hid myself."
Then he asked, "Who told you that you were naked?
You have eaten, then,
from the tree of which I had forbidden you to eat!"
The man replied, "The woman whom you put here with me—
she gave me fruit from the tree, and so I ate it."
The Lord God then asked the woman,
"Why did you do such a thing?"
The woman answered, "The serpent tricked me into it, so I ate it."

Then the Lord God said to the serpent:
"Because you have done this, you shall be banned from all the animals
and from all the wild creatures;
on your belly shall you crawl,
and dirt shall you eat
all the days of your life.
I will put enmity between you and the woman,
and between your offspring and hers;
he will strike at your head,
while you strike at his heel."

born of an immaculate mother, would deliver us from our slavery to sin.

The man called his wife Eve,
    because she became the mother of all the living.

The word of the Lord.

RESPONSORIAL PSALM: Ps 98:1, 2-3ab, 3cd-4 (℟.: 1a)

As we meditate upon the meaning of this feast, that God prepared the Blessed Virgin Mary in a miraculous way to be the mother of his Son, we are filled with gratitude and wonder. We break into song to celebrate God's goodness.

"The LORD has made his salvation known." There are two understandings of salvation in the New Testament. In Saint Paul's writings, we will be saved during the final judgment at the end of time. Jesus will intercede for us so that we might obtain the fullness of God's mercy.

According to Saint Luke, salvation is something that we already experience here upon the earth. Jesus has come into our lives with great signs of mercy and love. We already experience that here and now. Our lives have meaning because Jesus is a part of them.

℟. **Sing to the Lord a new song, for he has done marvelous deeds.**

Sing to the LORD a new song,
    for he has done wondrous deeds;
his right hand has won victory for him,
    his holy arm.

℟. **Sing to the Lord a new song, for he has done marvelous deeds.**

The LORD has made his salvation known:
    in the sight of the nations he has revealed his justice.
He has remembered his kindness and his faithfulness
    toward the house of Israel.

℟. **Sing to the Lord a new song, for he has done marvelous deeds.**

All the ends of the earth have seen
    the salvation by our God.
Sing joyfully to the LORD, all you lands;
    break into song; sing praise.

℟. **Sing to the Lord a new song, for he has done marvelous deeds.**

SECOND READING: Ephesians 1:3-6, 11-12

He chose us in Christ before the foundation of the world.

This reading is a hymn of praise to celebrate the fact that we were chosen by our Lord for salvation before the foundation of the world. This is the proper idea of predestination, that God has always called us to participate in his life.

A reading from the Letter of Saint Paul
to the Ephesians

Brothers and sisters:
Blessed be the God and Father of our Lord Jesus Christ,
who has blessed us in Christ

Predestination does not mean that we must do something, it means that we have the freedom to do it. We always have the possibility of saying no, but why would we want to?

The extent of God's favor is expressed in the fact that we have been adopted as God's children. We have become his chosen ones, his beloved.

It is Jesus who, through his death and resurrection, made all of this possible. He is our brother, and God is our "Abba," Father.

Our only possible response to this miracle is gratitude and praise. We live to praise the Lord.

with every spiritual blessing in the heavens,
    as he chose us in him, before the foundation of
        the world,
    to be holy and without blemish before him.
In love he destined us for adoption to himself
        through Jesus Christ,
    in accord with the favor of his will,
    for the praise of the glory of his grace
    that he granted us in the beloved.

In him we were also chosen,
    destined in accord with the purpose of the One
    who accomplishes all things according to the in-
        tention of his will,
    so that we might exist for the praise of his glory,
    we who first hoped in Christ.

The word of the Lord.

Lect.
No. 689

We honor Mary with the words which the archangel Gabriel used when he came to give her the glorious message that she was to be the Mother of God and blessed among all women.

ALLELUIA: cf. Luke 1:28

℟. **Alleluia, alleluia.**

Hail, Mary, full of grace, the Lord is with you;
blessed are you among women.

℟. **Alleluia, alleluia.**

Lect.
No. 689

GOSPEL: Luke 1:26-38

Hail, full of grace! The Lord is with you.

The annunciation in the Gospel of Luke is patterned after many of the annunciation stories found in the Old Testament. It is also a loose parallel to the annunciation of John the Baptist. While John's birth is great, that of Jesus is even greater. John's mother and father were elderly; Jesus' mother was a virgin.

A reading from the holy Gospel according to Luke

The angel Gabriel was sent from God
    to a town of Galilee called Nazareth,
    to a virgin betrothed to a man named Joseph,
    of the house of David,
    and the virgin's name was Mary.
And coming to her, he said,
    "Hail, full of grace! The Lord is with you."

The archangel Gabriel greets Mary by stating, "Hail, full of grace!" This greeting is actually an important scriptural proof for the dogma of the Immaculate Conception.

The phrase, "full of grace" is in the perfect tense in the original Greek version of this gospel. The perfect was used for things that began in the past and were still true in the present, such as saying that the flowers bloomed yesterday and were still in bloom today.

Mary was already full of grace even before the angel arrived. She had been protected from the effects of the original sin.

This is why Mary could respond with so much generosity to the invitation of the Lord. Those of us who have been wounded by sin tend to be selfish. Mary, on the other hand, was able to think in terms of service and vulnerability. She pronounced herself the handmaid of the Lord, placing herself at the service of God's plan.

The birth came about through the intervention of the Holy Spirit who overshadowed her, even as the cloud had overshadowed the Ark of the Covenant in the Old Testament.

But she was greatly troubled at what was said
and pondered what sort of greeting this might be.
Then the angel said to her,
"Do not be afraid, Mary,
for you have found favor with God.
Behold, you will conceive in your womb and bear a son,
and you shall name him Jesus.
He will be great and will be called Son of the Most High,
and the Lord God will give him the throne of David his father,
and he will rule over the house of Jacob forever,
and of his Kingdom there will be no end."
But Mary said to the angel,
"How can this be,
since I have no relations with a man?"
And the angel said to her in reply,
"The Holy Spirit will come upon you,
and the power of the Most High will overshadow you.
Therefore the child to be born
will be called holy, the Son of God.
And behold, Elizabeth, your relative,
has also conceived a son in her old age,
and this is the sixth month for her who was called barren;
for nothing will be impossible for God."
Mary said, "Behold, I am the handmaid of the Lord.
May it be done to me according to your word."
Then the angel departed from her.

The Gospel of the Lord.

PASTORAL REFLECTIONS

In an era that speaks about the long-term effects of dysfunctionality, it is a tremendous consolation to have a mother who can love us with a totally unconditional love.

December 9, 2012

SECOND SUNDAY OF ADVENT

Lect. No. 6

FIRST READING: Baruch 5:1-9

Jerusalem, God will show your splendor.

The First Reading comes from the Book of the Prophet Baruch. It is attributed to the secretary of Jeremiah the Prophet, although there are serious doubts that he actually wrote it (for there are indications throughout the book that it was written much later).

This passage is reminiscent of promises found in Second Isaiah that speak of the restoration of Israel and Jerusalem. She would no longer have to mourn. Her children would travel back to her from the distant corners of the earth.

Jerusalem had been dressed in clothes used during periods of mourning. Now she would be clothed in splendor.

She would wear the cloak of justice and she would put a mitre on her head (most probably referring to the mitre of Aaron, the high priest, meaning that she would be a holy, priestly city).

This reading speaks of the extravagant preparations that God makes for the restoration of his people. Even now he is making those same preparations so that we can turn our hearts to him during this Advent season.

A reading from the Book of the Prophet Baruch

Jerusalem, take off your robe of mourning and
    misery;
    put on the splendor of glory from God forever:
wrapped in the cloak of justice from God,
    bear on your head the mitre
    that displays the glory of the eternal name.
For God will show all the earth your splendor:
    you will be named by God forever
    the peace of justice, the glory of God's worship.

Up, Jerusalem! stand upon the heights;
    look to the east and see your children
gathered from the east and the west
    at the word of the Holy One,
    rejoicing that they are remembered by God.
Led away on foot by their enemies they left you:
    but God will bring them back to you
    borne aloft in glory as on royal thrones.
For God has commanded
    that every lofty mountain be made low,
and that the age-old depths and gorges
    be filled to level ground,
    that Israel may advance secure in the glory of
    God.
The forests and every fragrant kind of tree
    have overshadowed Israel at God's command;
for God is leading Israel in joy
    by the light of his glory,
    with his mercy and justice for company.

The word of the Lord.

| Lect. No. 6 | **RESPONSORIAL PSALM: Ps 126:1-2, 2-3, 4-5, 6 (℟.: 3)** |

The Responsorial Psalm continues the theme of restoration found in the First Reading and the Gospel. It presents an idealistic version of what the return from the Babylonian exile would be like for the people of Israel. It speaks of joy and laughter. It promises a return of fertility to the land.

During the season of Advent we are called to return to God from the exile that we have created for ourselves through our lives of sin and selfishness. We thought that these things would bring us joy, but they only brought us frustration and loneliness. God is the only one who can respond to our deepest need, the need for a love that will never go away and never make mistakes.

We cannot hope to change our hearts with our own strength. We are weak, and every time that we try to rely upon our discipline and self-control, we become frustrated because we only fall again. It is God who will change our frustration and grief into true joy. It is his love that will transform the desert of our hearts into a land overflowing with fertility.

℟. **The Lord has done great things for us, we are filled with joy.**

When the LORD brought back the captives of Zion,
    we were like men dreaming.
Then our mouth was filled with laughter,
    and our tongue with rejoicing.

℟. **The Lord has done great things for us, we are filled with joy.**

Then they said among the nations,
    "The LORD has done great things for them."
The LORD has done great things for us;
    we are glad indeed.

℟. **The Lord has done great things for us, we are filled with joy.**

Restore our fortunes, O LORD,
    like the torrents in the southern desert.
Those who sow in tears
    shall reap rejoicing.

℟. **The Lord has done great things for us, we are filled with joy.**

Although they go forth weeping,
    carrying the seed to be sown,
they shall come back rejoicing,
    carrying their sheaves.

℟. **The Lord has done great things for us, we are filled with joy.**

PASTORAL REFLECTIONS

The season of Advent is an excellent time to take stock of our spiritual lives and to participate in the Sacrament of Reconciliation, especially if we have not done that for a while.

Lect. No. 6

SECOND READING: Philippians 1:4-6, 8-11

Show yourselves pure and blameless for the day of Christ.

The Letter to the Philippians was written shortly after Saint Paul faced a period of persecution that taught him what was truly important and what was not.

This is why we see references to the Day of the Lord (for after almost dying, Paul was thinking about the end times). It is also why there is an affection in this letter that is almost extravagant. He wanted to say those truly important things to the Philippians while there was still time.

Paul prays that the members of this community might find those same insights: that they might discover what is pure and blameless.

This is a goal of the Advent season. We seek the truth with all our strength.

We purify our hearts so that we can be found blameless at the coming of the Lord (at the end of time and on Christmas day).

A reading from the Letter of Saint Paul to the Philippians

Brothers and sisters:
   I pray always with joy in my every prayer for all
      of you,
   because of your partnership for the gospel
   from the first day until now.
I am confident of this,
   that the one who began a good work in you
   will continue to complete it
   until the day of Christ Jesus.
God is my witness,
   how I long for all of you with the affection of
      Christ Jesus.
And this is my prayer:
   that your love may increase ever more and more
   in knowledge and every kind of perception,
   to discern what is of value,
   so that you may be pure and blameless for the day
      of Christ,
   filled with the fruit of righteousness
   that comes through Jesus Christ
   for the glory and praise of God.

The word of the Lord.

Lect. No. 6

The Alleluia Verse continues the theme found in all of the readings: the need to prepare the way of the Lord for the time is near. If we do that, we will experience the saving love of our God.

ALLELUIA: Luke 3:4, 6

℟. **Alleluia, alleluia.**

Prepare the way of the Lord, make straight his
   paths:
all flesh shall see the salvation of God.

℟. **Alleluia, alleluia.**

Lect.
No. 6

GOSPEL: Luke 3:1-6

All flesh shall see the salvation of God.

The Gospel speaks of the role of John the Baptist. He calls upon his people to prepare the way for the Lord. John preached that the fulfillment of God's promises was at hand. This meant that the people had to turn away from their sins so that they might embrace the salvation that God was offering.

John the Baptist also speaks to us as well. We cannot hope to embrace the babe of Bethlehem if we do not turn away from our sins.

Luke's version of this scene is typical of his Gospel. He gives a list of the names of those who held political power during this period.

Many scholars believe that Luke did this to demonstrate to the authorities of the Roman empire that Christians really good citizens (and they therefore should not be persecuted for their faith).

A reading from the holy Gospel according to Luke

In the fifteenth year of the reign of Tiberius Caesar, when Pontius Pilate was governor of Judea,
and Herod was tetrarch of Galilee,
and his brother Philip tetrarch of the region of Ituraea and Trachonitis,
and Lysanias was tetrarch of Abilene,
during the high priesthood of Annas and Caiaphas,
the word of God came to John the son of Zechariah in the desert.
John went throughout the whole region of the Jordan,
proclaiming a baptism of repentance for the forgiveness of sins,
as it is written in the book of the words of the prophet Isaiah:
A voice of one crying out in the desert:
"Prepare the way of the Lord,
make straight his paths.
Every valley shall be filled
and every mountain and hill shall be made low.
The winding roads shall be made straight,
and the rough ways made smooth,
and all flesh shall see the salvation of God."

The Gospel of the Lord.

PASTORAL REFLECTIONS

There is an established pattern to the Advent readings each year. The first week's readings continue the theme presented at the end of the previous Church year, the end of the world. The Second Sunday introduces the figure of John the Baptist. On the Third Sunday of Advent we hear John's preaching, and then on the Fourth Sunday we have an account of the Visitation of Mary to Elizabeth.

Lect. No. 9

FIRST READING: Zephaniah 3:14-18a

The Lord will rejoice over you with gladness.

The first part of the Book of the Prophet Zephaniah speaks of a period of terrible judgment upon the earth. Today's First Reading is taken from the latter part of the book.

It speaks of the restoration of Jerusalem. God would visit the city to protect it. He would bring a great period of rejoicing.

This reading expresses well the theme of the Third Sunday of Advent. It is called *Gaudete* Sunday, a Latin phrase that means "Rejoice."

We rejoice because the birth of Jesus is near, but also because we have been working to transform our hearts during this season of conversion.

A reading from the Book of the Prophet Zephaniah

Shout for joy, O daughter Zion!
　　Sing joyfully, O Israel!
Be glad and exult with all your heart,
　　O daughter Jerusalem!
The LORD has removed the judgment against you,
　　he has turned away your enemies;
the King of Israel, the LORD, is in your midst,
　　you have no further misfortune to fear.
On that day, it shall be said to Jerusalem:
　　Fear not, O Zion, be not discouraged!
The LORD, your God, is in your midst,
　　a mighty savior;
he will rejoice over you with gladness,
　　and renew you in his love,
he will sing joyfully because of you,
　　as one sings at festivals.

The word of the Lord.

PASTORAL REFLECTIONS

We often think of doing penance as something that is a bit depressing. "Having a good time" is interpreted as doing things to excess. Yet, the exact opposite is actually closer to the truth. When we sin, we deny our dignity as human beings. We do things that make us little better than the animals. When we convert, we are becoming what we always wanted to be. We are choosing to live in our dignity as children of God. Our conversion does not have to make us into joyless religious automatons. By doing penance, we are not rejecting the world; we are attempting to use it in the proper manner.

Lect. No. 9

RESPONSORIAL PSALM: Isaiah 12:2-3, 4, 5-6 (℟.:6)

The Responsorial Psalm is a hymn taken from the first part of the book of the Prophet Isaiah. Typical of the writings of Isaiah, it speaks of the salvation that the LORD would deliver to the city of Jerusalem, the city of Zion.

God's love and his intervention are so great that even the pagan nations should be informed of what God has done for his people.

The Response speaks of the joy that the people of God would experience because the LORD was present in their city. This continues the theme found in the First Reading that speaks of the fact that God is no longer far off, but has deigned to come into our midst.

While both of these passages from the Old Testament are referring to the future intervention in his people's history, we understand this passage to be fulfilled with the birth of Jesus into our world.

℟. **Cry out with joy and gladness: for among you is the great and Holy One of Israel.**

God indeed is my savior;
  I am confident and unafraid.
My strength and my courage is the LORD,
  and he has been my savior.
With joy you will draw water
  at the fountain of salvation.

℟. **Cry out with joy and gladness: for among you is the great and Holy One of Israel.**

Give thanks to the LORD, acclaim his name;
  among the nations make known his deeds,
  proclaim how exalted is his name.

℟. **Cry out with joy and gladness: for among you is the great and Holy One of Israel.**

Sing praise to the LORD for his glorious achievement;
  let this be known throughout all the earth.
Shout with exultation, O city of Zion,
  for great in your midst
  is the Holy One of Israel!

℟. **Cry out with joy and gladness: for among you is the great and Holy One of Israel.**

PASTORAL REFLECTIONS

There are two ways of understanding the word "salvation." It could mean that which happens to us when we die and go to heaven, or it could mean something that is already occurring in the here and now. In the former, Jesus saves us from eternal damnation; in the latter Jesus saves us from our worst enemies: sin, hate, alienation, etc.

During Advent, it would be good to reflect upon what one understands when one hears the phrase, "Jesus is my Savior."

SECOND READING: Philippians 4:4-7

The Lord is near.

This reading comes from the last part of the Letter to the Philippians. Saint Paul wrote that letter after he had been imprisoned and faced the possibility of being put to death. This gave him a clearer perspective on life and faith.

He wanted the Philippians to dedicate themselves to the only things that were really important. Thus, he speaks of prayer, petition, thanksgiving, and above all, joy. If God is the center of our lives, then we will find joy, no matter what might happen to us.

A reading from the Letter of Saint Paul to the Philippians

Brothers and sisters:
Rejoice in the Lord always.
I shall say it again: rejoice!
Your kindness should be known to all.
The Lord is near.
Have no anxiety at all, but in everything,
   by prayer and petition, with thanksgiving,
   make your requests known to God.
Then the peace of God that surpasses all understanding
   will guard your hearts and minds in Christ Jesus.
The word of the Lord.

ALLELUIA: Isaiah 61:1 (cited in Luke 4:18)

The Alleluia Verse speaks of the anointing of the Spirit that would come upon the Messiah. He would bring joy to those who were poor and felt themselves to be excluded from the Lord's blessings.

℞. **Alleluia, alleluia.**

The Spirit of the Lord is upon me,
because he has anointed me
to bring glad tidings to the poor.

℞. **Alleluia, alleluia.**

PASTORAL REFLECTIONS

Gaudete *Sunday, the Third Sunday of Advent, is supposed to be a day of joy. It is a good time to ask whether people would describe us as joy-filled people, or would they describe us as anxious, overwhelmed, and frustrated due to our Christmas preparations.*

Lect. No. 9

The Gospel presents the preaching of John the Baptist to the people of Israel. Like the accounts found in the other Synoptic Gospels, Luke speaks of the coming of the Day of the Lord. This would be a day of judgment upon Israel and upon the world. John the Baptist invites his listeners to turn away from their sins.

Unlike the accounts found in Matthew and Mark, Saint Luke's version speaks of how tax collectors and soldiers could convert their ways.

He did not require them to abandon their occupations. Rather, he simply asked them to exercise their responsibilities as honestly as they could.

God does not ask us to reject who we are, but rather simply asks us to be as virtuous as we possibly can be.

Yet the time had come for people to make a decision. God was going to separate the good from the evil as one separates wheat from chaff.

This Third Sunday of Advent is a time to make some serious decisions concerning how we live, work, play, etc. Like the tax collectors and soldiers who spoke to the Baptist, we are called to conform our ways to the Good News.

GOSPEL: Luke 3:10-18

What should we do?

A reading from the holy Gospel according to Luke

The crowds asked John the Baptist,
"What should we do?"
He said to them in reply,
"Whoever has two cloaks
should share with the person who has none.
And whoever has food should do likewise."
Even tax collectors came to be baptized and they said to him,
"Teacher, what should we do?"
He answered them,
"Stop collecting more than what is prescribed."
Soldiers also asked him,
"And what is it that we should do?"
He told them,
"Do not practice extortion,
do not falsely accuse anyone,
and be satisfied with your wages."

Now the people were filled with expectation,
and all were asking in their hearts
whether John might be the Christ.
John answered them all, saying,
"I am baptizing you with water,
but one mightier than I is coming.
I am not worthy to loosen the thongs of his sandals.
He will baptize you with the Holy Spirit and fire.
His winnowing fan is in his hand to clear his threshing floor
and to gather the wheat into his barn,
but the chaff he will burn with unquenchable fire."
Exhorting them in many other ways,
he preached good news to the people.

The Gospel of the Lord.

Lect. No. 12

FIRST READING: Micah 5:1-4a

From you shall come forth the ruler of Israel.

Today's First Reading is a classic example of a prophet saying more than he even realized. When Micah the Prophet pronounced these words, he was referring to events occurring in his own days.

Micah thought of the dynasty ruling in Jerusalem as so corrupt that it could not be salvaged. He was hoping that God would raise up a new king and a new dynasty that would have small town values (which is the reason for predicting that it would come from Bethlehem and not Jerusalem).

The Holy Spirit took his words and gave them a new meaning in the birth of Jesus in Bethlehem. Jesus is the true Good Shepherd who would bring peace to the whole world.

A reading from the Book of the Prophet Micah

Thus says the LORD:
    You, Bethlehem-Ephrathah,
    too small to be among the clans of Judah,
from you shall come forth for me
    one who is to be ruler in Israel;
whose origin is from of old,
    from ancient times.
Therefore the Lord will give them up, until the time
    when she who is to give birth has borne,
and the rest of his kindred shall return
    to the children of Israel.
He shall stand firm and shepherd his flock
    by the strength of the LORD,
    in the majestic name of the LORD, his God;
and they shall remain, for now his greatness
    shall reach to the ends of the earth;
    he shall be peace.

The word of the Lord.

PASTORAL REFLECTIONS

On these days before Christmas, we can reflect upon the fact that there are often different layers of meaning to what is going on. Things are often said during the holiday season that have a deeper meaning (e.g., sometimes referring to the past, sometimes reflecting one's hopes or fears, etc.).

Lect. No. 12

RESPONSORIAL PSALM: Ps 80:2-3, 15-16, 18-19 (℟.: 4)

The Responsorial Psalm expresses the anxious expectation for the day when we celebrate the birth of Jesus at Bethlehem. We call upon God to visit us and protect us. He is the only one who can truly save us. This is, in fact, what the name of Jesus means: that Yahweh saves. With his strength, we can change our ways and walk in God's love.

We are celebrating new life in this great feast. We experience the new life of the babe lying in the crib, but we also experience new life in ourselves. Jesus' birth gives us new possibilities. We are no longer tied to a futile life in which we seek pleasure from things that cannot truly satisfy us.

Now we will experience the only thing that will truly bring us peace and fulfillment: the love of God. This love will not simply be a theory, it will be visible in the child of Bethlehem, for Jesus is love incarnate.

℟. **Lord, make us turn to you; let us see your face and we shall be saved.**

O shepherd of Israel, hearken,
   from your throne upon the cherubim, shine forth.
Rouse your power,
   and come to save us.

℟. **Lord, make us turn to you; let us see your face and we shall be saved.**

Once again, O LORD of hosts,
   look down from heaven, and see;
take care of this vine,
   and protect what your right hand has planted,
   the son of man whom you yourself made strong.

℟. **Lord, make us turn to you; let us see your face and we shall be saved.**

May your help be with the man of your right hand,
   with the son of man whom you yourself made strong.
Then we will no more withdraw from you;
   give us new life, and we will call upon your name.

℟. **Lord, make us turn to you; let us see your face and we shall be saved.**

PASTORAL REFLECTIONS

How can I keep Christ before my eyes while I am so busy preparing things, entertaining, cleaning up, etc.? I might have to steal moments throughout the day to keep my perspective and balance so that I do not lose a sense of true Christmas joy.

Lect. No. 12

SECOND READING: Hebrews 10:5-10

Behold, I come to do your will.

There are two ideas in this reading that give us an indication of why it was chosen for this Sunday. First, it speaks of the fact that Christ came into the world. This was already seen in the Responsorial Psalm when the psalmist begged God to come and visit and save us.

The second theme is that Christ came in the flesh. God did not send a messenger to communicate his good will toward us. Rather, God took on our flesh and came to dwell among us.

This consecrates all that we are and all that we do, for it means that we do not have to reject our humanity to be God-like. Rather, we must be like Jesus who embraced humanity and made it a full expression of God's love.

A reading from the Letter to the Hebrews

Brothers and sisters:
When Christ came into the world, he said:
"Sacrifice and offering you did not desire,
    but a body you prepared for me;
in holocausts and sin offerings you took no delight.
Then I said, 'As is written of me in the scroll,
behold, I come to do your will, O God.'"

First he says, "Sacrifices and offerings,
    holocausts and sin offerings,
    you neither desired nor delighted in."
These are offered according to the law.
Then he says, "Behold, I come to do your will."
He takes away the first to establish the second.
By this "will," we have been consecrated
    through the offering of the body of Jesus Christ
        once for all.

The word of the Lord.

Lect. No. 12

ALLELUIA: Luke 1:38

The Alleluia Verse recalls the words that Mary spoke in response to the angel's invitation to become the mother of the Son of God.

℟. **Alleluia, alleluia.**
Behold, I am the handmaid of the Lord.
May it be done to me according to your word.

℟. **Alleluia, alleluia.**

Lect. No. 12

GOSPEL: Luke 1:39-45

And how does this happen to me, that the mother of my Lord should come to me?

The Gospel recalls what happened to Mary between the time that she agreed to be the mother of the Son of God and the actual birth of Jesus. Mary proved her generosity by forgetting her own problems and traveling to the home of her cousin Elizabeth, who was also with child, so that she might help her.

Even before a word is spoken, the baby in Elizabeth's womb, John the Baptist, recognizes the presence of Jesus and leaps to greet him. (The first person to recognize Jesus' presence in the world was an unborn child.)

Elizabeth greets Mary with great respect because the Holy Spirit had revealed the truth to her, that Mary was now the mother of her Lord. The entire scene is filled with a sense of awe and joy.

A reading from the holy Gospel according to Luke

Mary set out
and traveled to the hill country in haste
to a town of Judah,
where she entered the house of Zechariah
and greeted Elizabeth.
When Elizabeth heard Mary's greeting,
the infant leaped in her womb,
and Elizabeth, filled with the Holy Spirit,
cried out in a loud voice and said,
"Blessed are you among women,
and blessed is the fruit of your womb.
And how does this happen to me,
that the mother of my Lord should come to me?
For at the moment the sound of your greeting reached
my ears,
the infant in my womb leaped for joy.
Blessed are you who believed
that what was spoken to you by the Lord
would be fulfilled."
The Gospel of the Lord.

PASTORAL REFLECTIONS

This account of the Visitation reminds us of all the visitors we will have and how we will be visiting others. Sacred Scripture speaks of the obligation to hospitality. We should treat those who come into our homes as if they were Christ visiting our home. We should carry Christ's love to those whom we visit.

We should remember that hospitality should be shown most of all to those who need it most (and not necessarily to those who are the most entertaining).

Lect. No. 13

FIRST READING: Isaiah 62:1-5

The Lord delights in you.

This prophecy speaks of the restoration of the people of Israel. They had suffered terribly during the years of exile and during the difficult years when they first came back from exile. They wondered whether God had forgotten them or possibly was still angry with them.

This reading shows that this is not God's attitude. Using matrimonial symbolism, the prophet speaks of the remarkable restoration that will take place.

The LORD will espouse his people. They will be given a new name that expresses the delight of the LORD. This reading is filled with a sense of joy and new possibilities. The promise that it expresses was fulfilled when God established a new covenant with his chosen people.

The hymn is written with parallelism, saying the same thing over and over again with slightly different words to add emphasis.

A reading from the Book of the Prophet Isaiah

For Zion's sake I will not be silent,
for Jerusalem's sake I will not be quiet,
until her vindication shines forth like the dawn
and her victory like a burning torch.

Nations shall behold your vindication,
and all the kings your glory;
you shall be called by a new name
pronounced by the mouth of the LORD.
You shall be a glorious crown in the hand of the LORD,
a royal diadem held by your God.
No more shall people call you "Forsaken,"
or your land "Desolate,"
but you shall be called "My Delight,"
and your land "Espoused."
For the LORD delights in you
and makes your land his spouse.
As a young man marries a virgin,
your Builder shall marry you;
and as a bridegroom rejoices in his bride
so shall your God rejoice in you.

The word of the Lord.

RESPONSORIAL PSALM: Ps 89:4-5, 16-17, 27, 29 (℟.: 2a)

The psalm celebrates the covenant that God has made with his people as well as with King David. God will always remain faithful to his covenant. Even if we were to sin against God's goodness, God will not abandon his promises. We never have to worry about God hiding his face or forgetting us, for we will walk in its light.

The only possible response to this remarkable generosity is great joy. We are filled with awe at the goodness of God.

We are also filled with confidence, for we know that God will always defend us against our enemies. Thus, we can call God, "my father, my God, the rock, my savior."

℟. **Forever I will sing the goodness of the Lord.**

I have made a covenant with my chosen one,
    I have sworn to David my servant:
forever will I confirm your posterity
    and establish your throne for all generations.

℟. **Forever I will sing the goodness of the Lord.**

Blessed the people who know the joyful shout;
    in the light of your countenance, O LORD, they walk.
At your name they rejoice all the day,
    and through your justice they are exalted.

℟. **Forever I will sing the goodness of the Lord.**

He shall say of me, "You are my father,
    my God, the rock, my savior."
Forever I will maintain my kindness toward him,
    and my covenant with him stands firm.

℟. **Forever I will sing the goodness of the Lord.**

Lect. No. 13

SECOND READING: Acts 13:16-17, 22-25

Paul bears witness to Christ, the Son of David.

This speech presents a form of the early "kerygma," the things that Saint Paul would preach when he first entered a new city.

This kerygma is very Jewish in tone for Paul is speaking in a synagogue. He wants to present the message in such a way that they could understand who Jesus was and what he meant for them.

Notice that two kings are mentioned in the course of the speech: Saul and David. This is actually a subtle threat to the community.

A reading from the Acts of the Apostles

When Paul reached Antioch in Pisidia and entered the synagogue,
    he stood up, motioned with his hand, and said,
    "Fellow Israelites and you others who are God-fearing, listen.
The God of this people Israel chose our ancestors
    and exalted the people during their sojourn in the land of Egypt.
With uplifted arm he led them out of it.
Then he removed Saul and raised up David as king;
    of him he testified,
    'I have found David, son of Jesse, a man after my own heart;

Saul had been chosen by God to be king, but he displeased the Lord and was rejected. God then chose David to replace Saul and become the new king of Israel.

Paul was warning the community that the same could happen to them. They, too, considered themselves to be the chosen, but if they did not accept his message, they, too, could be rejected. Their only recourse was to accept Jesus as their Messiah and be baptized.

he will carry out my every wish.'

From this man's descendants God, according to his promise,
 has brought to Israel a savior, Jesus.
John heralded his coming by proclaiming a baptism of repentance
 to all the people of Israel;
 and as John was completing his course, he would say,
 'What do you suppose that I am? I am not he.
Behold, one is coming after me;
 I am not worthy to unfasten the sandals of his feet.'"

The word of the Lord.

ALLELUIA

℟. **Alleluia, alleluia.**

Tomorrow the wickedness of the earth will be destroyed:
the Savior of the world will reign over us.

℟. **Alleluia, alleluia.**

The birth of the child Jesus in Bethlehem destroys the power of wickedness upon the earth. He is love incarnate, and those forces which are opposed to that love have no power over him.

GOSPEL: 🅐 Longer Form: Matthew 1:1-25

The genealogy of Jesus Christ, the Son of David.

Matthew presents an extensive genealogy to show that Jesus is a true son of David, son of Abraham. This demonstrates that Jesus is the fulfillment of God's promise to his people.

Abraham was the founder of the Jewish people. By tracing Jesus' genealogy back to Abraham, Matthew is showing that Jesus is the Messiah whom Yahweh had sent to his chosen people.

A reading from the holy Gospel according to Matthew

The book of the genealogy of Jesus Christ, the son of David, the son of Abraham.

Abraham became the father of Isaac,
 Isaac the father of Jacob,
 Jacob the father of Judah and his brothers.
Judah became the father of Perez and Zerah,
 whose mother was Tamar.
Perez became the father of Hezron,
 Hezron the father of Ram,
 Ram the father of Amminadab.

David was the great king of Israel and model of what the Messiah should be. Jesus was a true son of David, and he would inherit his eternal throne.

The list of ancestors of Jesus is a bit unhistorical. Matthew tries to make three sets of fourteen names each. The middle set of names skips a few generations in order to make the list add up to fourteen names.

The number fourteen is important for that is the symbolic number for the name David. By producing three lists of fourteen, Matthew is saying that Jesus is three times more important than David. Hebrew had no superlative degree, so saying a word three times in a row was their way of expressing that idea (e.g., holy, holy, holy means the holiest). Jesus was three times "David," and he was therefore the "Davidest."

There are a number of women mentioned in the list. This is unusual. Normally genealogies only had names of men. Furthermore, the women mentioned had unusual pasts. One was an adulteress, one a foreigner, one committed incest, and one was a prostitute. Matthew was trying to say that God had worked in most unusual ways throughout history. He had chosen most unexpected people to be instruments of his will. This was also true of the fifth woman on his list, a poor virgin named Mary.

After the genealogy, we hear about the birth of Jesus.

Amminadab became the father of Nahshon,
  Nahshon the father of Salmon,
  Salmon the father of Boaz,
  whose mother was Rahab.
Boaz became the father of Obed,
  whose mother was Ruth.
Obed became the father of Jesse,
  Jesse the father of David the king.

David became the father of Solomon,
  whose mother had been the wife of Uriah.
Solomon became the father of Rehoboam,
  Rehoboam the father of Abijah,
  Abijah the father of Asaph.
Asaph became the father of Jehoshaphat,
  Jehoshaphat the father of Joram,
  Joram the father of Uzziah.
Uzziah became the father of Jotham,
  Jotham the father of Ahaz,
  Ahaz the father of Hezekiah.
Hezekiah became the father of Manasseh,
  Manasseh the father of Amos,
  Amos the father of Josiah.
Josiah became the father of Jechoniah and his brothers
  at the time of the Babylonian exile.

After the Babylonian exile,
  Jechoniah became the father of Shealtiel,
  Shealtiel the father of Zerubbabel,
  Zerubbabel the father of Abiud.
Abiud became the father of Eliakim,
  Eliakim the father of Azor,
  Azor the father of Zadok.
Zadok became the father of Achim,
  Achim the father of Eliud,
  Eliud the father of Eleazar.
Eleazar became the father of Matthan,
  Matthan the father of Jacob,
  Jacob the father of Joseph, the husband of Mary.

Mary and Joseph were betrothed. This means that they were engaged but not yet living together.

We hear that the child was conceived through the action of the Holy Spirit.

The phrase about Joseph being a righteous man is not clear. A truly righteous man (in the Jewish definition) would have had Mary killed. Matthew might have meant to say that although he was righteous, he decided to divorce her. Whatever Matthew might have meant, he probably wants to show Joseph as a truly righteous man (one who exhibits the traits of New Testament righteousness).

Joseph is warned in a dream to accept Mary and her child. Joseph is named after Joseph the Patriarch, the dreamer, of the Old Testament, so like him he received his revelations through dreams.

Matthew also shows how Jesus fulfills all of the predictions about the Messiah contained in the law and the prophets. Jesus is Emmanuel, a name that means God is with us.

The passage ends with us hearing that Joseph had no relations with his wife before the child was born. This does not mean that they had relations after, only that there could be absolutely no doubt that the child was the Son of God. Catholic tradition holds that Mary remained a virgin throughout her life.

Of her was born Jesus who is called the Christ.

Thus the total number of generations
　　from Abraham to David
　　is fourteen generations;
　　from David to the Babylonian exile,
　　fourteen generations;
　　from the Babylonian exile to the Christ,
　　fourteen generations.

Now this is how the birth of Jesus Christ came about.
When his mother Mary was betrothed to Joseph,
　　but before they lived together,
　　she was found with child through the Holy Spirit.
Joseph her husband, since he was a righteous man,
　　yet unwilling to expose her to shame,
　　decided to divorce her quietly.
Such was his intention when, behold,
　　the angel of the Lord appeared to him in a dream
　　　　and said,
　　"Joseph, son of David,
　　do not be afraid to take Mary your wife into your
　　　　home.
For it is through the Holy Spirit
　　that this child has been conceived in her.
She will bear a son and you are to name him Jesus,
　　because he will save his people from their sins."
All this took place to fulfill
　　what the Lord had said through the prophet:
　　　Behold, the virgin shall conceive and bear a son,
　　　　and they shall name him Emmanuel,
　　which means "God is with us."
When Joseph awoke,
　　he did as the angel of the Lord had commanded him
　　and took his wife into his home.
He had no relations with her until she bore a son,
　　and he named him Jesus.

The Gospel of the Lord.

GOSPEL: B Shorter Form: Matthew 1:18-25

Mary will give birth to a son, and you are to name him Jesus.

We hear that the child was conceived through the action of the Holy Spirit.

The phrase about Joseph being a righteous man is not clear. A truly righteous man (in the Jewish definition) would have had Mary killed. Matthew might have meant to say that although he was righteous, he decided to divorce her. Whatever Matthew might have meant, he probably wants to show Joseph as a truly righteous man (one who exhibits the traits of New Testament righteousness).

Joseph is warned in a dream to accept Mary and her child. Joseph is named after Joseph the Patriarch, the dreamer, of the Old Testament, so like him he received his revelations through dreams.

Matthew also shows how Jesus fulfills all of the predictions about the Messiah contained in the law and the prophets. Jesus is Emmanuel, a name that means God is with us.

The passage ends with us hearing that Joseph had no relations with his wife before the child was born. This does not mean that they had relations after, only that there could be absolutely no doubt that the child was the Son of God. Catholic tradition holds that Mary remained a virgin throughout her life.

A reading from the holy Gospel according to Matthew

This is how the birth of Jesus Christ came about.
   When his mother Mary was betrothed to Joseph,
   but before they lived together,
   she was found with child through the Holy Spirit.
Joseph her husband, since he was a righteous man,
   yet unwilling to expose her to shame,
   decided to divorce her quietly.
Such was his intention when, behold,
   the angel of the Lord appeared to him in a dream
      and said,
   "Joseph, son of David,
   do not be afraid to take Mary your wife into your
      home.
For it is through the Holy Spirit
   that this child has been conceived in her.
She will bear a son and you are to name him Jesus,
   because he will save his people from their sins."
All this took place to fulfill
   what the Lord had said through the prophet:
      Behold, the virgin shall conceive and bear a son,
         and they shall name him Emmanuel,
      which means "God is with us."
When Joseph awoke,
   he did as the angel of the Lord had commanded
      him
   and took his wife into his home.
He had no relations with her until she bore a son,
   and he named him Jesus.

The Gospel of the Lord.

THE NATIVITY OF THE LORD [CHRISTMAS]

AT THE MASS DURING THE NIGHT

Lect. No. 14

FIRST READING: Isaiah 9:1-6

A son is given us.

This passage is taken from a series of prophecies about the Messiah. Isaiah had long hoped that the kings of Israel would reform and prove to be faithful to their anointing. They all disappointed him, however, and Isaiah realized that things would change only if God sent a chosen one. This could not only be a messiah—it would have to be the Messiah.

This Messiah would change the world. The Israelites who were enslaved and burdened would be liberated. They had lived in gloom, but they would see a great light. They had been filled with sadness and confusion, but now they would be filled with joy.

The Messiah would have a series of symbolic names that would describe him. This was typical of ancient kings who would receive a series of symbolic names when they were enthroned.

He would be called Wonder-Counselor, God-Hero, Father-Forever, and Prince of Peace. He would inherit David's throne and reign forever. His reign would be marked by justice and peace.

A reading from the Book of the Prophet Isaiah

The people who walked in darkness
 have seen a great light;
upon those who dwelt in the land of gloom
 a light has shone.
You have brought them abundant joy
 and great rejoicing,
as they rejoice before you as at the harvest,
 as people make merry when dividing spoils.
For the yoke that burdened them,
 the pole on their shoulder,
and the rod of their taskmaster
 you have smashed, as on the day of Midian.
For every boot that tramped in battle,
 every cloak rolled in blood,
 will be burned as fuel for flames.
For a child is born to us, a son is given us;
 upon his shoulder dominion rests.
They name him Wonder-Counselor, God-Hero,
 Father-Forever, Prince of Peace.
His dominion is vast
 and forever peaceful,
from David's throne, and over his kingdom,
 which he confirms and sustains
by judgment and justice,
 both now and forever.
The zeal of the LORD of hosts will do this!

The word of the Lord.

35

| Lect. No. 14 | **RESPONSORIAL PSALM: Ps 96:1-2, 2-3, 11-12, 13 (℟.: Luke 2:11)** |

This hymn of praise invites us to sing a new song. There are two words for new in ancient languages. One word means that which is not old, the other means that which is radically new.

We are celebrating something radically new, an intervention of God in our history that makes all previous interventions seem insignificant. God becomes incarnate and thus fills this created world with his majesty.

The only possible response to this wondrous situation is to be filled with praise and awe. We even invite creation to praise God. Saint Paul tells us how creation was imprisoned in futility by our sin. Jesus now liberates it by becoming a creature. He restores creation to what God meant it to be when it was first created. Thus, the world and everyone who is in it should raise their voices to praise the Lord.

℟. **Today is born our Savior, Christ the Lord.**

Sing to the LORD a new song;
  sing to the LORD, all you lands.
Sing to the LORD; bless his name.

℟. **Today is born our Savior, Christ the Lord.**

Announce his salvation, day after day.
  Tell his glory among the nations;
  among all peoples, his wondrous deeds.

℟. **Today is born our Savior, Christ the Lord.**

Let the heavens be glad and the earth rejoice;
  let the sea and what fills it resound;
  let the plains be joyful and all that is in them!
Then shall all the trees of the forest exult.

℟. **Today is born our Savior, Christ the Lord.**

They shall exult before the LORD, for he comes;
  for he comes to rule the earth.
He shall rule the world with justice
  and the peoples with his constancy.

℟. **Today is born our Savior, Christ the Lord.**

| Lect. No. 14 | **SECOND READING: Titus 2:11-14** |

The grace of God has appeared to all.

The Second Reading reminds us that the birth of Jesus is not just a time to rejoice, it is also a time to call us to account.

Jesus is born into our world in order to sanctify us and call us to live a righteous life. Therefore, we must reject those things that separate us from God's love.

A reading from the Letter of Saint Paul to Titus

Beloved:
  The grace of God has appeared, saving all
  and training us to reject godless ways and worldly desires
  and to live temperately, justly, and devoutly in this age,
  as we await the blessed hope,

We also recall in this reading that while we celebrate the first coming of Jesus into the world, we also are preparing for his return in glory at the end of time. This, too, is a joyous expectation, for we do not fear the return of the Lord. Our prayer is *Maranatha,* "Come, Lord Jesus."

the appearance of the glory of our great God
and savior Jesus Christ,
who gave himself for us to deliver us from all law-
lessness
and to cleanse for himself a people as his own,
eager to do what is good.

The word of the Lord.

ALLELUIA: Luke 2:10-11

The Alleluia Verse repeats the words of the angels to the shepherds, that Jesus is our savior and he is born for us all. This is a message of great joy, for it means that we no longer have to live futile and pointless lives.

℞. **Alleluia, alleluia.**

I proclaim to you good news of great joy:
today a Savior is born for us,
Christ the Lord.

℞. **Alleluia, alleluia.**

GOSPEL: Luke 2:1-14

Today a Savior has been born for you.

Luke includes many of his major themes in this account of the birth of Jesus.

He starts his account by placing the birth in context of world history by reciting the names of kings and governors. By mentioning that the great Caesar Augustus called a worldwide census, Luke is reminding us that the child being born in a small village in the corner of the Roman empire would transform the entire world. We see this implicit prophecy fulfilled at the end of the Acts of the Apostles when Saint Paul proclaims the gospel in Rome, the political center of the world.

A reading from the holy Gospel according to Luke

In those days a decree went out from Caesar Augustus
that the whole world should be enrolled.
This was the first enrollment,
when Quirinius was governor of Syria.
So all went to be enrolled, each to his own town.
And Joseph too went up from Galilee from the town of Nazareth
to Judea, to the city of David that is called Bethlehem,
because he was of the house and family of David,
to be enrolled with Mary, his betrothed, who was with child.
While they were there,
the time came for her to have her child,

Certain of the details in this account are exactly the same as in Matthew's version of the story. Those common details have a high level of credibility. In both accounts, the mother is Mary, a virgin betrothed to a man named Joseph. The child's name is Jesus, a name revealed by God. The child was conceived through the power of the Holy Spirit. Jesus was born in Bethlehem and grew up in Nazareth. When one considers how many of the central details are in agreement, it is astounding. Some of the secondary details, e.g., whether shepherds or Magi visited the baby, etc. are not as important.

The story emphasizes the poverty of the Holy Family. The child is born in a cave and laid in a manger, for there was no room in the inn.

The first people in Luke's Gospel to visit baby Jesus were the shepherds. At the time of Jesus, shepherds were considered to be untrustworthy and their work made them ceremonially unclean. They were social outcasts. The message Luke is presenting is that God sent the message of salvation first to those who most needed it.

and she gave birth to her firstborn son.
She wrapped him in swaddling clothes and laid him
    in a manger,
    because there was no room for them in the inn.

Now there were shepherds in that region living in
    the fields
and keeping the night watch over their flock.
The angel of the Lord appeared to them
    and the glory of the Lord shone around them,
    and they were struck with great fear.
The angel said to them,
    "Do not be afraid;
    for behold, I proclaim to you good news of great
    joy
    that will be for all the people.
For today in the city of David
    a savior has been born for you who is Christ and
    Lord.
And this will be a sign for you:
    you will find an infant wrapped in swaddling
    clothes
    and lying in a manger."
And suddenly there was a multitude of the heavenly
    host with the angel,
    praising God and saying:
    "Glory to God in the highest
        and on earth peace to those on whom his
        favor rests."

The Gospel of the Lord.

PASTORAL REFLECTIONS

Something always goes wrong on Christmas Day. Reflecting on the messiness of the first Christmas can help us to keep perspective and not let the inevitable difficulties ruin our celebration.

December 25, 2012
THE NATIVITY OF THE LORD [CHRISTMAS]
AT THE MASS AT DAWN

Lect. No. 15

FIRST READING: Isaiah 62:11-12

Behold, your Savior comes!

The First Reading this morning celebrates the promise of salvation given to the community of Israel. It is a proclamation that should reach to the ends of the earth. They saw Israel's pain when she was punished, and now they must witness her restoration.

Israel will be a holy people. The word "holy" means that they are set apart for a sacred purpose, to proclaim the goodness of the LORD. They are also redeemed, bought back from slavery.

A reading from the Book of the Prophet Isaiah

See, the LORD proclaims
to the ends of the earth:
say to daughter Zion,
    your savior comes!
Here is his reward with him,
    his recompense before him.
They shall be called the holy people,
    the redeemed of the LORD,
and you shall be called "Frequented,"
    a city that is not forsaken.

The word of the Lord.

Lect. No. 15

RESPONSORIAL PSALM: Ps 97:1, 6, 11-12

Psalm 97 is an exuberant song of joy for the salvation that the LORD is accomplishing upon the earth.

When the psalmist speaks of the heavens and the earth rejoicing, he is using a typical Hebrew symbolism. By citing the two extremes, he means that everything in between is also engaged in this act of praise.

We are filled with joy, for once we were in the darkness and now we have seen the light: once we were imprisoned in sin and now we are free.

℟. **A light will shine on us this day: the Lord is born for us.**

The LORD is king; let the earth rejoice;
    let the many isles be glad.
The heavens proclaim his justice,
    and all peoples see his glory.

℟. **A light will shine on us this day: the Lord is born for us.**

Light dawns for the just;
    and gladness, for the upright of heart.
Be glad in the LORD, you just,
    and give thanks to his holy name.

℟. **A light will shine on us this day: the Lord is born for us.**

Lect.
No. 15

SECOND READING: Titus 3:4-7

Because of his mercy, he saved us.

This morning we celebrate new birth, that of the babe of Bethlehem and also our own re-birth through the Sacrament of Baptism. Both of these births are signs of mercy. We have not earned God's love; it is a gracious gift.

Justified by God's grace, we hear that we have become heirs in hope of eternal life. This means that God has established a relationship of peace with us through the death and resurrection of his Son Jesus. Now we live in hope, for if God would allow his Son to die for us, certainly he will call us into his glory.

A reading from the Letter of Saint Paul to Titus

Beloved:
When the kindness and generous love
    of God our savior appeared,
not because of any righteous deeds we had done
    but because of his mercy,
he saved us through the bath of rebirth
    and renewal by the Holy Spirit,
whom he richly poured out on us
    through Jesus Christ our savior,
so that we might be justified by his grace
    and become heirs in hope of eternal life.

The word of the Lord.

Lect.
No. 15

ALLELUIA: Luke 2:14

We join the angels as they sing to proclaim the glory of God in order to celebrate the birth of God's Son in Bethlehem. He is the one who truly brings peace to the earth.

℟. **Alleluia, alleluia.**

Glory to God in the highest,
and on earth peace to those
on whom his favor rests.

℟. **Alleluia, alleluia.**

PASTORAL REFLECTIONS

Our singing in church reflects and continues what the angels are doing in heaven, praising God in song. In that sense, our active participation in the music of the Mass is a sacred obligation and not something that is optional.

GOSPEL: Luke 2:15-20

The shepherds found Mary and Joseph and the infant.

This is the account of the shepherds who visited the baby and his parents. Everything in the account is filled with wonder and joy.

The last thing that the Holy Family would have expected is for shepherds to arrive in order to pay homage. Shepherds in the days of Jesus were feared and avoided. They were re-garded as untrustworthy and their work made them ceremo-nially unclean. They were social outcasts. Yet they pay homage to the newborn king of the Jews and give praise and glory to God for his wondrous deeds.

Mary ponders these things in her heart. In Biblical symbolism, the heart is the organ of think-ing, not feeling. (One feels with one's guts or stomach.) Thus, Mary is wondering about the meaning of the things that were happening.

A reading from the holy Gospel according to Luke

When the angels went away from them to heaven,
the shepherds said to one another,
"Let us go, then, to Bethlehem
to see this thing that has taken place,
which the Lord has made known to us."
So they went in haste and found Mary and Joseph,
and the infant lying in the manger.
When they saw this,
they made known the message
that had been told them about this child.
All who heard it were amazed
by what had been told them by the shepherds.
And Mary kept all these things,
reflecting on them in her heart.
Then the shepherds returned,
glorifying and praising God
for all they had heard and seen,
just as it had been told to them.

The Gospel of the Lord.

PASTORAL REFLECTIONS

The Gospel of Luke strongly emphasizes that Jesus came into this world for those who most needed him. The first to hear about his birth are the shepherds. The last to hear his invitation is the good thief (who obviously is not that good a thief considering that he was caught).

Who are those who today most need to hear about Jesus? Can I be an instrument of his love in their lives?

December 25, 2012
THE NATIVITY OF THE LORD [CHRISTMAS]
AT THE MASS DURING THE DAY

Lect. No. 16

FIRST READING: Isaiah 52:7-10

All the ends of the earth will behold the salvation of our God.

In this First Reading we hear of how the LORD comforts his people. This is, in fact, the major theme of this section of the Book of the Prophet Isaiah. It begins, "Comfort, be comforted my people" (Isaiah 40:1).

We also hear that it is the LORD himself who will comfort his people. Throughout these chapters the LORD insists that it is he himself who will intervene. We hear phrases like "I will rescue," "I will redeem," "I will create," etc. This is fulfilled in the birth of the babe of Bethlehem, for the child is God among us.

The prophet struggles to find words appropriate to this announcement, for it is glad tidings, an announcement of peace and of good news.

A reading from the Book of the Prophet Isaiah

How beautiful upon the mountains
    are the feet of him who brings glad tidings,
announcing peace, bearing good news,
    announcing salvation, and saying to Zion,
    "Your God is King!"

Hark! Your sentinels raise a cry,
    together they shout for joy,
for they see directly, before their eyes,
    the LORD restoring Zion.
Break out together in song,
    O ruins of Jerusalem!
For the LORD comforts his people,
    he redeems Jerusalem.
The LORD has bared his holy arm
    in the sight of all the nations;
all the ends of the earth will behold
    the salvation of our God.

The word of the Lord.

Lect. No. 16

RESPONSORIAL PSALM: Ps 98:1, 2-3, 3-4, 5-6 (℟.: 3c)

This entire psalm is a hymn of praise for the wondrous deeds that God has done for his chosen people.

Normally, when the people of Israel praised God for acts of

℟. **All the ends of the earth have seen the saving power of God.**

Sing to the LORD a new song,
    for he has done wondrous deeds;
his right hand has won victory for him,
    his holy arm.

42

salvation, it was a remembrance of the Exodus experience.

This psalm, however, seems to have been written later, and probably refers to the salvation that the LORD worked through the second exodus, the return of the Israelites from Babylon.

Yet, there is also a third application, that of the birth of Jesus, whose very name means "Yahweh saves."

The psalmist praises the LORD by singing a new song. There are two forms of the word new in Biblical languages. One word simply means that it is not old. The other word means that it is radically new.

The salvation of the LORD would be for all the nations of the earth. It was no longer restricted to one people or one time.

The psalmist calls upon the community to use every musical instrument to praise the LORD.

℞. **All the ends of the earth have seen the saving power of God.**

The LORD has made his salvation known:
in the sight of the nations he has revealed his justice.
He has remembered his kindness and his faithfulness
toward the house of Israel.

℞. **All the ends of the earth have seen the saving power of God.**

All the ends of the earth have seen
the salvation by our God.
Sing joyfully to the LORD, all you lands;
break into song; sing praise.

℞. **All the ends of the earth have seen the saving power of God.**

Sing praise to the LORD with the harp,
with the harp and melodious song.
With trumpets and the sound of the horn
sing joyfully before the King, the LORD.

℞. **All the ends of the earth have seen the saving power of God.**

SECOND READING: Hebrews 1:1-6

God has spoken to us through the Son.

The author of the Letter to the Hebrews combines Jewish learning and Greek philosophy to proclaim Jesus as our High Priest.

He speaks of how God revealed his word through the prophets of old. This was a wonderful gift, but the prophets could never fully communicate God's

A reading from the beginning of
the Letter to the Hebrews

Brothers and sisters:
In times past, God spoke in partial and various ways
to our ancestors through the prophets;
in these last days, he has spoken to us through the Son,
whom he made heir of all things

word in human words. Human words always fall short. That is why there had to be many prophets, because none was ever fully successful in revealing God's word to his people.

This is why God chose to send his own Son. Jesus, the only-begotten Son of God, is the Word of God, the perfect expression of who God is and what he asks of us. It is only through him that we can truly know God.

The last part of this reading tries to establish Jesus as superior to the angels. In Greek philosophy, totally spiritual beings were superior to material beings. Jesus took on our flesh, so some wondered if angels were superior to him. Our author argues that Jesus is the Son of God and above every angel.

and through whom he created the universe,
> who is the refulgence of his glory, the very imprint of his being,
and who sustains all things by his mighty word.
When he had accomplished purification from sins,
he took his seat at the right hand of the Majesty on high,
as far superior to the angels
as the name he has inherited is more excellent than theirs.

For to which of the angels did God ever say:
> *You are my son; this day I have begotten you?*
Or again:
> *I will be a father to him, and he shall be a son to me?*
And again, when he leads the firstborn into the world, he says:
> *Let all the angels of God worship him.*

The word of the Lord.

Lect.
No. 16

As the Lord Jesus comes to proclaim his Gospel to us, we rise to greet him and adore him as the light of the world. He lights a path for us through the darkness of our world.

ALLELUIA

℟. **Alleluia, alleluia.**

A holy day has dawned upon us.
Come, you nations, and adore the Lord.
For today a great light has come upon the earth.

℟. **Alleluia, alleluia.**

GOSPEL: A Longer Form: John 1:1-18

The Word became flesh and made his dwelling among us.

The Prologue of the Gospel of John speaks of Jesus as the Word of God. The author of this hymn is presenting Jesus as wisdom incarnate. This was a way of saying that even before Jesus was born in the flesh in Bethlehem, he already existed. Our author is saying that although the Old Testament authors did not know it, they were actually writing about Jesus whenever they wrote about Wisdom.

John the Baptist was a witness to the fact that Jesus is the Son of God. Unlike the other Gospels where John the Baptist is constantly calling people to conversion, in the Gospel of John he continuously gives witness to the identity of Jesus. John proclaims that Jesus is the Messiah and that he is not.

When this hymn speaks about the Word being in the world and the world not knowing it, it is not speaking about the rejection of Jesus. It is speaking about Israel's rejection of all of the prophets whom Yahweh sent to call her to conversion.

In verse 14 we begin to speak about Jesus incarnate. We hear that the Word became flesh. This means that God did not consider our material world to be evil, but rather decided to join us and thus bless and consecrate this created world.

A reading from the holy Gospel according to John

In the beginning was the Word,
    and the Word was with God,
    and the Word was God.
He was in the beginning with God.
All things came to be through him,
    and without him nothing came to be.
What came to be through him was life,
    and this life was the light of the human race;
the light shines in the darkness,
    and the darkness has not overcome it.
A man named John was sent from God.
He came for testimony, to testify to the light,
    so that all might believe through him.
He was not the light,
    but came to testify to the light.
The true light, which enlightens everyone,
    was coming into the world.
    He was in the world,
        and the world came to be through him,
        but the world did not know him.
    He came to what was his own,
        but his own people did not accept him.

But to those who did accept him
    he gave power to become children of God,
    to those who believe in his name,
    who were born not by natural generation
    nor by human choice nor by a man's decision
    but of God.
        And the Word became flesh
        and made his dwelling among us,
        and we saw his glory,
        the glory as of the Father's only Son,
        full of grace and truth.

Jesus is full of grace and truth. These two words are actually Old Testament ideas: that God loves us with a covenant love and God is always faithful. Jesus is God's love and faithfulness incarnate.

Jesus is the only Son of God. In the Old Testament, "Son of God" was often used as a synonym for hero, but here "Son of God" means the eternally begotten Son of God.

Finally, we hear that Jesus reveals who God is. As the wisdom of God, Jesus can fill us with knowledge of God. We cannot hope to understand who God is except through Jesus' revelation.

John testified to him and cried out, saying,
    "This was he of whom I said,
    'The one who is coming after me ranks ahead of me
    because he existed before me.'"
From his fullness we have all received,
    grace in place of grace,
    because while the law was given through Moses,
    grace and truth came through Jesus Christ.
No one has ever seen God.
The only Son, God, who is at the Father's side,
    has revealed him.

The Gospel of the Lord.

| Lect. No. 16 |

GOSPEL: B Shorter Form: John 1:1-5, 9-14

The Word became flesh and made his dwelling among us.

The Prologue of the Gospel of John speaks of Jesus as the Word of God. The author of this hymn is presenting Jesus as wisdom incarnate. This was a way of saying that even before Jesus was born in the flesh in Bethlehem, he already existed. Our author is saying that although the Old Testament authors did not know it, they were actually writing about Jesus whenever they wrote about Wisdom.

When this hymn speaks about the Word being in the world and the world not knowing it, it is not speaking about the rejection of Jesus. It is speaking about Israel's rejection of all of the prophets whom Yahweh sent to call her to conversion.

A reading from the holy Gospel according to John

In the beginning was the Word,
    and the Word was with God,
    and the Word was God.
He was in the beginning with God.
All things came to be through him,
    and without him nothing came to be.
What came to be through him was life,
    and this life was the light of the human race;
    and the darkness has not overcome it.
The true light, which enlightens everyone,
    was coming into the world.
He was in the world,
    and the world came to be through him,
    but the world did not know him.
He came to what was his own,
    but his own people did not accept him.

In verse 14 we begin to speak about Jesus incarnate. We hear that the Word became flesh. This means that God did not consider our material world to be evil, but rather decided to join us and thus bless and consecrate this created world.

Jesus is full of grace and truth. These two words are actually Old Testament ideas: that God loves us with a covenant love and God is always faithful. Jesus is God's love and faithfulness incarnate.

Jesus is the only Son of God. In the Old Testament, "Son of God" was often used as a synonym for hero, but here "Son of God" means the eternally begotten Son of God.

But to those who did accept him
> he gave power to become children of God,
> to those who believe in his name,
> who were born not by natural generation
> nor by human choice nor by a man's decision
> but of God.
> And the Word became flesh
> > and made his dwelling among us,
> > and we saw his glory,
> > the glory as of the Father's only Son,
> > full of grace and truth.

The Gospel of the Lord.

PASTORAL REFLECTIONS

There are different ways to speak about the Christmas story. Even the Gospels present Magi in one account (Matthew) and shepherds in another (Luke). Then in John, we have a philosophical presentation that speaks about the eternal Word of God that becomes human.

We retell the Christmas story in the way that we celebrate this day and season and in the way that we share God's love throughout the year. Christ and his message are reborn in our hearts and we make him present again to the world.

December 30, 2012
THE HOLY FAMILY OF JESUS, MARY, AND JOSEPH

The A, B, C readings given on pp. 52-55 may be used in place of these C readings.

Lect. No. 17 **FIRST READING: 1 Samuel 1:20-22, 24-28**

Samuel, as long as he lives, shall be dedicated to the Lord.

In chapter one of the First Book of Samuel, Hannah is presented as a faith-filled woman who was not able to have any children. She was berated by Peninnah, the other wife of her husband Elkanah. She therefore presented her plight to the LORD. She prayed that she would be given a child whom she promised would be dedicated to the service of the LORD.

While she was praying, the priest Eli saw her and assumed that she was drunk (for she was moving her lips but she was not saying anything).

The LORD listened to her prayer and she became pregnant. She bore a son whom she named Samuel (a name that means "God listens").

Hannah kept her promise and dedicated her son to the service of the LORD. She left him at the sanctuary in Shiloh where he assisted Eli and his sons who were priests of God.

Samuel was to be the last judge of Israel (a role that included priestly, prophetic, and kingly responsibilities). It was he who anointed first Saul and then David as kings of Israel.

A reading from the first Book of Samuel

In those days Hannah conceived, and at the end of her term bore a son
whom she called Samuel, since she had asked the LORD for him.
The next time her husband Elkanah was going up with the rest of his household
to offer the customary sacrifice to the LORD and to fulfill his vows,
Hannah did not go, explaining to her husband,
"Once the child is weaned,
I will take him to appear before the LORD
and to remain there forever;
I will offer him as a perpetual nazirite."

Once Samuel was weaned, Hannah brought him up with her,
along with a three-year-old bull,
an ephah of flour, and a skin of wine,
and presented him at the temple of the LORD in Shiloh.
After the boy's father had sacrificed the young bull,
Hannah, his mother, approached Eli and said:
"Pardon, my lord!
As you live, my lord,
I am the woman who stood near you here, praying to the LORD.
I prayed for this child, and the LORD granted my request.
Now I, in turn, give him to the LORD;
as long as he lives, he shall be dedicated to the LORD."
Hannah left Samuel there.

The word of the Lord.

48

Lect.
No. 17

RESPONSORIAL PSALM: Ps 84:2-3, 5-6, 9-10 (℞.: cf. 5a)

The Responsorial Psalm continues the theme of serving the LORD in his holy dwelling place. This is the same idea found in the Gospel today where we hear about Jesus who calls the temple in Jerusalem his Father's house.

Where is our true dwelling place? Where can we truly say that we are at home?

The psalm speaks of making pilgrimage to the LORD's house. This is the one place where we find ourselves at home, where we can experience the love of God in an unconditional manner.

Jesus came into the world, and we therefore no longer have to go to a particular shrine or church to experience his love. He is our home, for wherever we are upon the earth, we are dwelling in him.

℞. **Blessed are they who dwell in your house, O Lord.**

How lovely is your dwelling place, O LORD of hosts!
My soul yearns and pines for the courts of the LORD.
My heart and my flesh cry out for the living God.

℞. **Blessed are they who dwell in your house, O Lord.**

Happy they who dwell in your house!
Continually they praise you.
Happy the men whose strength you are!
Their hearts are set upon the pilgrimage.

℞. **Blessed are they who dwell in your house, O Lord.**

O LORD of hosts, hear our prayer;
hearken, O God of Jacob!
O God, behold our shield,
and look upon the face of your anointed.

℞. **Blessed are they who dwell in your house, O Lord.**

Lect.
No. 17

SECOND READING: 1 John 3:1-2, 21-24

We are called children of God. And so we are.

The first Letter of Saint John speaks of the incredible dignity that the Lord has bestowed upon us. We are not slaves or servants, we are children of God.

Yahweh treats us with the same respect and honor that he treats Jesus, his only-begotten Son. He calls us to share in his love and his mission here upon

A reading from the first Letter of Saint John

Beloved:
See what love the Father has bestowed on us
that we may be called the children of God.
And so we are.
The reason the world does not know us
is that it did not know him.
Beloved, we are God's children now;
what we shall be has not yet been revealed.

the earth, and in his glory in heaven.

The promise of heaven is that we will be like the one whom we love. We will not only share in the likeness and image of God, we will truly be one with him.

The way we know we are God's children is that we keep his commandments. We must live moral and giving lives.

The commandments are not rules that imprison us. They are guidelines that help us to choose what is right and good. They teach us virtue and generosity (especially if we live the greatest law, the law of love).

We do know that when it is revealed we shall be like him,
  for we shall see him as he is.

Beloved, if our hearts do not condemn us,
  we have confidence in God and receive from him whatever we ask,
  because we keep his commandments and do what pleases him.
And his commandment is this:
  we should believe in the name of his Son, Jesus Christ,
  and love one another just as he commanded us.
Those who keep his commandments remain in him, and he in them,
  and the way we know that he remains in us
  is from the Spirit he gave us.

The word of the Lord.

Lect. No. 17

The Alleluia Verse speaks of our need for the grace of God. Without it, we cannot hope to turn our minds and hearts to the Lord.

ALLELUIA: cf. Acts 16:14b

℟. **Alleluia, alleluia.**

Open our hearts, O Lord,
to listen to the words of your Son.

℟. **Alleluia, alleluia.**

Lect. No. 17

GOSPEL: Luke 2:41-52

His parents found Jesus sitting in the midst of the teachers.

The Gospel of Luke consistently shows the Holy Family to be good and observant Jews (for this was the will of God). They travel to Jerusalem for the Passover festival (something that was encouraged of those who were righteous).

A reading from the holy Gospel according to Luke

Each year Jesus' parents went to Jerusalem for the feast of Passover,
  and when he was twelve years old,
  they went up according to festival custom.

It is odd that this is the only story for the period of time between when Jesus was an infant and when he began his public ministry.

One must ask why Luke included this particular story in his Gospel. The answer seems to be that, according to Luke, it was when Jesus discerned that he was both human and divine.

A Jewish boy was considered to be a man when he was around twelve years old. Luke is saying that when Jesus knew what it meant to be a man, he also knew that he was God. That is why this is the first moment that Jesus proclaims God to be his Father in heaven.

The description of Jesus speaking with the doctors in the temple does not mean that he was teaching them. It could easily be that he was so sincere, so honest, that he astounded them.

This scene might also be a preparation for Mary, his mother. Jesus was lost for three days when he was about his Father's business. Later, when Jesus died for our sins and was buried for three days, Mary would have to trust that he was about the Father's business again.

After they had completed its days, as they were returning,
the boy Jesus remained behind in Jerusalem,
but his parents did not know it.
Thinking that he was in the caravan,
they journeyed for a day
and looked for him among their relatives and acquaintances,
but not finding him,
they returned to Jerusalem to look for him.
After three days they found him in the temple,
sitting in the midst of the teachers,
listening to them and asking them questions,
and all who heard him were astounded
at his understanding and his answers.
When his parents saw him,
they were astonished,
and his mother said to him,
"Son, why have you done this to us?
Your father and I have been looking for you with great anxiety."
And he said to them,
"Why were you looking for me?
Did you not know that I must be in my Father's house?"
But they did not understand what he said to them.
He went down with them and came to Nazareth,
and was obedient to them;
and his mother kept all these things in her heart.
And Jesus advanced in wisdom and age and favor
before God and man.

The Gospel of the Lord.

The following A, B, C readings may be used in place of the previous readings.

Lect. No. 17

FIRST READING: Sirach 3:2-6, 12-14

Those who fear the Lord honor their parents.

The Book of Sirach was written late in the Old Testament period when Jewish society was strongly influenced by Greek culture.

A Greek ideal was to live an ordered life that would give public witness to the values that were the core of one's beliefs.

The author of Sirach combined this ideal with the traditional respect for parents and the family. Together these ideas produce this beautiful appeal for a family life in which one's parents are treated with great respect.

Although this portrait is idealized, it also shows signs of realism. It acknowledges that the situation might arise in which one's parents are no longer mentally alert. Nevertheless, care for parents is a sacred responsibility.

A reading from the Book of Sirach

God sets a father in honor over his children;
 a mother's authority he confirms over her sons.
Whoever honors his father atones for sins,
 and preserves himself from them.
When he prays, he is heard;
 he stores up riches who reveres his mother.
Whoever honors his father is gladdened by children,
 and, when he prays, is heard.
Whoever reveres his father will live a long life;
 he who obeys his father brings comfort to his
 mother.

My son, take care of your father when he is old;
 grieve him not as long as he lives.
Even if his mind fail, be considerate of him;
 revile him not all the days of his life;
kindness to a father will not be forgotten,
 firmly planted against the debt of your sins
 —a house raised in justice to you.

The word of the Lord.

Lect. No. 17

RESPONSORIAL PSALM: Ps 128:1-2, 3, 4-5 (℟.: cf. 1)

Like the First Reading, Psalm 128 is taken from the Wisdom tradition of Old Testament literature. Wisdom literature answered the question, "How can we live a good and virtuous life?"

This psalm responds that one must fear the LORD. This expression is often misunderstood. People sometimes think

℟. **Blessed are those who fear the Lord and walk in his ways.**

Blessed is everyone who fears the LORD,
 who walks in his ways!
For you shall eat the fruit of your handiwork;
 blessed shall you be, and favored.

℟. **Blessed are those who fear the Lord and walk in his ways.**

that we should be afraid that God might condemn us for our sins and send us to Hell.

Fear of the LORD is really a profound sense of reverence and awe when one considers the greatness of God. We are creatures, while God is the creator of all. We cannot even begin to understand the wonder of God's majesty.

If we have this attitude toward God, our everyday lives will reflect it and we will observe his law. Then our families will be blessed, for our life-styles will be respectful and gracious. We will not be selfish and egocentric.

Your wife shall be like a fruitful vine
   in the recesses of your home;
your children like olive plants
   around your table.

R/. **Blessed are those who fear the Lord and walk in his ways.**

Behold, thus is the man blessed
   who fears the LORD.
The LORD bless you from Zion:
   may you see the prosperity of Jerusalem
   all the days of your life.

R/. **Blessed are those who fear the Lord and walk in his ways.**

Lect. No. 17   **SECOND READING:** 🅰 **Longer Form: Colossians 3:12-21**

Family life in the Lord.

The first part of this reading exhorts the community to a life of virtue. Early Christians felt that it was essential for them to live at peace with one another so that pagans could see how virtuous their calling was and might be led to conversion. This is why they were to live in compassion, kindness, humility, gentleness, and patience, etc. Christ would lead them to virtue and peace.

This ideal is just as important today. One often hears of people who go to Mass but do not live their faith on an everyday basis, especially in the way they treat their own family.

We cannot hope to live our Christian calling if we are not filled with a sense of gratitude. It is the virtue that reminds us how much we depend upon

A reading from the Letter of Saint Paul
to the Colossians

Brothers and sisters:
Put on, as God's chosen ones, holy and beloved,
   heartfelt compassion, kindness, humility, gentleness, and patience,
   bearing with one another and forgiving one another,
   if one has a grievance against another;
   as the Lord has forgiven you, so must you also do.
And over all these put on love,
   that is, the bond of perfection.
And let the peace of Christ control your hearts,
   the peace into which you were also called in one body.
And be thankful.
Let the word of Christ dwell in you richly,
   as in all wisdom you teach and admonish one another,

the Lord. This reading encourages expressions of gratitude toward the Lord for all that we have received.

The latter part of the reading exhorts family members to live lives of mutual respect (for it was God who established the various family relationships).

Notice, that rather than emphasizing the control of one member over another, the letter emphasizes the mutual responsibilities of one family member toward the others.

singing psalms, hymns, and spiritual songs
   with gratitude in your hearts to God.
And whatever you do, in word or in deed,
   do everything in the name of the Lord Jesus,
   giving thanks to God the Father through him.

Wives, be subordinate to your husbands,
   as is proper in the Lord.
Husbands, love your wives,
   and avoid any bitterness toward them.
Children, obey your parents in everything,
   for this is pleasing to the Lord.
Fathers, do not provoke your children,
   so they may not become discouraged.

The word of the Lord.

Lect. No. 17

SECOND READING: B Shorter Form: Colossians 3:12-17

Family life in the Lord.

The first part of this reading exhorts the community to a life of virtue. Early Christians felt that it was essential for them to live at peace with one another so that pagans could see how virtuous their calling was and might be led to conversion. This is why they were to live in compassion, kindness, humility, gentleness, and patience, etc. Christ would lead them to virtue and peace.

This ideal is just as important today. One often hears of people who go to Mass but do not live their faith on an everyday basis, especially in the way they treat their own family.

We cannot hope to live our Christian calling if we are not filled with a sense of gratitude. It is the virtue that reminds us how much we depend upon

A reading from the Letter of Saint Paul to the Colossians

Brothers and sisters:
   Put on, as God's chosen ones, holy and beloved,
   heartfelt compassion, kindness, humility, gentleness, and patience,
   bearing with one another and forgiving one another,
   if one has a grievance against another;
   as the Lord has forgiven you, so must you also do.
And over all these put on love,
   that is, the bond of perfection.
And let the peace of Christ control your hearts,
   the peace into which you were also called in one body.
And be thankful.
Let the word of Christ dwell in you richly,
   as in all wisdom you teach and admonish one another,

the Lord. This reading encourages expressions of gratitude toward the Lord for everything we have, for everything that we have comes from the Lord.

singing psalms, hymns, and spiritual songs
with gratitude in your hearts to God.
And whatever you do, in word or in deed,
do everything in the name of the Lord Jesus,
giving thanks to God the Father through him.

The word of the Lord.

ALLELUIA: Colossians 3:15a, 16a

The only way that our families can be peace-filled is by making Christ the center of our lives.

℟. **Alleluia, alleluia.**

Let the peace of Christ control your hearts;
let the word of Christ dwell in you richly.

℟. **Alleluia, alleluia.**

GOSPEL: Luke 2:41-52

His parents found Jesus sitting in the midst of the teachers.

See p. 50.

PASTORAL REFLECTIONS

The Feast of the Holy Family reminds us that our faith must be expressed not only in our individual lives but also in that of our families. Pope Paul VI said that one's family is the first Church that most people attend. Our families are the source of our faith and also an expression of that faith.

This does not mean that any of our families is perfect. None of them is. Sometimes it is in our acceptance of the brokenness of our families and the striving to make them better that we give our most important witness to our commitment to our faith.

January 1, 2013

THE OCTAVE DAY OF THE NATIVITY OF THE LORD [CHRISTMAS]

SOLEMNITY OF MARY, THE HOLY MOTHER OF GOD

Lect.
No. 18

FIRST READING: Numbers 6:22-27

They shall invoke my name upon the Israelites, and I will bless them.

The First Reading for this feast records the blessing that the LORD gave to Moses that he was to invoke over the people of Israel.

It is the presence of God in our lives that is the true definition of blessing. Our lives, in fact, only have meaning inasmuch as we make God the center.

This blessing is also called the blessing of Saint Francis, for he recommended this greeting to his followers.

A reading from the Book of Numbers

The LORD said to Moses:
    "Speak to Aaron and his sons and tell them:
    This is how you shall bless the Israelites.
Say to them:
    The LORD bless you and keep you!
    The LORD let his face shine upon you, and be gracious to you!
    The LORD look upon you kindly and give you peace!
So shall they invoke my name upon the Israelites,
    and I will bless them."

The word of the Lord.

Lect.
No. 18

RESPONSORIAL PSALM: Ps 67:2-3, 5, 6, 8 (℟.: 2a)

The psalm continues the theme that the only true blessing is that which is found in the presence of the LORD. God is the source of mercy. God is the source of our salvation.

We should remember that there are two meanings for the word salvation.

Saint Paul always speaks about salvation as what will

℟. **May God bless us in his mercy.**

May God have pity on us and bless us;
    may he let his face shine upon us.
So may your way be known upon earth;
    among all nations, your salvation.

℟. **May God bless us in his mercy.**

May the nations be glad and exult
    because you rule the peoples in equity;
    the nations on the earth you guide.

happen to us when God welcomes us into heaven.

Saint Luke speaks about salvation as something that is already happening to us now. The minute we make Jesus a part of our lives, we are already experiencing the joys of heaven.

℟. **May God bless us in his mercy.**

May the peoples praise you, O God;
    may all the peoples praise you!
May God bless us,
    and may all the ends of the earth fear him!

℟. **May God bless us in his mercy.**

Lect. No. 18

SECOND READING: Galatians 4:4-7

God sent his Son, born of a woman.

There are two words for time in Greek. One word simply means the passing of one minute to the next. The other, that which Saint Paul uses here, signifies time that is sacred time.

This is the first reference in Scripture to the birth of Jesus (written over a decade before the first Gospel).

God sends the Holy Spirit into our hearts so that we can know how much God loves us. This means that when we ask ourselves what we would most like to hear from God, the answer is not so much ours as that of the Spirit speaking in our hearts.

A reading from the Letter of Saint Paul to the Galatians

Brothers and sisters:
    When the fullness of time had come, God sent his Son,
    born of a woman, born under the law,
    to ransom those under the law,
    so that we might receive adoption as sons.
As proof that you are sons,
    God sent the Spirit of his Son into our hearts,
    crying out, "Abba, Father!"
So you are no longer a slave but a son,
    and if a son then also an heir, through God.

The word of the Lord.

Lect. No. 18

ALLELUIA: Hebrews 1:1-2

The Alleluia Verse quotes the first couple of verses of the Letter to the Hebrews. While God revealed many words to Israel throughout history, he revealed the one Word of God in the birth of his only Son.

℟. **Alleluia, alleluia.**

In the past God spoke to our ancestors through the prophets;
in these last days, he has spoken to us through the Son.

℟. **Alleluia, alleluia.**

Lect.
No. 18

GOSPEL: Luke 2:16-21

They found Mary and Joseph and the infant.
When the eight days were completed, he was named Jesus.

This passage from the Gospel of Luke recounts some of the wondrous events that accompanied the birth of Jesus. Note especially that Mary pondered all of these things in her heart. In Biblical symbolism, the heart is where one thinks. Thus, Mary is pictured as wondering what the meaning of all these things could be.

It is also important to remember that shepherds were not considered to be reputable people. They were social outcasts, thieves, and worse. The message of salvation was given first of all to those who most needed it.

Mary and Joseph, being good Jews, fulfill all of the prescriptions of the law by circumcising Jesus eight days after he was born and giving him the name that had been revealed to them by the archangel Gabriel.

A reading from the holy Gospel according to Luke

The shepherds went in haste to Bethlehem and found Mary and Joseph,
and the infant lying in the manger.
When they saw this,
they made known the message
that had been told them about this child.
All who heard it were amazed
by what had been told them by the shepherds.
And Mary kept all these things,
reflecting on them in her heart.
Then the shepherds returned,
glorifying and praising God
for all they had heard and seen,
just as it had been told to them.

When eight days were completed for his circumcision,
he was named Jesus, the name given him by the angel
before he was conceived in the womb.

The Gospel of the Lord.

PASTORAL REFLECTIONS

In 431 A.D., bishops from all over the world met in Ephesus (Turkey) and declared Mary to be the Mother of God. (The term they used was Theotokos.*) This declaration actually had more to do with Jesus than Mary. By it, the Council Fathers were declaring that the Word of God did not pretend to unite with human flesh. Jesus truly had two natures (human and divine) united in one person. This feast of the Blessed Virgin reminds us that our devotion to Mary should always be Christ-centered, for she always points to her Son and says, "Follow him!"*

January 6, 2013

THE EPIPHANY OF THE LORD

Lect.
No. 20

FIRST READING: Isaiah 60:1-6

The glory of the Lord shines upon you.

This part of the Book of the Prophet Isaiah was written shortly after the Jews returned from exile in Babylon (c. 539 B.C.).

In the previous part of the Book of Isaiah, we heard how Yahweh would restore the fortune of his beloved people. Thus, when the Persian emperor Cyrus allowed the Jewish people to return to their homeland, they were exultant. Yet, when they arrived home, all they found was devastation.

In this part of Isaiah, we hear that God would still fulfill the promises found in Second Isaiah (chs. 40—55).

The glory of God would be upon Israel to such an extent that even the Gentile peoples would come in pilgrimage to Jerusalem to pay homage to the LORD. No longer would the pagans carry the Israelites off into exile. Now the pagans would bring their riches and submit themselves to the God of Israel. This promise would be fulfilled with the arrival of the Magi.

A reading from the Book of the Prophet Isaiah

Rise up in splendor, Jerusalem! Your light has
    come,
    the glory of the Lord shines upon you.
See, darkness covers the earth,
    and thick clouds cover the peoples;
but upon you the LORD shines,
    and over you appears his glory.
Nations shall walk by your light,
    and kings by your shining radiance.
Raise your eyes and look about;
    they all gather and come to you:
your sons come from afar,
    and your daughters in the arms of their nurses.

Then you shall be radiant at what you see,
    your heart shall throb and overflow,
for the riches of the sea shall be emptied out before
        you,
    the wealth of nations shall be brought to you.
Caravans of camels shall fill you,
    dromedaries from Midian and Ephah;
all from Sheba shall come
    bearing gold and frankincense,
    and proclaiming the praises of the LORD.

The word of the Lord.

Lect. No. 20

RESPONSORIAL PSALM: Ps 72:1-2, 7-8, 10-11, 12-13 (℟.: cf. 11)

Psalm 72 gives a description of the perfect king of Israel. He would be someone who was filled with wisdom like Solomon, as well as a great warrior who could enlarge the boundaries of Israel from sea to sea, an accomplishment of David, and someone who guaranteed justice in the land, especially to the poor.

As with the First Reading, we hear that even Gentile kings would recognize the splendor of that king's reign and come to pay him homage.

None of the kings of Israel could fulfill all of these expectations. Every time that the prophets spoke of a king whom they hoped would finally do the will of the LORD, they ended up being disillusioned. Thus, they began to speak about an anointed one in the future who would be unlike all of the other kings of Israel.

The arrival of the Magi to pay homage to baby Jesus, the Messiah of the LORD, was the fulfillment of this prophecy.

℟. **Lord, every nation on earth will adore you.**

O God, with your judgment endow the king,
  and with your justice, the king's son;
he shall govern your people with justice
  and your afflicted ones with judgment.

℟. **Lord, every nation on earth will adore you.**

Justice shall flower in his days,
  and profound peace, till the moon be no more.
May he rule from sea to sea,
  and from the River to the ends of the earth.

℟. **Lord, every nation on earth will adore you.**

The kings of Tarshish and the Isles shall offer gifts;
  the kings of Arabia and Seba shall bring tribute.
All kings shall pay him homage,
  all nations shall serve him.

℟. **Lord, every nation on earth will adore you.**

For he shall rescue the poor when he cries out,
  and the afflicted when he has no one to help him.
He shall have pity for the lowly and the poor;
  the lives of the poor he shall save.

℟. **Lord, every nation on earth will adore you.**

Lect. No. 20

SECOND READING: Ephesians 3:2-3a, 5-6

Now it has been revealed that the Gentiles are coheirs of the promise.

In the Old Covenant, only the Jewish people received the promise. They were the chosen people and heirs of the promises that God had made to the patriarchs and the prophets of Israel.

A reading from the Letter of Saint Paul
to the Ephesians

Brothers and sisters:
  You have heard of the stewardship of God's grace
that was given to me for your benefit,

In the New Covenant all peoples will participate in the grace of the Lord. There will be no distinction between Jew and Greek, slave or free, male or female. They all are chosen by the Lord. All will participate in the promise of the Gospel. They all are part of the body of Christ, which is the Church. This is the mystery of salvation: the bounty of God's love for all people.

namely, that the mystery was made known to me
  by revelation.
It was not made known to people in other generations
  as it has now been revealed
  to his holy apostles and prophets by the Spirit:
  that the Gentiles are coheirs, members of the
    same body,
  and copartners in the promise in Christ Jesus
    through the gospel.

The word of the Lord.

ALLELUIA: Matthew 2:2

Lect. No. 20

The Magi saw a star rising in the sky and risked all to pay homage to the newborn king of the Jews. As we proclaim this Alleluia Verse, we promise to follow their example.

℞. **Alleluia, alleluia.**

We saw his star at its rising
and have come to do him homage.

℞. **Alleluia, alleluia.**

GOSPEL: Matthew 2:1-12

Lect. No. 20

We saw his star at its rising and have come to do him homage.

The feast of the Epiphany celebrates the arrival of the Magi to pay homage to baby Jesus. Epiphany means manifestation, for we are commemorating the day when the glory of God's Messiah was made manifest to the pagans (in the person of the Magi).

Magi were astrologers. They were not kings (although that title is often used for them) nor does it say that there were three (that is the number of gifts). The account speaks of them coming from the east (possibly Persia or Babylon).

A reading from the holy Gospel according
to Matthew

When Jesus was born in Bethlehem of Judea,
  in the days of King Herod,
  behold, magi from the east arrived in Jerusalem,
    saying,
  "Where is the newborn king of the Jews?
We saw his star at its rising
  and have come to do him homage."
When King Herod heard this,
  he was greatly troubled,
  and all Jerusalem with him.
Assembling all the chief priests and the scribes of
  the people,

It is possible that the star that they saw was the elision of three planets, Mars, Jupiter, and Saturn, which occurred around 7 B.C. The technical name for this type of elision is syzygy.

The Magi would naturally have gone to Jerusalem to inquire about the birth of a Jewish king. Herod intends to use them to murder what he considers to be a rival to his throne. From many sources we know that Herod was a murderous paranoid when it came to his throne. He murdered a wife, three sons, and a brother-in-law, who was the high priest.

Jewish scholars used a passage taken from Micah to determine that the Messiah was to be born in Bethlehem. This is typical of Matthew who always shows how Jesus fulfills the law and the prophets.

The Magi bring gold, frankincense, and myrrh. They would have brought these products because they were easy to carry and valuable. Later authors found symbolic meaning in these gifts. They spoke of gold as a gift one would give a king, frankincense as an incense one would burn to honor a god, and myrrh as an ointment used in burials, foretelling how Jesus would save us from our sins.

he inquired of them where the Christ was to be born.

They said to him, "In Bethlehem of Judea,
  for thus it has been written through the prophet:
    And you, Bethlehem, land of Judah,
      are by no means least among the rulers of Judah;
    since from you shall come a ruler,
      who is to shepherd my people Israel."

Then Herod called the magi secretly
  and ascertained from them the time of the star's appearance.

He sent them to Bethlehem and said,
  "Go and search diligently for the child.

When you have found him, bring me word,
  that I too may go and do him homage."

After their audience with the king they set out.

And behold, the star that they had seen at its rising preceded them,
  until it came and stopped over the place where the child was.

They were overjoyed at seeing the star,
  and on entering the house
  they saw the child with Mary his mother.

They prostrated themselves and did him homage.

Then they opened their treasures
  and offered him gifts of gold, frankincense, and myrrh.

And having been warned in a dream not to return to Herod,
  they departed for their country by another way.

The Gospel of the Lord.

PASTORAL REFLECTIONS

This feast with its star and the arrival of the Magi reminds us that God has a plan that is worked out in time (whether Biblical time or the time of our own lives).

January 13, 2013

THE BAPTISM OF THE LORD

(First Sunday in Ordinary Time)

The A, B, C readings given on pp. 67-69
may be used in place of these C readings.

Lect. No. 21 | **FIRST READING: Isaiah 40:1-5, 9-11**

The First Reading comes from the beginning of the second section of the Book of the Prophet Isaiah. It was actually written during the Babylonian exile (587-539 B.C.).

The people had suffered terribly during the war that led to the fall of Jerusalem and during their exile from their homeland. They wondered whether God would be angry at them forever.

Second Isaiah (an anonymous prophet whose writings were attached to those of the Prophet Isaiah) spoke of the consolation that the LORD was about to offer.

God would restore the good fortune of the people. God would bring the people of Israel back to their homeland. There would be no barrier that would prevent the people from going home.

This good news was to be proclaimed on the mountaintops. During the exile, the people had to be circumspect about how they gave witness to their faith (for they were living in exile), but now they could shout it out.

The glory of the Lord shall be revealed and all people shall see it.

A reading from the Book of the Prophet Isaiah

omfort, give comfort to my people,
says your God.
Speak tenderly to Jerusalem, and proclaim to her
that her service is at an end,
her guilt is expiated;
indeed, she has received from the hand of the
LORD
double for all her sins.

A voice cries out:
In the desert prepare the way of the LORD!
Make straight in the wasteland a highway for
our God!
Every valley shall be filled in,
every mountain and hill shall be made low;
the rugged land shall be made a plain,
the rough country, a broad valley.
Then the glory of the LORD shall be revealed,
and all people shall see it together;
for the mouth of the LORD has spoken.

Go up onto a high mountain,
Zion, herald of glad tidings;
cry out at the top of your voice,
Jerusalem, herald of good news!
Fear not to cry out
and say to the cities of Judah:
Here is your God!

It was God himself who would intervene for God loved the people of Israel. He treats them with the same compassion that one would expect from a faithful shepherd.

Here comes with power
　the Lord GOD,
　who rules by a strong arm;
here is his reward with him,
　his recompense before him.
Like a shepherd he feeds his flock;
　in his arms he gathers the lambs,
carrying them in his bosom,
　and leading the ewes with care.

The word of the Lord.

Lect. No. 21 RESPONSORIAL PSALM: Psalm 104:1b-2, 3-4, 24-25, 27-28, 29-30

The Responsorial Psalm is a hymn of praise that proclaims the glory and power of God. This psalm is used for today we celebrate the beginning of the public ministry of Jesus (with his Baptism in the Jordan).

The ministry of Jesus is seen as a victory of the Godly forces against the forces of evil. While John could only baptize with water, Jesus' Baptism would be one of the Holy Spirit and fire.

Typical of this type of hymn, God is first proclaimed as the creator and ruler of all that exists. Creation is seen as a victory over the forces of chaos.

God defeated even the evil forces that dwell in the sea (often called Leviathan in hymns like this one). But God not only subdues these forces, he also nourishes them and cares for them.

Not least of all God's works of power and beneficence is the fact that God created us. We

℟. **O bless the Lord, my soul.**

O LORD, my God, you are great indeed!
　you are clothed with majesty and glory,
robed in light as with a cloak.
　You have spread out the heavens like a tent-cloth.

℟. **O bless the Lord, my soul.**

You have constructed your palace upon the waters.
　You make the clouds your chariot;
you travel on the wings of the wind.
　You make the winds your messengers,
and flaming fire your ministers.

℟. **O bless the Lord, my soul.**

How manifold are your works, O LORD!
　In wisdom you have wrought them all—
the earth is full of your creatures;
　the sea also, great and wide,
in which are schools without number
　of living things both small and great.

℟. **O bless the Lord, my soul.**

They look to you to give them food in due time.
　When you give it to them, they gather it;
when you open your hand, they are filled with good
　things.

are fragile creatures (little more than mud with a bit of breath to hold us in being), but God loves and protects us.

℟. **O bless the Lord, my soul.**

If you take away their breath, they perish and return
   to the dust.

When you send forth your spirit, they are created,
and you renew the face of the earth.

℟. **O bless the Lord, my soul.**

Lect. No. 21

SECOND READING: Titus 2:11-14; 3:4-7

*Jesus Christ saved us through the bath of rebirth
and renewal by the Holy Spirit.*

On this feast of the Baptism of Jesus, we hear about the "bath of rebirth and renewal by the Holy Spirit" that we have received. This rebirth was not due to anything that we had done to deserve it. It was the gift of a merciful and gracious God.

Baptism is an expression of our faith. Faith is a gift from God. We cannot do anything to earn that gift.

Yet, once we have received that gift from God, we must respond to it by being baptized and living as children of God.

This reading reminds us that receiving the Sacrament of Baptism is not enough. It is not a magical act that fulfills our responsibility to live as God's children.

We must also live what Baptism signifies. We must reject those things which are opposed to the truth ("our godless ways") and live lives filled with virtue.

A reading from the Letter of Saint Paul to Titus

Beloved:
The grace of God has appeared, saving all
and training us to reject godless ways and worldly
   desires
and to live temperately, justly, and devoutly in this
   age,
as we await the blessed hope,
the appearance of the glory of our great God
and savior Jesus Christ,
who gave himself for us to deliver us from all law-
   lessness
and to cleanse for himself a people as his own,
eager to do what is good.

   When the kindness and generous love
      of God our savior appeared,
   not because of any righteous deeds we had
      done
      but because of his mercy,
   he saved us through the bath of rebirth
      and renewal by the Holy Spirit,
   whom he richly poured out on us
      through Jesus Christ our savior,
   so that we might be justified by his grace
      and become heirs in hope of eternal life.

The word of the Lord.

Lect. No. 21

The Alleluia Verse reminds us that John the Baptist proclaimed that Jesus would offer us a Baptism that was so much more powerful than John's Baptism of conversion.

ALLELUIA: cf. Luke 3:16

℟. **Alleluia, alleluia.**

John said: One mightier than I is coming;
he will baptize you with the Holy Spirit and with fire.

℟. **Alleluia, alleluia.**

Lect. No. 21

GOSPEL: Luke 3:15-16, 21-22

When Jesus had been baptized and was praying, heaven was opened.

When John the Baptist began his ministry of preaching conversion, many wondered whether he might be the Messiah of God.

John himself gave witness that he was not the Messiah, that another would come along who was much greater than he. He only baptized with water, but the Messiah would baptize with the Holy Spirit and fire. (The role of the Holy Spirit is central in the writings of Luke.)

While John's Baptism only gave us the possibility of turning from our sins, Jesus' Baptism made us into children of God. It invites us into the life of the Trinity (which is why we hear the voice of the Father and see the Holy Spirit in the form of the dove).

A reading from the holy Gospel according to Mark

The people were filled with expectation,
and all were asking in their hearts
whether John might be the Christ.
John answered them all, saying,
"I am baptizing you with water,
but one mightier than I is coming.
I am not worthy to loosen the thongs of his sandals.
He will baptize you with the Holy Spirit and fire."

After all the people had been baptized
and Jesus also had been baptized and was praying,
heaven was opened and the Holy Spirit descended upon him
in bodily form like a dove.
And a voice came from heaven,
"You are my beloved Son;
with you I am well pleased."

The Gospel of the Lord.

The following A, B, C readings may be used in place of the previous readings.

FIRST READING: Isaiah 42:1-4, 6-7

Behold my servant with whom I am well pleased.

This is the first of four hymns in Isaiah that speak about a mysterious figure called the Suffering Servant of Yahweh (the LORD). They are scattered throughout the second part of the Book of the Prophet Isaiah.

In this hymn we hear that the Servant is a chosen one of the LORD. He is called a "beloved" (even as Jesus is called "beloved" during his Baptism).

The Servant was to be a gentle figure who would bring justice to the entire world (and not just to the people of Israel).

Throughout the Old Testament it is never quite clear who this Servant was supposed to be. Some suggested that it was the nation of Israel, others that it was one of the prophets.

Jesus applied this prophecy to himself wherever he spoke about his mission, especially his suffering and death on the cross.

A reading from the Book of the Prophet Isaiah

Thus says the LORD:
  Here is my servant whom I uphold,
  my chosen one with whom I am pleased,
upon whom I have put my spirit;
  he shall bring forth justice to the nations,
not crying out, not shouting,
  not making his voice heard in the street.
A bruised reed he shall not break,
  and a smoldering wick he shall not quench,
until he establishes justice on the earth;
  the coastlands will wait for his teaching.

I, the LORD, have called you for the victory of justice,
  I have grasped you by the hand;
I formed you, and set you
  as a covenant of the people,
  a light for the nations,
to open the eyes of the blind,
  to bring out prisoners from confinement,
  and from the dungeon, those who live in darkness.

The word of the Lord.

RESPONSORIAL PSALM: Ps 29:1-2, 3-4, 3, 9-10 (℟.: 11b)

This psalm is an ancient hymn to Yahweh. It was probably originally a Canaanite hymn to Baal, the god of the storms. The phrase, "voice of the LORD," is actually a Hebrew phrase for thunder.

At some point a Jewish author replaced the name Baal

℟. **The Lord will bless his people with peace.**

Give to the LORD, you sons of God,
  give to the LORD glory and praise,
give to the LORD the glory due his name;
  adore the LORD in holy attire.

℟. **The Lord will bless his people with peace.**

with the name of the Israelite God, Yahweh (transcribed here as LORD). This was an act of faith, for this person was proclaiming that Yahweh was the true source of fertility and life for the land.

The same Jewish author then tied this psalm more closely to the Jewish faith by speaking of the temple of the LORD (referring to the temple in Jerusalem).

The voice of the LORD is over the waters,
   the LORD, over vast waters.
The voice of the LORD is mighty;
   the voice of the LORD is majestic.

℟. **The Lord will bless his people with peace.**

The God of glory thunders,
   and in his temple all say, "Glory!"
The LORD is enthroned above the flood;
   the LORD is enthroned as king forever.

℟. **The Lord will bless his people with peace.**

Lect. No. 21

SECOND READING: Acts 10:34-38

God anointed him with the Holy Spirit.

Immediately before this passage from the Acts of the Apostles, we hear how Saint Peter was invited to the house of Cornelius, a Roman pagan who wanted to become a Christian. He was a God-fearer, meaning a pagan who sympathized with Jewish ways.

In Peter's address we hear how the Holy Spirit gave a sign to the early Christian community that both Jew and Gentile are being invited into the life of the Lord, for the Holy Spirit had descended upon Cornelius even before he was baptized.

In the discourse, Peter mentions two Baptisms. The first is that given by John the Baptist, and it was a Baptism of conversion. The second Baptism is that given by Jesus, and it was a Baptism of both conversion and the reception of the Holy Spirit.

A reading from the Acts of the Apostles

Peter proceeded to speak to those gathered
   in the house of Cornelius, saying:
"In truth, I see that God shows no partiality.
Rather, in every nation whoever fears him and acts
      uprightly
   is acceptable to him.
You know the word that he sent to the Israelites
   as he proclaimed peace through Jesus Christ, who
      is Lord of all,
   what has happened all over Judea,
   beginning in Galilee after the baptism
   that John preached,
   how God anointed Jesus of Nazareth
   with the Holy Spirit and power.
He went about doing good
   and healing all those oppressed by the devil,
   for God was with him."

The word of the Lord.

Lect. No. 21

Today, as we celebrate the feast of the Baptism of Jesus, we are remembering that Jesus is not simply a person who is being baptized by John the Baptist, he is also the only-begotten Son of God.

ALLELUIA: cf. Mark 9:7

℟. **Alleluia, alleluia.**

The heavens were opened and the voice of the Father thundered:
This is my beloved Son, listen to him.

℟. **Alleluia, alleluia.**

Lect. No. 21

GOSPEL: Luke 3:15-16, 21-22

When Jesus had been baptized and was praying, heaven was opened.

See p. 66.

PASTORAL REFLECTIONS

As we celebrate the feast of the Baptism of Jesus, we are invited to reflect upon the significance of our own Baptisms. Do I really believe that I have died to one form of life so that I might live in Christ? What does it mean for me to be a child of God? Do I renew my Baptismal promises every time I sign myself with the Sign of the Cross with holy water whenever I enter or leave my church?

Do I celebrate the anniversary date of my Baptism? Have I ever visited the Baptismal font in which I was baptized? Do I fulfill my responsibilities to the children of whom I am a godparent?

January 20, 2013

SECOND SUNDAY IN ORDINARY TIME

FIRST READING: Isaiah 62:1-5

The bridegroom rejoices in his bride.

This beautiful hymn is taken from the third part of the Book of the Prophet Isaiah. It celebrates the vindication and restoration that God would visit upon Israel. She had suffered terribly during the exile in Babylon and things had not been much better for her when she returned to Israel after that exile (for the land was totally devastated).

The passage uses matrimonial imagery to describe the new relationship between God and his people. This is a theme that Hosea had developed when he compared the love between Yahweh and his people to the love between a husband and a wife.

This is also the idea presented in the Gospel where Jesus saves the wedding feast of the couple at Cana by changing water into wine (and thus prefigures his own marriage to the Church).

A reading from the Book of the Prophet Isaiah

For Zion's sake I will not be silent,
for Jerusalem's sake I will not be quiet,
until her vindication shines forth like the dawn
and her victory like a burning torch.

Nations shall behold your vindication,
and all the kings your glory;
you shall be called by a new name
pronounced by the mouth of the LORD.
You shall be a glorious crown in the hand of the LORD,
a royal diadem held by your God.
No more shall people call you "Forsaken,"
or your land "Desolate,"
but you shall be called "My Delight,"
and your land "Espoused."
For the LORD delights in you
and makes your land his spouse.
As a young man marries a virgin,
your Builder shall marry you;
and as a bridegroom rejoices in his bride
so shall your God rejoice in you.

The word of the Lord.

PASTORAL REFLECTIONS

The imagery of this reading presents a tremendously intimate portrait of the relationship between God and Israel (the Church). The Eucharist, which is the union of Christ's flesh with ours, is a continuation and strengthening of that commitment.

RESPONSORIAL PSALM: Ps 96:1-2, 2-3, 7-8, 9-10 (℟.: 3)

The Responsorial Psalm is an exuberant hymn of praise. This is a new song, for God has given us new signs of his glory and love.

It is not only the people of Israel who should give praise to God. All the nations on the earth are called to join in this song. They have all witnessed his goodness toward the people of God.

This is one of the reasons why we gather together on Sunday: to sing the praise and glory of God. We are called upon to tremble before him.

This is not fear caused by terror of what God might do to us. It is a sense of awe that we have when we observe the works of God in our midst.

℟. **Proclaim his marvelous deeds to all the nations.**

Sing to the LORD a new song;
　sing to the LORD, all you lands.
Sing to the LORD; bless his name.

℟. **Proclaim his marvelous deeds to all the nations.**

Announce his salvation, day after day.
Tell his glory among the nations;
　among all peoples, his wondrous deeds.

℟. **Proclaim his marvelous deeds to all the nations.**

Give to the LORD, you families of nations,
　give to the LORD glory and praise;
　give to the LORD the glory due his name!

℟. **Proclaim his marvelous deeds to all the nations.**

Worship the LORD in holy attire.
　Tremble before him, all the earth;
say among the nations: The LORD is king.
　He governs the peoples with equity.

℟. **Proclaim his marvelous deeds to all the nations.**

SECOND READING: 1 Corinthians 12:4-11

One and the same Spirit distributing them individually to each person as he wishes.

Saint Paul wrote this letter to the community in Corinth. There were members of the community who overemphasized the importance of certain gifts of the Holy Spirit. This was especially true of the gifts that were more spectacular such as the gift of tongues.

Paul reminds them that all of the gifts come from the Holy Spirit. They are given for the sake of the community.

A reading from the first Letter of Saint Paul to the Corinthians

Brothers and sisters:
There are different kinds of spiritual gifts but the same Spirit;
there are different forms of service but the same Lord;
there are different workings but the same God who produces all of them in everyone.
To each individual the manifestation of the Spirit is given for some benefit.

Therefore, they should not cause one to develop a sense of arrogance. They do not belong to any of us. They were given to us to be held in trust (for they are from God and are to be rendered back to God in the way that we use them).

Paul subtly argues that the more spectacular gifts of the Spirit (such as the gift of tongues) are really less important than others. Those which are truly the most important are those which serve to build up the community (e.g., wisdom, knowledge, faith, etc.).

To one is given through the Spirit the expression of wisdom;
to another, the expression of knowledge according to the same Spirit;
to another, faith by the same Spirit;
to another, gifts of healing by the one Spirit;
to another, mighty deeds;
to another, prophecy;
to another, discernment of spirits;
to another, varieties of tongues;
to another, interpretation of tongues.
But one and the same Spirit produces all of these,
distributing them individually to each person as he wishes.

The word of the Lord.

Lect. No. 66

ALLELUIA: cf. 2 Thessalonians 2:14

God has called us to share in his glory. In the Gospel of John, the word "glory" does not mean power or prestige; it means a willingness to love and serve.

℟. **Alleluia, alleluia.**

God has called us through the Gospel
to possess the glory of our Lord Jesus Christ.

℟. **Alleluia, alleluia.**

Lect. No. 66

GOSPEL: John 2:1-11

Jesus did this as the beginning of his signs at Cana in Galilee.

The Gospel today describes the first miracle (or, as the Gospel of John describes it, the first sign of glory) that Jesus performed.

The passage does not call Mary by her name. It calls her the mother of Jesus. This is typical of the Gospel of John, for whenever a character plays a symbolic role, that person is not called by name. She is being

A reading from the holy Gospel according to John

There was a wedding at Cana in Galilee,
and the mother of Jesus was there.
Jesus and his disciples were also invited to the wedding.
When the wine ran short,
the mother of Jesus said to him,
"They have no wine."
And Jesus said to her,
"Woman, how does your concern affect me?

presented as queen mother who prepares the wedding feast for her son.

Jesus' response to his mother's request is not a sign of disrespect (it is simply the way that one would say that it was none of their business in Aramaic). Nevertheless, Mary orders the servants to listen to her son (something that Mary always does).

There are six stone jars. Six is one less than seven (which is the perfect number in the Bible). The Jewish custom is thus shown to fall short of perfection.

Throughout the Gospel of John, Jesus replaces the customs of the Old Testament with his love.

There is too much wine. An abundance of wine is a sign of the Messianic banquet in heaven. Jesus serves the better wine (the New Covenant) that replaces the earlier, not as good wine (the Old Covenant).

This miracle prefigures the event that would give us access to the heavenly banquet: the cross (which is why Jesus spoke of his hour, the hour of glory).

My hour has not yet come."
His mother said to the servers,
    "Do whatever he tells you."
Now there were six stone water jars there for Jewish ceremonial washings,
    each holding twenty to thirty gallons.
Jesus told them,
    "Fill the jars with water."
So they filled them to the brim.
Then he told them,
    "Draw some out now and take it to the headwaiter."
So they took it.
And when the headwaiter tasted the water that had become wine,
    without knowing where it came from
    —although the servers who had drawn the water knew —,
    the headwaiter called the bridegroom and said to him,
    "Everyone serves good wine first,
and then when people have drunk freely, an inferior one;
but you have kept the good wine until now."
Jesus did this as the beginning of his signs at Cana in Galilee
    and so revealed his glory,
    and his disciples began to believe in him.

The Gospel of the Lord.

PASTORAL REFLECTIONS

This passage from the Gospel of John gives us a glimpse into the extensive symbolism of the Gospel of John. It would not be a waste of time to study a commentary on that Gospel about which St. Augustine said, "It is shallow enough for a child to play in, but profound enough for an elephant to swim in."

January 27, 2013

THIRD SUNDAY IN ORDINARY TIME

Lect. No. 69 FIRST READING: Nehemiah 8:2-4a, 5-6, 8-10

*They read from the book of the Law and
they understood what was read.*

The First Reading is a description of the proclamation of the law of the LORD to the people of Israel. This is something that had to happen periodically in the history of Israel. The people would slowly drift away from ways of the LORD and adopt the practices followed by their pagan neighbors.

This is why God would send a prophet or a leader who would lead his people back to the law.

The law is not a series of ordinances that robs people of their freedom. Rather, it is the word of God. It teaches the people what God really wants from them.

This is liberating, for they could now be what God called them to be. They would no longer have to be slaves to their passions, but could do what was good and righteous.

This particular renewal of the Covenant occurred in the fifth century B.C. The governor Nehemiah had been sent from Persia to administer the promised land as a Persian province.

He realized that the people had become decadent and he and the priest Ezra called the people together and had the law of the LORD proclaimed to them.

A reading from the Book of Nehemiah

Ezra the priest brought the law before the assembly,
which consisted of men, women,
and those children old enough to understand.
Standing at one end of the open place that was before the Water Gate,
he read out of the book from daybreak till midday,
in the presence of the men, the women,
and those children old enough to understand;
and all the people listened attentively to the book of the law.
Ezra the scribe stood on a wooden platform
that had been made for the occasion.
He opened the scroll
so that all the people might see it
—for he was standing higher up than any of the people—;
and, as he opened it, all the people rose.
Ezra blessed the LORD, the great God,
and all the people, their hands raised high, answered,
"Amen, amen!"
Then they bowed down and prostrated themselves before the LORD,
their faces to the ground.
Ezra read plainly from the book of the law of God,
interpreting it so that all could understand what was read.
Then Nehemiah, that is, His Excellency, and Ezra the priest-scribe
and the Levites who were instructing the people

As the law was read, the people realized how far they had wandered from God's ways. They began to weep and mourn for their sins.

Ezra and Nehemiah ordered them not to weep. They had not read the law to condemn the people, but rather to offer them a new beginning.

This was to be a source of joy, for now the people could fulfill their God-given destiny to be God's holy people.

said to all the people:
"Today is holy to the LORD your God.
Do not be sad, and do not weep"—
    for all the people were weeping as they heard the words of the law.
He said further: "Go, eat rich foods and drink sweet drinks,
    and allot portions to those who had nothing prepared;
    for today is holy to our LORD.
Do not be saddened this day,
    for rejoicing in the LORD must be your strength!"

The word of the Lord.

Lect. No. 69

RESPONSORIAL PSALM: Ps 19:8, 9, 10, 15 (℟.: cf. Jn 6:63c)

The Responsorial Psalm comes from the second half of Psalm 19. It begins with six synonyms for the law of the LORD, praising God for the law's goodness.

It is odd, however, that there would only be six synonyms. Seven was the perfect number in the Bible, and six references to the law would imply that it somehow lacked perfection.

The last section clarifies why the psalmist formed this pattern. He speaks of the words of his mouth and the thoughts of his heart. This is the seventh reference.

The law is only perfect when it is interiorized (found in the thoughts of one's heart) and when one gives witness to it in the way one lives (the words of one's mouth).

℟. **Your words, Lord, are Spirit and life.**

The law of the LORD is perfect,
    refreshing the soul;
the decree of the LORD is trustworthy,
    giving wisdom to the simple.

℟. **Your words, Lord, are Spirit and life.**

The precepts of the LORD are right,
    rejoicing the heart;
the command of the LORD is clear,
    enlightening the eye.

℟. **Your words, Lord, are Spirit and life.**

The fear of the LORD is pure,
    enduring forever;
the ordinances of the LORD are true,
    all of them just.

℟. **Your words, Lord, are Spirit and life.**

Let the words of my mouth and the thought of my heart
    find favor before you,
O LORD, my rock and my redeemer.

℟. **Your words, Lord, are Spirit and life.**

Lect. No. 69 **SECOND READING:** ◼ **Longer Form: 1 Corinthians 12:12-30**

You are Christ's body and individually parts of it.

The Second Reading is a continuation of the passage found in last week's Second Reading. Saint Paul had written to the community in Corinth to correct an arrogant attitude that some of the community members had developed. They believed that they had received special gifts from the Holy Spirit that made them superior to others.

They especially gloried in the gift of tongues (ecstatic utterances that they claimed came from the Holy Spirit). They felt that this was the best of gifts for the Spirit was completely in control of what they were saying.

Paul argued in the earlier part of chapter 12 that the Holy Spirit gave many gifts and that the gifts that were most important were those that helped to build up the community.

In today's reading he uses the metaphor of the Church being a body and we being parts of that body.

This is an idea found in Stoic philosophy, a philosophy that was popular in this particular era. Paul uses its ideas here and in other passages of his letters.

He is teaching the community that we need each other. None of us has received all of the gifts of the Spirit. None of us is complete in him/herself.

A reading from the first Letter of Saint Paul to the Corinthians

Brothers and sisters:
As a body is one though it has many parts,
and all the parts of the body, though many, are one body,
so also Christ.
For in one Spirit we were all baptized into one body,
whether Jews or Greeks, slaves or free persons,
and we were all given to drink of one Spirit.

Now the body is not a single part, but many.
If a foot should say,
"Because I am not a hand I do not belong to the body,"
it does not for this reason belong any less to the body.
Or if an ear should say,
"Because I am not an eye I do not belong to the body,"
it does not for this reason belong any less to the body.
If the whole body were an eye, where would the hearing be?
If the whole body were hearing, where would the sense of smell be?
But as it is, God placed the parts,
each one of them, in the body as he intended.
If they were all one part, where would the body be?
But as it is, there are many parts, yet one body.
The eye cannot say to the hand, "I do not need you,"
nor again the head to the feet, "I do not need you."
Indeed, the parts of the body that seem to be weaker
are all the more necessary,
and those parts of the body that we consider less honorable

We have been given gifts to share with those who do not have them, and they have been given gifts to respond to our need. Thus, our different gifts should not separate us; they should unite us.

This reading is one of the sources for the idea of the Mystical Body of Christ. The Holy Spirit unifies the members of the Church so that we form a manifestation of the presence of Christ in the world.

Paul closes this section by listing a series of gifts of the Spirit. Speaking in tongues is at the end of the list to show that it is not as important as the other gifts. He also places apostles at the beginning of the list.

Some in the community were amazed that he dared tell them how to use their Spirit-given gifts. His response is that he, as an apostle, had been given the authority from the Spirit to guide the life of the community.

we surround with greater honor,
and our less presentable parts are treated with greater propriety,
whereas our more presentable parts do not need this.
But God has so constructed the body
as to give greater honor to a part that is without it,
so that there may be no division in the body,
but that the parts may have the same concern for one another.
If one part suffers, all the parts suffer with it;
if one part is honored, all the parts share its joy.

Now you are Christ's body, and individually parts of it.
Some people God has designated in the church
to be, first, apostles; second, prophets; third, teachers;
then, mighty deeds;
then gifts of healing, assistance, administration,
and varieties of tongues.
Are all apostles? Are all prophets? Are all teachers?
Do all work mighty deeds? Do all have gifts of healing?
Do all speak in tongues? Do all interpret?

The word of the Lord.

PASTORAL REFLECTIONS

There is always a tension between our charisms (God-given gifts) and authority (the God-given responsibility to guide how the gifts are to be used). God speaks both in a horizontal and in a vertical manner, through the grass-roots insights given to individuals in the Church and through the pronouncements of the Magisterium. Both must be respected if we are to respond most fully to the Spirit of God working in our midst.

SECOND READING: B Shorter Form: 1 Corinthians 12:12-14, 27

You are Christ's body and individually parts of it.

Saint Paul is reminding the members of the community in Corinth that none of us is autonomous. We depend upon each other, and the Spirit has given each of us gifts to share with one another.

This passage is one of the sources for the development of the idea of the Mystical Body of Christ, the idea that the Spirit unites us to form a manifestation of the presence of Christ in the world.

A reading from the first Letter of Saint Paul to the Corinthians

Brothers and sisters:
As a body is one though it has many parts,
and all the parts of the body, though many, are one body,
so also Christ.
For in one Spirit we were all baptized into one body,
whether Jews or Greeks, slaves or free persons,
and we were all given to drink of one Spirit.
Now the body is not a single part, but many.
You are Christ's body, and individually parts of it.

The word of the Lord.

ALLELUIA: cf. Luke 4:18

The Alleluia Verse cites the statement made by Jesus when he spoke in the synagogue of Nazareth, his hometown. He proclaimed himself to be the fulfillment of this prophecy.

R̸. **Alleluia, alleluia.**

The Lord sent me to bring glad tidings to the poor,
and to proclaim liberty to captives.

R̸. **Alleluia, alleluia.**

GOSPEL: Luke 1:1-4; 4:14-21

Today this Scripture passage is fulfilled.

The Gospel today is a combination of two texts from the Gospel of Luke. The first is the introduction to the Gospel.

In it Saint Luke explains his reason for writing the Gospel (and the fact that he is trying to improve upon the material that had already been written about Jesus).

A reading from the holy Gospel according to Luke

Since many have undertaken to compile a narrative of the events
that have been fulfilled among us,
just as those who were eyewitnesses from the beginning

He claims that he is writing for a certain Theophilus. It is unclear if this is a royal official, or a rich patron, or if this is a symbolic name.

The Greek word "theos" means "God" and "phileo" means "to love," so this could be a symbolic name for anyone who loves God (hence, any Christian).

The second part of the Gospel is taken from the passage that describes Jesus' preaching in the synagogue of Nazareth.

Jesus speaks of his being anointed by the Spirit to proclaim a tremendous liberation from the forces of evil.

The Jewish people celebrated every fiftieth year as a Jubilee Year, a time of favor to the Lord. Debts were forgiven, slaves were set free, property was given back to its original owners, etc.

Jesus is saying that he is the fulfillment of everything that the Jubilee Year was supposed to be. One does not have to wait for fifty years.

Jesus, by his very presence, calls us to experience his love so that we might be liberated from all that enslaves us.

He also calls us to share that liberation with those who most need it.

and ministers of the word have handed them down
to us,
I too have decided,
after investigating everything accurately anew,
to write it down in an orderly sequence for you,
most excellent Theophilus,
so that you may realize the certainty of the teachings
you have received.

Jesus returned to Galilee in the power of the Spirit,
and news of him spread throughout the whole region.
He taught in their synagogues and was praised by all.

He came to Nazareth, where he had grown up,
and went according to his custom
into the synagogue on the sabbath day.
He stood up to read and was handed a scroll of the
prophet Isaiah.
He unrolled the scroll and found the passage where it
was written:
The Spirit of the Lord is upon me,
because he has anointed me
to bring glad tidings to the poor.
He has sent me to proclaim liberty to captives
and recovery of sight to the blind,
to let the oppressed go free,
and to proclaim a year acceptable to the Lord.
Rolling up the scroll, he handed it back to the attendant and sat down,
and the eyes of all in the synagogue looked intently
at him.
He said to them,
"Today this Scripture passage is fulfilled in your
hearing."

The Gospel of the Lord.

February 3, 2013

FOURTH SUNDAY IN ORDINARY TIME

Lect. No. 72

FIRST READING: Jeremiah 1:4-5, 17-19

A prophet to the nations I appointed you.

The First Reading begins to develop the theme that God has given each of us a mission to proclaim the Good News (this is Jeremiah's role in this reading and that of Jesus in the Gospel).

Yet, there will also be a price to pay. If we try to live a good life and do what is right, we will face opposition. There is a saying that no good deed goes unpunished.

This is why it is important to remember that we are not doing this on our own. God reminds Jeremiah that it is he who called Jeremiah to do what he was doing.

God knew that Jeremiah could not do it on his own. He did not expect him to do that. God would accompany him and give him the courage to proclaim the truth to his community.

A reading from the Book of the Prophet Jeremiah

The word of the LORD came to me, saying:
Before I formed you in the womb I knew you,
    before you were born I dedicated you,
    a prophet to the nations I appointed you.

But do you gird your loins;
    stand up and tell them
    all that I command you.
Be not crushed on their account,
    as though I would leave you crushed before
        them;
for it is I this day
    who have made you a fortified city,
a pillar of iron, a wall of brass,
    against the whole land:
against Judah's kings and princes,
    against its priests and people.
They will fight against you but not prevail over
        you,
    for I am with you to deliver you, says the LORD.

The word of the Lord.

PASTORAL REFLECTIONS

We often tell ourselves that we can't do something (e.g., forgive someone, share our faith publicly, perform a particular ministry, etc.). While it is probably true that we can't do these things on our own, our recognition of our inability can actually be a moment of conversion in which we reach out to God who can give us the strength to do what we think is impossible.

Lect. No. 72 **RESPONSORIAL PSALM: Ps 71:1-2, 3-4, 5-6, 15, 17 (℟.: cf. 15ab)**

The Responsorial Psalm continues the themes found in the First Reading. We are called to proclaim the justice of God.

We have been taught God's ways from our youth. We have to proclaim those ways both in word and deed.

This is not simply a job to do as if we can live our faith when it is convenient. This is who we are, for this is why God created us.

Yet, we cannot do this on our own. We have neither the necessary talents nor the courage. We must depend on God's strength because he will accomplish great things in and through us.

God is our rock and our fortress. He is our refuge in times of difficulty. He is the only one who can rescue us from the hands of the wicked.

℟. **I will sing of your salvation.**

In you, O LORD, I take refuge;
    let me never be put to shame.
In your justice rescue me, and deliver me;
    incline your ear to me, and save me.

℟. **I will sing of your salvation.**

Be my rock of refuge,
    a stronghold to give me safety,
    for you are my rock and my fortress.
O my God, rescue me from the hand of the wicked.

℟. **I will sing of your salvation.**

For you are my hope, O Lord;
    my trust, O God, from my youth.
On you I depend from birth;
    from my mother's womb you are my strength.

℟. **I will sing of your salvation.**

My mouth shall declare your justice,
    day by day your salvation.
O God, you have taught me from my youth,
    and till the present I proclaim your wondrous deeds.

℟. **I will sing of your salvation.**

Lect. No. 72 **SECOND READING:** ◼ **Longer Form:1 Corinthians 12:31—13:13**

So faith, hope, love remain, these three; but the greatest of these is love.

Over the past couple of weeks we have heard readings from the first Letter to the Corinthians. Saint Paul wrote this letter to correct a tendency to exaggerate the importance of certain gifts of the Holy Spirit. Some of the Corinthians felt that speaking in tongues was more important than other gifts

A reading from the first Letter of Saint Paul to the Corinthians

Brothers and sisters:
Strive eagerly for the greatest spiritual gifts.
But I shall show you a still more excellent way.

If I speak in human and angelic tongues,
    but do not have love,
    I am a resounding gong or a clashing cymbal.

(including some gifts that served to build up the community). Paul taught them that gifts are given for service of others.

In chapter 13 Paul quotes a hymn on love to give the most important criterion by which these gifts of the Spirit should be used. (Paul probably did not write this hymn himself.) Love should be the measure of all that we do.

This hymn is especially important for us today, for the word "love" has been misused by our society. Paul is not speaking about affection, or sexual attraction, or neediness, or any of the other ideas that are called "love" today.

He is speaking about the willingness to serve and even die for the other. This hymn could serve as an examination of conscience to help us determine whether our actions and attitudes are really based upon love.

Toward the end of the reading, Paul speaks of his former attitude (that of a child). By this he means that he once thought only of himself (he is speaking of the selfishness that children can sometimes display).

Now he has learned to be generous and think more of others than of himself. This is what heaven means: not being concerned with ourselves, but being a totally giving person for all eternity.

And if I have the gift of prophecy,
   and comprehend all mysteries and all knowledge;
   if I have all faith so as to move mountains,
   but do not have love, I am nothing.
If I give away everything I own,
   and if I hand my body over so that I may boast,
   but do not have love, I gain nothing.

Love is patient, love is kind.
It is not jealous, it is not pompous,
   it is not inflated, it is not rude,
   it does not seek its own interests,
   it is not quick-tempered, it does not brood over injury,
   it does not rejoice over wrongdoing but rejoices with the truth.
It bears all things, believes all things,
   hopes all things, endures all things.

Love never fails.
If there are prophecies, they will be brought to nothing;
   if tongues, they will cease;
   if knowledge, it will be brought to nothing.
For we know partially and we prophesy partially,
   but when the perfect comes, the partial will pass away.
When I was a child, I used to talk as a child,
   think as a child, reason as a child;
   when I became a man, I put aside childish things.
At present we see indistinctly, as in a mirror,
   but then face to face.
At present I know partially;
   then I shall know fully, as I am fully known.
So faith, hope, love remain, these three;
   but the greatest of these is love.

The word of the Lord.

SECOND READING: B Shorter Form: 1 Corinthians 13:4-13

So faith, hope, love remain, these three; but the greatest of these is love.

In chapter 13 Paul quotes a hymn on love to give the most important criterion by which the gifts of the Spirit should be used. Love should be the measure of all that we do.

This hymn is especially important for us today, for the word "love" has been misused by our society. Paul is not speaking about affection, or sexual attraction, or neediness, or any of the other ideas that are called "love" today.

He is speaking about the willingness to serve and even die for the other. This hymn could serve as an examination of conscience to help us determine whether our actions and attitudes are really based upon love.

Toward the end of the reading, Paul speaks of his former attitude (that of a child). By this he means that he once thought only of himself (he is speaking of the selfishness that children can sometimes display).

Now he has learned to be generous and think more of others than of himself. This is what heaven means: not being concerned with ourselves, but being a totally giving person for all eternity.

A reading from the first Letter of Saint Paul to the Corinthians

Brothers and sisters:
   Love is patient, love is kind.
It is not jealous, it is not pompous,
   it is not inflated, it is not rude,
   it does not seek its own interests,
   it is not quick-tempered, it does not brood over injury,
   it does not rejoice over wrongdoing but rejoices with the truth.
It bears all things, believes all things,
   hopes all things, endures all things.

Love never fails.
If there are prophecies, they will be brought to nothing;
   if tongues, they will cease;
   if knowledge, it will be brought to nothing.
For we know partially and we prophesy partially,
   but when the perfect comes, the partial will pass away.
When I was a child, I used to talk as a child,
   think as a child, reason as a child;
   when I became a man, I put aside childish things.
At present we see indistinctly, as in a mirror,
   but then face to face.
At present I know partially;
   then I shall know fully, as I am fully known.
So faith, hope, love remain, these three;
   but the greatest of these is love.

The word of the Lord.

The Alleluia Verse is a recitation of the proclamation that Jesus made when he preached in the synagogue in Nazareth proclaiming his mission to be one of consolation.

ALLELUIA: Luke 4:18

℟. **Alleluia, alleluia.**

The Lord sent me to bring glad tidings to the poor, to proclaim liberty to captives.

℟. **Alleluia, alleluia.**

GOSPEL: Luke 4:21-30

Like Elijah and Elisha, Jesus was not sent only to the Jews.

The first part of the Gospel tells of the rejection that Jesus received in his home village of Nazareth.

As we heard last month, Jesus had just proclaimed himself to be the fulfillment of the prophecy contained in the Book of the Prophet Isaiah, that he was the anointed one of the Lord.

He came to give consolation to those who were poor and rejected.

One would think that the reaction to this would be great joy. Yet, the reaction is the exact opposite. The people he came to help decided to reject him. Why would this happen?

One of the reasons is that we do not like to depend upon others. We like to believe that we can solve our own problems. We like to be autonomous.

When Jesus teaches the people in his village that they need him, they become enraged and try to kill him.

A reading from the holy Gospel according to Luke

Jesus began speaking in the synagogue, saying:
"Today this Scripture passage is fulfilled in your hearing."
And all spoke highly of him
and were amazed at the gracious words that came from his mouth.
They also asked, "Isn't this the son of Joseph?"
He said to them, "Surely you will quote me this proverb,
'Physician, cure yourself,' and say,
'Do here in your native place
the things that we heard were done in Capernaum.'"
And he said, "Amen, I say to you,
no prophet is accepted in his own native place.
Indeed, I tell you,
there were many widows in Israel in the days of Elijah
when the sky was closed for three and a half years
and a severe famine spread over the entire land.
It was to none of these that Elijah was sent,
but only to a widow in Zarephath in the land of Sidon.
Again, there were many lepers in Israel
during the time of Elisha the prophet;

Ironically, this means that the Good News is not something that people will readily accept. The Good News calls us to conversion and vulnerability. It calls us to recognize that we are no better than the widow of Zarephath and Naaman, the Syrian.

It is only when we are willing to admit this that we can open our hearts to the healing that Jesus is offering.

yet not one of them was cleansed, but only Naaman the Syrian."
When the people in the synagogue heard this,
    they were all filled with fury.
They rose up, drove him out of the town,
    and led him to the brow of the hill
    on which their town had been built,
    to hurl him down headlong.
But Jesus passed through the midst of them and went away.

The Gospel of the Lord.

PASTORAL REFLECTIONS

It can often be difficult to see the goodness of the people who are the closest to us. We see their flaws all too easily and we can be blind to their better qualities. This is why the relatives and acquaintances of Jesus could not recognize what he was when he entered the synagogue. They knew him too well. This is why Jesus tells them that foreigners would fare better in the kingdom than they would.

This passage certainly challenges us to see the talents and good qualities in those around us, and also to be less judgmental concerning their flaws. Maybe they are trying their hardest, and maybe God appreciates their efforts more than our efforts (for they could easily be trying harder because they might have received fewer gifts from God, but they are using those gifts better than we use ours).

February 10, 2013

FIFTH SUNDAY IN ORDINARY TIME

Lect. No. 75

FIRST READING: Isaiah 6:1-2a, 3-8

Here I am! Send me.

The First Reading speaks of the vision that Isaiah had at the beginning of his prophetic ministry. Isaiah was in the temple when he experienced the holiness of God.

In the Bible, holiness means that God is totally beyond our understanding. He is truly great and awesome.

The cry of "holy, holy, holy," speaks of the incredible holiness of God. There is no comparative or superlative degree in Hebrew.

The speaker had to repeat that word two or three times. Hence, the cry means that God is the "holiest" of all.

Isaiah is filled with fear and recognizes his sinfulness. When we encounter the holy, we realize how broken and limited we are. This is what fear of God means.

It is not terror, it is awe. But God cleanses us of our sin and gives us the courage to do those things that we cannot do on our own.

A reading from the Book of the Prophet Isaiah

In the year King Uzziah died,
I saw the Lord seated on a high and lofty throne,
with the train of his garment filling the temple.
Seraphim were stationed above.

They cried one to the other,
"Holy, holy, holy is the Lord of hosts!
All the earth is filled with his glory!"
At the sound of that cry, the frame of the door shook
and the house was filled with smoke.

Then I said, "Woe is me, I am doomed!
For I am a man of unclean lips,
living among a people of unclean lips;
yet my eyes have seen the King, the Lord of
hosts!"
Then one of the seraphim flew to me,
holding an ember that he had taken with tongs
from the altar.

He touched my mouth with it, and said,
"See, now that this has touched your lips,
your wickedness is removed, your sin purged."

Then I heard the voice of the Lord saying,
"Whom shall I send? Who will go for us?"
"Here I am," I said; "send me!"

The word of the Lord.

RESPONSORIAL PSALM: Ps 138:1-2, 2-3, 4-5, 7-8 (℟.: 1c)

The Responsorial Psalm continues the theme found in the First Reading. It is a celebration of the tremendous holiness of God.

We cannot even begin to comprehend the greatness and glory of our God. Our human mind and human experience are limited, but God is not.

Our only possible response to this encounter with the holiness of God is to praise the glory of God. We join in the hymn sung by the angels that proclaims the holiness of God.

Whenever we enter the temple of God (or our parish church or a shrine or any place where God's holiness is evident), we are filled to overflowing with a sense of joy and gratitude and wonder.

Yet, our God is not just great in the heavens, ruling over all of creation in splendor. Our God is also great in the way he has intervened in our own personal history.

God has rescued us when we were in danger (his right hand has saved us). God has answered us and will always answer us in the future when we call upon him.

℟. **In the sight of the angels I will sing your praises, Lord.**

I will give thanks to you, O LORD, with all my heart,
for you have heard the words of my mouth;
in the presence of the angels I will sing your praise;
I will worship at your holy temple
and give thanks to your name.

℟. **In the sight of the angels I will sing your praises, Lord.**

Because of your kindness and your truth;
for you have made great above all things
your name and your promise.
When I called, you answered me;
you built up strength within me.

℟. **In the sight of the angels I will sing your praises, Lord.**

All the kings of the earth shall give thanks to you, O LORD,
when they hear the words of your mouth;
and they shall sing of the ways of the LORD:
"Great is the glory of the LORD."

℟. **In the sight of the angels I will sing your praises, Lord.**

Your right hand saves me.
The LORD will complete what he has done for me;
your kindness, O LORD, endures forever;
forsake not the work of your hands.

℟. **In the sight of the angels I will sing your praises, Lord.**

SECOND READING: A Longer Form: 1 Corinthians 15:1-11

So we preached and so you believe.

The Second Reading is a recitation of the kerygma of the early Church. The kerygma is the proclamation that an apostle would make when he first arrived in a new city. It told of how Jesus died for our sins, was buried, and rose from the dead.

This passage speaks of the various apparitions of Jesus after the resurrection. He appeared to Cephas and the twelve (Cephas is the Aramaic name for Peter).

He appeared to over five hundred at one time. This account is not contained in the Gospel, which means that the Gospels do not contain all the details of what happened in those days.

Jesus also appeared to James and the apostles. It is odd that the phrase "the twelve" and then "the apostles" are used, as if they are somehow two different groups.

Paul also speaks of the revelation that was made to him. While he does not specifically speak of the appearance on the road to Damascus, what he says is consistent with what is contained in Acts.

He is filled with awe at the fact that God would have chosen him (when he had persecuted the Church). God showers his grace upon those whom he wills.

A reading from the first Letter of Saint Paul to the Corinthians

I am reminding you, brothers and sisters,
of the gospel I preached to you,
which you indeed received and in which you also stand.
Through it you are also being saved,
if you hold fast to the word I preached to you,
unless you believed in vain.
For I handed on to you as of first importance what I also received:
that Christ died for our sins in accordance with the Scriptures;
that he was buried;
that he was raised on the third day in accordance with the Scriptures;
that he appeared to Cephas, then to the Twelve.
After that, he appeared to more than five hundred brothers at once,
most of whom are still living,
though some have fallen asleep.
After that he appeared to James,
then to all the apostles.
Last of all, as to one born abnormally,
he appeared to me.
For I am the least of the apostles,
not fit to be called an apostle,
because I persecuted the church of God.
But by the grace of God I am what I am,
and his grace to me has not been ineffective.
Indeed, I have toiled harder than all of them;
not I, however, but the grace of God that is with me.
Therefore, whether it be I or they,
so we preach and so you believed.

The word of the Lord.

Lect. No. 75 · **SECOND READING:** **Shorter Form: 1 Corinthians 15:3-8, 11**

So we preached and so you believe.

The Second Reading is a recitation of the kerygma (the proclamation that an apostle would make when he first arrived in a new city). It told of how Jesus died for our sins, was buried, and rose from the dead.

This passage speaks of the apparitions after the resurrection. Jesus appeared to Cephas (Peter) and the twelve.

He appeared to over five hundred at one time. This account is not contained in the Gospel, which means that the Gospels do not contain all the details of what happened in those days.

Jesus also appears to James and the apostles.

Paul also speaks of the revelation that was made to him. He is filled with awe at the fact that God would have chosen him (when he had persecuted the Church).

A reading from the first Letter of Saint Paul to the Corinthians

Brothers and sisters,
I handed on to you as of first importance what I also received:
that Christ died for our sins in accordance with the Scriptures;
that he was buried;
that he was raised on the third day in accordance with the Scriptures;
that he appeared to Cephas, then to the Twelve.
After that, he appeared to more than five hundred brothers at once,
most of whom are still living,
though some have fallen asleep.
After that he appeared to James,
then to all the apostles.
Last of all, as to one born abnormally,
he appeared to me.
Therefore, whether it be I or they,
so we preach and so you believed.

The word of the Lord.

Lect. No. 75

The Alleluia Verse is the invitation that Jesus gives Peter (and each one of us). We are to share the gift of faith we have received from God.

ALLELUIA: Matthew 4:19

℟. **Alleluia, alleluia.**

Come after me
and I will make you fishers of men.

℟. **Alleluia, alleluia.**

Lect. No. 75

GOSPEL: Luke 5:1-11

They left everything and followed Jesus.

The Gospel continues the themes found in the First Reading. Like that reading, we hear the story of a call to do ministry. This call occurs in the context of a manifestation of the glory of God.

The one who is called is filled with a sense of awe and fear, yet God promises to supply all that person needs to be able to respond.

In this passage, we hear of the call of Peter. He was a fisherman on the Lake of Gennesaret (the Sea of Galilee). He had fished all night and had not caught anything. Jesus uses his boat as a platform to preach to the crowd that had gathered. He then told Peter to toss his nets out into the water.

This is highly unusual, for one fishes at night on the Sea of Galilee. In the morning, the surface of the water tends to heat up quickly and the fish swim to lower, cooler waters.

Thus, the net should have been empty when Peter pulled it in. The tremendous catch that Peter actually pulled in was clearly something that was miraculous.

Peter reacts to this suspension of the rules of nature with terror. He recognizes that something very holy was happening, and this filled him with great fear.

A reading from the holy Gospel according to Luke

While the crowd was pressing in on Jesus and listening to the word of God,
  he was standing by the Lake of Gennesaret.
He saw two boats there alongside the lake;
  the fishermen had disembarked and were washing their nets.
Getting into one of the boats, the one belonging to Simon,
  he asked him to put out a short distance from the shore.
Then he sat down and taught the crowds from the boat.
After he had finished speaking, he said to Simon,
  "Put out into deep water and lower your nets for a catch."
Simon said in reply,
  "Master, we have worked hard all night and have caught nothing,
  but at your command I will lower the nets."
When they had done this, they caught a great number of fish
  and their nets were tearing.
They signaled to their partners in the other boat
  to come to help them.
They came and filled both boats
  so that the boats were in danger of sinking.
When Simon Peter saw this, he fell at the knees of Jesus and said,
  "Depart from me, Lord, for I am a sinful man."
For astonishment at the catch of fish they had made seized him
  and all those with him,

He knew that he was a sinner, and that he did not deserve to be in Jesus' presence. But, as with Isaiah and Paul, we are called to service not because we deserve it, but rather because God will work in and through us.

and likewise James and John, the sons of Zebedee,
  who were partners of Simon.
Jesus said to Simon, "Do not be afraid;
  from now on you will be catching men."
When they brought their boats to the shore,
  they left everything and followed him.

The Gospel of the Lord.

PASTORAL REFLECTIONS

In the Old Testament, one tended to encounter the holiness of God by going up a mountain or entering the Holy of Holies in the temple. When Jesus died on the cross, though, the veil of the temple split open from top to bottom. This was symbolic, for it tells us that the holiness of God is no longer shut up in a particular room in the temple. It has come crashing out into the world.

We can see this in the Sacraments. Jesus and the Church have chosen everyday things to be instruments of God's love: bread, wine, water, oil, words, breath, and touch.

We can also encounter the holiness of God in so many everyday things around us: sunrise, leaves and flowers, food, etc. God communicates his goodness and holiness in many, many ways.

February 13, 2013
ASH WEDNESDAY

Lect.
Vol. II
No. 219

FIRST READING: Joel 2:12-18

Rend your hearts, not your garments.

Lent is a time to examine our lives carefully and to root out those things that keep us from loving God and each other.

In the First Reading, Joel speaks of how God is ready to forgive us. We, however, must decide to seek that pardon. If we are not willing to admit that we are sinners and broken, then God cannot heal us.

It is not that God does not want to heal us, only that we cannot receive his healing until we open our hearts to it.

It is never too late to turn back to God. Consider the story of the owner of the vineyard who rewarded everyone who worked for him, even those who worked for only a very short while.

At the same time, however, we cannot presume upon God's mercy. We must use this blessed season to change our ways.

The reading speaks of weeping and mourning as signs of our willingness to turn away from sin and to return to God. Our sign today is ashes, which are an external sign of our own willingness to change both our hearts and our actions.

A reading from the Book of the Prophet Joel

Even now, says the LORD,
   return to me with your whole heart,
    with fasting, and weeping, and mourning;
Rend your hearts, not your garments,
    and return to the LORD, your God.
For gracious and merciful is he,
    slow to anger, rich in kindness,
    and relenting in punishment.
Perhaps he will again relent
    and leave behind him a blessing,
Offerings and libations
    for the LORD, your God.

Blow the trumpet in Zion!
    proclaim a fast,
    call an assembly;
Gather the people,
    notify the congregation;
Assemble the elders,
    gather the children
    and the infants at the breast;
Let the bridegroom quit his room
    and the bride her chamber.
Between the porch and the altar
    let the priests, the ministers of the LORD, weep,
And say, "Spare, O LORD, your people,
    and make not your heritage a reproach,
    with the nations ruling over them!
Why should they say among the peoples,
    'Where is their God?'"

When we do this, we can truly accept the love and mercy that God offers us in this holy season.

Then the Lord was stirred to concern for his land
and took pity on his people.

The word of the Lord.

RESPONSORIAL PSALM: Ps 51:3-4, 5-6ab, 12-13, 14 and 17 (℟.: 3)

Psalm 51 is a beautiful penitential psalm. It is dedicated to the memory of that moment when the Prophet Nathan confronted King David concerning his act of adultery with Bathsheba and his murder of Uriah the Hittite.

The psalm recognizes many of the facets of turning away from sin and back to God. It speaks of how we can only be cleansed through the intervention of God.

We recognize the fact that we are sinners and worthy of condemnation. Yet, we beseech God for healing.

If God recreates us with his Spirit, we will be alive in God again. Our sin has made us like creatures that have lost their life, but now God has breathed his Spirit back into us. We will be filled with the joy of God, for he is the source of our salvation.

℟. **Be merciful, O Lord, for we have sinned.**

Have mercy on me, O God, in your goodness;
in the greatness of your compassion wipe out my
offense.
Thoroughly wash me from my guilt
and of my sin cleanse me.

℟. **Be merciful, O Lord, for we have sinned.**

For I acknowledge my offense,
and my sin is before me always:
"Against you only have I sinned,
and done what is evil in your sight."

℟. **Be merciful, O Lord, for we have sinned.**

A clean heart create for me, O God,
and a steadfast spirit renew within me.
Cast me not out from your presence,
and your Holy Spirit take not from me.

℟. **Be merciful, O Lord, for we have sinned.**

Give me back the joy of your salvation,
and a willing spirit sustain in me.
O Lord, open my lips,
and my mouth shall proclaim your praise.

℟. **Be merciful, O Lord, for we have sinned.**

SECOND READING: 2 Corinthians 5:20—6:2

Be reconciled to God. Behold, now is the acceptable time.

Saint Paul speaks of being an ambassador for the message of salvation. His entire life work was to proclaim the salvation that God offers us through

A reading from the second Letter of Saint Paul
to the Corinthians

Brothers and sisters:
We are ambassadors for Christ,
as if God were appealing through us.

the death and resurrection of Jesus.

Now is the time to accept that salvation into our lives. The beginning of Lent is a blessed time when we have the opportunity to turn from our mistaken ways and find the path of truth.

This is all that God wants of us. We see this in the fact that Jesus took our human condition upon himself, even suffering and dying, although he had done nothing wrong. He became sin (adopted our sinful flesh) to set us free from our sin.

We implore you on behalf of Christ,
    be reconciled to God.
For our sake he made him to be sin who did not
    know sin,
    so that we might become the righteousness of
    God in him.

Working together, then,
    we appeal to you not to receive the grace of God
    in vain.
For he says:

    In an acceptable time I heard you,
        and on the day of salvation I helped you.

Behold, now is a very acceptable time;
    behold, now is the day of salvation.

The word of the Lord.

Lect. Vol. II No. 219

VERSE BEFORE THE GOSPEL: See Psalm 95:8

Now is the time to turn from our sin and to embrace God with all our heart. Today is the day of our salvation.

If today you hear his voice,
harden not your hearts.

Lect. Vol. II No. 219

GOSPEL: Matthew 6:1-6,16-18

Your Father who sees in secret will repay you.

When the temple in Jerusalem was destroyed in 70 A.D., the Jewish people lost the place where they could expiate their sins. Previously, they had performed sacrifices through which they would obtain forgiveness for their sins.

Sin had brought death into their lives. The blood of their sacrifices gave them life again (for blood was a sign of life).

The people asked the rabbis what they could do to obtain for-

A reading from the holy Gospel according
to Matthew

Jesus said to his disciples:
"Take care not to perform righteous deeds
    in order that people may see them;
    otherwise, you will have no recompense from
    your heavenly Father.
When you give alms,
    do not blow a trumpet before you,
    as the hypocrites do in the synagogues and in the
    streets
to win the praise of others.

giveness for their sins now that there was nowhere that they could offer sacrifices.

The rabbis answered that there were three things that brought forgiveness of sins: almsgiving, fasting, and praying.

These are the exact things that our reading asks us to do. Saint Matthew's message is that the rabbis were right, but they were wrong in the way that they did these things. They often did them to look good before others.

That is not the reason why we should do these things. We should do them out of a profound willingness to change our lives. They should be reflections of a change of heart. Without that, they are nothing more than superficial deeds that do us no good.

And so today we dedicate ourselves to acts of penance These actions are signs of our willingness to make this Lent meaningful. We commit ourselves to prayer, to acts of charity, and to acts of mortification.

These things do not have to be spectacular (in fact, it is always prudent to plan things that are reasonable lest we overcommit ourselves and lose heart after a few days). But they must be honest signs of willingness to live for and in God our Father.

Amen, I say to you,
    they have received their reward.
But when you give alms,
    do not let your left hand know what your right is
        doing.
    so that your almsgiving may be secret.
And your Father who sees in secret will repay you.

"When you pray,
    do not be like the hypocrites,
    who love to stand and pray in the synagogues and
        on street corners
    so that others may see them.
Amen, I say to you,
    they have received their reward.
But when you pray, go to your inner room,
    close the door, and pray to your Father in secret.
And your Father who sees in secret will repay you.

"When you fast,
    do not look gloomy like the hypocrites.
They neglect their appearance,
    so that they may appear to others to be fasting.
Amen, I say to you, they have received their reward.
But when you fast,
    anoint your head and wash your face,
    so that you may not appear to be fasting,
    except to your Father who is hidden.
And your Father who sees what is hidden will repay
        you."

The Gospel of the Lord.

FIRST SUNDAY OF LENT

FIRST READING: Deuteronomy 26:4-10

The confession of faith of the chosen people.

The First Reading presents an example of absolute dependence upon the LORD. The Israelites were to bring their offerings to the LORD and profess their faith in the God who rescued them from slavery in Egypt.

It was the LORD who did this for them. They did not save themselves with their own strength and cunning.

This is the exact opposite of what Satan tempts Jesus to do in the Gospel reading. He seeks to force Jesus to use his powers to assist himself and not to trust in the Father.

This is ultimately the difference between having true faith and living a self-centered life. With the former, one recognizes that all one has and all that one is comes from God. Everything is a gift for which we are profoundly grateful. With the latter, one thinks that all one has or is comes from one's own efforts.

(Lectors, please be cautious in how you pronounce the word "Aramean." It is one of the most frequently mispronounced words in Scripture.)

A reading from the Book of Deuteronomy

Moses spoke to the people, saying:
"The priest shall receive the basket from you
and shall set it in front of the altar of the LORD,
your God.
Then you shall declare before the LORD, your God,
'My father was a wandering Aramean
who went down to Egypt with a small household
and lived there as an alien.
But there he became a nation
great, strong, and numerous.
When the Egyptians maltreated and oppressed us,
imposing hard labor upon us,
we cried to the LORD, the God of our fathers,
and he heard our cry
and saw our affliction, our toil, and our oppression.
He brought us out of Egypt
with his strong hand and outstretched arm,
with terrifying power, with signs and wonders;
and bringing us into this country,
he gave us this land flowing with milk and honey.
Therefore, I have now brought you the firstfruits
of the products of the soil
which you, O LORD, have given me.'
And having set them before the LORD, your God,
you shall bow down in his presence."

The word of the Lord.

RESPONSORIAL PSALM: Ps 91:1-2, 10-11, 12-13, 14-15 (℟.: cf. 15b)

The Responsorial Psalm contains the saying that Satan would quote when he was tempting Jesus in the desert: "For to his angels he has given command about you, that they guard you in all your ways. Upon their hands they shall bear you up, lest you dash your foot against a stone."

The irony of Satan quoting this saying is that it is contained in a psalm that professes a radical trust in God. The psalmist speaks of God being his refuge and his fortress.

Satan, on the other hand, uses the saying to try to tempt Jesus away from trusting the providence of God. He wants Jesus to orchestrate a situation in which he would force the Father to rescue him.

This would not be an act of trust, but a form of manipulation. When one truly trusts and loves another, one does not play games with that person's love.

℟. **Be with me, Lord, when I am in trouble.**

You who dwell in the shelter of the Most High,
    who abide in the shadow of the Almighty,
say to the LORD, "My refuge and fortress,
    my God in whom I trust."

℟. **Be with me, Lord, when I am in trouble.**

No evil shall befall you,
    nor shall affliction come near your tent,
for to his angels he has given command about you,
    that they guard you in all your ways.

℟. **Be with me, Lord, when I am in trouble.**

Upon their hands they shall bear you up,
    lest you dash your foot against a stone.
You shall tread upon the asp and the viper;
    you shall trample down the lion and the dragon.

℟. **Be with me, Lord, when I am in trouble.**

Because he clings to me, I will deliver him;
    I will set him on high because he acknowledges
        my name.
He shall call upon me, and I will answer him;
    I will be with him in distress;
I will deliver him and glorify him.

℟. **Be with me, Lord, when I am in trouble.**

Lect. No. 24

SECOND READING: Romans 10:8-13

The confession of faith of all believers in Christ.

The Second Reading reminds us of the need to profess our faith in God. The word "faith" means that we trust in someone else. We believe in others and place our hope in them.

A reading from the Letter of Saint Paul
to the Romans

Brothers and sisters:
    What does Scripture say?
The word is near you,

FIRST SUNDAY OF LENT   98

Saint Paul states that if we believe in our hearts, we are justified. This means that we are at peace with God, for we have accepted the peace and forgiveness that he offers.

If we profess that Jesus is Lord, we will be saved.

Paul thought of salvation as something that occurs on the last day. We must live our faith if we expect to be saved in our final judgment.

Lent is a time to ask two questions: What do I really believe and what do I really express with my life? This is a time to transform both our hearts and our lives.

in your mouth and in your heart
—that is, the word of faith that we preach—,
for, if you confess with your mouth that Jesus is Lord
and believe in your heart that God raised him from the dead,
you will be saved.
For one believes with the heart and so is justified,
and one confesses with the mouth and so is saved.
For the Scripture says,
No one who believes in him will be put to shame.
For there is no distinction between Jew and Greek;
the same Lord is Lord of all,
enriching all who call upon him.
For "everyone who calls on the name of the Lord will be saved."

The word of the Lord.

VERSE BEFORE THE GOSPEL: Matthew 4:4b

The Verse Before the Gospel quotes the saying that Jesus cited to the devil, that we need the word of God to survive.

One does not live on bread alone,
but on every word that comes forth from the mouth of God.

GOSPEL: Luke 4:1-13

Jesus was led by the Spirit into the desert and was tempted.

The temptation in the desert marks a moment when Jesus can purify the intentions for his public ministry. He is not going out into the world to gain fame or power. He is preaching and healing in order to obey the will of the Father.

There are three versions of the temptation in the desert (one in each of the Synoptic Gospels). Mark is the simplest.

A reading from the holy Gospel according to Luke

Filled with the Holy Spirit, Jesus returned from the Jordan
and was led by the Spirit into the desert for forty days,
to be tempted by the devil.
He ate nothing during those days,
and when they were over he was hungry.

He does not even give the three separate temptations.

Matthew and Luke are similar, except they reverse the order of the last two temptations (possibly because mountains are important in Matthew and Jerusalem was important in Luke).

The temptations ask Jesus to misuse the power he has been given by the Father. Satan tells him to think of himself and to seek his own comfort.

He tells Jesus to put the Father's love to the test (trying to place a kernel of doubt in Jesus' heart). In all of this, Satan tries to show himself reasonable.

But Jesus is not using the logic of this world. He has placed himself entirely in the Father's hands.

It is important to remember that Satan's temptations often sound reasonable and even logical. They tell us that we are being fools for not thinking of ourselves, that we deserve what we have, that God is at our beck and call.

Jesus reminds us that God's logic goes beyond earthly logic and calls us to sacrifice and radical trust in God.

The devil said to him,
    "If you are the Son of God,
    command this stone to become bread."
Jesus answered him,
    "It is written, *One does not live on bread alone*."
Then he took him up and showed him
    all the kingdoms of the world in a single instant.
The devil said to him,
    "I shall give to you all this power and glory;
    for it has been handed over to me,
    and I may give it to whomever I wish.
All this will be yours, if you worship me."
Jesus said to him in reply,
    "It is written:
    *You shall worship the Lord, your God,
        and him alone shall you serve*."
Then he led him to Jerusalem,
    made him stand on the parapet of the temple, and
        said to him,
    "If you are the Son of God,
    throw yourself down from here, for it is written:
        *He will command his angels concerning you, to
            guard you,*
    and:
        *With their hands they will support you,
        lest you dash your foot against a stone*."
Jesus said to him in reply,
    "It also says,
    You shall not put the Lord, your God, to the test."
When the devil had finished every temptation,
    he departed from him for a time.

The Gospel of the Lord.

February 24, 2013
SECOND SUNDAY OF LENT

Lect. No. 27

FIRST READING:

Genesis 15:5-12, 17-18

God made a covenant with Abraham, his faithful servant.

The First Reading describes the way in which God established a covenant with Abraham (here called Abram, for his name had not yet been changed by God).

A covenant was a treaty or pact made between two nations, a sovereign and his subjects, or two friends.

The people of Israel used this term to describe the fact that God had chosen them to be his people.

Part of every covenant was a series of blessings and curses that the parties would call down upon themselves.

They were to be blessed if they fulfilled all of the prescriptions to which they were committing themselves, but cursed if they deviated from the stipulations of the covenant.

This is the reason for the splitting of the animals. By passing through the midst of the animals, God was stating, "May I be torn asunder like these animals if I do not keep my covenant with Abram."

The astounding thing in this account is that he did not ask Abram to pass through the midst of the animals.

A reading from the Book of Genesis

The Lord God took Abram outside and said,
"Look up at the sky and count the stars, if you can.
Just so," he added, "shall your descendants be."
Abram put his faith in the LORD,
   who credited it to him as an act of righteousness.

He then said to him,
   "I am the LORD who brought you from Ur of the Chaldeans
to give you this land as a possession."
"O Lord GOD," he asked,
   "how am I to know that I shall possess it?"
He answered him,
   "Bring me a three-year-old heifer, a three-year-old she-goat,
   a three-year-old ram, a turtledove, and a young pigeon."
Abram brought him all these, split them in two,
   and placed each half opposite the other;
   but the birds he did not cut up.
Birds of prey swooped down on the carcasses,
   but Abram stayed with them.
As the sun was about to set, a trance fell upon Abram,
   and a deep, terrifying darkness enveloped him.

When the sun had set and it was dark,
   there appeared a smoking fire pot and a flaming torch,
   which passed between those pieces.
It was on that occasion that the LORD made a covenant with Abram,

100

The description of Abraham's inheritance fits the description of the land of Israel during the reign of King David, from the Nile to the Euphrates.

saying: "To your descendants I give this land, from the Wadi of Egypt to the Great River, the Euphrates."

The word of the Lord.

Lect. No. 27

RESPONSORIAL PSALM: Ps 27:1, 7-8, 8-9, 13-14 (℟.: 1a)

The Responsorial Psalm is a series of verses taken from Psalm 27, an individual lament. The way that the verses have been chosen, however, makes this psalm more of a psalm of trust. The psalmist is sure that God will intervene in his cause and rescue him from the hands of his enemies.

In Lent, we ask what the enemies are from which God delivers us. Could they be sin and selfishness and the loneliness that we bring into our lives every time that we consciously or subtly reject God?

The middle verses are appropriate: "Your presence, O Lord, I seek. Hide not your face from me." In the First Reading we heard how God did not hide from Abram, but rather made a binding commitment to him. In the Gospel we hear how Jesus is shown to be the Son of God in the glory of the Transfiguration.

℟. **The Lord is my light and my salvation.**

The Lord is my light and my salvation;
   whom should I fear?
The Lord is my life's refuge;
   of whom should I be afraid?

℟. **The Lord is my light and my salvation.**

Hear, O Lord, the sound of my call;
   have pity on me, and answer me.
Of you my heart speaks; you my glance seeks.

℟. **The Lord is my light and my salvation.**

Your presence, O Lord, I seek.
   Hide not your face from me;
do not in anger repel your servant.
   You are my helper: cast me not off.

℟. **The Lord is my light and my salvation.**

I believe that I shall see the bounty of the Lord
   in the land of the living.
Wait for the Lord with courage;
   be stouthearted, and wait for the Lord.

℟. **The Lord is my light and my salvation.**

Lect. No. 27

SECOND READING: Longer Form: Philippians 3:17—4:1

Christ will change our lowly body to conform with his glorified body.

Saint Paul often uses himself as a model of what the Christian life is. This is not arrogant pride as much as an honest recognition that he had turned his life over to the Lord.

A reading from the Letter of Saint Paul
to the Philippians

Join with others in being imitators of me, brothers and sisters,

The Christian life is not always easy. We are tempted by the things of this world. God created the world to be good, but we often misuse the things of this world (e.g., food, wealth, sex, etc.).

Rather than their being used to serve our legitimate needs, they become prisons that trap us. We become enslaved to our passions.

The only way to break out of this prison is to keep the proper perspective. We are living in this world, but we cannot live for it.

We are citizens of heaven, and we must live with a certain detachment toward anything in this world that would drag us down. We have to be willing to ask ourselves, "Is this the way a saint would act?"

and observe those who thus conduct themselves
according to the model you have in us.
For many, as I have often told you
and now tell you even in tears,
conduct themselves as enemies of the cross of Christ.
Their end is destruction.
Their God is their stomach;
their glory is in their "shame."
Their minds are occupied with earthly things.
But our citizenship is in heaven,
and from it we also await a savior, the Lord Jesus Christ.
He will change our lowly body
to conform with his glorified body
by the power that enables him also
to bring all things into subjection to himself.

Therefore, my brothers and sisters,
whom I love and long for, my joy and crown,
in this way stand firm in the Lord.

The word of the Lord.

| Lect. No. 27 | **SECOND READING:** **B** Shorter Form: Philippians 3:20—4:1 |

Christ will change our lowly body to conform with his glorified body.

God created the world to be good, but we often misuse the things of this world (e.g., food, wealth, sex, etc.). We become enslaved to our passions.

The only way to break out of this prison is to keep the proper perspective. We are living in this world, but we cannot live for it.

We are citizens of heaven, and we must live with a certain detachment toward anything in this world that would drag us down and make us forget our true homeland.

A reading from the Letter of Saint Paul
to the Philippians

Brothers and sisters:
Our citizenship is in heaven,
and from it we also await a savior, the Lord Jesus Christ.
He will change our lowly body
to conform with his glorified body
by the power that enables him also
to bring all things into subjection to himself.

Therefore, my brothers and sisters,
whom I love and long for, my joy and crown,
in this way stand firm in the Lord, beloved.

The word of the Lord.

VERSE BEFORE THE GOSPEL: cf. Matthew 17:5

The Verse Before the Gospel repeats the words heard on the day of the Transfiguration.

From the shining cloud the Father's voice is heard:
This is my beloved Son, hear him.

GOSPEL: Luke 9:28b-36

*While he was praying his face changed in appearance
and his clothing became dazzling white.*

The account of the Transfiguration opens in a typical manner for the Gospel of Luke: Jesus went up the mountain to pray.

Jesus prays in this Gospel so that he might discern and obey the will of the Father.

Moses and Elijah appear with Jesus to show that Jesus is the fulfillment of the law (represented by Moses) and the prophets (represented by Elijah).

Furthermore, both of them were associated with the coming of the Messiah, for Moses prayed for someone who would be greater than himself, and Elijah was to appear to prepare the chosen people for the Day of the Lord.

The disciples are confused. As often happens when we come into contact with the Holy, they could not fully understand the meaning of it all.

God the Father proclaims Jesus as his chosen Son. This is something also heard at the Baptism, and even under the cross when Jesus is proclaimed to be the Son of God.

A reading from the holy Gospel according to Luke

Jesus took Peter, John, and James
and went up the mountain to pray.
While he was praying his face changed in appearance
and his clothing became dazzling white.
And behold, two men were conversing with him,
Moses and Elijah,
who appeared in glory and spoke of his exodus
that he was going to accomplish in Jerusalem.
Peter and his companions had been overcome by
sleep,
but becoming fully awake,
they saw his glory and the two men standing with
him.
As they were about to part from him, Peter said to
Jesus,
"Master, it is good that we are here;
let us make three tents,
one for you, one for Moses, and one for Elijah."
But he did not know what he was saying.
While he was still speaking,
a cloud came and cast a shadow over them,
and they became frightened when they entered the
cloud.
Then from the cloud came a voice that said,
"This is my chosen Son; listen to him."
After the voice had spoken, Jesus was found alone.
They fell silent and did not at that time
tell anyone what they had seen.

The Gospel of the Lord.

March 3, 2013
THIRD SUNDAY OF LENT

The readings given for Year A, no. 28, pp. 109-116, may be used in place of these readings for Year C.

 FIRST READING: Exodus 3:1-8a, 13-15

"I AM" sent me to you.

This Sunday's First Reading continues the presentation of important moments in salvation history.

Last week we heard about the covenant that God made with Abraham. This Sunday we have the story of Moses and the burning bush.

Moses has a typical reaction when he encounters the presence of God. First of all, he is attracted to the burning bush. When we experience the Holy, we want to draw near.

Yet, as soon as Moses arrives there, he realizes that the Holy also creates a sense of fear (not terror—it is more a sense of awe to be in the presence of God).

God identifies himself as the God of Abraham, Isaac and Jacob, the God who promised that they would inherit the land flowing with milk and honey.

Thus, Moses learns that this is not a new God whom the Israelites had never met before, but rather it is the God who had already called the Patriarchs and prepared the way for his holy people.

Moses asks God what his name is so that he could tell the

A reading from the Book of Exodus

Moses was tending the flock of his father-in-law Jethro,
  the priest of Midian.
Leading the flock across the desert, he came to Horeb,
  the mountain of God.
There an angel of the LORD appeared to Moses in fire
  flaming out of a bush.
As he looked on, he was surprised to see that the bush,
  though on fire, was not consumed.
So Moses decided,
  "I must go over to look at this remarkable sight,
  and see why the bush is not burned."

When the LORD saw him coming over to look at it more closely,
  God called out to him from the bush, "Moses! Moses!"
He answered, "Here I am."
God said, "Come no nearer!
Remove the sandals from your feet,
  for the place where you stand is holy ground.
I am the God of your fathers," he continued,
  "the God of Abraham, the God of Isaac, the God of Jacob."
Moses hid his face, for he was afraid to look at God.
But the LORD said,
  "I have witnessed the affliction of my people in Egypt
  and have heard their cry of complaint against their slave drivers,

people when he recounted what had happened to him. God answers that his name is Yahweh, "I am."

The rabbis had two explanations for this name. They said that it could mean, "I am who I am, and it is none of your business who I am."

This would mean that God was a God of mystery, and we should accept that we will never fully know or understand who God is.

The other explanation for the name was that Yahweh meant, "I am who I am for you, who I have always been for you, who I will always be for you." In other words, God describes himself as being at the service of his chosen people.

He further demonstrates that attitude by listening to the groans of his people and sending Moses to lead them out of the land of their suffering.

so I know well what they are suffering.
Therefore I have come down to rescue them
    from the hands of the Egyptians
    and lead them out of that land into a good and spacious land,
    a land flowing with milk and honey."

Moses said to God, "But when I go to the Israelites
    and say to them, 'The God of your fathers has sent me to you,'
    if they ask me, 'What is his name?' what am I to tell them?"
God replied, "I am who am."
Then he added, "This is what you shall tell the Israelites:
    I AM sent me to you."

God spoke further to Moses, "Thus shall you say to the Israelites:
    The Lord, the God of your fathers,
    the God of Abraham, the God of Isaac, the God of Jacob,
    has sent me to you.

"This is my name forever;
    thus am I to be remembered through all generations."

The word of the Lord.

PASTORAL REFLECTIONS

Names were very important for ancient peoples. To know someone's name was to have power over that person. This is why it is so significant that God would reveal his name to Moses. This is also why the name could only be pronounced out loud once a year: on the Feast of Yom Kippur, the Day of Atonement.

Lect.
No. 30

RESPONSORIAL PSALM: Ps 103:1-2, 3-4, 6-7, 8, 11 (℟.: 8a)

The First Reading identified God as the God who hears our pleas and responds to our needs with generosity. Psalm 103 is a thanksgiving to render gratitude to that God.

The psalm is filled with words that describe the caring and compassionate attitude that God demonstrates to the people of Israel and to us, words such as kindness, compassion, merciful, gracious.

This fills us with a sense of awe, for God's kindness and generosity are truly beyond our comprehension.

Justice means giving each person what that person truly deserves.

If God practiced strict justice, then we could not survive, for we have all sinned and all deserve God's punishment. But God has put aside our guilt and surrounded us with mercy and love.

℟. **The Lord is kind and merciful.**

Bless the LORD, O my soul;
  and all my being, bless his holy name.
Bless the LORD, O my soul,
  and forget not all his benefits.

℟. **The Lord is kind and merciful.**

He pardons all your iniquities,
  he heals all your ills.
He redeems your life from destruction,
  he crowns you with kindness and compassion.

℟. **The Lord is kind and merciful.**

The LORD secures justice
  and the rights of all the oppressed.
He has made known his ways to Moses,
  and his deeds to the children of Israel.

℟. **The Lord is kind and merciful.**

Merciful and gracious is the LORD,
  slow to anger and abounding in kindness.
For as the heavens are high above the earth,
  so surpassing is his kindness toward those who
    fear him.

℟. **The Lord is kind and merciful.**

PASTORAL REFLECTIONS

One of the Gospel injunctions is that we are to go out into the world and preach the forgiveness of sins. We are to proclaim God's mercy to those who desperately need to hear about it.

We have to ask ourselves whether we and our parish have done this. Do we spend our time and resources to share the Good News with the unchurched?

Lect. No. 30

SECOND READING: 1 Corinthians 10:1-6, 10-12

The life of the people with Moses in the desert was written down as a warning to us.

Saint Paul reminds the people of Corinth that every gift from God also carries responsibility. If God has revealed his love and goodness to us, then we must respond appropriately.

Paul speaks of how the people of the Old Testament received God's revelation. They, in a sense, experienced a prefiguring of the sacraments of Baptism and Eucharist. Yet they rejected God and sinned, and for this they were severely punished.

How much more is the Christian community responsible, for what they received was not a prefiguring of the sacraments, but the actual sacraments themselves.

In the course of this passage, Paul speaks of the rock that gave water to the Israelites in the desert, and he says that the rock was Jesus.

This was an attempt to show that, even before Jesus was born in Bethlehem, he already existed as God.

A reading from the first Letter of Saint Paul to the Corinthians

I do not want you to be unaware, brothers and sisters, that our ancestors were all under the cloud
and all passed through the sea,
and all of them were baptized into Moses
in the cloud and in the sea.
All ate the same spiritual food,
and all drank the same spiritual drink,
for they drank from a spiritual rock that followed them,
and the rock was the Christ.
Yet God was not pleased with most of them,
for they were struck down in the desert.

These things happened as examples for us,
so that we might not desire evil things, as they did.
Do not grumble as some of them did,
and suffered death by the destroyer.
These things happened to them as an example,
and they have been written down as a warning to us,
upon whom the end of the ages has come.
Therefore, whoever thinks he is standing secure
should take care not to fall.

The word of the Lord.

Lect. No. 30

VERSE BEFORE THE GOSPEL: Matthew 4:17

We are reminded that Lent is a season of repentance.

Repent, says the Lord;
the kingdom of heaven is at hand.

Lect.
No. 30

GOSPEL: Luke 13:1-9

If you do not repent, you will all perish as they did.

The Gospel recalls the theme found in the Second Reading today, that those who have received God's grace are responsible for what they have received.

Lent is a season when we are invited to honestly examine our lives and to remove anything that keeps us from loving God and neighbor from our hearts. It is not to be squandered, for we honestly do not know how much time we have to turn to the Lord's ways. We do not know how much time we have to live. We see disasters on TV, we pass car accidents on the highway, we hear of relatives who died suddenly.

Every moment is precious. In a sense, we are living on borrowed time, and this season of repentance is too valuable not to use well.

There is also a positive dimension to the parable found at the end of today's Gospel passage. Lent is a time to dig around our roots and fertilize them (with the word of God, prayer, penitential practices, reception of the sacraments, etc.) so that, even if we have not really borne fruit yet, we might still have a chance to do so.

We cannot let our past failures paralyze us; we must courageously use every opportunity for growth that God provides for us.

A reading from the holy Gospel according to Luke

Some people told Jesus about the Galileans
　whose blood Pilate had mingled with the blood of
　　their sacrifices.
Jesus said to them in reply,
　"Do you think that because these Galileans suffered in this way
　they were greater sinners than all other Galileans?
By no means!
But I tell you, if you do not repent,
　you will all perish as they did!
Or those eighteen people who were killed
　when the tower at Siloam fell on them—
　do you think they were more guilty
　than everyone else who lived in Jerusalem?
By no means!
But I tell you, if you do not repent,
　you will all perish as they did!"

And he told them this parable:
　"There once was a person who had a fig tree
　　planted in his orchard,
　and when he came in search of fruit on it but
　　found none,
　he said to the gardener,
　'For three years now I have come in search of fruit
　　on this fig tree
　but have found none.
So cut it down.
Why should it exhaust the soil?'
He said to him in reply,
　'Sir, leave it for this year also,
　and I shall cultivate the ground around it and fertilize it;
　it may bear fruit in the future.
If not you can cut it down.'"

The Gospel of the Lord.

The following readings given for Year A may be used in place of the previous readings.

Lect. No. 28

FIRST READING: Exodus 17:3-7

Give us water, so that we may drink.

The people of Israel had an astounding talent for showing ingratitude. The LORD had just freed them from slavery in Egypt. He had performed great miracles to force Pharaoh to let his people go free. Yet, they refused to trust in him.

In spite of their lack of gratitude, the LORD performed yet another act of generosity on their behalf. He provided them with water from the rock.

This was a pattern that occurred over and over again throughout the Exodus experience. This is why the Israelites had to remain in the desert for forty years, to learn how to trust in the LORD.

Before we condemn the Israelites, though, it is good to admit that, in spite of all the ways we have seen God's goodness in our lives, we still doubt his presence all too often. We often hedge our bets by relying on God but also by trying to rely upon our own resources.

A reading from the Book of Exodus

In those days, in their thirst for water,
   the people grumbled against Moses,
   saying, "Why did you ever make us leave Egypt?
Was it just to have us die here of thirst
   with our children and our livestock?"
So Moses cried out to the LORD,
   "What shall I do with this people?
A little more and they will stone me!"
The LORD answered Moses,
   "Go over there in front of the people,
   along with some of the elders of Israel,
   holding in your hand, as you go,
   the staff with which you struck the river.
I will be standing there in front of you on the rock in
      Horeb.
Strike the rock, and the water will flow from it
   for the people to drink."
This Moses did, in the presence of the elders of
      Israel.
The place was called Massah and Meribah,
   because the Israelites quarreled there
   and tested the LORD, saying,
"Is the LORD in our midst or not?"

The word of the Lord.

Lect. No. 28

RESPONSORIAL PSALM: Ps 95:1-2, 6-7, 8-9 (℟.: 8)

This is above all a hymn of praise for the LORD who is our strength and salvation. We must recognize how much we need God to be a part of our lives.

When we acknowledge how important God is for us, then we

℟. **If today you hear his voice, harden not your hearts.**

Come, let us sing joyfully to the LORD;
   let us acclaim the Rock of our salvation.
Let us come into his presence with thanksgiving;
   let us joyfully sing psalms to him.

must fall down on our knees to worship him.

One of the goals of Lent is to do exactly that. We must discover those things that we have set at the center of our lives in the place of God and root them out. We must return God to his proper place in our lives. We must fall down on our knees in gratitude and awe.

This is why the last part of our Responsorial Psalm is a warning against arrogance and pride. We always are being tempted by the illusion that we can solve all of our problems if we just try hard enough. Only in God can we find a response to our need: only in our heavenly Father can we find peace.

℞. **If today you hear his voice, harden not your hearts.**

Come, let us bow down in worship;
   let us kneel before the LORD who made us.
For he is our God,
   and we are the people he shepherds, the flock he guides.

℞. **If today you hear his voice, harden not your hearts.**

Oh, that today you would hear his voice:
   "Harden not your hearts as at Meribah,
   as in the day of Massah in the desert.
Where your fathers tempted me;
   they tested me though they had seen my works."

℞. **If today you hear his voice, harden not your hearts.**

Lect. No. 28

SECOND READING: Romans 5:1-2, 5-8

The love of God has been poured into our hearts through the Holy Spirit that has been given to us.

Saint Paul outlines his theology of salvation in this letter to the Christian community in Rome.

According to Paul, Christ paid the price for our redemption on the cross. When we accept the free gift of his love through our response of faith, we are justified. Justification means that we are living at peace with our God.

This gift is incredible. It was given to us not because of something that we have done, but quite the opposite. We have sinned and rejected God's love, and God responded to that offense with a greater outpouring of love.

A reading from the Letter of Saint Paul
to the Romans

Brothers and sisters:
   Since we have been justified by faith,
   we have peace with God through our Lord Jesus Christ,
   through whom we have gained access by faith
   to this grace in which we stand,
   and we boast in hope of the glory of God.

And hope does not disappoint,
   because the love of God has been poured out into our hearts
   through the Holy Spirit who has been given to us.
For Christ, while we were still helpless,
   died at the appointed time for the ungodly.

If God did this for us while we were sinners, then what is in store for us now that we are living at peace with him (justified)! Paul marvels at the greatness of God's love and the glory into which we have been called to live for all eternity.

Indeed, only with difficulty does one die for a just person,
 though perhaps for a good person one might even find courage to die.
But God proves his love for us
 in that while we were still sinners Christ died for us.

The word of the Lord.

Lect. No. 28

VERSE BEFORE THE GOSPEL: cf. John 4:42, 15

Jesus is both the savior of the world and our own individual savior. We thirst for his love and grace, and he responds to our need with great generosity.

Lord, you are truly the Savior of the world;
give me living water, that I may never thirst again.

GOSPEL: **A** Longer Form: John 4:5-42

The water that I shall give will become a spring of eternal life.

Throughout the Old Testament there are several "well" stories. In each of them, a person meets his or her spouse (e.g., Isaac, Jacob, Moses, and Ruth). The technical term for this type of pattern is "leitmotif." The differences in each of the stories give us insights into the characters involved in these encounters.

The evangelist used the well story pattern in this account to speak of God's relationship to the Samaritans and pagans. They had not been part of the original covenant, which was a type of marriage between God and the people of Israel. God was now going to invite them into the new covenant.

The Samaritan woman in this story represents the Samaritans and pagans. This is typical

A reading from the holy Gospel according to John

Jesus came to a town of Samaria called Sychar, near the plot of land that Jacob had given to his son Joseph.
Jacob's well was there.
Jesus, tired from his journey, sat down there at the well.
It was about noon.

A woman of Samaria came to draw water.
Jesus said to her,
 "Give me a drink."
His disciples had gone into the town to buy food.
The Samaritan woman said to him,
 "How can you, a Jew, ask me, a Samaritan woman, for a drink?"
—For Jews use nothing in common with Samaritans.—
Jesus answered and said to her,

of John's Gospel, for every time that a character is referred to by a title and not a name (e.g., man born blind, Samaritan woman), that character plays a symbolic role.

The woman goes to the well at the the sixth hour, which is noon. That is unusual, for it was too hot at that hour to go to the well for water. This woman was afraid to meet others because of her reputation, and so she avoided them by going to the well when they were not there.

Even when Jesus begins to speak to her, she is hesitant. Jesus continues to treat her with great dignity and respect— one could say with more respect than she would have treated herself.

Jesus offers her "living water." This phrase is ambiguous for it could mean flowing water or water that gives life. She only understands flowing water.

Jesus promises that this water will become a font overflowing within her. This means that she will be filled to overflowing with God's grace and life.

The woman does not understand anything that Jesus is saying, so he instructs her to call her husband. She has had five and is now living with another man, which makes six. These husbands represent all of the gods that her people have served.

The perfect number in the Bible is seven. Jesus, by offering her water, is becoming her

"If you knew the gift of God
and who is saying to you, 'Give me a drink,'
you would have asked him
and he would have given you living water."
The woman said to him,
"Sir, you do not even have a bucket and the cistern is deep;
where then can you get this living water?
Are you greater than our father Jacob,
who gave us this cistern and drank from it himself
with his children and his flocks?"
Jesus answered and said to her,
"Everyone who drinks this water will be thirsty again;
but whoever drinks the water I shall give will never thirst;
the water I shall give will become in him
a spring of water welling up to eternal life."
The woman said to him,
"Sir, give me this water, so that I may not be thirsty
or have to keep coming here to draw water."

Jesus said to her,
"Go call your husband and come back."
The woman answered and said to him,
"I do not have a husband."
Jesus answered her,
"You are right in saying, 'I do not have a husband.'
For you have had five husbands,
and the one you have now is not your husband.
What you have said is true."
The woman said to him,
"Sir, I can see that you are a prophet.
Our ancestors worshiped on this mountain;
but you people say that the place to worship is in Jerusalem."
Jesus said to her,
"Believe me, woman, the hour is coming

seventh. He is inviting the Samaritan people and the pagans into a marriage (covenant) with God. (Always remember that this is a symbolic marriage.)

The Samaritan woman asks whether Jesus might be the Messiah. The Samaritan concept of the Messiah was very different from the Jewish concept. The Jewish people expected a conquering hero, but the Samaritans expected one who would reveal the secrets of God to them. This was exactly what Jesus was doing, for he was able to reveal all of the woman's secrets.

We hear that we are to worship the Father in Spirit and in Truth. The Spirit is the Holy Spirit, and the Truth is Jesus. We worship the Father in and through Jesus and the Holy Spirit.

The woman leaves her water jar, for, as Jesus promised, his grace has become a font of living water inside of her. She proclaims her message to the people from her village. Before she avoided them (going to the well at noon to avoid speaking to them); now she shares her discovery with them and she helps to bring them to salvation.

Jesus does not need the nourishment that the disciples can offer for he is totally sustained by the Father.

Jesus tells his disciples that the grain is already white for the harvest ("ripe" is a bit of a mistranslation). He is not pointing

when you will worship the Father
neither on this mountain nor in Jerusalem.
You people worship what you do not understand;
we worship what we understand,
because salvation is from the Jews.
But the hour is coming, and is now here,
when true worshipers will worship the Father in Spirit and truth;
and indeed the Father seeks such people to worship him.
God is Spirit, and those who worship him
must worship in Spirit and truth."
The woman said to him,
"I know that the Messiah is coming, the one called the Christ;
when he comes, he will tell us everything."
Jesus said to her,
"I am he, the one who is speaking with you."

At that moment his disciples returned,
and were amazed that he was talking with a woman,
but still no one said, "What are you looking for?"
or "Why are you talking with her?"
The woman left her water jar
and went into the town and said to the people,
"Come see a man who told me everything I have done.
Could he possibly be the Christ?"
They went out of the town and came to him.
Meanwhile, the disciples urged him, "Rabbi, eat."
But he said to them,
"I have food to eat of which you do not know."
So the disciples said to one another,
"Could someone have brought him something to eat?"
Jesus said to them,
"My food is to do the will of the one who sent me and to finish his work.

at the grain fields, he is pointing at the Samaritans who were coming out of the village. Samaritans wore white robes, and they were the harvest of which Jesus was speaking. The one who sowed that harvest was the Samaritan woman; now the disciples were being called to harvest what she had planted.

The Samaritans then encounter Jesus and come to a more profound faith. They no longer believe in him because of what the woman said, but because they had experienced him themselves.

This is a powerful story of conversion. A woman who previously had been filled with fear was now filled to overflowing with love.

This is also the story of a people who had searched for love in the many gods whom they worshiped, but had not found true love or peace.

Finally, this is an invitation for us to leave the false gods whom we have worshiped (e.g., work, possessions, power, etc.).

Do you not say, 'In four months the harvest will be here'?
I tell you, look up and see the fields ripe for the harvest.
The reaper is already receiving payment
    and gathering crops for eternal life,
    so that the sower and reaper can rejoice together.
For here the saying is verified that 'One sows and another reaps.'
I sent you to reap what you have not worked for;
    others have done the work,
    and you are sharing the fruits of their work."

Many of the Samaritans of that town began to believe in him
    because of the word of the woman who testified,
    "He told me everything I have done."
When the Samaritans came to him,
    they invited him to stay with them;
    and he stayed there two days.
Many more began to believe in him because of his word,
    and they said to the woman,
    "We no longer believe because of your word;
    for we have heard for ourselves,
    and we know that this is truly the savior of the world."

The Gospel of the Lord.

Lect. No. 28
GOSPEL: B Shorter Form: John 4:5-15, 19b-26, 39a, 40-42

The water that I shall give will become a spring of eternal life.

Throughout the Old Testament there are several "well" stories. In each of them, a person meets his or her spouse (e.g., Isaac, Jacob, Moses, and Ruth). The technical term for this type of pattern is "leitmotif." The differences in each of the stories give us insights into the characters involved in these encounters.

A reading from the holy Gospel according to John

Jesus came to a town of Samaria called Sychar, near the plot of land that Jacob had given to his son Joseph.
Jacob's well was there.
Jesus, tired from his journey, sat down there at the well.
It was about noon.

The Samaritan woman in this story represents the Samaritans and the pagans. When Jesus begins to speak to the Samaritan woman at the well, she is hesitant. Jesus treats her with great dignity and respect—one could say with more respect than she would have treated herself.

Jesus offers her "living water." This phrase is ambiguous for it could mean flowing water or water that gives life. She only understands flowing water.

Jesus promises that this water will become a font overflowing within her. This means that she will be filled to overflowing with God's grace and life.

The woman does not understand anything that Jesus is saying, so he instructs her to call her husband.

She has had five and is now living with another man, which makes six.

These husbands represent all of the gods that her people have served.

The perfect number in the Bible is seven. Jesus, by offering her water, is becoming her seventh.

He is inviting the Samaritan people and the pagans into a marriage (covenant) with God. (Always remember that this is a symbolic marriage).

The Samaritan woman asks whether Jesus might be the Messiah. The Samaritan concept of Messiah was very differ-

A woman of Samaria came to draw water.
Jesus said to her,
    "Give me a drink."
His disciples had gone into the town to buy food.
The Samaritan woman said to him,
    "How can you, a Jew, ask me, a Samaritan
        woman, for a drink?"
—For Jews use nothing in common with Samaritans.—
Jesus answered and said to her,
    "If you knew the gift of God
    and who is saying to you, 'Give me a drink,'
    you would have asked him
    and he would have given you living water."
The woman said to him,
    "Sir, you do not even have a bucket and the cistern is deep;
    where then can you get this living water?
Are you greater than our father Jacob,
    who gave us this cistern and drank from it himself
    with his children and his flocks?"
Jesus answered and said to her,
    "Everyone who drinks this water will be thirsty
        again;
    but whoever drinks the water I shall give will
        never thirst;
    the water I shall give will become in him
    a spring of water welling up to eternal life."
The woman said to him,
    "Sir, give me this water, so that I may not be thirsty
    or have to keep coming here to draw water.

"I can see that you are a prophet.
Our ancestors worshiped on this mountain;
    but you people say that the place to worship is in
        Jerusalem."
Jesus said to her,
    "Believe me, woman, the hour is coming

ent from the Jewish concept. The Jewish people expected a conquering hero, but the Samaritans expected one who would reveal the secrets of God to them. This was exactly what Jesus was doing, for he was able to reveal all of the woman's secrets.

We hear that we are to worship the Father in Spirit and in Truth. The Spirit is the Holy Spirit, and the Truth is Jesus. We worship the Father in and through Jesus and the Holy Spirit.

The woman leaves her water jar, for, as Jesus promised, his grace has become a font of living water inside of her. She proclaims her message to the people from her village. Before she avoided them (going to the well at noon to avoid speaking to them); now she shares her discovery with them and she helps to bring them to salvation.

The Samaritans then encounter Jesus and come to a more profound faith. They no longer believe in him because of what the woman said, but because they had experienced him themselves.

Finally, this is an invitation for us to leave the false gods whom we have worshiped (e.g., work, possessions, power, etc.).

when you will worship the Father
neither on this mountain nor in Jerusalem.
You people worship what you do not understand;
we worship what we understand,
because salvation is from the Jews.
But the hour is coming, and is now here,
when true worshipers will worship the Father in Spirit and truth;
and indeed the Father seeks such people to worship him.
God is Spirit, and those who worship him
must worship in Spirit and truth."
The woman said to him,
"I know that the Messiah is coming, the one called the Christ;
when he comes, he will tell us everything."
Jesus said to her,
"I am he, the one who is speaking with you."

Many of the Samaritans of that town began to believe in him.
When the Samaritans came to him,
they invited him to stay with them;
and he stayed there two days.
Many more began to believe in him because of his word,
and they said to the woman,
"We no longer believe because of your word;
for we have heard for ourselves,
and we know that this is truly the savior of the world."

The Gospel of the Lord.

PASTORAL REFLECTIONS

It is easy to point to the many mistakes others have made (e.g., the Samaritan woman), not realizing that we are probably just as bad as they are (only our faults are more subtle or hidden, e.g., judgmentalism).

March 10, 2013

FOURTH SUNDAY OF LENT

The readings given for Year A, no. 31, pp. 121-129, may be used in place of these readings for Year C.

Lect. No. 33

FIRST READING: Joshua 5:9a, 10-12

The people of God entered the promised land and there kept the Passover.

A reading from the Book of Joshua

The LORD said to Joshua,
"Today I have removed the reproach of Egypt from you."

While the Israelites were encamped at Gilgal on the
    plains of Jericho,
    they celebrated the Passover
    on the evening of the fourteenth of the month.
On the day after the Passover,
    they ate of the produce of the land
    in the form of unleavened cakes and parched grain.
On that same day after the Passover,
    on which they ate of the produce of the land, the
    manna ceased.
No longer was there manna for the Israelites,
    who that year ate of the yield of the land of Canaan.

The word of the Lord.

The First Reading continues the series of readings on the important moments of salvation history that we have seen over the past few weeks. This week we hear of the first celebration of the Passover in the promised land, the land flowing with milk and honey.

This is a moment of celebration, for the people could now grow their own crops and depend upon their own efforts to provide for their needs (and not have to depend upon the manna that the LORD provided).

This is also a moment of danger, however, for the people could henceforth begin to believe that they were masters of their own destiny.

Lect. No. 33

RESPONSORIAL PSALM: Ps 34:2-3, 4-5, 6-7 (℟.: 9a)

The Responsorial Psalm is a celebration of God's goodness. We have been given an opportunity during Lent to turn back to his ways.

That is an experience that should fill us with joy. Lent is not a time for grief and gloom. It is a season of renewal and rebirth.

℟. **Taste and see the goodness of the Lord.**

I will bless the LORD at all times;
    his praise shall be ever in my mouth.
Let my soul glory in the LORD;
    the lowly will hear me and be glad.

℟. **Taste and see the goodness of the Lord.**

Glorify the LORD with me,
    let us together extol his name.

The latter part of the psalm gives us the two options that are placed before us. We can blush with shame if we refuse to use this Lenten season well, or we can look to God with faces that are radiant with joy.

God is always willing to hear our call, but we have to be willing to call out.

I sought the LORD, and he answered me
  and delivered me from all my fears.

℟. **Taste and see the goodness of the Lord.**

Look to him that you may be radiant with joy,
  and your faces may not blush with shame.
When the poor one called out, the LORD heard,
  and from all his distress he saved him.

℟. **Taste and see the goodness of the Lord.**

SECOND READING: 2 Corinthians 5:17-21

God reconciled us to himself through Christ.

The Second Reading continues the theme of renewal. We hear that Christ died so that we might be reconciled to God. Jesus paid the price for our sins.

Saint Paul says that Jesus became sin, meaning that he took the curse of our sins upon himself. He put the old ways (of selfishness and alienation) to death. Now we have to choose life and love.

There are a number of passages in the New Testament that present the idea that we are a new creation. When Jesus is buried in the Gospel of John, he is buried in a garden (signifying the garden of Eden).

He breathes on his disciples after the resurrection (just as God breathed into the mud to create Adam). The Spirit is a great wind on the Day of Pentecost (just as the Spirit hovered over the waters on the day of creation).

A reading from the second Letter of Saint Paul
to the Corinthians

Brothers and sisters:
  Whoever is in Christ is a new creation:
  the old things have passed away;
  behold, new things have come.
And all this is from God,
  who has reconciled us to himself through Christ
  and given us the ministry of reconciliation,
  namely, God was reconciling the world to himself
    in Christ,
  not counting their trespasses against them
  and entrusting to us the message of reconciliation.
So we are ambassadors for Christ,
  as if God were appealing through us.
We implore you on behalf of Christ,
  be reconciled to God.
For our sake he made him to be sin who did not
    know sin,
  so that we might become the righteousness of
    God in him.

The word of the Lord.

VERSE BEFORE THE GOSPEL: Luke 15:18

We are all called to abandon our sinful ways and return to our merciful Father.

I will get up and go to my Father and shall say to him:
Father, I have sinned against heaven and against you.

GOSPEL: Luke 15:1-3, 11-32

Your brother was dead and has come to life again.

The Gospel presents the beautiful parable of the Prodigal Son.

It is easy to take this story for granted, for we have heard it so often. Yet there are details in the story that continue to jump out and fill us with awe.

The Pharisees studied the law of God with great enthusiasm. They earnestly tried to be blameless in their observance of that law.

The danger was that it was easy for them to become self-righteous (not unlike the brother of the Prodigal Son who did not rejoice in the fact that his father had forgiven his brother).

Furthermore, because they observed the law so scrupulously, they could easily begin to think that they did not need the mercy of God (for they could feel that they had done nothing wrong).

This is why Jesus presents a picture of God as the all-merciful one, the loving parent who forgives our every fault.

It is interesting to note that the Prodigal Son does not really seem to be sorry for what he

A reading from the holy Gospel according to Luke

Tax collectors and sinners were all drawing near to listen to Jesus,
but the Pharisees and scribes began to complain, saying,
"This man welcomes sinners and eats with them."
So to them Jesus addressed this parable:
"A man had two sons, and the younger son said to his father,
'Father give me the share of your estate that should come to me.'
So the father divided the property between them.
After a few days, the younger son collected all his belongings
and set off to a distant country
where he squandered his inheritance on a life of dissipation.
When he had freely spent everything,
a severe famine struck that country,
and he found himself in dire need.
So he hired himself out to one of the local citizens
who sent him to his farm to tend the swine.
And he longed to eat his fill of the pods on which the swine fed,
but nobody gave him any.
Coming to his senses he thought,
'How many of my father's hired workers
have more than enough food to eat,
but here am I, dying from hunger.

has done. He is sorry that he is hungry.

He prepares his apology to the father, almost as if he would say whatever was needed just to be received back into the good graces of his father.

The father is waiting for his son, catching sight of him from a great distance.

This is unusual, for Jewish fathers at the time of Jesus would not have been standing outside, waiting for their sons to come back to them. Rather, they would have been waiting in their houses. If their sons did return, they could fall down on their knees and beg for their father's mercy.

This father actively seeks out his son.

Furthermore, the father forgives the son even before the son can apologize for what he had done (almost as if the father knew that the apology was not quite as sincere as it could have been).

The father calls for a feast to be prepared to celebrate the safe return of his son.

This is a common element in the Gospel of Luke, for food is a symbol for the bounty and goodness of God. Even heaven is described as being a heavenly banquet.

The brother's reaction is pathetic. He loved his father for what he could receive from him, not out of pure, disinterested love.

I shall get up and go to my father and I shall say to him,
    "Father, I have sinned against heaven and against you.
I no longer deserve to be called your son;
    treat me as you would treat one of your hired workers."'
So he got up and went back to his father.
While he was still a long way off,
    his father caught sight of him, and was filled with compassion.
He ran to his son, embraced him and kissed him.
His son said to him,
    'Father, I have sinned against heaven and against you;
    I no longer deserve to be called your son.'
But his father ordered his servants,
    'Quickly bring the finest robe and put it on him;
    put a ring on his finger and sandals on his feet.
Take the fattened calf and slaughter it.
Then let us celebrate with a feast,
    because this son of mine was dead, and has come to life again;
    he was lost, and has been found.'
Then the celebration began.
Now the older son had been out in the field
    and, on his way back, as he neared the house,
    he heard the sound of music and dancing.
He called one of the servants and asked what this might mean.
The servant said to him,
    'Your brother has returned
    and your father has slaughtered the fattened calf
    because he has him back safe and sound.'
He became angry,
    and when he refused to enter the house,
    his father came out and pleaded with him.

Thus, he views his father's pardon of his brother as an act of betrayal.

If the brother had truly loved his father, he would have been filled with joy when the father experienced the joy of being able to pardon his errant son.

How joyful will we be if our greatest enemy is pardoned by God? Remember, Saint Paul teaches in First Corinthians that true love does not rejoice in bad things that happen to others but rather only rejoices in the good. In Romans he offers to go to hell if that would save his fellow Jews.

He said to his father in reply,
'Look, all these years I served you
and not once did I disobey your orders;
yet you never gave me even a young goat to feast
on with my friends.
But when your son returns
who swallowed up your property with prostitutes,
for him you slaughter the fattened calf.'
He said to him,
'My son, you are here with me always;
everything I have is yours.
But now we must celebrate and rejoice,
because your brother was dead and has come to
life again;
he was lost and has been found.'"
The Gospel of the Lord.

The following readings given for Year A may be used in place of the previous readings.

FIRST READING: 1 Samuel 16:1b, 6-7, 10-13a

David is anointed as king of Israel.

The Israelites had asked the LORD for a king to rule over them. The LORD indicated to Samuel, the last of the judges, that Saul was to be that king. (Judges were charismatically chosen leaders who acted as king, prophet, priest, and judge.) For a while, all went well and Saul led Israel against their enemies. But Saul did what was evil in the sight of the LORD. So the LORD rejected Saul and sent Samuel to anoint another king of Israel in his place.

The LORD sent Samuel to Bethlehem, a small city in the area settled by the tribe of Judah. There Samuel spoke to Jesse and asked to see his sons. He saw one after another

A reading from the first Book of Samuel

The LORD said to Samuel:
"Fill your horn with oil, and be on your way.
I am sending you to Jesse of Bethlehem,
for I have chosen my king from among his sons."

As Jesse and his sons came to the sacrifice,
Samuel looked at Eliab and thought,
"Surely the LORD's anointed is here before him."
But the LORD said to Samuel:
"Do not judge from his appearance or from his
lofty stature,
because I have rejected him.
Not as man sees does God see,
because man sees the appearance
but the LORD looks into the heart."

of the sons, and all of them seemed to be handsome and courageous. If Samuel had made the choice on appearances, he could have chosen any one of them.

But the LORD chooses according to what is in a person's heart. David was to be the new king of Israel, for he was a man according to the LORD's own heart.

Samuel anointed David, making him an anointed of the Lord. Remember that the word "anointed" in Hebrew is messiah. But while David was a messiah, only Jesus would be the Messiah. Nevertheless, David would be regarded as the model of what the future Messiah should be. This is why the Gospel of Matthew mentions that Jesus is a son of David in its genealogy.

The Spirit of the LORD rushed upon David, even as the Spirit of the LORD would anoint Jesus to proclaim a year of favor.

In the same way Jesse presented seven sons before Samuel,
 but Samuel said to Jesse,
 "The LORD has not chosen any one of these."
Then Samuel asked Jesse,
 "Are these all the sons you have?"
Jesse replied,
 "There is still the youngest, who is tending the sheep."
Samuel said to Jesse,
 "Send for him;
 we will not begin the sacrificial banquet until he arrives here."
Jesse sent and had the young man brought to them.
He was ruddy, a youth handsome to behold
 and making a splendid appearance.
The LORD said,
 "There—anoint him, for this is the one!"
Then Samuel, with the horn of oil in hand,
 anointed David in the presence of his brothers;
 and from that day on, the spirit of the LORD rushed upon David.

The word of the Lord.

Lect. No. 31

RESPONSORIAL PSALM: Ps 23:1-3a, 3b-4, 5, 6 (℞.: 1)

This psalm is a beautiful hymn of trust in the goodness of the LORD. It was probably written during the exile in Babylon when the people of Israel desperately needed the consolation of knowing that the LORD was leading them and had not forgotten or abandoned them because of their sinfulness.

Before the exile, the prophets had often complained that the kings of Israel were evil shepherds who did not guide their

℞. **The Lord is my shepherd; there is nothing I shall want.**

The LORD is my shepherd; I shall not want.
 In verdant pastures he gives me repose;
beside restful waters he leads me;
 he refreshes my soul.

℞. **The Lord is my shepherd; there is nothing I shall want.**

He guides me in right paths
 for his name's sake.

flocks in the ways of the L ORD. Now God himself would guide them.

There are several images presented in the first part of the psalm to show how God is a good shepherd. He brings the flock to verdant pastures, leads them to restful waters (remember the importance of that in an arid climate), and he leads them through dangerous places. The valley through which we are led is called the "dark valley" (more popularly known as the "valley of death"). The Hebrew meaning is a valley that is dark as death.

His rod and staff give us comfort for while we are wandering in the dark, we can nevertheless feel his presence as he gently touches us with them.

Even though I walk in the dark valley
    I fear no evil; for you are at my side
with your rod and your staff
    that give me courage.

    ℟. **The Lord is my shepherd; there is nothing I shall want.**

You spread the table before me
    in the sight of my foes;
you anoint my head with oil;
    my cup overflows.

    ℟. **The Lord is my shepherd; there is nothing I shall want.**

Only goodness and kindness follow me
    all the days of my life;
and I shall dwell in the house of the L ORD
    for years to come.

    ℟. **The Lord is my shepherd; there is nothing I shall want.**

Lect. No. 31

SECOND READING: Ephesians 5:8-14

Arise from the dead, and Christ will give you light.

The Second Reading develops the theme of light and darkness. These two opposites were often used as a synonym for good and evil. We must choose the good and reject evil. Otherwise, we will be children of the dark, children of the evil one.

We see this same theme developed in other places in Scripture. Jesus, for example, calls himself the light of the world. He gives light to the man born blind. On the other hand, we hear that after Judas departed from the Last Supper it was dark.

A reading from the Letter of Saint Paul to the Ephesians

Brothers and sisters:
    You were once darkness,
    but now you are light in the Lord.
Live as children of light,
    for light produces every kind of goodness
    and righteousness and truth.
Try to learn what is pleasing to the Lord.
Take no part in the fruitless works of darkness;
    rather expose them, for it is shameful even to mention
    the things done by them in secret;
    but everything exposed by the light becomes visible,

One of the goals of our Lenten conversion is transparency. We should do everything in such a way that we will never be embarrassed if others see what we are doing. We have to allow the light of Christ to shine through us.

for everything that becomes visible is light.
Therefore, it says:

> "Awake, O sleeper,
> and arise from the dead,
> and Christ will give you light."

The word of the Lord.

VERSE BEFORE THE GOSPEL: John 8:12

Jesus is the light of the world. He is the source of guidance for our journey and the light toward which we all travel.

I am the light of the world, says the Lord;
whoever follows me will have the light of life.

GOSPEL: **A** Longer Form: John 9:1-41

*The man who was blind went off and washed himself
and came back able to see.*

This story is presented at two levels of meaning. The first (superficial) level is the story of a miracle that Jesus performed during his public ministry. The second (deeper symbolic level) is a story of a community that came to faith in Jesus Christ as the light of the world.

The disciples ask whether the man born blind is a sinner or whether his parents are sinners to explain why he should have been born blind. They are using a theology in which individual maladies are the result of particular sins.

Jesus rejects their question (which was rude considering that the blind man could hear what they were saying). He speaks of God manifesting his power through him. Jesus treats the man with great respect, beginning the healing of his spirit

A reading from the holy Gospel according to John

As Jesus passed by he saw a man blind from birth. His disciples asked him,
"Rabbi, who sinned, this man or his parents,
that he was born blind?"
Jesus answered,
"Neither he nor his parents sinned;
it is so that the works of God might be made visible through him.
We have to do the works of the one who sent me while it is day.
Night is coming when no one can work.
While I am in the world, I am the light of the world."
When he had said this, he spat on the ground
and made clay with the saliva,
and smeared the clay on his eyes, and said to him,
"Go wash in the Pool of Siloam"—which means Sent—.
So he went and washed, and came back able to see.

even before he heals him physically.

Jesus uses saliva to heal the man, something that many miracle workers in his day would have done. (The Pharisees would later object for the very act of making mud was considered to be work, an act forbidden on the Sabbath.) He then sends the man to wash at the pool of Siloam.

The man was immediately healed. The people who were his neighbors never really knew him as a person, they only knew him as a disability. (Notice, that they do not use his name.) That is why they cannot identify him when he is healed.

The man is brought before the Pharisees. It is only then that we hear that Jesus healed the man on the Sabbath. This is intentional, for while it was not important to Jesus that it was the Sabbath, it was important to the Pharisees. They could not understand why Jesus would not wait until the next day to heal him, for it was against the law to heal him if he were not in danger of death. Jesus, on the other hand, would not make him wait even one more minute.

The fact that the man is interrogated only before the Pharisees and not, as one would expect, before the full Sanhedrin (which was composed of both Pharisees and the Sadducees), is a sign that this story has a second level, one that occurred toward the end of the century when the Sadducees had ceased to exist.

His neighbors and those who had seen him earlier
as a beggar said,
"Isn't this the one who used to sit and beg?"
Some said, "It is,"
but others said, "No, he just looks like him."
He said, "I am."
So they said to him, "How were your eyes opened?"
He replied,
"The man called Jesus made clay and anointed my eyes
and told me, 'Go to Siloam and wash.'
So I went there and washed and was able to see."
And they said to him, "Where is he?"
He said, "I don't know."

They brought the one who was once blind to the
Pharisees.
Now Jesus had made clay and opened his eyes on a
sabbath.
So then the Pharisees also asked him how he was
able to see.
He said to them,
"He put clay on my eyes, and I washed, and now I
can see."
So some of the Pharisees said,
"This man is not from God,
because he does not keep the sabbath."
But others said,
"How can a sinful man do such signs?"
And there was a division among them.
So they said to the blind man again,
"What do you have to say about him,
since he opened your eyes?"
He said, "He is a prophet."

Now the Jews did not believe
that he had been blind and gained his sight
until they summoned the parents of the one who
had gained his sight.

The man born blind is not given a name because he also plays a symbolic role in this Gospel. He represents the members of the community of the beloved disciple that had come to believe in Jesus.

Before they converted they had been blind, for they had not known the light of the world. Jesus came into their lives, and he healed them. He brought them to faith and they were able to see the truth. But like the man born blind, they suffered for their beliefs, for they were expelled from the synagogue.

The parents of the man born blind seem to represent that part of the Christian community that denied their faith in order to remain within the synagogue. They are often called crypto-Christians, a name that means hidden Christians. They let fear guide their lives, and they thus denied the one whom they knew to be the Messiah. They are a warning to us when we subtly deny our faith by failing to give witness to who or what we are.

The man born blind humiliates the great doctors of the law with his simplicity and truth. He has no formal learning, but his wisdom is much more profound than theirs. It is the wisdom of the cross being more powerful than the wisdom of the world.

Throughout the account the man born blind has used various titles for Jesus such as "the man called Jesus," "a prophet," "a man . . . from God," etc. After he is expelled from the presence of the Pharisees (which represents the synagogue), he comes to recognize

They asked them,
　"Is this your son, who you say was born blind?
How does he now see?"
His parents answered and said,
　"We know that this is our son and that he was
　　born blind.
We do not know how he sees now,
　nor do we know who opened his eyes.
Ask him, he is of age;
　he can speak for himself."
His parents said this because they were afraid
　of the Jews, for the Jews had already agreed
　that if anyone acknowledged him as the Christ,
　he would be expelled from the synagogue.
For this reason his parents said,
　"He is of age; question him."

So a second time they called the man who had been
　blind
　and said to him, "Give God the praise!
We know that this man is a sinner."
He replied,
　"If he is a sinner, I do not know.
One thing I do know is that I was blind and now I
　see."
So they said to him,
　"What did he do to you?
　How did he open your eyes?"
He answered them,
　"I told you already and you did not listen.
Why do you want to hear it again?
Do you want to become his disciples, too?"
They ridiculed him and said,
　"You are that man's disciple;
　we are disciples of Moses!
We know that God spoke to Moses,
　but we do not know where this one is from."

who Jesus is for him. He calls him his "Lord" and he worships him. "Lord" is a title used for Yahweh in the Old Testament. The name Yahweh was so holy that whenever one found it in Scripture, one would pronounce its substitute word, *Adonai,* which meant the "Lord." By saying that Jesus is "Lord," the author is saying that Jesus is the same thing that Yahweh is: God. Also, one only worships God; so when the man worships Jesus, he is proclaiming him as God.

It was when the man suffered and was expelled from the synagogue that he came to recognize who Jesus was for him. The same is often true for us, that it is in times of suffering that we finally recognize who God really is for us.

Throughout this story there has been a recurring theme of sin. The disciples thought that the man was blind as a punishment for sin. The Pharisees accused both Jesus and the man born blind of being sinners.

It is the Pharisees who are the true sinners for they had the ability to recognize who Jesus was, and they refused to see. They chose to remain in their blindness, so they were condemned to remain in the hell they had made for themselves.

Throughout this Gospel we hear that Jesus has come for judgment. He does not want to condemn us. We condemn ourselves if we choose against the Lord and against the truth. Likewise, by choosing Jesus to be the center of our lives, we have already received our reward, for Jesus will be a part of our lives.

The man answered and said to them,
"This is what is so amazing,
that you do not know where he is from, yet he opened my eyes.
We know that God does not listen to sinners,
but if one is devout and does his will, he listens to him.
It is unheard of that anyone ever opened the eyes of a person born blind.
If this man were not from God,
he would not be able to do anything."
They answered and said to him,
"You were born totally in sin,
and are you trying to teach us?"
Then they threw him out.

When Jesus heard that they had thrown him out,
he found him and said, "Do you believe in the Son of Man?"
He answered and said,
"Who is he, sir, that I may believe in him?"
Jesus said to him,
"You have seen him,
and the one speaking with you is he."
He said,
"I do believe, Lord," and he worshiped him.
Then Jesus said,
"I came into this world for judgment,
so that those who do not see might see,
and those who do see might become blind."

Some of the Pharisees who were with him heard this
and said to him, "Surely we are not also blind, are we?"
Jesus said to them,
"If you were blind, you would have no sin;
but now you are saying, 'We see,' so your sin remains."

The Gospel of the Lord.

GOSPEL: B Shorter Form: John 9:1, 6-9, 13-17, 34-38

The man who was blind went off and washed himself
and came back able to see.

This story is presented at two levels of meaning. The first (superficial) level is the story of a miracle that Jesus performed during his public ministry. The second (deeper symbolic level) is a story of a community that came to faith in Jesus Christ as the light of the world.

Jesus uses saliva to heal the man born blind and sends him to wash at the pool of Siloam.

The man born blind is not given a name because he also plays a symbolic role in this Gospel. He represents the members of the community of the beloved disciple that had come to believe in Jesus.

Before they converted they had been blind, for they had not known the light of the world. Jesus came into their lives, and he healed them. He brought them to faith and they were able to see the truth. But like the man born blind, they suffered for their beliefs, for they were expelled from the synagogue. The man born blind humiliates the great doctors of the law with his simplicity and truth. He has no formal learning, but his wisdom is much more profound than theirs. It is the wisdom of the cross being more powerful than the wisdom of the world.

Throughout the account the man born blind has used various titles for Jesus such as "the man called Jesus," "a prophet," "a man . . . from God,"

A reading from the holy Gospel according to John

As Jesus passed by he saw a man blind from birth. He spat on the ground and made clay with the saliva,
and smeared the clay on his eyes, and said to him,
"Go wash in the Pool of Siloam"—which means Sent—.
So he went and washed, and came back able to see.

His neighbors and those who had seen him earlier as a beggar said,
"Isn't this the one who used to sit and beg?"
Some said, "It is,"
but others said, "No, he just looks like him."
He said, "I am."

They brought the one who was once blind to the Pharisees.
Now Jesus had made clay and opened his eyes on a sabbath.
So then the Pharisees also asked him how he was able to see.
He said to them,
"He put clay on my eyes, and I washed, and now I can see."
So some of the Pharisees said,
"This man is not from God,
because he does not keep the sabbath."
But others said,
"How can a sinful man do such signs?"
And there was a division among them.
So they said to the blind man again,
"What do you have to say about him,
since he opened your eyes?"
He said, "He is a prophet."

etc. After he is expelled from the presence of the Pharisees (which represents the synagogue), he comes to recognize who Jesus is for him. He calls him his "Lord" and he worships him. "Lord" is a title used for Yahweh in the Old Testament. The name Yahweh was so holy that whenever one found it in Scripture, one would pronounce its substitute word, *Adonai,* which meant the "Lord." By saying that Jesus is "Lord," the author is saying that Jesus is the same thing that Yahweh is: God. Furthermore, one only worships God; so when the man worships Jesus, he is proclaiming him as God.

They answered and said to him,
    "You were born totally in sin,
    and are you trying to teach us?"
Then they threw him out.

When Jesus heard that they had thrown him out,
    he found him and said, "Do you believe in the Son
        of Man?"
He answered and said,
    "Who is he, sir, that I may believe in him?"
Jesus said to him,
    "You have seen him,
    and the one speaking with you is he."
He said,
    "I do believe, Lord," and he worshiped him.

The Gospel of the Lord.

PASTORAL REFLECTIONS

Suffering is one of the most difficult issues in faith and philosophy. Throughout most of the Old Testament, it was believed that suffering was a punishment for one's sins. If one were suffering, then it meant that one must have sinned.

Job calls this conclusion into question. While Job agrees with his friends that he is a sinner (for all people have sinned), he argues that he did not do enough to deserve the terrible suffering he was experiencing.

In this passage, Jesus states that the blindness of the man born blind was not a punishment. It was so that God's plan could be fulfilled.

In spite of the fact that we cannot figure out why there is suffering, whether it is caused by God or allowed by God, we are still called to respond to it with trust.

March 17, 2013

FIFTH SUNDAY OF LENT

The readings given for Year A, no. 34, pp. 134-141, may be used in place of these readings for Year C.

Lect. No. 36

FIRST READING: Isaiah 43:16-21

See, I am doing something new and I give my people drink.

The First Reading comes from the part of the Book of the Prophet Isaiah written by an anonymous prophet during the Babylonian exile (589-539 B.C.).

The prophet recalls the great things that God did during the Exodus from Egypt. He then tells his listeners to forget those events, for they would seem as nothing compared with the great things that the LORD was about to do to liberate his people from their exile in Babylon.

He, himself, would do these things, for he loved his chosen people.

This reading reminds us that God is still doing great things in our own days, especially during Lent, to liberate us from all those things that hold us in bondage (e.g., sin, selfishness, etc.).

A reading from the Book of the Prophet Isaiah

Thus says the LORD,
who opens a way in the sea
and a path in the mighty waters,
who leads out chariots and horsemen,
a powerful army,
till they lie prostrate together, never to rise,
snuffed out and quenched like a wick.
Remember not the events of the past,
the things of long ago consider not;
see, I am doing something new!
Now it springs forth, do you not perceive it?
In the desert I make a way,
in the wasteland, rivers.
Wild beasts honor me,
jackals and ostriches,
for I put water in the desert
and rivers in the wasteland
for my chosen people to drink,
the people whom I formed for myself,
that they might announce my praise.

The word of the Lord.

PASTORAL REFLECTIONS

This reading provides us with the question of what God is doing in our lives to call us to conversion. Has God sent certain people into our lives to challenge us? Is our dissatisfaction with our lives a sign that we need to change things? Does God sometimes let us feel the consequences of our actions so that we will recognize that they are problematic?

Lect. No. 36

RESPONSORIAL PSALM: Ps 126:1-2, 2-3, 4-5, 6 (℟.: 3)

This psalm is both a thanksgiving for the great things that the LORD did to bring his chosen people back from their exile in Babylon and an appeal to continue to help them.

The people expected that, once they returned from exile, everything would be fine. Yet, when they arrived in Israel, it was anything but fine.

The city of Jerusalem and the temple had been destroyed.

The fields were barren and overgrown. Drought afflicted them year after year.

The people could not defend themselves from the depredations of the desert nomads (for they had not yet rebuilt the city walls).

The people therefore prayed that the LORD would intervene once again and bless their efforts with an abundant harvest. On the one hand, this psalm can almost seem like the attitude that says, "What have you done for me lately?"

But it could also be understood to be a profession of trust that God would always continue to intervene to help his beloved people.

℟. **The Lord has done great things for us; we are filled with joy.**

When the LORD brought back the captives of Zion,
  we were like men dreaming.
Then our mouth was filled with laughter,
  and our tongue with rejoicing.

℟. **The Lord has done great things for us; we are filled with joy.**

Then they said among the nations,
  "The LORD has done great things for them."
The LORD has done great things for us;
  we are glad indeed.

℟. **The Lord has done great things for us; we are filled with joy.**

Restore our fortunes, O LORD,
  like the torrents in the southern desert.
Those that sow in tears
  shall reap rejoicing.

℟. **The Lord has done great things for us; we are filled with joy.**

Although they go forth weeping,
  carrying the seed to be sown,
they shall come back rejoicing,
  carrying their sheaves.

℟. **The Lord has done great things for us; we are filled with joy.**

PASTORAL REFLECTIONS

Am I as ready to pray and trust in God when things don't work out as much as I would be when they work out to my satisfaction?

Lect.
No. 36

SECOND READING: Philippians 3:8-14

Because of Christ, I consider everything as a loss, being conformed to his death.

This letter was written toward the end of Saint Paul's life. Paul now realizes what is truly important, and what is not all that significant.

The only thing that has truly sustained him throughout his long and difficult years of ministry is his holding on to the love of the Lord.

Before his conversion, Paul was proud of his religious ancestry and Pharasaic practice. He would have been considered to be a very religious person. But Paul now realized that what is important is not what we do for the Lord, but what the Lord does for us.

God loves us unconditionally. All that he asks us to do is to trust in his love (this is what Paul means by having faith in Christ).

There is another sign of Paul's deepening conversion in the latter part of the letter. He often held himself up as a model of what it means to follow Jesus. In this passage he admits that he is not yet fully converted, but he does know what his goal is.

He therefore pursues that goal with all his strength. We cannot yet be perfect, but we can certainly strive to be faithful.

A reading from the Letter of Saint Paul
to the Philippians

Brothers and sisters:
I consider everything as a loss
    because of the supreme good of knowing Christ
        Jesus my Lord.
For his sake I have accepted the loss of all things
    and I consider them so much rubbish,
    that I may gain Christ and be found in him,
    not having any righteousness of my own based on
        the law
    but that which comes through faith in Christ,
    the righteousness from God,
    depending on faith to know him and the power of
        his resurrection
    and the sharing of his sufferings by being con-
        formed to his death,
    if somehow I may attain the resurrection from the
        dead.

It is not that I have already taken hold of it
    or have already attained perfect maturity,
    but I continue my pursuit in hope that I may pos-
        sess it,
    since I have indeed been taken possession of by
        Christ Jesus.
Brothers and sisters, I for my part
    do not consider myself to have taken possession.
Just one thing: forgetting what lies behind
    but straining forward to what lies ahead,
    I continue my pursuit toward the goal,
    the prize of God's upward calling, in Christ Jesus.

The word of the Lord.

VERSE BEFORE THE GOSPEL: Joel 2:12-13

The LORD calls us to conversion so that we might experience the mercy and love that he has for us.

Even now, says the Lord,
return to me with your whole heart;
for I am gracious and merciful.

GOSPEL: John 8:1-11

Let the one among you who is without sin be the first to throw a stone at her.

This story is not found in many ancient manuscripts of the Gospel of John.

This does not mean that it is not authentic, however, for it accurately portrays the mercy of Jesus toward sinners.

It seems as if the Pharisees and the scribes wanted to trap Jesus. They knew that he associated with sinners.

They wanted to see whether he would reject the law of Moses in the way that he treated the woman.

Jesus told them that the one who is without sin should cast the first stone.

This reminds one of the saying in which he tells his listeners to take the plank out of their own eye before they try to take the sliver out of the eye of another.

It is not clear what Jesus was writing on the ground. There is no indication of his writing the sins of his listeners (as is sometimes suggested). It might be a sign of his disinterest in what they were doing.

A reading from the holy Gospel according to John

Jesus went to the Mount of Olives.
　But early in the morning he arrived again in the temple area,
　and all the people started coming to him,
　and he sat down and taught them.
Then the scribes and the Pharisees brought a woman
　who had been caught in adultery
　and made her stand in the middle.
They said to him,
　"Teacher, this woman was caught
　in the very act of committing adultery.
Now in the law, Moses commanded us to stone such women.
So what do you say?"
They said this to test him,
　so that they could have some charge to bring against him.
Jesus bent down and began to write on the ground with his finger.
But when they continued asking him,
　he straightened up and said to them,
　"Let the one among you who is without sin
　be the first to throw a stone at her."
Again he bent down and wrote on the ground.
And in response, they went away one by one,
　beginning with the elders.

He finally pronounces the woman forgiven, telling her not to sin again. While the Pharisees had treated her as a test case and an object of derision, Jesus treated her with mercy and respect. Yet, he ordered her to treat herself with respect by not sinning again.

So he was left alone with the woman before him.
Then Jesus straightened up and said to her,
    "Woman, where are they?
Has no one condemned you?"
She replied, "No one, sir."
Then Jesus said, "Neither do I condemn you.
Go, and from now on do not sin any more."

The Gospel of the Lord.

The following readings given for Year A may be used in place of the previous readings.

Lect. No. 34

FIRST READING: Ezekiel 37:12-14

I will put my spirit in you that you may live.

This prophecy is taken from a passage that speaks about the resurrection of the dead. Ezekiel describes a plain filled with the dry bones of those who had died. He preaches to the bones and they are filled with God's breath and Spirit and brought back to life.

It appears as if Ezekiel was originally speaking about the resurrection of the nation, but his words could also be applied to the resurrection of the individual.

It is the Spirit of God who gives us true life, life that will never end.

A reading from the Book of the Prophet Ezekiel

Thus says the Lord GOD:
    O my people, I will open your graves
    and have you rise from them,
    and bring you back to the land of Israel.
Then you shall know that I am the LORD,
    when I open your graves and have you rise from
        them,
    O my people!
I will put my spirit in you that you may live,
    and I will settle you upon your land;
    thus you shall know that I am the LORD.
I have promised, and I will do it, says the LORD.

The word of the Lord.

Lect. No. 34

RESPONSORIAL PSALM: Ps 130:1-2, 3-4, 5-6, 7-8 (R̤.: 7)

Psalm 130 is an individual lament. It begins with an almost desperate appeal to the LORD for an intervention. Then there is a series of verses that speak of the things tormenting the psalmist. Finally, there is a *todah.* This is a thanksgiving for

R̤. **With the Lord there is mercy and fullness of redemption.**

Out of the depths I cry to you, O LORD;
    Lord, hear my voice!
Let your ears be attentive
    to my voice in supplication.

the deliverance that the psalmist is sure Yahweh would give.

There is a sense of urgency in this psalm, as if things had gone so far that there were only moments of life left. The image of the sentinel waiting for the dawn is especially appropriate. The dark is filled with danger and confusion, but with the dawn comes a restoration of hope. Throughout the Old Testament, the dawn was considered to be the hour of the day when God would intervene.

The psalmist readily admits that the disasters that had befallen him were probably due to his own sins. He even states that if the LORD were to mark his iniquities, he would have no chance of standing. He and Israel deserve everything that they were getting. Nevertheless. he is filled with hope that the LORD will deliver them from their dangers, for the LORD is truly merciful and gracious.

℞. **With the Lord there is mercy and fullness of redemption.**

If you, O LORD, mark iniquities,
  Lord, who can stand?
But with you is forgiveness,
  that you may be revered.

℞. **With the Lord there is mercy and fullness of redemption.**

I trust in the LORD;
  my soul trusts in his word.
More than sentinels wait for the dawn,
  let Israel wait for the LORD.

℞. **With the Lord there is mercy and fullness of redemption.**

For with the LORD is kindness
  and with him is plenteous redemption;
and he will redeem Israel
  from all their iniquities.

℞. **With the Lord there is mercy and fullness of redemption.**

Lect. No. 34

SECOND READING: Romans 8:8-11

The Spirit of the One who raised Jesus from the dead dwells in you.

In this passage from Saint Paul's Letter to the Romans we hear of the contrast between living according to the flesh and living according to the Spirit. By using the word flesh, Paul is not speaking about our bodies or the created world. He is speaking about that part of us which drags us down, which will lead us to sin. Saint Augustine calls this concupiscence.

The Spirit, on the other hand, is the gift of the Holy Spirit that we have received in our Bap-

A reading from the Letter of Saint Paul
to the Romans

Brothers and sisters:
  Those who are in the flesh cannot please God.
But you are not in the flesh;
  on the contrary, you are in the spirit,
  if only the Spirit of God dwells in you.
Whoever does not have the Spirit of Christ does not
    belong to him.
But if Christ is in you,
  although the body is dead because of sin,
  the spirit is alive because of righteousness.

tism. We can live in the Spirit by choosing to live in God's love.

The life that we receive from the Spirit is so profound that even our mortal bodies will be filled with eternal life in the resurrection from the dead.

If the Spirit of the One who raised Jesus from the
 dead dwells in you,
 the One who raised Christ from the dead
 will give life to your mortal bodies also,
 through his Spirit dwelling in you.

The word of the Lord.

VERSE BEFORE THE GOSPEL: John 11:25a, 26

Jesus is the source and the goal of our lives. Life has no meaning if it is not lived in him and for him.

I am the resurrection and the life, says the Lord;
 whoever believes in me, even if he dies, will never
 die.

GOSPEL: **A** Longer Form: John 11:1-45

I am the resurrection and the life.

Lazarus was a common name at the time of Jesus (a form of the name Eliezer, which means that "God aids") and this Lazarus should not be confused with the poor Lazarus of the parable in Luke's Gospel.

Jesus stayed at the house of Lazarus and his sisters Martha and Mary during the Jewish feast days. There were so many pilgrims in Jerusalem at those times that pilgrims often stayed in the suburbs of Jerusalem. Bethany, the town where Lazarus, Mary, and Martha lived, was only a short distance outside of Jerusalem.

Although Mary does not anoint the feet of Jesus until chapter 12, the action is placed in the past tense. In this Gospel the readers and the author already know all of the events recorded in this Gospel.

It is odd that Jesus remained where he was after he had heard

A reading from the holy Gospel according to John

Now a man was ill, Lazarus from Bethany,
 the village of Mary and her sister Martha.
Mary was the one who had anointed the Lord with
 perfumed oil
 and dried his feet with her hair;
 it was her brother Lazarus who was ill.
So the sisters sent word to Jesus saying,
 "Master, the one you love is ill."
When Jesus heard this he said,
 "This illness is not to end in death,
 but is for the glory of God,
 that the Son of God may be glorified through it."
Now Jesus loved Martha and her sister and
 Lazarus.
So when he heard that he was ill,
 he remained for two days in the place where he
 was.
Then after this he said to his disciples,
 "Let us go back to Judea."
The disciples said to him,

of the illness of his friend. It is almost as if he wanted him to die. This is only explainable if one remembers that this will be a powerful sign of God's love. In fact, it will be a sign of God's glory.

Jesus' hour of glory in this Gospel is the cross and not the resurrection as one might expect. In the greatest irony of the Gospel, Jesus is put to death by the Jewish leaders specifically because he brought Lazarus back to life. The Jewish leaders wanted people to be under their control; they did not want them to be free or truly alive.

We hear that Lazarus was dead for four days already. The Jewish people believed that the soul remained in the body for the first three days after the person died. To say that someone was dead for four days was to say that they were irretrievably dead.

Martha and Mary both respond to Jesus' arrival with statements that show both a mix of annoyance at the fact that he had taken so long to get there and an expression of hope that he would still do something to help them.

Jesus responds that he is "the resurrection and the life." What is interesting about this phrase is that he is not saying that he will grant the resurrection; he is saying that he is the resurrection.

When one comes to know Jesus, one is already in some way risen. One's life is so full and profound that even if one

"Rabbi, the Jews were just trying to stone you,
    and you want to go back there?"
Jesus answered,
    "Are there not twelve hours in a day?
If one walks during the day, he does not stumble,
    because he sees the light of this world.
But if one walks at night, he stumbles,
    because the light is not in him."
He said this, and then told them,
    "Our friend Lazarus is asleep,
    but I am going to awaken him."
So the disciples said to him,
    "Master, if he is asleep, he will be saved."
But Jesus was talking about his death,
    while they thought that he meant ordinary sleep.
So then Jesus said to them clearly,
    "Lazarus has died.
And I am glad for you that I was not there,
    that you may believe.
Let us go to him."
So Thomas, called Didymus, said to his fellow disciples,
    "Let us also go to die with him."

When Jesus arrived, he found that Lazarus
    had already been in the tomb for four days.
Now Bethany was near Jerusalem, only about two
    miles away.
And many of the Jews had come to Martha and
    Mary
    to comfort them about their brother.
When Martha heard that Jesus was coming,
    she went to meet him;
    but Mary sat at home.
Martha said to Jesus,
    "Lord, if you had been here,
    my brother would not have died.
But even now I know that whatever you ask of God,

were to die, one would continue to live in him. Eschatology speaks about the things that will occur at the end of time. This Gospel has a "realized eschatology," for we do not have to wait until the end of time to receive our eternal reward. We have already begun to experience it when we came to know Jesus (although we will experience it even more fully after we die).

Jesus is described as being perturbed and deeply troubled. At first we might think that he is disturbed because the Jewish people and Mary are crying (which he might have interpreted as a sign of the lack of faith in him), but he himself cries within a few minutes. It is more probable that he is angry at death itself, which has robbed him of his beloved friend. He also cries to express his grief at the death of Lazarus.

Christian hope at the death of a beloved does not mean that we have to deny our emotions. It means that we express them, but also try to maintain hope.

There are several expressions of irony throughout the story. Thomas says that the disciples should follow Jesus to die with him (when they do the exact opposite). The people watching Jesus cry ask whether he could not have saved Lazarus from death (which he, of course, could have). This is typical of the Gospel of John where we, the readers, often know more than the characters involved in the story.

God will give you."
Jesus said to her,
  "Your brother will rise."
Martha said to him,
  "I know he will rise,
  in the resurrection on the last day."
Jesus told her,
  "I am the resurrection and the life;
  whoever believes in me, even if he dies, will live,
  and everyone who lives and believes in me will
    never die.
Do you believe this?"
She said to him, "Yes, Lord.
I have come to believe that you are the Christ, the
    Son of God,
  the one who is coming into the world."

When she had said this,
  she went and called her sister Mary secretly, saying,
  "The teacher is here and is asking for you."
As soon as she heard this,
  she rose quickly and went to him.
For Jesus had not yet come into the village,
  but was still where Martha had met him.
So when the Jews who were with her in the house
    comforting her
  saw Mary get up quickly and go out,
  they followed her,
  presuming that she was going to the tomb to weep
    there.
When Mary came to where Jesus was and saw him,
  she fell at his feet and said to him,
  "Lord, if you had been here,
  my brother would not have died."
When Jesus saw her weeping and the Jews who had
    come with her weeping,
  he became perturbed and deeply troubled, and
    said,

Jesus proclaims a rather unusual prayer. It is almost as if it is being said for the sake of the audience, so that they will know that Jesus is doing this deed of power through the intervention of the Father. Jesus does absolutely nothing in this Gospel on his own. Everything he does is in obedience to the will of the Father.

Lazarus is not actually resurrected, he is reanimated. The difference is that Lazarus is brought back to life, but he would still have to die again some day.

Jesus, on the other hand, when he is resurrected, will never die again. He has a glorified body that is not subject to the limitations of our mortal bodies. Such is not the case with Lazarus who someday would die again.

Jesus instructs those with him to untie Lazarus. This has often been used as an image of how Jesus unbinds us from everything that imprisons us, whether it be sin or fear or the habits that leave us lonely and confused. We cannot do this by ourselves; we must seek the assistance of Jesus to set us free.

The end of the account speaks of those who had come to see Mary and Martha. The purpose is to show that this was a very public miracle and it explains why this particular miracle would be brought to the attention of the leaders of the Jews in the next verses of this story.

"Where have you laid him?"
They said to him, "Sir, come and see."
And Jesus wept.
So the Jews said, "See how he loved him."
But some of them said,
    "Could not the one who opened the eyes of the
        blind man
    have done something so that this man would not
        have died?"

So Jesus, perturbed again, came to the tomb.
It was a cave, and a stone lay across it.
Jesus said, "Take away the stone."
Martha, the dead man's sister, said to him,
    "Lord, by now there will be a stench;
    he has been dead for four days."
Jesus said to her,
    "Did I not tell you that if you believe
    you will see the glory of God?"
So they took away the stone.
And Jesus raised his eyes and said,
    "Father, I thank you for hearing me.
I know that you always hear me;
    but because of the crowd here I have said this,
    that they may believe that you sent me."
And when he had said this,
    he cried out in a loud voice,
    "Lazarus, come out!"
The dead man came out,
    tied hand and foot with burial bands,
    and his face was wrapped in a cloth.
So Jesus said to them,
    "Untie him and let him go."

Now many of the Jews who had come to Mary
    and seen what he had done began to believe in him.

The Gospel of the Lord.

GOSPEL: B Shorter Form: John 11:3-7, 17, 20-27, 33b-45

I am the resurrection and the life.

It is odd that Jesus remained where he was after he had heard of the illness of his friend Lazarus. It is almost as if he wanted him to die. This is only explainable if one remembers that this will be a powerful sign of God's love. In fact, it will be a sign of God's glory.

We hear that Lazarus was dead for four days already. The Jewish people believed that the soul remained in the body for the first three days after the person died. To say that someone was dead for four days was to say that that person was irretrievably dead.

Martha and Mary both respond to Jesus' arrival with statements that show both a mix of annoyance at the fact that he had taken so long to get there and an expression of hope that he would still do something to help them.

Jesus responds that he is "the resurrection and the life." What is interesting about this phrase is that he is not saying that he will grant the resurrection; he is saying that he is the resurrection.

When one comes to know Jesus, one is already in some way risen. One's life is so full and profound that even if one were to die, one would continue to live in him. Eschatology speaks about the things that will occur at the end of time. This Gospel has a "realized eschatology," for we do not have to wait until the end of time to re-

A reading from the holy Gospel according to John

The sisters of Lazarus sent word to Jesus, saying, "Master, the one you love is ill."
When Jesus heard this he said,
　"This illness is not to end in death,
　but is for the glory of God,
　that the Son of God may be glorified through it."
Now Jesus loved Martha and her sister and Lazarus.
So when he heard that he was ill,
　he remained for two days in the place where he
　　was.
Then after this he said to his disciples,
　"Let us go back to Judea."

When Jesus arrived, he found that Lazarus
　had already been in the tomb for four days.
When Martha heard that Jesus was coming,
　she went to meet him;
　but Mary sat at home.
Martha said to Jesus,
　"Lord, if you had been here,
　my brother would not have died.
But even now I know that whatever you ask of God,
　God will give you."
Jesus said to her,
　"Your brother will rise."
Martha said,
　"I know he will rise,
　in the resurrection on the last day."
Jesus told her,
　"I am the resurrection and the life;
　whoever believes in me, even if he dies, will live,
　and everyone who lives and believes in me will
　　never die.
Do you believe this?"
She said to him, "Yes, Lord.

ceive our eternal reward. We have already begun to experience it when we came to know Jesus (although we will experience it even more fully after we die).

Jesus is described as being perturbed and deeply troubled. At first we might think that he is disturbed because the Jewish people and Mary are crying (which he might have interpreted as a sign of the lack of faith in him), but he himself cries within a few minutes. It is more probable that he is angry at death itself, which has robbed him of his beloved friend. He also cries to express his grief at the death of Lazarus.

Christian hope at the death of a beloved does not mean that we have to deny our emotions. It means that we express them, but also try to maintain hope.

Lazarus is not actually resurrected, he is reanimated. The difference is that Lazarus is brought back to life, but he would still have to die again some day.

Jesus, on the other hand, when he is resurrected, will never die again. He has a glorified body that is not subject to the limitations of our mortal bodies. Such is not the case with Lazarus who someday would die again.

The end of the account speaks of those who had come to see Mary and Martha. The purpose is to show that this was a very public miracle and it explains why this particular miracle would be brought to the attention of the leaders of the Jews in the next verses of this story.

I have come to believe that you are the Christ, the Son of God,
    the one who is coming into the world."

He became perturbed and deeply troubled, and said, "Where have you laid him?"
They said to him, "Sir, come and see."
And Jesus wept.
So the Jews said, "See how he loved him."
But some of them said,
    "Could not the one who opened the eyes of the blind man
    have done something so that this man would not have died?"

So Jesus, perturbed again, came to the tomb.
It was a cave, and a stone lay across it.
Jesus said, "Take away the stone."
Martha, the dead man's sister, said to him,
    "Lord, by now there will be a stench;
    he has been dead for four days."
Jesus said to her,
    "Did I not tell you that if you believe
    you will see the glory of God?"
So they took away the stone.
And Jesus raised his eyes and said,
    "Father, I thank you for hearing me.
I know that you always hear me;
    but because of the crowd here I have said this,
    that they may believe that you sent me."
And when he had said this,
    he cried out in a loud voice,
    "Lazarus, come out!"
The dead man came out,
    tied hand and foot with burial bands,
    and his face was wrapped in a cloth.
So Jesus said to them,
    "Untie him and let him go."

Now many of the Jews who had come to Mary
    and seen what he had done began to believe in him.

The Gospel of the Lord.

March 24, 2013

PALM SUNDAY OF THE PASSION OF THE LORD

At the Procession with Palms

Lect. No. 37

GOSPEL: Luke 19:28-40

Blessed is he who comes in the name of the Lord.

Jesus begins his triumphant entrance into Jerusalem from the Mount of Olives. This mount had always been associated with the Day of the LORD in Hebrew Scriptures.

Jesus rides into Jerusalem on a colt. The Prophet Zechariah spoke of how the Messiah would enter Jerusalem on a donkey, the colt of a donkey.

He was emphasizing the humility of the Jewish Messiah in contrast to the haughty arrogance of the kings of the Gentiles who rode about on great war horses.

The crowd pays Jesus what could only be described as royal honors. At the time of the feast of Passover, large crowds of pilgrims entered Jerusalem. The city, which had a population of around 60,000 people, suddenly became a city of around 300,000 people.

This made the leaders of the Jews and the Romans very nervous, for this was the perfect time for rebellion. This might be why the Pharisees tell Jesus to silence the crowd.

A reading from the holy Gospel according to Luke

Jesus proceeded on his journey up to Jerusalem.
  As he drew near to Bethphage and Bethany
  at the place called the Mount of Olives,
  he sent two of his disciples.
He said, "Go into the village opposite you,
  and as you enter it you will find a colt tethered
  on which no one has ever sat.
Untie it and bring it here.
And if anyone should ask you,
  'Why are you untying it?'
  you will answer,
  'The Master has need of it.'"
So those who had been sent went off
  and found everything just as he had told them.
And as they were untying the colt, its owners said to
      them,
  "Why are you untying this colt?"
They answered,
  "The Master has need of it."
So they brought it to Jesus,
  threw their cloaks over the colt,
  and helped Jesus to mount.
As he rode along,
  the people were spreading their cloaks on the
      road;
  and now as he was approaching the slope of the
      Mount of Olives,

Jesus responds that even if he were to silence the crowd, the stones themselves would cry out (possibly a reference to the stones of the temple being thrown down during its destruction in 70 A.D.).

Notice that the crowd does not use the Aramaic word "hosanna." Luke was writing for a Gentile audience that would not have understood that phrase (which means "Lord, save us."). He thus avoids using that term just as he avoids using Aramaic terms throughout the Gospel.

the whole multitude of his disciples
began to praise God aloud with joy
for all the mighty deeds they had seen.
They proclaimed:
    "Blessed is the king who comes
        in the name of the Lord.
    Peace in heaven
        and glory in the highest."
Some of the Pharisees in the crowd said to him,
    "Teacher, rebuke your disciples."
He said in reply,
    "I tell you, if they keep silent,
    the stones will cry out!"

The Gospel of the Lord.

At the Mass

Lect. No. 38

FIRST READING: Isaiah 50:4-7

My face I did not shield from buffets and spitting, knowing that I shall not be put to shame.

This reading is taken from the third song of the Suffering Servant. It speaks of the Servant as one who brings consolation to the weary, even while he is the subject of terrible suffering. We will hear in the fourth song that he suffers to bring us forgiveness of our sins.

It was never exactly clear who this figure was supposed to be during Old Testament times. Jesus, through many of the things he said, showed that he considered himself to be the fulfillment of this prophecy.

In spite of the agony of the Servant, he remained obedient to the will of God. He professed his faith in the Lord for he knew that God would deliver him from all of his distress. This deliverance was fulfilled when the Father raised Jesus from the dead on Easter Sunday.

A reading from the Book of the Prophet Isaiah

The Lord GOD has given me
    a well-trained tongue,
that I might know how to speak to the weary
    a word that will rouse them.
Morning after morning
    he opens my ear that I may hear;
and I have not rebelled,
    have not turned back.
I gave my back to those who beat me,
    my cheeks to those who plucked my beard;
my face I did not shield
    from buffets and spitting.

The Lord GOD is my help,
    therefore I am not disgraced;
I have set my face like flint,
    knowing that I shall not be put to shame.

The word of the Lord.

RESPONSORIAL PSALM: Ps 22:8-9, 17-18, 19-20, 23-24 (R⁄.: 2a)

This is the psalm that Jesus quoted while he was hanging on the cross. It is a lamentation, and typical of all lamentations, it begins with an appeal, continues with a list of the sufferings that the psalmist is undergoing, and closes with a short hymn of praise in which the psalmist declares his faith in his eventual deliverance.

When Jesus quoted the first verse of this psalm, he was identifying with the psalmist's feeling of abandonment, but he was at the same time professing his faith in the fact that God would deliver him. He agreed with the sentiments found in the psalm, "I will proclaim your name to my brethren; in the midst of the assembly I will praise you."

The similarities between this psalm and what actually occurred to Jesus on the cross are astounding. It speaks of hands and feet being pierced, garments being divided, lots being cast, etc.

We can easily forget that Psalm 22 was written several hundreds of years before the time of Jesus. It fills us with a sense of awe, for here we see the Holy Spirit inspiring the psalmist in a powerful way.

R⁄. **My God, my God, why have you abandoned me?**

All who see me scoff at me;
    they mock me with parted lips, they wag their
        heads:
"He relied on the LORD; let him deliver him,
    let him rescue him, if he loves him."

R⁄. **My God, my God, why have you abandoned me?**

Indeed, many dogs surround me,
    a pack of evildoers closes in upon me;
they have pierced my hands and my feet;
    I can count all my bones.

R⁄. **My God, my God, why have you abandoned me?**

They divide my garments among them,
    and for my vesture they cast lots.
But you, O LORD, be not far from me;
    O my help, hasten to aid me.

R⁄. **My God, my God, why have you abandoned me?**

I will proclaim your name to my brethren;
    in the midst of the assembly I will praise you:
"You who fear the LORD, praise him;
    all you descendants of Jacob, give glory to him;
    revere him, all you descendants of Israel!"

R⁄. **My God, my God, why have you abandoned me?**

SECOND READING: Philippians 2:6-11

Christ humbled himself. Because of this, God greatly exalted him.

Saint Paul presents this hymn as an example of the profound humility of Jesus. It is also a teaching about Jesus who surrendered his prerogatives as God to serve us as a human.

The phrase, "form of God," means that Jesus is God, even as God the Father is God. Yet Jesus emptied himself of his godliness. The word "empty," *kenosis* in Greek, signifies a spirituality of surrender and humility. It does not mean that he stopped being God.

The ultimate degree of humility was to be obedient to the Father, even to the point of dying on the cross. We might think that this expression of humility was humiliating for Jesus, but he did not see it that way. He saw it as the fullest expression of his love and trust in the Father. God the Father responded to this trust by proclaiming Jesus as Lord, a title that affirms his divinity.

A reading from the Letter of Saint Paul to the Philippians

Christ Jesus, though he was in the form of God,
did not regard equality with God
    something to be grasped.
Rather, he emptied himself,
    taking the form of a slave,
    coming in human likeness;
    and found human in appearance,
    he humbled himself,
    becoming obedient to the point of death,
    even death on a cross.
Because of this, God greatly exalted him
    and bestowed on him the name
    which is above every name,
    that at the name of Jesus
    every knee should bend,
    of those in heaven and on earth and under the
        earth,
    and every tongue confess that
    Jesus Christ is Lord,
    to the glory of God the Father.

The word of the Lord.

VERSE BEFORE THE GOSPEL: Philippians 2:8-9

The Verse Before the Gospel repeats the heart of the Philippians' hymn. It celebrates the obedience of Jesus upon the cross and his exaltation in his resurrection.

Christ became obedient to the point of death,
even death on a cross.
Because of this, God greatly exalted him
and bestowed on him the name which is above
    every name.

GOSPEL: **A** Longer Form: Luke 22:14—23:56

The Passion of our Lord Jesus Christ.

In the beginning of the account, Jesus speaks of not celebrating the Passover again until the kingdom of God comes.

Every time that we celebrate the Eucharist, we are celebrating the dawning of the glory of that kingdom. In Luke's Gospel, the promises associated with our heavenly reward have already begun to be fulfilled in our present days.

The words over the cup are similar to those found in the writings of Saint Paul. They speak of "the cup of the new covenant in my blood." This softens the words that Jesus probably used at the Last Supper.

Mark and Matthew probably have a more original version in which Jesus says that the cup is his blood in the new covenant. In their version, the cup really has blood, while in Luke and Paul, it contains the new covenant that was initiated by blood.

Luke's version of the Last Supper is similar to John's in the fact that Jesus offers important teachings on discipleship in the course of the meal. Luke had emphasized the importance of meals all throughout his Gospel, so it is not a surprise that he should have Jesus give this important teaching in the context of a meal.

The Passion of our Lord Jesus Christ
according to Luke

When the hour came,
   Jesus took his place at table with the apostles.
He said to them,
   "I have eagerly desired to eat this Passover with
      you before I suffer,
   for, I tell you, I shall not eat it again
   until there is fulfillment in the kingdom of God."
Then he took a cup, gave thanks, and said,
   "Take this and share it among yourselves;
   for I tell you that from this time on
   I shall not drink of the fruit of the vine
   until the kingdom of God comes."
Then he took the bread, said the blessing,
   broke it, and gave it to them, saying,
   "This is my body, which will be given for you;
   do this in memory of me."
And likewise the cup after they had eaten, saying,
   "This cup is the new covenant in my blood,
   which will be shed for you.

"And yet behold, the hand of the one who is to be-
      tray me
   is with me on the table;
   for the Son of Man indeed goes as it has been de-
      termined;
   but woe to that man by whom he is betrayed."
And they began to debate among themselves
   who among them would do such a deed.

Then an argument broke out among them
   about which of them should be regarded as the
      greatest.
He said to them,
   "The kings of the Gentiles lord it over them

Jesus describes the role of the disciples as being one of service and not one of prestige. Jesus' entire ministry, and even his giving of the Eucharist at the Last Supper, was an extended lesson on service.

In the course of his instruction, Jesus addresses Simon Peter. He tells him that Satan would strive to sift the community like wheat.

A similar idea is found in Matthew when Peter is given the keys of the kingdom. He is told that the gates of the underworld would not prevail against the Church.

Peter is told to strengthen his brethren when he would turn back. The meaning of that phrase follows immediately, for Jesus predicts Peter's denial.

It is interesting that Jesus would mention Peter's weakness in the same context as his call to be the chief of the apostles.

Peter is called to this responsibility not because he is perfect. He is reminded that he will fall like all of us. Yet God will strengthen him.

When the disciples first went out to preach the Good News, they were told to rely upon the providence of God. Now, because great and terrible events were upon them, they are told to be prepared.

The sayings about the money bag, sack, and sword are most probably intended to be understood symbolically (as can be

and those in authority over them are addressed as
    'Benefactors';
but among you it shall not be so.
Rather, let the greatest among you be as the youngest,
    and the leader as the servant.
For who is greater:
    the one seated at table or the one who serves?
Is it not the one seated at table?
I am among you as the one who serves.
It is you who have stood by me in my trials;
    and I confer a kingdom on you,
    just as my Father has conferred one on me,
    that you may eat and drink at my table in my
        kingdom;
    and you will sit on thrones
    judging the twelve tribes of Israel.

"Simon, Simon, behold Satan has demanded
    to sift all of you like wheat,
    but I have prayed that your own faith may not fail;
    and once you have turned back,
    you must strengthen your brothers."
He said to him,
    "Lord, I am prepared to go to prison and to die
        with you."
But he replied,
    "I tell you, Peter, before the cock crows this day,
    you will deny three times that you know me."

He said to them,
    "When I sent you forth without a money bag or a
        sack or sandals,
    were you in need of anything?"
"No, nothing," they replied.
He said to them,
    "But now one who has a money bag should take it,
    and likewise a sack,
    and one who does not have a sword
    should sell his cloak and buy one.
For I tell you that this Scripture must be fulfilled in me,

seen when one of the disciples speaks of having two swords. Jesus, almost in exasperation at the incomprehension of the disciples, cries out, "Enough!").

There are two details in the agony of the garden that are particular to Luke. The first is that an angel comes from heaven to console Jesus. This is consistent with the general theme of consolation that is found throughout the Gospel.

The second detail is that the agony of Jesus was so profound that he sweats blood. The Greek in this particular phrase is very ambiguous.

It might mean that he was sweating so profoundly that it was as if he were bleeding.

Or, it could mean that he was actually sweating blood (which occasionally occurs when people are subjected to incredible turmoil).

Judas identifies Jesus with a kiss. The garden would have been dark, and the guards of the temple probably did not know Jesus very well, so this would have been a good way to let them know whom they were to arrest (even if the affection shown in the sign is ironically tragic).

When one of the disciples cuts off the ear of the servant of the high priest, Jesus touches the ear and heals it (this is typical of the Gospel of Luke, for Jesus has come into the world to heal those who are broken).

namely, *He was counted among the wicked;*
and indeed what is written about me is coming to fulfillment."
Then they said,
"Lord, look, there are two swords here."
But he replied, "It is enough!"

Then going out, he went, as was his custom, to the Mount of Olives,
and the disciples followed him.
When he arrived at the place he said to them,
"Pray that you may not undergo the test."
After withdrawing about a stone's throw from them and kneeling,
he prayed, saying, "Father, if you are willing,
take this cup away from me;
still, not my will but yours be done."
And to strengthen him an angel from heaven appeared to him.
He was in such agony and he prayed so fervently
that his sweat became like drops of blood
falling on the ground.
When he rose from prayer and returned to his disciples,
he found them sleeping from grief.
He said to them, "Why are you sleeping?
Get up and pray that you may not undergo the test."

While he was still speaking, a crowd approached
and in front was one of the Twelve, a man named Judas.
He went up to Jesus to kiss him.
Jesus said to him,
"Judas, are you betraying the Son of Man with a kiss?"
His disciples realized what was about to happen, and they asked,
"Lord, shall we strike with a sword?"
And one of them struck the high priest's servant
and cut off his right ear.

Jesus berates the troops for seizing him at night when they could have arrested him in the temple during the day. The soldiers did this so that their action would not start a riot. Yet it was also symbolic of their service to the forces of darkness and not of the light.

Jesus was taken to the house of the high priest. The plot against Jesus seems to have been initiated by the high priest and his friends (who would have belonged to the Sadducees).

They were rich and had the most to lose if Jesus caused some sort of rebellion, so they decided to get rid of him in order to protect their possessions and privilege.

Peter followed Jesus when he was arrested. He was accused three times (by three different people) of being a follower of Jesus, and all three times he denied it (fulfilling Jesus' prophecy at the Last Supper).

The people would have known he was a Galilean by his accent, for there was a significant difference in the accent of people from Galilee and those from Jerusalem.

This is the only Gospel where Jesus turns and looks at Peter after he had denied him.

This does not seem to be a look of accusation as much as one of compassion. Peter's response is great grief.

But Jesus said in reply,
    "Stop, no more of this!"
Then he touched the servant's ear and healed him.
And Jesus said to the chief priests and temple guards
    and elders who had come for him,
    "Have you come out as against a robber, with swords and clubs?
Day after day I was with you in the temple area,
    and you did not seize me;
    but this is your hour, the time for the power of darkness."

After arresting him they led him away
    and took him into the house of the high priest;
    Peter was following at a distance.
They lit a fire in the middle of the courtyard and sat around it,
    and Peter sat down with them.
When a maid saw him seated in the light,
    she looked intently at him and said,
    "This man too was with him."
But he denied it saying,
    "Woman, I do not know him."
A short while later someone else saw him and said,
    "You too are one of them";
    but Peter answered, "My friend, I am not."
About an hour later, still another insisted,
    "Assuredly, this man too was with him,
    for he also is a Galilean."
But Peter said,
    "My friend, I do not know what you are talking about."
Just as he was saying this, the cock crowed,
    and the Lord turned and looked at Peter;
    and Peter remembered the word of the Lord,
    how he had said to him,
    "Before the cock crows today, you will deny me three times."

In Luke the trial of Jesus takes place before the whole Sanhedrin (and not just before the high priest and his associates as in Mark). Jesus is mocked and beaten as they interrogate him.

He is asked whether he is the Christ (Messiah). He does not respond directly (for, as he himself states, they would not listen to him).

He calls himself the Son of Man who is seated at the right hand of God, recalling the prophecy in Daniel 7 that the Son of Man would receive power and dominion.

Finally, he accepts their accusation that he considers himself to be the Son of God.

It is significant that the Jewish leaders have to lie when they bring Jesus before Pilate, for he is not concerned with their religious arguments.

They accuse Jesus of opposing taxes paid to Caesar and of making himself a king, both of which would be capital offenses under Roman law.

However, Pilate is in no way convinced by their accusations.

Pilate represents Roman authority, and Luke is trying to show that any good Roman authority should be able to discern the innocence of Jesus (and of his followers).

We only find the episode of Pilate sending Jesus to Herod (this is the son of Herod the Great) in the Gospel of Luke. There are some typical Lucan elements in this story.

He went out and began to weep bitterly.

The men who held Jesus in custody were ridiculing and beating him.

They blindfolded him and questioned him, saying, "Prophesy! Who is it that struck you?"

And they reviled him in saying many other things against him.

When day came the council of elders of the people met,
both chief priests and scribes,
and they brought him before their Sanhedrin.

They said, "If you are the Christ, tell us,"
but he replied to them, "If I tell you, you will not believe,
and if I question, you will not respond.

But from this time on the Son of Man will be seated at the right hand of the power of God."

They all asked, "Are you then the Son of God?"

He replied to them, "You say that I am."

Then they said, "What further need have we for testimony?

We have heard it from his own mouth."

Then the whole assembly of them arose and brought him before Pilate.

They brought charges against him, saying,
"We found this man misleading our people;
he opposes the payment of taxes to Caesar
and maintains that he is the Christ, a king."

Pilate asked him, "Are you the king of the Jews?"

He said to him in reply, "You say so."

Pilate then addressed the chief priests and the crowds, "I find this man not guilty."

But they were adamant and said,
"He is inciting the people with his teaching throughout all Judea,
from Galilee where he began even to here."

On hearing this Pilate asked if the man was a Galilean;

Luke consistently mentions the names and titles of kings and governors. Furthermore, he speaks of how Jesus brought peace and well-being to all those whom he encountered.

This even extends to those who are putting him on trial, for up to this time Herod and Pilate were enemies, but after Jesus comes into their lives, they become the best of friends.

Jesus was dressed in resplendent garb while he was being questioned and mocked in front of Herod.

This was intended to be an action that humiliated him, but it was actually a type of prophecy that revealed who Jesus really was.

Again, Pilate proclaims Jesus to be innocent, but the crowd would not allow his release.

They demand the release of Barabbas, a man who had been involved in rebellion and even murder.

Ironically, these are the very things that they falsely accused Jesus of having done.

The crowds insist that Jesus be crucified.

Pilate spoke to them three times, trying to find a way to release Jesus, but they would not listen.

He even had Jesus flogged in the hope that it would satisfy the blood lust of the crowd, but it did not do any good.

and upon learning that he was under Herod's jurisdiction,
he sent him to Herod who was in Jerusalem at that time.
Herod was very glad to see Jesus;
he had been wanting to see him for a long time,
for he had heard about him
and had been hoping to see him perform some sign.
He questioned him at length,
but he gave him no answer.
The chief priests and scribes, meanwhile,
stood by accusing him harshly.
Herod and his soldiers treated him contemptuously and mocked him,
and after clothing him in resplendent garb,
he sent him back to Pilate.
Herod and Pilate became friends that very day,
even though they had been enemies formerly.
Pilate then summoned the chief priests, the rulers, and the people
and said to them, "You brought this man to me
and accused him of inciting the people to revolt.
I have conducted my investigation in your presence
and have not found this man guilty
of the charges you have brought against him,
nor did Herod, for he sent him back to us.
So no capital crime has been committed by him.
Therefore I shall have him flogged and then release him."

But all together they shouted out,
"Away with this man!
Release Barabbas to us."
—Now Barabbas had been imprisoned for a rebellion
that had taken place in the city and for murder.—
Again Pilate addressed them, still wishing to release Jesus,
but they continued their shouting,
"Crucify him! Crucify him!"

Finally he gave in to their demands and handed Jesus over to them to be crucified.

Note that even at this moment, Luke makes it clear that this was not a legal process as much as a politically expedient action.

Jesus would have carried the crossbar of the cross (the upright portion would be fixed in the ground). He was assisted by a certain Simon, a Cyrenian.

In his Gospel (15:21), Mark identifies this Simon as "the father of Alexander and Rufus," possibly because the sons became followers of Christ. In his Letter to the Romans (16:13), Paul sends greetings to a certain "Rufus, chosen in the Lord."

There is an ancient legend that Simon was carrying eggs to market, and when he touched them with his bloodied hands, they changed to red (supposedly the origin of the custom of coloring Easter eggs).

Along the way, Jesus meets a group of women who are mourning and lamenting for him.

Typical of this Gospel, Jesus is not concerned with his own difficulties. He stops and "consoles" the women.

His words of consolation, however, turn out to be a prophecy of the disaster that would befall Jerusalem when it was conquered by the Romans during a rebellion in 70 A.D.

Jesus is crucified at the place of the Skull (so named because the mound resembled a skull).

Pilate addressed them a third time,
"What evil has this man done?
I found him guilty of no capital crime.
Therefore I shall have him flogged and then release him."
With loud shouts, however,
they persisted in calling for his crucifixion,
and their voices prevailed.
The verdict of Pilate was that their demand should be granted.
So he released the man who had been imprisoned
for rebellion and murder, for whom they asked,
and he handed Jesus over to them to deal with as they wished.

As they led him away
they took hold of a certain Simon, a Cyrenian,
who was coming in from the country;
and after laying the cross on him,
they made him carry it behind Jesus.
A large crowd of people followed Jesus,
including many women who mourned and lamented him.
Jesus turned to them and said,
"Daughters of Jerusalem, do not weep for me;
weep instead for yourselves and for your children,
for indeed, the days are coming when people will say,
'Blessed are the barren,
the wombs that never bore
and the breasts that never nursed.'
At that time people will say to the mountains,
'Fall upon us!'
and to the hills, 'Cover us!'
for if these things are done when the wood is green
what will happen when it is dry?"
Now two others, both criminals,
were led away with him to be executed.

Note that Luke does not give the Hebrew title Golgotha because his readers did not know that language.

Even as Jesus is being crucified, he is concerned with forgiveness of sin. He asks his Father to forgive the very people who were putting him to death.

The crowds mock Jesus with titles such as the "chosen one of God," "the Christ of God," and the "King of the Jews."

All of these are true titles, but this would only be seen when Jesus had risen from the dead.

They call upon Jesus to save himself as he had saved others. The irony is that he was saving others in the very act of not saving himself.

This is the only Gospel that speaks of the good thief. Again, this is typical of the Gospel of Luke, for Jesus has come to save those who were lost and most needed his love.

Jesus forgives the good thief and invites him into paradise.

(The good thief has been given the name Dismas, and the other is known as Gestas. According to popular legend, Dismas was rewarded because he had protected Mary and her child at the time of the flight into Egypt. The feast day of St. Dismas is March 25, and he is venerated as the patron of those in prison.)

The darkness that covered the whole land is a symbol of the apparent triumph of the sons of darkness.

When they came to the place called the Skull,
  they crucified him and the criminals there,
  one on his right, the other on his left.
Then Jesus said,
  "Father, forgive them, they know not what they do."
They divided his garments by casting lots.
The people stood by and watched;
  the rulers, meanwhile, sneered at him and said,
  "He saved others, let him save himself
  if he is the chosen one, the Christ of God."
Even the soldiers jeered at him.
As they approached to offer him wine they called out,
  "If you are King of the Jews, save yourself."
Above him there was an inscription that read,
  "This is the King of the Jews."

Now one of the criminals hanging there reviled Jesus, saying,
  "Are you not the Christ?
  Save yourself and us."
The other, however, rebuking him, said in reply,
  "Have you no fear of God,
  for you are subject to the same condemnation?
And indeed, we have been condemned justly,
  for the sentence we received corresponds to our crimes,
  but this man has done nothing criminal."
Then he said,
  "Jesus, remember me when you come into your kingdom."
He replied to him,
  "Amen, I say to you,
  today you will be with me in Paradise."

It was now about noon and darkness came over the whole land
  until three in the afternoon
  because of an eclipse of the sun.
Then the veil of the temple was torn down the middle.

The veil in the temple separated people from the holiness of God which was found in the Holy of Holies.

With the death of Jesus, we can encounter that holiness everywhere upon the earth. In a sense, his blood consecrated the world to his love.

Jesus is obedient to the Father until the last moment of his life, entrusting his Spirit into the Father's hands. His obedience healed our disobedience.

The centurion affirms what we already saw in the trial before Pilate, that Jesus was truly the innocent one.

Even those who had gathered for the spectacle recognized the travesty that had occurred and beat their breasts to beg for forgiveness.

Joseph of Arimathea is described as being a virtuous and righteous man. He was awaiting the Kingdom of God. Throughout the Gospel of Luke, it was those who were pure of heart who were always ready to follow Jesus.

Joseph buries Jesus in a new tomb (a great act of generosity and compassion).

The women who followed took note of where Jesus was buried, for they intended to return to anoint his body on the day after the Sabbath (Easter Sunday).

Jesus cried out in a loud voice,
  "Father, into your hands I commend my spirit";
  and when he had said this he breathed his last.

Here all kneel and pause for a short time.

The centurion who witnessed what had happened glorified God and said,
  "This man was innocent beyond doubt."
When all the people who had gathered for this spectacle saw what had happened,
  they returned home beating their breasts;
  but all his acquaintances stood at a distance,
  including the women who had followed him from Galilee
  and saw these events.

Now there was a virtuous and righteous man named Joseph who,
  though he was a member of the council,
  had not consented to their plan of action.
He came from the Jewish town of Arimathea
  and was awaiting the kingdom of God.
He went to Pilate and asked for the body of Jesus.
After he had taken the body down,
  he wrapped it in a linen cloth
  and laid him in a rock-hewn tomb
  in which no one had yet been buried.
It was the day of preparation,
  and the sabbath was about to begin.
The women who had come from Galilee with him followed behind,
  and when they had seen the tomb
  and the way in which his body was laid in it,
  they returned and prepared spices and perfumed oils.
Then they rested on the sabbath according to the commandment.

The Gospel of the Lord.

Lect. No. 38

GOSPEL: B Shorter Form: Luke 23:1-49

The Passion of our Lord Jesus Christ.

It is significant that the Jewish leaders have to lie when they bring Jesus before Pilate. He is not concerned with their religious arguments.

They accuse Jesus of opposing taxes paid to Caesar and of making himself a king, both of which would be capital offenses under Roman law.

However, Pilate is in no way convinced by their accusations.

Pilate represents Roman authority, and Luke is trying to show that any good Roman authority should be able to discern the innocence of Jesus (and of his followers).

We only find the episode of Pilate sending Jesus to Herod (this is the son of Herod the Great) in the Gospel of Luke. There are some typical Lucan elements in this story.

Luke consistently mentions the names and titles of kings and governors. Furthermore, he speaks of how Jesus brought peace and well-being to all those whom he encountered.

This even extends to those who are putting him on trial, for up to this time Herod and Pilate were enemies, but after Jesus comes into their lives, they become the best of friends.

Jesus was dressed in resplendent garb while he was being questioned and mocked in front of Herod.

The Passion of our Lord Jesus Christ according to Luke

The elders of the people, chief priests and scribes, arose and brought Jesus before Pilate.
They brought charges against him, saying,
  "We found this man misleading our people;
  he opposes the payment of taxes to Caesar
  and maintains that he is the Christ, a king."
Pilate asked him, "Are you the king of the Jews?"
He said to him in reply, "You say so."
Pilate then addressed the chief priests and the crowds,
  "I find this man not guilty."
But they were adamant and said,
  "He is inciting the people with his teaching
    throughout all Judea,
  from Galilee where he began even to here."

On hearing this Pilate asked if the man was a
    Galilean;
  and upon learning that he was under Herod's ju-
    risdiction,
  he sent him to Herod who was in Jerusalem at
    that time.
Herod was very glad to see Jesus;
  he had been wanting to see him for a long time,
  for he had heard about him
  and had been hoping to see him perform some sign.
He questioned him at length,
  but he gave him no answer.
The chief priests and scribes, meanwhile,
  stood by accusing him harshly.
Herod and his soldiers treated him contemptuously
    and mocked him,
  and after clothing him in resplendent garb,
  he sent him back to Pilate.

This was intended to be an action that humiliated him, but it was actually a type of prophecy that revealed who Jesus really was.

Again, Pilate proclaims Jesus to be innocent, but the crowd will not allow his release.

They demand the release of Barabbas, a man who had been involved in rebellion and even murder.

Ironically, these are the very things that they falsely accused Jesus of having done.

The crowds insist that Jesus be crucified.

Pilate spoke to them three times, trying to find a way to release Jesus, but they would not listen.

He even had Jesus flogged in the hope that it would satisfy the blood lust of the crowd, but it did not do any good.

Finally he gave in to their demands and handed Jesus over to them to be crucified.

Note that even at this moment, Luke makes it clear that this was not a legal process as much as a politically expedient action.

Jesus would have carried the crossbar of the cross (the upright portion would be fixed in the ground). He was assisted by a certain Simon, a Cyrenian.

In his Gospel (15:21), Mark identifies this Simon as "the father of Alexander and Rufus," possibly because the sons became followers of Christ. In his Letter to the Romans (16:13),

Herod and Pilate became friends that very day,
    even though they had been enemies formerly.
Pilate then summoned the chief priests, the rulers,
        and the people
    and said to them, "You brought this man to me
    and accused him of inciting the people to revolt.
I have conducted my investigation in your presence
    and have not found this man guilty
    of the charges you have brought against him,
    nor did Herod, for he sent him back to us.
So no capital crime has been committed by him.
Therefore I shall have him flogged and then release
        him."

But all together they shouted out,
    "Away with this man!
    Release Barabbas to us."
—Now Barabbas had been imprisoned for a rebellion
    that had taken place in the city and for murder.—
Again Pilate addressed them, still wishing to release
        Jesus,
    but they continued their shouting,
    "Crucify him! Crucify him!"
Pilate addressed them a third time,
    "What evil has this man done?
    I found him guilty of no capital crime.
Therefore I shall have him flogged and then release
        him."
With loud shouts, however,
    they persisted in calling for his crucifixion,
    and their voices prevailed.
The verdict of Pilate was that their demand should
        be granted.
So he released the man who had been imprisoned
    for rebellion and murder, for whom they asked,
    and he handed Jesus over to them to deal with as
        they wished.

Paul sends greetings to a certain "Rufus, chosen in the Lord."

There is an ancient legend that Simon was carrying eggs to market, and when he touched them with his bloodied hands, they changed to red (supposedly the origin of the custom of coloring Easter eggs).

Along the way Jesus meets a group of women who are mourning and lamenting for him.

Typical of this Gospel, Jesus is not concerned with his own difficulties. He stops and "consoles" the women.

His words of consolation, however, turn out to be a prophecy of the disaster that would befall Jerusalem when it was conquered by the Romans during a rebellion in 70 A.D.

Jesus is crucified at the place of the Skull (so named because the mound resembled a skull).

Note that Luke does not give the Hebrew title Golgotha because his readers did not know that language.

Even as Jesus is being crucified, he is concerned with forgiveness of sin. He asks his Father to forgive the very people who were putting him to death.

The crowds mock Jesus with titles such as the "chosen one of God," "the Christ of God," and the "King of the Jews."

All of these are true titles, but this would only be seen when Jesus had risen from the dead.

They call upon Jesus to save himself as he had saved others. The irony is that he was saving others in the very act of not saving himself.

As they led him away
they took hold of a certain Simon, a Cyrenian,
who was coming in from the country;
and after laying the cross on him,
they made him carry it behind Jesus.
A large crowd of people followed Jesus,
including many women who mourned and lamented him.
Jesus turned to them and said,
"Daughters of Jerusalem, do not weep for me;
weep instead for yourselves and for your children,
for indeed, the days are coming when people will say,
'Blessed are the barren,
the wombs that never bore
and the breasts that never nursed.'
At that time people will say to the mountains,
'Fall upon us!'
and to the hills, 'Cover us!'
for if these things are done when the wood is green
what will happen when it is dry?"
Now two others, both criminals,
were led away with him to be executed.

When they came to the place called the Skull,
they crucified him and the criminals there,
one on his right, the other on his left.
Then Jesus said,
"Father, forgive them, they know not what they do."
They divided his garments by casting lots.
The people stood by and watched;
the rulers, meanwhile, sneered at him and said,
"He saved others, let him save himself
if he is the chosen one, the Christ of God."
Even the soldiers jeered at him.
As they approached to offer him wine they called out,
"If you are King of the Jews, save yourself."

This is the only Gospel that speaks of the good thief. Again, this is typical of the Gospel of Luke, for Jesus has come to save those who were lost and most needed his love.

Jesus forgives the good thief and invites him into paradise.

(The good thief has been given the name Dismas, and the other is known as Gestas. According to popular legend, Dismas was rewarded because he had protected Mary and her child at the time of the flight into Egypt. The feast day of St. Dismas is March 25, and he is venerated as the patron of those in prison.)

The darkness that covered the whole land is a symbol of the apparent triumph of the sons of darkness.

The veil in the temple separated people from the holiness of God which was found in the Holy of Holies.

With the death of Jesus, we can encounter that holiness everywhere upon the earth. In a sense, his blood consecrated the world to his love.

Jesus is obedient to the Father until the last moment of his life, entrusting his Spirit into the Father's hands.

The centurion affirms what we already saw in the trial before Pilate, that Jesus was truly the innocent one.

Even those who had gathered for the spectacle recognized the travesty that had occurred and beat their breasts to beg for forgiveness.

Above him there was an inscription that read,
   "This is the King of the Jews."

Now one of the criminals hanging there reviled Jesus, saying,
   "Are you not the Christ?
   Save yourself and us."
The other, however, rebuking him, said in reply,
   "Have you no fear of God,
   for you are subject to the same condemnation?
And indeed, we have been condemned justly,
   for the sentence we received corresponds to our crimes,
   but this man has done nothing criminal."
Then he said,
   "Jesus, remember me when you come into your kingdom."
He replied to him,
   "Amen, I say to you,
   today you will be with me in Paradise."

It was now about noon and darkness came over the whole land
   until three in the afternoon
   because of an eclipse of the sun.
Then the veil of the temple was torn down the middle.
Jesus cried out in a loud voice,
   "Father, into your hands I commend my spirit";
   and when he had said this he breathed his last.

   Here all kneel and pause for a short time.
The centurion who witnessed what had happened glorified God and said,
   "This man was innocent beyond doubt."
When all the people who had gathered for this spectacle saw what had happened,
   they returned home beating their breasts;
   but all his acquaintances stood at a distance,
   including the women who had followed him from Galilee
   and saw these events.

The Gospel of the Lord.

THURSDAY OF HOLY WEEK
[HOLY THURSDAY]
THE CHRISM MASS

Lect. No. 260

FIRST READING:

Isaiah 61:1-3ab, 6a, 8b-9

The LORD has anointed me; and sent me to bring glad tidings
to the lowly, and to give them oil of gladness.

This passage is taken from the third part of the Book of the Prophet Isaiah, a part written by an anonymous author named Trito-Isaiah. He wrote after the exile when the people of Israel had returned from exile in Babylon.

The author speaks of an anointed one who would bring a year of favor to his people. This was to be the fulfillment of the Jubilee Year.

Every seven years the people did not plant crops because they wanted to show their faith in the providence of the LORD. Every seventh seven there was a Jubilee Year. Debts were forgiven, slaves were freed, properties were returned to their original owners, etc. It was to be a year of profound dedication to justice. The people were to share the providence they had received from the LORD.

The Messiah spoken of in this passage was to establish that year of favor. He was to bring consolation to a people burdened by their difficulties. He would be able to do this because he was filled with the anointing of the Spirit of the LORD.

A reading from the Book of the Prophet Isaiah

The Spirit of the Lord GOD is upon me,
   because the LORD has anointed me;
He has sent me to bring glad tidings to the lowly,
   to heal the brokenhearted,
To proclaim liberty to the captives
   and release to the prisoners,
To announce a year of favor from the LORD
   and a day of vindication by our God,
   to comfort all who mourn;
To place on those who mourn in Zion
   a diadem instead of ashes,
To give them oil of gladness in place of mourning,
   a glorious mantle instead of a listless spirit.

You yourselves shall be named priests of the LORD,
   ministers of our God shall you be called.

I will give them their recompense faithfully,
   a lasting covenant I will make with them.
Their descendants shall be renowned among the nations,
   and their offspring among the peoples;
All who see them shall acknowledge them
   as a race the LORD has blessed.

The word of the Lord.

RESPONSORIAL PSALM: Ps 89:21-22, 25 and 27 (℟.: 2a)

At the Chrism Mass we bless the sacred oils that will be used throughout the year. This oil will be used for consecrating, anointing for healing, setting apart for God.

These verses speak of the effects of an anointing. David, the anointed of the LORD, was filled with the strength, faithfulness, and kindness of the LORD.

Anointing establishes a special relationship between us and God, who is our father, our rock, and our savior.

℟. **For ever I will sing the goodness of the Lord.**

"I have found David, my servant;
　with my holy oil I have anointed him.
That my hand may be always with him;
　and that my arm may make him strong."

℟. **For ever I will sing the goodness of the Lord.**

"My faithfulness and my kindness shall be with him,
　and through my name shall his horn be exalted.
He shall say of me, 'You are my father,
　my God, the Rock, my savior!' "

℟. **For ever I will sing the goodness of the Lord.**

SECOND READING: Revelation 1:5-8

He has made us into a kingdom, priests for his God and Father.

The Book of Revelation is filled with liturgical hymns. This one lauds Jesus who is the faithful witness. The word for witness in Greek is "Martureo," the source of the English word "martyr."

Jesus has made us co-heirs with him in the glory of God, for he has adopted us as his brothers and sisters.

We have also become priests through our baptismal anointing. We share in the priesthood of Jesus, and like him, we are both the priest offering up the sacrifice and the sacrifice itself. We lift up an offering of our life and love, our successes and failures, our hopes and even our fears.

God is our Alpha and Omega for he is the source of everything we have and are, and also the goal toward which we journey.

A reading from the Book of Revelation

[Grace to you and peace] from Jesus Christ,
who is the faithful witness,
　the firstborn of the dead and ruler of the kings of
　the earth.
To him who loves us and has freed us from our sins by
　his Blood,
　who has made us into a Kingdom, priests for his
　God and Father,
to him be glory and power forever and ever. Amen.

　Behold, he is coming amid the clouds,
　　and every eye will see him,
　　even those who pierced him.
　All the peoples of the earth will lament him.
　　Yes. Amen.

"I am the Alpha and the Omega," says the Lord God,
　"the one who is and who was
　　and who is to come, the Almighty."

The word of the Lord.

VERSE BEFORE THE GOSPEL: Isaiah 61:1 (cited in Luke 4:18)

This Verse Before the Gospel speaks of the sacred anointing through which the Holy Spirit calls us to serve the poorest of the poor.

The Spirit of the LORD is upon me;
for he sent me to bring glad tidings to the poor.

GOSPEL: Luke 4:16-21

The Spirit of the Lord is upon me, because of which he has anointed me.

Early in his public ministry, Jesus goes into the synagogue in his home town and identifies himself as the anointed one of God.

This anointing proclaims Jesus as the fulfillment of the Jubilee Year of the Lord. No longer would we have to wait fifty years in order to experience God's justice. When we encounter Jesus and the love he offers, we are changed.

We can no longer treat ourselves and others with the lack of respect that we sometimes showed them. We must love them with the same love with which Jesus loved us. This is especially true of those who most need our care and love, those who are broken and hurting.

As we receive the anointing of the Spirit of the Lord (using the oils blessed at this Mass), we share in Jesus' ministry to proclaim that year of favor to the world.

A reading from the holy Gospel according to Luke

Jesus came to Nazareth, where he had grown up,
and went according to his custom
into the synagogue on the sabbath day.
He stood up to read and was handed a scroll of the
    prophet Isaiah.
He unrolled the scroll and found the passage
    where it was written:
    The Spirit of the Lord is upon me,
    because he has anointed me
        to bring glad tidings to the poor.
    He has sent me to proclaim liberty to captives
        and recovery of sight to the blind,
        to let the oppressed go free,
    and to proclaim a year acceptable to the Lord.
Rolling up the scroll, he handed it back to the
    attendant and sat down,
and the eyes of all in the synagogue looked intently at him.
He said to them,
    "Today this Scripture passage is fulfilled in your
    hearing."

The Gospel of the Lord.

March 28, 2013

THURSDAY OF THE LORD'S SUPPER [HOLY THURSDAY]

AT THE EVENING MASS

Lect. No. 39 FIRST READING: Exodus 12:1-8, 11-14

The law regarding the Passover meal.

The First Reading for Holy Thursday is a recounting of the events of the first Passover of the Exodus. Scholars now believe that the Jewish people celebrated Passover before the Exodus as an agricultural feast (possibly associated with the birth of the Spring lambs). The Hebrew word for Passover, "Pesach," means leaping, probably referring to the leaping of the newborn lambs.

After the Exodus, it was linked with the events that occurred in Egypt. The passing over was now understood both as the angel of death passing over Egypt and the Israelites passing over the Red Sea.

The month of the Passover was to be considered the first month of the year. This changed when the Israelites were in exile in Babylon. During the exile they adopted the Babylonian calendar, which marked the fall as the beginning of the year. Jewish people celebrate Rosh Hashana (New Year's Day) in September.

The meal was to be eaten as if they were preparing for a journey (with loins girt and sandals on their feet). They were, in fact, to relive the events every time they commemorated them.

A reading from the Book of Exodus

The LORD said to Moses and Aaron in the land of Egypt,

"This month shall stand at the head of your calendar;

you shall reckon it the first month of the year.

Tell the whole community of Israel:

On the tenth of this month every one of your families

must procure for itself a lamb, one apiece for each household.

If a family is too small for a whole lamb,

it shall join the nearest household in procuring one

and shall share in the lamb

in proportion to the number of persons who partake of it.

The lamb must be a year-old male and without blemish.

You may take it from either the sheep or the goats.

You shall keep it until the fourteenth day of this month,

and then, with the whole assembly of Israel present,

it shall be slaughtered during the evening twilight.

They shall take some of its blood

and apply it to the two doorposts and the lintel

of every house in which they partake of the lamb.

That same night they shall eat its roasted flesh

with unleavened bread and bitter herbs.

The Israelites ate a lamb and used the blood of the lamb to mark their doorposts and lintel. This mark protected them from the depredations of the angel of death who destroyed the first-born of all of the Egyptians.

It is appropriate that the doorposts should be marked with blood. In Old Testament symbolism blood signified life. The blood saved the lives of the Israelites.

The closing verses of this reading remind the Israelites that this was to be a celebration among the Jews forever, and also that it was intended to be a pilgrimage festival. During the days of Jesus, it was believed that as many as a quarter of a million pilgrims arrived in Jerusalem to celebrate the feast.

"This is how you are to eat it:
with your loins girt, sandals on your feet and your staff in hand,
you shall eat like those who are in flight.
It is the Passover of the LORD.
For on this same night I will go through Egypt,
striking down every firstborn of the land, both man and beast,
and executing judgment on all the gods of Egypt—I, the LORD!
But the blood will mark the houses where you are.
Seeing the blood, I will pass over you;
thus, when I strike the land of Egypt,
no destructive blow will come upon you.

"This day shall be a memorial feast for you,
which all your generations shall celebrate
with pilgrimage to the LORD, as a perpetual institution."
The word of the Lord.

Lect.
No. 39

RESPONSORIAL PSALM: Ps 116:12-13, 15-16bc, 17-18

(℟.: cf. 1 Corinthians 10:16)

Psalm 116 is a thanksgiving psalm prayed in gratitude to the LORD for a deliverance. The psalmist had been at the point of death, but the LORD had loosed his bonds (the bonds of death).

The LORD had granted him the cup of salvation (allowed him to taste the effects of the LORD's salvation). Now, he would offer him a sacrifice of thanksgiving.

Both of these sacrificial images are appropriate for our celebration this evening. The Eucharist is both a powerful gift of salvation (celebrating the salvation offered upon the cross)

℟. **Our blessing-cup is a communion with the Blood of Christ.**

How shall I make a return to the LORD
for all the good he has done for me?
The cup of salvation I will take up,
and I will call upon the name of the LORD.

℟. **Our blessing-cup is a communion with the Blood of Christ.**

Precious in the eyes of the LORD
is the death of his faithful ones.
I am your servant, the son of your handmaid;
you have loosed my bonds.

℟. **Our blessing-cup is a communion with the Blood of Christ.**

and an act of thanksgiving. The word "Eucharist" in Greek actually means "to give thanks." Our only possible response to the incredible generosity and benevolence of God is to live our commitments to him with integrity.

To you will I offer sacrifice of thanksgiving,
    and I will call upon the name of the LORD.
My vows to the LORD I will pay
    in the presence of all his people.

℟. **Our blessing-cup is a communion with the Blood of Christ.**

Lect.
No. 39

SECOND READING: 1 Corinthians 11:23-26

*For as often as you eat this bread and drink the cup,
you proclaim the death of the Lord.*

Paul wrote this account of the institution of the Eucharist to the Corinthian community because they seem to have forgotten the significance of this event. They were celebrating the Lord's Supper but not living in communion with their sisters and brothers. Some in the community had more than enough to eat when they gathered together, while others were all but starving.

Paul accused them of sinning against the communion they were celebrating when they participated in the Eucharist. He told them to examine their consciences before they received the Eucharist. In other words, they were to make absolutely sure they understood the significance of what they were doing.

A reading from the first Letter of Saint Paul to the Corinthians

Brothers and sisters:
    I received from the Lord what I also handed on
        to you,
    that the Lord Jesus, on the night he was handed
        over,
    took bread, and, after he had given thanks,
    broke it and said, "This is my body that is for you.
Do this in remembrance of me."
In the same way also the cup, after supper, saying,
    "This cup is the new covenant in my blood.
Do this, as often as you drink it, in remembrance of
    me."
For as often as you eat this bread and drink the cup,
    you proclaim the death of the Lord until he
        comes.
The word of the Lord.

Lect.
No. 39

VERSE BEFORE THE GOSPEL: John 13:34

This command to love one another is the core of the Sacrament we are celebrating.

I give you a new commandment, says the Lord:
love one another as I have loved you.

Lect.
No. 39

GOSPEL: John 13:1-15

Jesus loved them to the end.

The account of the Last Supper found in the Gospel of John does not include an account of the institution of the Eucharist. Rather, it speaks of how Jesus washed the feet of his disciples and invited them to do the same to each other. It is not that this Gospel ignores the Eucharist (quite the opposite, for it speaks of the Eucharist here, in chapter 6, and also in chapter 21).

Rather, John presents this scene to teach us the spiritual significance of the Sacrament of the Eucharist. It is the Sacrament through which Jesus serves us in a most profound manner, and in which he invites us to be of service to each other. This is what his ministry in this Gospel is all about. Jesus came into this world to save us.

This is why the beginning of the account mentions certain things. First of all, we hear that the feast of the Passover was near (in John the Last Supper is an anticipation of the Passover meal, for in this Gospel Passover does not begin until Good Friday night).

We also hear that Jesus is acting in the love of the Father. Thus, his action of humility is not one performed because he did not know he was God, but rather the opposite. As we hear in the First Letter of John, God is love. Therefore, we hear of the great love he had for his disciples, a love shown in humble service.

A reading from the holy Gospel according to John

Before the feast of Passover, Jesus knew that his hour had come
to pass from this world to the Father.
He loved his own in the world and he loved them to the end.
The devil had already induced Judas, son of Simon the Iscariot, to hand him over.
So, during supper,
fully aware that the Father had put everything into his power
and that he had come from God and was returning to God,
he rose from supper and took off his outer garments.
He took a towel and tied it around his waist.
Then he poured water into a basin
and began to wash the disciples' feet
and dry them with the towel around his waist.
He came to Simon Peter, who said to him,
"Master, are you going to wash my feet?"
Jesus answered and said to him,
"What I am doing, you do not understand now,
but you will understand later."
Peter said to him, "You will never wash my feet."
Jesus answered him,
"Unless I wash you, you will have no inheritance with me."
Simon Peter said to him,
"Master, then not only my feet, but my hands and head as well."
Jesus said to him,
"Whoever has bathed has no need except to have his feet washed,
for he is clean all over;
so you are clean, but not all."

Peter does not want his feet to be washed, possibly because he fears vulnerability (being served). Yet, both service and vulnerability are necessary dimensions of the love of Christ. We must both serve and allow ourselves to be served.

This chapter presents the Sacrament of the Eucharist as a verb, an act of service, and an invitation to serve others. This portrayal is balanced by chapter 6 where the Eucharist is presented as a noun (the real presence of Jesus) and chapter 21, where the meal on the shore after the miraculous catch of fish has Eucharistic overtones and presents the Eucharist as a call to mission.

For he knew who would betray him;
  for this reason, he said, "Not all of you are clean."

So when he had washed their feet
  and put his garments back on and reclined at table again,
  he said to them, "Do you realize what I have done for you?
You call me 'teacher' and 'master,' and rightly so, for indeed I am.
If I, therefore, the master and teacher, have washed your feet,
  you ought to wash one another's feet.
I have given you a model to follow,
  so that as I have done for you, you should also do."

The Gospel of the Lord.

PASTORAL REFLECTIONS

The commemoration of the Lord's Last Supper ends with a Eucharistic procession. The Blessed Sacrament is carried from its normal tabernacle to a repository where it will be reserved until the Liturgy of the Lord's Passion and Death on Friday afternoon.

It is appropriate to have a period of silent adoration after the liturgy on Thursday. We are told, though, that it should not continue beyond midnight.

We experience a certain emptiness after the liturgy on Thursday when the altar is stripped and the tabernacle is left open. This feeling is even more evident when we walk into church on Good Friday and we notice that there is no need to genuflect.

This is the feeling we have when someone suddenly dies. It is almost as if we cannot believe that what is happening is real. Something is very wrong, but we are not sure what it is or how it could be made better.

This is all appropriate, for we are remembering and in some way reliving the death of Jesus, our loved one, the one who gives meaning to our lives.

FRIDAY OF THE PASSION OF THE LORD [GOOD FRIDAY]

Lect. No. 40 **FIRST READING: Isaiah 52:13—53:12**

He himself was wounded for our sins.
(Fourth oracle of the Servant of the Lord.)

This is the fourth of the songs of the Suffering Servant of Yahweh. These songs were incorporated into the second part of the Book of the Prophet Isaiah. They are attributed to an anonymous author called Second Isaiah (he prophesied during the Babylonian exile).

These songs speak about a mysterious figure who would suffer to fulfill the mission of the LORD. This mission was to bring about an era of justice and peace. This wondrous future would be given not only to the people of the nation of Israel, but also to all the nations (the Hebrew phrase for the Gentiles).

The Servant would not bring about this new dispensation through violence. He would be meek and gentle and would not crush a bruised reed.

The author of the song speaks of the awe that this figure evokes (both at his willingness to suffer and at the extent of that suffering).

It was not known in ancient times who this Servant was. Some said that it was the personification of the nation of Israel, others that it was one of the prophets (possibly Jeremiah). It was Jesus who first applied these prophecies to himself.

A reading from the Book of the Prophet Isaiah

See, my servant shall prosper,
he shall be raised high and greatly exalted.
Even as many were amazed at him—
so marred was his look beyond human semblance
and his appearance beyond that of the sons of man—
so shall he startle many nations,
because of him kings shall stand speechless;
for those who have not been told shall see,
those who have not heard shall ponder it.

Who would believe what we have heard?
To whom has the arm of the LORD been revealed?
He grew up like a sapling before him,
like a shoot from the parched earth;
there was in him no stately bearing to make us look at him,
nor appearance that would attract us to him.
He was spurned and avoided by people,
a man of suffering, accustomed to infirmity,
one of those from whom people hide their faces,
spurned, and we held him in no esteem.

Yet it was our infirmities that he bore,
our sufferings that he endured,
while we thought of him as stricken,
as one smitten by God and afflicted.
But he was pierced for our offenses,
crushed for our sins;

The fourth song is the most poignant in its description. It contains two elements that were not part of the theology of the era in which it was written.

First of all, it speaks about the ultimate exaltation of the Servant after he had been killed in the service of the LORD. This means his resurrection from the dead, an idea that had not yet become fully developed in theology of Israel.

Even stranger for this era was the idea that this Servant would bear the sins of the people upon himself: expiation. The Jewish people did not believe that the suffering and death of any person could bring about good. Their Messiah was to conquer, not to be killed.

What is being described is what Saint Paul speaks of as being the wisdom of God or the wisdom of the cross. In that wisdom, one must die in order to live forever.

The description of the sufferings of this Servant are similar to those of Psalm 22 and are uncannily similar to what actually happened to Jesus. He was like a sheep led to the slaughter, cut off from the land of the living, buried among wrongdoers, crushed.

Yet, because he was obedient to the will of the Father, he won pardon for our offenses and would be exalted in glory and proclaimed as Lord of everything that exists in heaven, on the earth, and under the earth.

upon him was the chastisement that makes us whole,
   by his stripes we were healed.
We had all gone astray like sheep,
   each following his own way;
but the LORD laid upon him
   the guilt of us all.

Though he was harshly treated, he submitted
   and opened not his mouth;
like a lamb led to the slaughter
   or a sheep before the shearers,
   he was silent and opened not his mouth.
Oppressed and condemned, he was taken away,
   and who would have thought any more of his destiny?
When he was cut off from the land of the living,
   and smitten for the sin of his people,
a grave was assigned him among the wicked
   and a burial place with evildoers,
though he had done no wrong
   nor spoken any falsehood.
But the LORD was pleased
   to crush him in infirmity.

If he gives his life as an offering for sin,
   he shall see his descendants in a long life,
   and the will of the LORD shall be accomplished
      through him.

Because of his affliction
   he shall see the light in fullness of days;
through his suffering, my servant shall justify many,
   and their guilt he shall bear.
Therefore I will give him his portion among the great,
   and he shall divide the spoils with the mighty,
because he surrendered himself to death
   and was counted among the wicked;
and he shall take away the sins of many,
   and win pardon for their offenses.

The word of the Lord.

RESPONSORIAL PSALM: Ps 31:2, 6, 12-13, 15-16, 17, 25

(℞.: Luke 23:46)

Psalm 31 is a psalm of thanksgiving written by one who had been delivered from horrible life-threatening dangers. It expresses faith in the fact that God would surely deliver that person, for the LORD is truly a refuge.

It might seem odd to be reciting this psalm today, since it almost seems too positive in tone. Yet, there is a strong sense of hope in our commemoration for we are certain that the defeat on the cross will be followed by the triumph of the resurrection. This also reminds us that not all of our deliverances will be in this life. We must live in hope of a future fulfillment of God's promises in our resurrection from the dead.

Even on Good Friday Jesus expressed this same hope. He was citing Psalm 22 when he prayed, "My God, my God, why have you forsaken me?" These are the first words of this psalm of lamentation. All lamentations end with a profession of faith in God's ultimate deliverance. While Jesus was expressing feelings of abandonment, he was also professing his faith that the LORD, his Father, would deliver him.

℞. **Father, into your hands I commend my spirit.**

In you, O LORD, I take refuge;
    let me never be put to shame.
In your justice rescue me.
Into your hands I commend my spirit;
    you will redeem me, O LORD, O faithful God.

℞. **Father, into your hands I commend my spirit.**

For all my foes I am an object of reproach,
    a laughingstock to my neighbors, and a dread to
        my friends;
they who see me abroad flee from me.
I am forgotten like the unremembered dead;
    I am like a dish that is broken.

℞. **Father, into your hands I commend my spirit.**

But my trust is in you, O LORD;
    I say, "You are my God.
In your hands is my destiny; rescue me
    from the clutches of my enemies and my persecu-
        tors."

℞. **Father, into your hands I commend my spirit.**

Let your face shine upon your servant;
    save me in your kindness.
Take courage and be stouthearted,
    all you who hope in the LORD.

℞. **Father, into your hands I commend my spirit.**

SECOND READING: Hebrews 4:14-16; 5:7-9

*Jesus learned obedience and became the source of salvation
for all who obey him.*

One of the major themes developed in the Letter to the Hebrews is that Jesus is our High Priest. Unlike the high priests of the Old Testament, Jesus was not a sinner. Being totally sinless, he therefore did not have to perform sacrifices for his own sins. His sacrifice was performed totally for our benefit.

Yet, in spite of the fact that Jesus was perfect and without sin, he nevertheless was able to empathize with us (because he shared our human condition). He was like us in all things but sin.

The second part of the reading speaks of Jesus' obedience to the will of the Father. This should not be understood as a blind obedience that denigrated Jesus. Rather, by being obedient, he was most fully who he really is. He was perfect in his response to God's will. Likewise, when we sin we are rejecting who God made us to be, while when we live in obedience to God's will, we are actually most fully ourselves.

A reading from the Letter to the Hebrews

Brothers and sisters:
   Since we have a great high priest who has
      passed through the heavens,
Jesus, the Son of God,
let us hold fast to our confession.
For we do not have a high priest
   who is unable to sympathize with our weaknesses,
   but one who has similarly been tested in every
      way,
   yet without sin.
So let us confidently approach the throne of grace
   to receive mercy and to find grace for timely help.

In the days when Christ was in the flesh,
   he offered prayers and supplications with loud
      cries and tears
   to the one who was able to save him from death,
   and he was heard because of his reverence.
Son though he was, he learned obedience from what
      he suffered;
   and when he was made perfect,
   he became the source of eternal salvation for all
      who obey him.

The word of the Lord.

VERSE BEFORE THE GOSPEL: Philippians 2:8-9

This verse, taken from the Philippians' hymn, speaks of Jesus' profound obedience to the will of the Father and his exaltation as Lord.

Christ became obedient to the point of death,
even death on a cross.
Because of this, God greatly exalted him
and bestowed on him the name which is above
   every other name.

Lect. No. 40

GOSPEL: John 18:1—19:42

The Passion of our Lord Jesus Christ.

The passion narrative in the Gospel of John agrees with the other Gospels in most details except for those that are specifically Johannine. One example of this is that wherever possible the divinity of Jesus is emphasized. Jesus knows all things and controls all things from the beginning to the end of the account.

Although the place where Jesus led the disciples is not mentioned by name, it is obviously the garden of Gethsemane. We can see the violent intent of the soldiers of the high priests by the weapons they are carrying. This contrasts with the way that Jesus meets the troops, totally without arms. He is able to defeat them with the truth.

Jesus asks them whom they seek. They respond, "Jesus the Nazarene," and he tells them, "I AM." This phrase is the same as the meaning of the name of God in the Old Testament: Yahweh. Thus, Jesus is identifying himself as God. Those who had come to arrest Jesus fall down in fear and awe, for they are in the presence of the living God.

Peter tries to defend Jesus with a sword, cutting off Malchus's ear. This is the only Gospel in which Peter is identified as the violent disciple. Jesus tells him to put away his sword because he is not going to confront violence with vio-

The Passion of our Lord Jesus Christ according to John

Jesus went out with his disciples across the Kidron valley
　to where there was a garden,
　into which he and his disciples entered.
Judas his betrayer also knew the place,
　because Jesus had often met there with his disciples.
So Judas got a band of soldiers and guards
　from the chief priests and the Pharisees
　and went there with lanterns, torches, and weapons.
Jesus, knowing everything that was going to happen to him,
　went out and said to them, "Whom are you looking for?"
They answered him, "Jesus the Nazorean."
He said to them, "I AM."
Judas his betrayer was also with them.
When he said to them, "I AM,"
　they turned away and fell to the ground.
So he again asked them,
　"Whom are you looking for?"
They said, "Jesus the Nazorean."
Jesus answered,
　"I told you that I AM.
So if you are looking for me, let these men go."
This was to fulfill what he had said,
　"I have not lost any of those you gave me."
Then Simon Peter, who had a sword, drew it,
　struck the high priest's slave, and cut off his right ear.
The slave's name was Malchus.

lence. Jesus wants to show that only love conquers.

Jesus is brought to the high priest's house. We hear how Caiaphas had predicted that it was better that one person die for the sake of the people. Caiaphas had meant that it was better to kill him before a rebellion began, but the Holy Spirit had given him a revelation that he did not even understand. Jesus was going to die for the people, for the forgiveness of their sins.

The leaders of the Jews were offended by the fact that Jesus claimed divine prerogatives for himself. He was also considered to be a political danger, for the Jewish leaders feared he might start a rebellion in which they would lose their privileges.

The other disciple, who is probably the beloved disciple, enters the high priest's house. He also arranges to bring Peter into the courtyard.

Jesus answers the questions of the high priest with diffidence. He is the very presence of God, and it is absurd that they should be questioning him. Furthermore, he is truth itself, and had spoken in the light. They were the ones who were working to hide their evil deeds in the dark.

The temple guards are enraged that Jesus would respond to the high priest in this manner and one strikes Jesus. He is trying to protect the dignity of the high priest, but there is an

Jesus said to Peter,
  "Put your sword into its scabbard.
Shall I not drink the cup that the Father gave me?"

So the band of soldiers, the tribune, and the Jewish guards seized Jesus,
  bound him, and brought him to Annas first.
He was the father-in-law of Caiaphas,
  who was high priest that year.
It was Caiaphas who had counseled the Jews
  that it was better that one man should die rather than the people.

Simon Peter and another disciple followed Jesus.
Now the other disciple was known to the high priest,
  and he entered the courtyard of the high priest with Jesus.
But Peter stood at the gate outside.
So the other disciple, the acquaintance of the high priest,
  went out and spoke to the gatekeeper and brought Peter in.
Then the maid who was the gatekeeper said to Peter,
  "You are not one of this man's disciples, are you?"
He said, "I am not."
Now the slaves and the guards were standing around a charcoal fire
  that they had made, because it was cold,
  and were warming themselves.
Peter was also standing there keeping warm.

The high priest questioned Jesus
  about his disciples and about his doctrine.
Jesus answered him,
  "I have spoken publicly to the world.
I have always taught in a synagogue
  or in the temple area where all the Jews gather,

irony here. How much more important is Jesus, and yet the guard fails to recognize the honor he should be paying him.

We hear of Peter's denial of Jesus (an abbreviated version as compared to the Synoptic version). Typical of this Gospel is the subtle comparison between Peter who denies Jesus and the beloved disciple who is courageous enough to accompany Jesus to the cross.

Jesus is brought to the palace of Pilate. The leaders of the Jews do not want to enter the palace because that would make them ritually impure and they would not be able to celebrate the Passover meal that night. John's Gospel presents the Last Supper as an anticipated Passover meal. In the Gospel of John, Jesus dies on Good Friday, but Passover begins on Friday night and not on Thursday night as in the Synoptic Gospels. The best studies on this topic have suggested that John was probably right.

The interrogation of Jesus before Pilate is a brilliant scene. There are seven sections to the drama (divided by leaving or entering the palace). The first and last, second and second last, third and third last sections are related. The central section is the passage where Jesus is hailed as the King of the Jews. This is the core message of this extended section. Jesus, despite appearances, is the true King of the Jews. Yet, he is a King who rules from the cross, and his crown is not one of gold but one made of thorns.

and in secret I have said nothing. Why ask me?
Ask those who heard me what I said to them.
They know what I said."
When he had said this,
    one of the temple guards standing there struck Jesus and said,
    "Is this the way you answer the high priest?"
Jesus answered him,
    "If I have spoken wrongly, testify to the wrong;
    but if I have spoken rightly, why do you strike me?"
Then Annas sent him bound to Caiaphas the high priest.

Now Simon Peter was standing there keeping warm.
And they said to him,
    "You are not one of his disciples, are you?"
He denied it and said,
    "I am not."
One of the slaves of the high priest,
    a relative of the one whose ear Peter had cut off, said,
    "Didn't I see you in the garden with him?"
Again Peter denied it.
And immediately the cock crowed.

Then they brought Jesus from Caiaphas to the praetorium.
It was morning.
And they themselves did not enter the praetorium,
    in order not to be defiled so that they could eat the Passover.
So Pilate came out to them and said,
    "What charge do you bring against this man?"
They answered and said to him,
    "If he were not a criminal,
    we would not have handed him over to you."
At this, Pilate said to them,

In the first and last sections, Pilate uses Jesus as a pawn to get back at the Jews (whom he hated). He tells the Jews to judge him according to their own law. They respond that they cannot put him to death (which is quoting Roman law and not Jewish law). They have thus implicitly denied their own law.

Likewise, in the last section Pilate asks whether he should put their King to death. They respond that they have no king but Caesar. By saying that, they are denying their true King (both Jesus and Yahweh).

In the second and second last portions we see Pilate questioning Jesus. In the second there are questions concerning Jesus' kingdom and truth, and in the second last section there are questions concerning Pilate's authority. Both of these sections examine who has the real authority, Pilate or Jesus.

The way that Jesus responds to Pilate throughout this section shows that Jesus possesses true authority while Pilate's authority is illusory. All authority comes from God (even that exercised by earthly rulers).

Furthermore, when Pilate asks the question, "What is truth?" he is not asking a philosophical question. He is stating a political opinion, "What does truth matter when he could gain political advantage." He knew that Jesus was innocent, but yet he would let Jesus die in order to get back at the Jews.

"Take him yourselves, and judge him according to
  your law."
The Jews answered him,
  "We do not have the right to execute anyone,"
  in order that the word of Jesus might be fulfilled
  that he said indicating the kind of death he would
    die.
So Pilate went back into the praetorium
  and summoned Jesus and said to him,
  "Are you the King of the Jews?"
Jesus answered,
  "Do you say this on your own
  or have others told you about me?"
Pilate answered,
  "I am not a Jew, am I?
Your own nation and the chief priests handed you
    over to me.
What have you done?"
Jesus answered,
  "My kingdom does not belong to this world.
If my kingdom did belong to this world,
  my attendants would be fighting
  to keep me from being handed over to the Jews.
But as it is, my kingdom is not here."
So Pilate said to him,
  "Then you are a king?"
Jesus answered,
  "You say I am a king.
For this I was born and for this I came into the
    world,
  to testify to the truth.
Everyone who belongs to the truth listens to my
    voice."
Pilate said to him, "What is truth?"

When he had said this,
  he again went out to the Jews and said to them,
  "I find no guilt in him.

In the third and third last sections we see Pilate speaking with the Jewish leaders. He gives them a choice between Jesus and Barabbas in the third, and presents the beaten and humiliated Jesus in the third last. Neither of these presentations quiets their bloodlust. They still seek to crucify him.

As mentioned above, the core to understanding all that is going on in this trial is found in the central section where the soldiers treat Jesus as a king. They intend to humiliate him, but in great irony they are actually proclaiming the hidden truth about Jesus.

All of the characters involved (Pilate, the leaders of the Jews, the soldiers) thought that they were controlling what was going on. Jesus is the true King, and he was in control in spite of what they thought.

The purple cloak they use is a bit problematic. Purple cloth was very rare and it was not clear how they would have obtained it. The Gospel of Matthew speaks of a scarlet robe.

Pilate asks Jesus where he is from. This is a common theme throughout the Gospel. People often wonder where Jesus comes from, for they do not recognize that he comes from the Father. He comes from above, and he leads us back there.

After this drama is played out, it is time for all to be completed. Jesus is led out to the place of judgment.

But you have a custom that I release one prisoner to
    you at Passover.
Do you want me to release to you the King of the
    Jews?"
They cried out again,
    "Not this one but Barabbas!"
Now Barabbas was a revolutionary.

Then Pilate took Jesus and had him scourged.
And the soldiers wove a crown out of thorns and
    placed it on his head,
    and clothed him in a purple cloak,
    and they came to him and said,
    "Hail, King of the Jews!"
And they struck him repeatedly.
Once more Pilate went out and said to them,
    "Look, I am bringing him out to you,
    so that you may know that I find no guilt in him."
So Jesus came out,
    wearing the crown of thorns and the purple cloak.
And he said to them, "Behold, the man!"
When the chief priests and the guards saw him they
    cried out,
    "Crucify him, crucify him!"
Pilate said to them,
    "Take him yourselves and crucify him.
I find no guilt in him."
The Jews answered,
    "We have a law, and according to that law he
        ought to die,
    because he made himself the Son of God."
Now when Pilate heard this statement,
    he became even more afraid,
    and went back into the praetorium and said to
        Jesus,
    "Where are you from?"
Jesus did not answer him.
So Pilate said to him,

It is important to remember that all of this is occurring on the preparation day for the Passover celebration. Jesus was being led out to his crucifixion at the very moment that the Passover lambs were being taken to the temple to be killed. In this we see how Jesus is the new Passover Lamb. This symbolism is continued later in the account where we hear about the fact that none of his bones was broken. This was one of the requirements for the Passover lamb, and it was true of Jesus as well.

The leaders of the Jews are strongly blamed for the death of Jesus in this Gospel. This Gospel and Matthew have often been used as proof texts for anti-Semitism. That is not a correct reading of these texts. It was not "the Jews" who had Jesus put to death. It was their leaders with the collaboration of the Roman authorities. We should remember, however, that we are ultimately responsible for the death of Jesus. He died because of our sins.

Pilate proclaims Jesus as King of the Jews in the inscription that he ordered to be hung over the head of Jesus. The leaders of the Jews objected to the phrase "King of the Jews," but Pilate insisted that it remain.

Jesus is crucified on Golgotha, a small outcropping of rock in a used-out quarry. His cross was anchored in a rock that had a natural flaw and was therefore rejected by the builders (hence, the fulfillment of the verse that speaks of the stone rejected by the builders becoming the cornerstone).

"Do you not speak to me?
Do you not know that I have power to release you
    and I have power to crucify you?"
Jesus answered him,
    "You would have no power over me
    if it had not been given to you from above.
For this reason the one who handed me over to you
    has the greater sin."
Consequently, Pilate tried to release him; but the
    Jews cried out,
    "If you release him, you are not a Friend of Caesar.
Everyone who makes himself a king opposes Caesar."

When Pilate heard these words he brought Jesus out
    and seated him on the judge's bench
    in the place called Stone Pavement, in Hebrew,
    Gabbatha.
It was preparation day for Passover, and it was
    about noon.
And he said to the Jews,
    "Behold, your king!"
They cried out,
    "Take him away, take him away! Crucify him!"
Pilate said to them,
    "Shall I crucify your king?"
The chief priests answered,
    "We have no king but Caesar."
Then he handed him over to them to be crucified.

So they took Jesus, and, carrying the cross himself,
    he went out to what is called the Place of the
    Skull,
    in Hebrew, Golgotha.
There they crucified him, and with him two others,
    one on either side, with Jesus in the middle.
Pilate also had an inscription written and put on the
    cross.

The leaders of the Jews object to the inscription placed over the head of Jesus stating that he was the King of the Jews. Ironically, it was a pagan who insisted upon sustaining the truth while Jesus' own people were rejecting their own King.

The soldiers divide Jesus' garments, but they do not cut his cloak, which was a seamless garment.

The mother of Jesus is standing below the cross along with Mary, the wife of Clopas, Mary of Magdala, and the beloved disciple.

Jesus hands his mother over into the care of the beloved disciple. Tradition holds that he cared for her for the rest of her life.

This passage also has a symbolic meaning. Jesus married the Church on the cross (in fulfillment of the matrimonial symbolism found throughout the Gospel). According to Jewish tradition, if a man died without having children, his next of kin was to marry the widow to have a child who would bear the deceased man's name.

Jesus had no children from his marriage to the Church, so he adopted the beloved disciple to be his brother so that he might produce children who would bear his name (Christians).

Jesus is in control until the very minute of his death. He fulfills all that was prophesied

It read,
"Jesus the Nazorean, the King of the Jews."
Now many of the Jews read this inscription,
    because the place where Jesus was crucified was
        near the city;
    and it was written in Hebrew, Latin, and Greek.
So the chief priests of the Jews said to Pilate,
    "Do not write 'The King of the Jews,'
    but that he said, 'I am the King of the Jews.'"
Pilate answered,
    "What I have written, I have written."

When the soldiers had crucified Jesus,
    they took his clothes and divided them into four
        shares,
    a share for each soldier.
They also took his tunic, but the tunic was seamless,
    woven in one piece from the top down.
So they said to one another,
    "Let's not tear it, but cast lots for it to see whose it
        will be,"
    in order that the passage of Scripture might be
        fulfilled that says:
        They divided my garments among them,
            and for my vesture they cast lots.
This is what the soldiers did.
Standing by the cross of Jesus were his mother
    and his mother's sister, Mary the wife of Clopas,
    and Mary of Magdala.
When Jesus saw his mother and the disciple there
        whom he loved
    he said to his mother, "Woman, behold, your son."
Then he said to the disciple,
    "Behold, your mother."
And from that hour the disciple took her into his
        home.

After this, aware that everything was now finished,
    in order that the Scripture might be fulfilled,

about his death, and he then hands over his spirit. It was he who decided when it was time to die.

The soldiers were sent to break the legs of those who had been crucified. One died on the cross due to suffocation when one no longer had the strength to push one's body up to catch one's breath. By breaking the legs of those who had been crucified, the soldiers hastened their death (for they could not push up to breathe).

When they came to Jesus, he was already dead. They therefore did not break his legs.

This fulfilled the Paschal Lamb symbolism, that none of the lamb's bones were to be broken.

It also fulfilled matrimonial symbolism. God created Eve by placing Adam in a deep sleep and taking a rib from his side. God created the second Adam's (Jesus') wife, the Church, by allowing Jesus to descend into a deep sleep (death) and opening his side (the side pierced with the lance). It gave forth blood and water (the symbols for the Eucharist and Baptism).

The burial is problematic. The Synoptics speak of the women going to the tomb on Easter morning to anoint the body because there had been no time to do so on Good Friday. The myrrh and aloes, therefore, must be symbolic to show that they buried the body of Jesus with great care and love.

Jesus said, "I thirst."
There was a vessel filled with common wine.
So they put a sponge soaked in wine on a sprig of hyssop
    and put it up to his mouth.
When Jesus had taken the wine, he said,
    "It is finished."
And bowing his head, he handed over the spirit.

Here all kneel and pause for a short time.

Now since it was preparation day,
    in order that the bodies might not remain on the cross on the sabbath,
    for the sabbath day of that week was a solemn one,
    the Jews asked Pilate that their legs be broken
    and that they be taken down.
So the soldiers came and broke the legs of the first
    and then of the other one who was crucified with Jesus.
But when they came to Jesus and saw that he was already dead,
    they did not break his legs,
    but one soldier thrust his lance into his side,
    and immediately blood and water flowed out.
An eyewitness has testified, and his testimony is true;
    he knows that he is speaking the truth,
    so that you also may come to believe.
For this happened so that the Scripture passage might be fulfilled:
Not a bone of it will be broken.
And again another passage says:
They will look upon him whom they have pierced.

After this, Joseph of Arimathea,
    secretly a disciple of Jesus for fear of the Jews,
    asked Pilate if he could remove the body of Jesus.
And Pilate permitted it.

This is the only Gospel where we see Nicodemus assisting Joseph of Arimathea. Nicodemus appears three times in this Gospel. The first time is when he comes to Jesus by night (for he was afraid). The second time is when it is suggested in the Sanhedrin that Jesus be put to death. Nicodemus objects that this is not the proper legal procedure. Notice that he is not defending Jesus as much as defending the law.

This is the third time we see Nicodemus. Here he courageously assists in the burial of Jesus, a criminal convicted according to Roman law. He risks his life to render this sign of respect toward Jesus. These three appearances show a growth in his faith from fear to lukewarm commitment to the point where he is willing to die for Jesus.

So he came and took his body.
Nicodemus, the one who had first come to him at
     night,
     also came bringing a mixture of myrrh and aloes
     weighing about one hundred pounds.
They took the body of Jesus
     and bound it with burial cloths along with the
     spices,
     according to the Jewish burial custom.
Now in the place where he had been crucified there
     was a garden,
     and in the garden a new tomb, in which no one
     had yet been buried.
So they laid Jesus there because of the Jewish
     preparation day;
     for the tomb was close by.

The Gospel of the Lord.

PASTORAL REFLECTIONS

Why did Jesus have to die for us? In the Gospel of John, his death is the ultimate revelation of how much God loves us. Because of our sinfulness and brokenness, we are filled with self-doubt and self-loathing. (Sin is, after all, an act of self-hate.) We would never be able to believe that we were this loved until someone died for us.

This is why the Father wanted his Son to die on the cross. It was not because God could not forgive us in any other way. It was because God wanted Jesus to be as loving as possible, and he wanted us to experience that love. This love was best expressed through the death of Jesus. (This is why there is matrimonial symbolism in the account of the Passion—for it was the fulfillment of God's promise of love for us.)

March 30, 2013

THE EASTER VIGIL

FIRST READING:

A Longer Form: Genesis 1:1—2:2

God looked at everything he had made, and he found it very good.

We begin our Easter Vigil readings with the Priestly account of creation. This account was written during the Babylonian exile, and shows signs of either agreeing with or rejecting the theology that the Jewish people encountered there.

By using the phrases, "In the beginning" and "create," the author is speaking about creation *ex nihilo*, the fact that God created everything that exists from nothing.

The first thing that God creates is light. Ancient people believed that light was the most ethereal of all the things that existed, so it was the first thing created. One should not ask where the light came from (the sun and moon and stars are not created until the fourth day). God is the ultimate source of light.

God creates through the word. He speaks and all is made. This creation story, in fact, has God speaking ten times. The law of God was very important to the authors who wrote this account, and so God is seen as creating with the ten words (the phrase decalogue means both ten words and ten commandments). God also names all the things that he creates, showing that he has dominion over them all.

A reading from the Book of Genesis

In the beginning, when God created the heavens and the earth,
the earth was a formless wasteland, and darkness covered the abyss,
while a mighty wind swept over the waters.

Then God said,
"Let there be light," and there was light.
God saw how good the light was.
God then separated the light from the darkness.
God called the light "day," and the darkness he called "night."
Thus evening came, and morning followed—the first day.

Then God said,
"Let there be a dome in the middle of the waters,
to separate one body of water from the other."
And so it happened:
God made the dome,
and it separated the water above the dome from the water below it.
God called the dome "the sky."
Evening came, and morning followed—the second day.

Then God said,
"Let the water under the sky be gathered into a single basin,
so that the dry land may appear."

God not only creates, he also separates. He separates the light from darkness, water from dry land, etc. God places order in our universe and gives it certain laws that it must obey. This is the source for the idea of the "laws of nature" (and also "the natural law").

The ancients pictured the sky as a type of bowl that protected the world from the flood of waters over it. Thus, when the great flood occurs in the day of Noah, God opens the floodgates in the heavens. This reminds us of the fragility of creation. If God were to withhold his care for but a minute, it would cease to exist.

On the third day God commands the earth to bring forth vegetation. This phrasing retains a bit of the idea of Mother Nature, for God uses the earth as his intermediary. Plants were not considered to be living creatures by the Jews. Things had to have breath and blood in order to be considered living creatures.

When God creates the lights in the heavens, he names neither the sun nor the moon. The reason for this is that the names for Moon and Sun in Hebrew were also names of pagan gods. In order to keep all traces of pagan beliefs out of this account, the author does not even mention the names of these heavenly bodies (lest a reader believe that Yahweh had created the moon and the sun as minor deities). They are clearly creatures created by and subject to the LORD alone.

And so it happened:
   the water under the sky was gathered into its basin,
   and the dry land appeared.
God called the dry land "the earth,"
   and the basin of the water he called "the sea."
God saw how good it was.
Then God said,
   "Let the earth bring forth vegetation:
   every kind of plant that bears seed
   and every kind of fruit tree on earth
   that bears fruit with its seed in it."
And so it happened:
   the earth brought forth every kind of plant that bears seed
   and every kind of fruit tree on earth
   that bears fruit with its seed in it.
God saw how good it was.
Evening came, and morning followed—the third day.

Then God said:
   "Let there be lights in the dome of the sky,
   to separate day from night.
Let them mark the fixed times, the days and the years,
   and serve as luminaries in the dome of the sky,
   to shed light upon the earth."
And so it happened:
   God made the two great lights,
   the greater one to govern the day,
   and the lesser one to govern the night;
   and he made the stars.
God set them in the dome of the sky,
   to shed light upon the earth,
   to govern the day and the night,
   and to separate the light from the darkness.
God saw how good it was.

Note that evening precedes the morning throughout the account. Jewish people believe the day begins with sunset (specifically, when one can look into the sky and see three stars at the same glance).

On the fifth day God creates fish, sea creatures, and birds. These creatures are at the edge of the world in which we exist. Those creatures closer to us are created the sixth day. Note that the author uses the word "create" on the fifth day. This is the second use of this phrase, for on the first day God created things that were not living, and he was now creating living creatures.

God even created the sea creatures. This is a reference to Leviathan and Rahab, the primordial sea creatures. Pagans believed them to be gods. This author states clearly that they were created by the Lord God. One of the psalms even speaks of how God created them so that he could play with them, as if they were a child's playthings.

The rabbis speculated on when God created the angels. They had two possible answers. Some said that God created the angels on the second day for that is when he created the heavens. Others said that he created the angels on the fifth day, for that is when he created winged creatures.

Throughout the account we continue to hear how good creation is. God created this world to be good. Evil entered through sin, not because the world had been created that way.

Evening came, and morning followed—the fourth day.

Then God said,
   "Let the water teem with an abundance of living creatures,
   and on the earth let birds fly beneath the dome of the sky."
And so it happened:
   God created the great sea monsters
   and all kinds of swimming creatures with which the water teems,
   and all kinds of winged birds.
God saw how good it was, and God blessed them, saying,
   "Be fertile, multiply, and fill the water of the seas;
   and let the birds multiply on the earth."
Evening came, and morning followed—the fifth day.

Then God said,
   "Let the earth bring forth all kinds of living creatures:
   cattle, creeping things, and wild animals of all kinds."
And so it happened:
   God made all kinds of wild animals, all kinds of cattle,
   and all kinds of creeping things of the earth.
God saw how good it was.

Then God said:
   "Let us make man in our image, after our likeness.
Let them have dominion over the fish of the sea,
   the birds of the air, and the cattle,
   and over all the wild animals
   and all the creatures that crawl on the ground."
God created man in his image;
      in the image of God he created him;
      male and female he created them.

The creation of the human race involves a special intervention on God's part (notice the three uses of the word "create"). Humanity is created as both male and female, implying that we are not complete without each other.

We are created in God's likeness and image. This means that we have been given dominion over all that was created. We have been made God's viceroys and representatives upon the earth. This does not mean that we should be arrogant and misuse creation.

Psalm 8 explains that dominion is treating the world as a small child might who sings the glory of God's creation. Dominion means to celebrate creation, not abuse it.

All that was created is placed at our disposition. This is how greatly God esteems us.

On the seventh day God rests and consecrates the Sabbath. The weekly day of rest is not another commandment that we must obey, but rather a time when we can imitate God himself. As Jesus said, the Sabbath was created for us, for it gives us a chance to rest, meditate on life and praise God for all his goodness.

God blessed them, saying:
    "Be fertile and multiply;
    fill the earth and subdue it.
Have dominion over the fish of the sea, the birds of
        the air,
    and all the living things that move on the earth."
God also said:
    "See, I give you every seed-bearing plant all over
        the earth
    and every tree that has seed-bearing fruit on it to
        be your food;
    and to all the animals of the land, all the birds of
        the air,
    and all the living creatures that crawl on the
        ground,
    I give all the green plants for food."
And so it happened.
God looked at everything he had made, and he
        found it very good.
Evening came, and morning followed—the sixth
        day.

Thus the heavens and the earth and all their array
        were completed.
Since on the seventh day God was finished
    with the work he had been doing,
    he rested on the seventh day from all the work he
        had undertaken.

The word of the Lord.

PASTORAL REFLECTIONS

Both work and rest are activities which show that we are created in God's image and likeness. When we work, we continue God's work of creation. When we rest, we continue God's childlike awe and wonder as he reflects upon creation and pronounces it to be "good, good, very good."

Lect. No. 41

FIRST READING: **B** Shorter Form: Genesis 1:1, 26-31a

God looked at everything he had made, and he found it very good.

We begin our Easter Vigil readings with the Priestly account of creation. By using the phrases, "In the beginning" and "create," the author is speaking about creation *ex nihilo*, the fact that God created everything that exists from nothing.

God creates through the word. He speaks and everything is made, and all that God makes is good.

The creation of the human race involves a special intervention on God's part (notice the three uses of the word "create"). Humanity is created as both male and female, implying that we are not complete without each other.

We are created in God's likeness and image. This means that we have been given dominion over all that was created.

We have been made God's viceroys and representatives upon the earth. This does not mean that we should be arrogant and misuse creation.

Psalm 8 explains that dominion is treating the world as a small child might who sings the glory of God's creation. Dominion means to celebrate creation, not abuse it.

All that was created is placed at our disposition. This is how greatly God esteems us.

A reading from the Book of Genesis

In the beginning, when God created the heavens
  and the earth,
  God said: "Let us make man in our image, after
    our likeness.
Let them have dominion over the fish of the sea,
  the birds of the air, and the cattle,
  and over all the wild animals
  and all the creatures that crawl on the ground."
God created man in his image;
    in the image of God he created him;
    male and female he created them.
God blessed them, saying:
  "Be fertile and multiply;
  fill the earth and subdue it.
Have dominion over the fish of the sea, the birds of
    the air,
  and all the living things that move on the earth."
God also said:
  "See, I give you every seed-bearing plant all over
    the earth
  and every tree that has seed-bearing fruit on it to
    be your food;
  and to all the animals of the land, all the birds of
    the air,
  and all the living creatures that crawl on the
    ground,
  I give all the green plants for food."
And so it happened.
God looked at everything he had made, and he
    found it very good.

The word of the Lord.

Lect. No. 41 RESPONSORIAL PSALM: **A** Ps 104:1-2, 5-6, 10, 12, 13-14, 24, 35 (R̷.: 30)

Psalm 104 is a hymn of thanksgiving to praise the LORD as the God of creation.

The response requests that God send forth his Spirit and renew the face of the earth. This is a recognition that God created everything that exists through his Spirit.

The word for Spirit in Hebrew is the same word as breath and wind. God spoke, sent forth the breath of his mouth, and all was created.

On Easter, we celebrate the first creation and also the new creation which occurred in the death and resurrection of Jesus and the descent of the Holy Spirit upon the earth.

In this hymn we see both the power of the LORD (for he can command the earth and waters to occupy a place from which they will not move) and also God's loving concern (for he waters the earth, gives vegetation for the needs of its animals, etc.).

Just by looking at the world and all that it contains, the psalmist is led to glorify the God of creation. One cannot look at a bird or flower and not realize that it was created by a loving God. One cannot look into a microscope or a telescope and not realize that God is great and generous and good. It fills us with a sense of awe and gratitude.

R̷. **Lord, send out your Spirit, and renew the face of the earth.**

Bless the LORD, O my soul!
  O LORD, my God, you are great indeed!
You are clothed with majesty and glory,
  robed in light as with a cloak.

R̷. **Lord, send out your Spirit, and renew the face of the earth.**

You fixed the earth upon its foundation,
  not to be moved forever;
with the ocean, as with a garment, you covered it;
  above the mountains the waters stood.

R̷. **Lord, send out your Spirit, and renew the face of the earth.**

You send forth springs into the watercourses
  that wind among the mountains.
Beside them the birds of heaven dwell;
  from among the branches they send forth their song.

R̷. **Lord, send out your Spirit, and renew the face of the earth.**

You water the mountains from your palace;
  the earth is replete with the fruit of your works.
You raise grass for the cattle,
  and vegetation for man's use,
producing bread from the earth.

R̷. **Lord, send out your Spirit, and renew the face of the earth.**

How manifold are your works, O LORD!
  In wisdom you have wrought them all—
the earth is full of your creatures.
Bless the LORD, O my soul!

R̷. **Lord, send out your Spirit, and renew the face of the earth.**

RESPONSORIAL PSALM: 🅱 **Ps 33:4-5, 6-7, 12-13, 20 and 22 (℟.: 5b)**

Psalm 33 is both a hymn to praise the God of creation and a hymn of trust in the goodness of the LORD.

God's word created the world in goodness. He continuously proclaimed all that he created to be good. His word is trustworthy. His law manifests his justice and righteousness, for the law is an expression of his divine will.

Blessed, indeed, is the nation that has such a just and merciful God. This is a God who not only created all things, but also continues to care for them with gentle compassion.

We might sometimes wonder if God could really be concerned with us. We wonder if God knows what is happening to us or cares. This psalm celebrates the fact that God, who created all things, will still respond to our every need. We truly can place our hope in him. He is our shield and refuge, our help and our hope.

℟. **The earth is full of the goodness of the Lord.**

Upright is the word of the LORD,
　and all his works are trustworthy.
He loves justice and right;
　of the kindness of the LORD the earth is full.

℟. **The earth is full of the goodness of the Lord.**

By the word of the LORD the heavens were made;
　by the breath of his mouth all their host.
He gathers the waters of the sea as in a flask;
　in cellars he confines the deep.

℟. **The earth is full of the goodness of the Lord.**

Blessed the nation whose God is the LORD,
　the people he has chosen for his own inheritance.
From heaven the LORD looks down;
　he sees all mankind.

℟. **The earth is full of the goodness of the Lord.**

Our soul waits for the LORD,
　who is our help and our shield.
May your kindness, O LORD, be upon us
　who have put our hope in you.

℟. **The earth is full of the goodness of the Lord.**

SECOND READING: 🅰 **Longer Form: Genesis 22:1-18**

The sacrifice of Abraham, our father in faith.

The Second Reading this evening is the story of the sacrifice of Isaac (this is also called the binding of Isaac in Jewish literature). It is an esteemed story in both the Jewish and the Christian tradition.

A reading from the Book of Genesis

God put Abraham to the test.
　He called to him, "Abraham!"
"Here I am," he replied.
Then God said:

God calls Abraham and asks him to sacrifice his only son to the LORD. There is tremendous irony in this request, for Abraham had had another son, Ishmael. Ishmael tried to harm Isaac, and Ishmael was sent away into the desert to die. Furthermore, God asks for the son "whom you love." God knew exactly how great this sacrifice would be for Abraham.

He is also asking for a tremendous act of trust, for the boy Isaac was the only visible sign of God's fulfillment of his promise. Even though God had promised a great land and a descendance as numerous as the sand on the shore of the sea and the stars in the sky, Abraham nevertheless did not yet have any land and only one son (for as far as Abraham knew, his other son Ishmael was dead or at least as good as dead to Abraham).

But Abraham proves his obedience to the will of the LORD by taking his son to Mount Moriah where he fully intends to sacrifice him. The journey is made pathetic by the fact that Abraham carries the knife and fire on the journey up the mountain while his son carries the wood. Abraham is carrying those objects that might harm the boy.

Then it is even worse when the son asks where the sacrifice is, and Abraham responds that the LORD will provide. Abraham is saying this thinking of the son that the LORD had already provided, but the LORD would give these words new meaning.

"Take your son Isaac, your only one, whom you love,
    and go to the land of Moriah.
There you shall offer him up as a holocaust
    on a height that I will point out to you."
Early the next morning Abraham saddled his donkey,
    took with him his son Isaac and two of his servants as well,
    and with the wood that he had cut for the holocaust,
    set out for the place of which God had told him.

On the third day Abraham got sight of the place from afar.
Then he said to his servants:
    "Both of you stay here with the donkey,
    while the boy and I go on over yonder.
We will worship and then come back to you."
Thereupon Abraham took the wood for the holocaust
    and laid it on his son Isaac's shoulders,
    while he himself carried the fire and the knife.
As the two walked on together, Isaac spoke to his father Abraham:
    "Father!" Isaac said.
"Yes, son," he replied.
Isaac continued, "Here are the fire and the wood,
    but where is the sheep for the holocaust?"
"Son," Abraham answered,
    "God himself will provide the sheep for the holocaust."
Then the two continued going forward.

When they came to the place of which God had told him,
    Abraham built an altar there and arranged the wood on it.
Next he tied up his son Isaac,
    and put him on top of the wood on the altar.

When the LORD saw that Abraham was totally obedient, he halted the sacrifice. What Abraham had said about the LORD providing was fulfilled when Abraham saw a ram caught in the thicket and sacrificed that animal in place of his son.

Some scholars say that this was originally a story of how the Israelite people rejected human sacrifices. That might even be true, but the form of the story contained in Genesis is clearly a story about the demands of faith. One must be willing to die to oneself and sacrifice everything in order to follow God's will.

This event is a prefiguring of what happened to Jesus on the cross. We had sinned and deserved to be punished. We were to be the holocaust, but God sent a substitute in our place: Jesus, his only beloved Son. Thus, he saved his beloved children through the death of his only Son.

Why did God test Abraham in this manner? Certainly he knew Abraham's faith. Is it possible that this test was for Abraham's benefit, so that he could learn the depths of his trust? This is true in our own faith lives, for we often learn what trust means in times of suffering.

The account closes with a reaffirmation of God's covenantial promises to Abraham. Until the day he died Abraham would have to continue to trust, for his immediate descendance was not very numerous nor did he possess much land (for he only owned his burial cave).

Then he reached out and took the knife to slaughter his son.
But the LORD's messenger called to him from heaven,
　"Abraham, Abraham!"
"Here I am," he answered.
"Do not lay your hand on the boy," said the messenger.
"Do not do the least thing to him.
I know now how devoted you are to God,
　since you did not withhold from me your own beloved son."
As Abraham looked about,
　he spied a ram caught by its horns in the thicket.
So he went and took the ram
　and offered it up as a holocaust in place of his son.
Abraham named the site Yahweh-yireh;
　hence people now say, "On the mountain the LORD will see."

Again the LORD's messenger called to Abraham from heaven and said:
　"I swear by myself, declares the LORD,
　that because you acted as you did
　in not withholding from me your beloved son,
　I will bless you abundantly
　and make your descendants as countless
　as the stars of the sky and the sands of the seashore;
　your descendants shall take possession
　of the gates of their enemies,
　and in your descendants all the nations of the earth shall find blessing—
　all this because you obeyed my command."

The word of the Lord.

Lect.
No. 41
SECOND READING: B Shorter Form: Genesis 22:1-2, 9a, 10-13, 15-18

The sacrifice of Abraham, our father in faith.

God calls Abraham and asks him to sacrifice his only son to the LORD. He is asking for the son "whom you love." God knew exactly how great this sacrifice would be for Abraham.

He is also asking for a tremendous act of trust, for the boy Isaac was the only visible sign of God's fulfillment of his promise. Even though God had promised a great land and a descendance as numerous as the sand on the shore of the sea and the stars in the sky, Abraham nevertheless did not yet have any land and only one son (for as far as Abraham knew, his other son Ishmael was dead or at least as good as dead to Abraham).

But Abraham proves his obedience to the will of the LORD by taking his son to Mount Moriah where he fully intends to sacrifice him.

When the LORD saw that Abraham was totally obedient, he halted the sacrifice. What Abraham had said about the LORD providing was fulfilled when Abraham saw a ram caught in the thicket and sacrificed that animal in place of his son.

This story is clearly about the demands of faith. One must be willing to die to self and sacrifice everything in order to follow God's will.

A reading from the Book of Genesis

God put Abraham to the test.
He called to him, "Abraham!"
"Here I am," he replied.
Then God said:
  "Take your son Isaac, your only one, whom you love,
  and go to the land of Moriah.
There you shall offer him up as a holocaust
  on a height that I will point out to you."

When they came to the place of which God had told him,
  Abraham built an altar there and arranged the wood on it.
Then he reached out and took the knife to slaughter his son.
But the LORD'S messenger called to him from heaven,
  "Abraham, Abraham!"
"Here I am," he answered.
"Do not lay your hand on the boy," said the messenger.
"Do not do the least thing to him.
I know now how devoted you are to God,
  since you did not withhold from me your own beloved son."
As Abraham looked about,
  he spied a ram caught by its horns in the thicket.
So he went and took the ram
  and offered it up as a holocaust in place of his son.

Again the LORD'S messenger called to Abraham from heaven and said:

This event is a prefiguring of what happened to Jesus on the cross. We had sinned and deserved to be punished, but God sent a substitute in our place: Jesus, his only beloved Son. Thus, he saved his beloved children through the death of his only Son.

Why did God test Abraham in this manner? Certainly he knew Abraham's faith. Is it possible that this test was for Abraham's benefit, so that he could learn the depths of his trust? This is true in our own lives, for we often learn what trust means in times of suffering.

"I swear by myself, declares the LORD,
that because you acted as you did
in not withholding from me your beloved son,
I will bless you abundantly
and make your descendants as countless
as the stars of the sky and the sands of the seashore;
your descendants shall take possession
of the gates of their enemies,
and in your descendants all the nations of the earth shall find blessing—
all this because you obeyed my command."

The word of the Lord.

Lect.
No. 41

RESPONSORIAL PSALM: Ps 16:5, 8, 9-10, 11 (R/.: 1)

Psalm 16 is a powerful expression of trust in the LORD. Not only will God deliver us; God is our entire inheritance. He is our allotted portion and our cup.

This is an appropriate response to the story that we have just read. Abraham risked everything on the LORD. He believed in the LORD'S promise even when there was no sign that the LORD was going to be faithful.

God was just as faithful to his own Son when he died on the cross. He did not allow his Son to undergo corruption or to be abandoned to the netherworld. This is also true of us, for we have become adopted children of the LORD. We are heirs to his promise and coheirs with Jesus.

R/. **You are my inheritance, O Lord.**

O LORD, my allotted portion and my cup,
    you it is who hold fast my lot.
I set the LORD ever before me;
    with him at my right hand I shall not be disturbed.

R/. **You are my inheritance, O Lord.**

Therefore my heart is glad and my soul rejoices,
    my body, too, abides in confidence;
because you will not abandon my soul to the netherworld,
    nor will you suffer your faithful one to undergo corruption.

R/. **You are my inheritance, O Lord.**

You will show me the path to life,
    fullness of joys in your presence,
    the delights at your right hand forever.

R/. **You are my inheritance, O Lord.**

THIRD READING: Exodus 14:15—15:1

The Israelites marched on dry land through the midst of the sea.

Our Third Reading tells us of the Exodus of the Israelites from slavery in Egypt to freedom in the promised land.

Although the Pharaoh had promised to let the Israelites go free, he repented his decision and followed them with all of his troops. He intended to cut them off and kill them.

The LORD ordered Moses to hold his staff over the waters of the Red Sea. The waters split, and the Israelites were able to pass through the sea without harm.

Various explanations have been given in recent years to interpret what happened. Some have spoken of earthquakes, volcanic explosions, El Niño, etc. God often works through natural means to further his plan. Whatever, the Israelites and we have one explanation for what happened: God delivered his chosen people from certain destruction at the hands of Pharaoh and his soldiers.

We could also speak about the soldiers. God did not want the Israelites to travel to the promised land by the sea route lest they become afraid and return to Egypt. He knew that his people were not courageous. Maybe they even needed the soldiers at their backs to force them across the sea lest they

A reading from the Book of Exodus

The LORD said to Moses, "Why are you crying out to me?
Tell the Israelites to go forward.
And you, lift up your staff and, with hand outstretched over the sea,
split the sea in two,
that the Israelites may pass through it on dry land.
But I will make the Egyptians so obstinate
that they will go in after them.
Then I will receive glory through Pharaoh and all his army,
his chariots and charioteers.
The Egyptians shall know that I am the LORD,
when I receive glory through Pharaoh
and his chariots and charioteers."

The angel of God, who had been leading Israel's camp,
now moved and went around behind them.
The column of cloud also, leaving the front,
took up its place behind them,
so that it came between the camp of the Egyptians
and that of Israel.
But the cloud now became dark, and thus the night passed
without the rival camps coming any closer together all night long.
Then Moses stretched out his hand over the sea,
and the LORD swept the sea
with a strong east wind throughout the night
and so turned it into dry land.

turn back out of fear. This has often been used as a symbol of the fact that God often allows us to feel the consequences of our sins in order to push us across the sea from slavery to sin into the freedom of God's children.

We become bogged down in our sinful habits, and it often looks more comfortable to stay in our sins than to convert from them. The sins have become familiar (even if they are a form of slavery), while conversion is the unknown (like marching off into the desert).

God brings us to the point where staying in our sins grows so uncomfortable that we finally have the courage to leave them and wander into the unknown. We have to recognize for ourselves how much our sins are hurting us before we can reject them and choose the freedom of the children of God.

The Egyptians followed the Israelites, but their heavy chariots became clogged down in the mud of the recently dried sea bottom. Thus, when Moses stretched his hands out over the sea again and the waters flowed back, they could not extricate themselves and they drowned. The defeat was total, for one cannot fight against the LORD.

The Israelites, who had by now reached dry land, were filled with a sense of awe and wonder. They realized that they owed their entire victory to the LORD. The only thing they could do was to thank and praise the LORD.

When the water was thus divided,
    the Israelites marched into the midst of the sea on
        dry land,
    with the water like a wall to their right and to
        their left.

The Egyptians followed in pursuit;
    all Pharaoh's horses and chariots and charioteers
        went after them
    right into the midst of the sea.
In the night watch just before dawn
    the LORD cast through the column of the fiery cloud
    upon the Egyptian force a glance that threw it
        into a panic;
    and he so clogged their chariot wheels
    that they could hardly drive.
With that the Egyptians sounded the retreat before
        Israel,
    because the LORD was fighting for them against
        the Egyptians.

Then the LORD told Moses, "Stretch out your hand
        over the sea,
    that the water may flow back upon the Egyptians,
    upon their chariots and their charioteers."
So Moses stretched out his hand over the sea,
    and at dawn the sea flowed back to its normal
        depth.
The Egyptians were fleeing head on toward the sea,
    when the LORD hurled them into its midst.
As the water flowed back,
    it covered the chariots and the charioteers of
        Pharaoh's whole army
    which had followed the Israelites into the sea.
Not a single one of them escaped.
But the Israelites had marched on dry land
    through the midst of the sea,
    with the water like a wall to their right and to
        their left.

The Israelites sang a great victory song to celebrate their wondrous deliverance. Their song, which is called the Song of Miriam, is one of the oldest parts of the Old Testament to have been written. It represents a very ancient tradition.

By studying the language of the hymn, scholars have determined that it dates back to at least the 11th century B.C. In other words, the hymn that is now found in the Book of Exodus might be the actual hymn that the Israelites sang on that glorious day when the Lord led them through the sea on dry land.

Thus the Lord saved Israel on that day
from the power of the Egyptians.
When Israel saw the Egyptians lying dead on the seashore
and beheld the great power that the Lord
had shown against the Egyptians,
they feared the Lord and believed in him and in his servant Moses.

Then Moses and the Israelites sang this song to the Lord:
I will sing to the Lord, for he is gloriously triumphant;
horse and chariot he has cast into the sea.

The word of the Lord.

Lect. No. 41

RESPONSORIAL PSALM: Exodus 15:1-2, 3-4, 5-6, 17-18 (℟.: 1b)

As we have just seen, this might be one of the oldest hymns of the Bible. It was sung in celebration of the victory that God had given to the Israelite people at the Reed Sea.

One of the important aspects of the hymn is the pattern of parallelism that occurs throughout the hymn. The author repeats the same idea over and over again using slightly different words each time.

In this hymn the Lord is lauded as being a great warrior. He defeated both the forces of Pharaoh and also the forces of the sea.

In the Old Testament, the sea was often thought of as being opposed to the will of God. It was where the great sea monster Leviathan lived. If God can

℟. **Let us sing to the Lord; he has covered himself in glory.**

I will sing to the Lord, for he is gloriously triumphant;
horse and chariot he has cast into the sea.
My strength and my courage is the Lord,
and he has been my savior.
He is my God, I praise him;
the God of my father, I extol him.

℟. **Let us sing to the Lord; he has covered himself in glory.**

The Lord is a warrior,
Lord is his name!
Pharaoh's chariots and army he hurled into the sea;
the elite of his officers were submerged in the Red Sea.

℟. **Let us sing to the Lord; he has covered himself in glory.**

use it to further his plans, then he is truly LORD of earth and sea.

God not only redeemed the Israelites, he also brought them and planted them on the mountain of his inheritance.

Some scholars believe that this part of the hymn was written at a later date, for it speaks of Mount Zion (the mountain upon which Solomon built the temple in Jerusalem a few hundred years after the Exodus). But others argue that it actually represents the same ancient tradition in which God is pictured as living on a great mountain (like Mount Sinai).

The flood waters covered them,
    they sank into the depths like a stone.
Your right hand, O LORD, magnificent in power,
    your right hand, O LORD, has shattered the enemy.

℟. **Let us sing to the Lord; he has covered himself in glory.**

You brought in the people you redeemed
    and planted them on the mountain of your inheritance—
the place where you made your seat, O LORD,
    the sanctuary, LORD, which your hands established.
The LORD shall reign forever and ever.

℟. **Let us sing to the Lord; he has covered himself in glory.**

Lect.
No. 41

FOURTH READING: Isaiah 54:5-14

With enduring love, the Lord, your redeemer, takes pity on you.

This reading comes from the Book of the Prophet Isaiah, from the section of the book written by Second Isaiah. It was composed during the exile in Babylon, and it is a promise of consolation for a people who had been sorely tried by their suffering.

When Israel had been defeated by the Babylonians, they wondered why the LORD had allowed them to lose to their enemies. They wondered whether Yahweh might be less powerful than Marduk, the national god of the Babylonians. Or else, might Yahweh be angry with them and have rejected them? Was he still angry at them? Would he ever forgive them?

A reading from the Book of the Prophet Isaiah

The One who has become your husband is your Maker;
    his name is the LORD of hosts;
your redeemer is the Holy One of Israel,
    called God of all the earth.
The LORD calls you back,
    like a wife forsaken and grieved in spirit,
    a wife married in youth and then cast off,
    says your God.
For a brief moment I abandoned you,
    but with great tenderness I will take you back.
In an outburst of wrath, for a moment
    I hid my face from you;
but with enduring love I take pity on you,
    says the LORD, your redeemer.

This reading speaks of the commitment that God had made toward them. He was their maker, their spouse. He might have been angry at them for a while, but they were now forgiven. The LORD speaks of his anger as being something that was momentary, forever to be forgotten.

Even though nature itself would be shaken, even though mountains and hills were brought low, God's love for Israel would never be in question. God would rebuild their cities with great splendor. He himself would redeem them and deliver them from the hands of their enemies.

The LORD would also instruct his people so that they would know his will and never again fall from his favor. They would live in God's justice and peace forever.

This is for me like the days of Noah,
   when I swore that the waters of Noah
   should never again deluge the earth;
so I have sworn not to be angry with you,
   or to rebuke you.
Though the mountains leave their place
   and the hills be shaken,
my love shall never leave you
   nor my covenant of peace be shaken,
   says the LORD, who has mercy on you.
O afflicted one, storm-battered and unconsoled,
   I lay your pavements in carnelians,
   and your foundations in sapphires;
I will make your battlements of rubies,
   your gates of carbuncles,
   and all your walls of precious stones.
All your children shall be taught by the LORD,
   and great shall be the peace of your children.
In justice shall you be established,
   far from the fear of oppression,
   where destruction cannot come near you.

The word of the Lord.

Lect. No. 41

RESPONSORIAL PSALM: Ps 30:2, 4, 5-6, 11-12, 13 (℟.: 2a)

Psalm 30 is a thanksgiving for a deliverance. The psalmist was at the point of death and was sure that he had fallen into the hands of his enemies.

The LORD intervened in a miraculous manner and saved him from all of his enemies' plots. The LORD is truly merciful and generous. Even when he becomes angry at people for their sins, his anger lasts but a moment and then the Lord renews his favor.

℟. **I will praise you, Lord, for you have rescued me.**

I will extol you, O LORD, for you drew me clear
   and did not let my enemies rejoice over me.
O LORD, you brought me up from the netherworld;
   you preserved me from among those going down
      into the pit.

℟. **I will praise you, Lord, for you have rescued me.**

Sing praise to the LORD, you his faithful ones,
   and give thanks to his holy name.

We can ask how to apply this psalm to our Christian lives. It is obvious that we are reading this psalm at the Easter Vigil because we are celebrating Jesus' defeat over our worst enemies: sin, alienation, death, etc.

Our other enemies, people who hurt us, are no longer to be hated because we are a Gospel people. We do not want to hurt or destroy them, we want to love them into healing (just as God has done to us).

For his anger lasts but a moment;
    a lifetime, his good will.
At nightfall, weeping enters in,
    but with the dawn, rejoicing.

℞. **I will praise you, Lord, for you have rescued me.**

Hear, O LORD, and have pity on me;
    O LORD, be my helper.
You changed my mourning into dancing;
    O LORD, my God, forever will I give you thanks.

℞. **I will praise you, Lord, for you have rescued me.**

Lect. No. 41

FIFTH READING: Isaiah 55:1-11

Come to me that you may have life.
I will renew with you an everlasting covenant.

The Fifth Reading is another passage from the Book of the Prophet Isaiah, from the writings of Second Isaiah.

The central theme of this prophet is consolation. The first words of his prophecy are, in fact, "be consoled." (Is 40:1)

This consolation is not something to be earned. God has already paid the price. We should not seek after other sources of comfort for the pain in our hearts. God alone can provide that love and that healing which will bring us true peace.

This healing is so powerful that nations will seek it from afar. If we give witness to the peace we have found in God, people will seek to find the same peace in their own lives. Even if we never mention the name of the LORD, they will

A reading from the Book of the Prophet Isaiah

Thus says the LORD:
    All you who are thirsty,
    come to the water!
You who have no money,
    come, receive grain and eat;
come, without paying and without cost,
    drink wine and milk!
Why spend your money for what is not bread,
    your wages for what fails to satisfy?
Heed me, and you shall eat well,
    you shall delight in rich fare.
Come to me heedfully,
    listen, that you may have life.
I will renew with you the everlasting covenant,
    the benefits assured to David.
As I made him a witness to the peoples,
    a leader and commander of nations,
so shall you summon a nation you knew not,
    and nations that knew you not shall run to you,

see that there is something different about us and they will ask to share in the gift that we have received.

Now is the time to seek God. It is time to abandon all foolishness and sinfulness. We must admit our fundamental need for the mercy of God and seek him with all our strength. This is not a time for compromise or hesitation. We must make a leap of faith and place our trust in God.

This leap of faith means adopting a different way of viewing reality, for we must look at things through the eyes of God. This means learning the wisdom of God and living by its precepts.

The word of God has been showered down upon the earth and into our hearts. We must allow it to take root and become fertile. God's word is effective (remember how the world was created through God's word), but God also gives us freedom. God will not force himself upon us: we must choose to make our hearts a home for his word.

because of the LORD, your God,
  the Holy One of Israel, who has glorified you.

Seek the LORD while he may be found,
  call him while he is near.
Let the scoundrel forsake his way,
  and the wicked man his thoughts;
let him turn to the LORD for mercy;
  to our God, who is generous in forgiving.
For my thoughts are not your thoughts,
  nor are your ways my ways, says the LORD.
As high as the heavens are above the earth,
  so high are my ways above your ways
  and my thoughts above your thoughts.

For just as from the heavens
  the rain and snow come down
and do not return there
  till they have watered the earth,
  making it fertile and fruitful,
giving seed to the one who sows
  and bread to the one who eats,
so shall my word be
  that goes forth from my mouth;
my word shall not return to me void,
  but shall do my will,
  achieving the end for which I sent it.

The word of the Lord.

Lect.
No. 41

RESPONSORIAL PSALM: Isaiah 12:2-3, 4, 5-6 (℞.: 3)

This Responsorial Psalm is not even a psalm; it is a hymn found in the first part of the Book of the Prophet Isaiah.

It celebrates the actions of the LORD who is Israel's savior. When this hymn was written, it especially meant that God would save Israel from their earthly enemies. But, as we

℞. **You will draw water joyfully from the springs of salvation.**

God indeed is my savior;
  I am confident and unafraid.
My strength and my courage is the LORD,
  and he has been my savior.
With joy you will draw water
  at the fountain of salvation.

have seen in the previous readings, we must spiritualize this hymn and speak of how God saves us from the worst of our enemies: sin, fear, alienation, death, etc.

We must proclaim God as our deliverer. We must praise God with great gratitude. We recognize how God has showered his blessing upon us and we give thanks.

This is already an action that produces a powerful witness to our faith, for when we speak about how God has blessed us, people will begin to see God working in their own lives.

℟. **You will draw water joyfully from the springs of salvation.**

Give thanks to the LORD, acclaim his name;
    among the nations make known his deeds,
    proclaim how exalted is his name.

℟. **You will draw water joyfully from the springs of salvation.**

Sing praise to the LORD for his glorious achievement;
    let this be known throughout all the earth.
Shout with exultation, O city of Zion,
    for great in your midst
    is the Holy One of Israel!

℟. **You will draw water joyfully from the springs of salvation.**

Lect.
No. 41

SIXTH READING: Baruch 3:9-15, 32—4:4

Walk toward the splendor of the Lord.

This Sixth Reading has been attributed to Baruch, the secretary of Jeremiah the Prophet. The book is actually a collection of various fragments that have been assembled together. It is not clear if it was actually written by Baruch.

This particular section speaks about wisdom and the law. Wisdom was considered to be the revelation of the will of God. We could not possibly know what God wanted if he had not revealed it to us.

The fullest expression of this revelation, according to this reading, is the law. God had not left us in the darkness like

A reading from the Book of the Prophet Baruch

Hear, O Israel, the commandments of life:
    listen, and know prudence!
How is it, Israel,
    that you are in the land of your foes,
    grown old in a foreign land,
defiled with the dead,
    accounted with those destined for the netherworld?
You have forsaken the fountain of wisdom!
    Had you walked in the way of God,
    you would have dwelt in enduring peace.
Learn where prudence is,
    where strength, where understanding;
that you may know also
    where are length of days, and life,
    where light of the eyes, and peace.

other peoples. They did not know how to please the LORD. God has revealed exactly what is pleasing in his sight through the law.

That is why we should reexamine our ways and observe the law with all our heart. If we live the law, then we will find true joy. Our lives will be filled with meaning. If we do not follow it, then we will find that we have abandoned the will of God and we will not find peace.

This wisdom, the law of the LORD, is already ingrained in creation. We saw this in the First Reading that we heard this evening, when we saw how God created with ten words (the Decalogue).

These ten words, the ten commandments, are the foundation and blueprint of creation. If we observe nature, we should be able to see the order that exists in it and be able to learn what God wants of us.

As Christians, our law is the law of love seen in the Gospels. We do not observe precepts for the sake of consistency, but rather as a response to God's revelation of love for us. Only by living God's law can our hearts be receptive to the love of God.

Who has found the place of wisdom,
    who has entered into her treasuries?

The One who knows all things knows her;
    he has probed her by his knowledge—
the One who established the earth for all time,
    and filled it with four-footed beasts;
he who dismisses the light, and it departs,
    calls it, and it obeys him trembling;
before whom the stars at their posts
    shine and rejoice;
when he calls them, they answer, "Here we are!"
    shining with joy for their Maker.
Such is our God;
    no other is to be compared to him:
he has traced out the whole way of understanding,
    and has given her to Jacob, his servant,
    to Israel, his beloved son.

Since then she has appeared on earth,
    and moved among people.
She is the book of the precepts of God,
    the law that endures forever;
all who cling to her will live,
    but those will die who forsake her.
Turn, O Jacob, and receive her:
    walk by her light toward splendor.
Give not your glory to another,
    your privileges to an alien race.
Blessed are we, O Israel;
    for what pleases God is known to us!

The word of the Lord.

PASTORAL REFLECTIONS

St. Paul speaks of how the law we observe is not outside of us. It is not an externally written set of regulations that rob us of our freedom. The law of God was written on our hearts (or we could say breathed into our hearts with the breath of God's Spirit). Thus, when we follow the law, we are only fulfilling our destiny and living in the dignity God always intended for us.

RESPONSORIAL PSALM: Ps 19:8, 9, 10, 11 (℟.: John 6:68c)

Psalm 19 is a perfect response to the reading we have just heard from Baruch. The first part is a hymn to celebrate the God of creation. The second part celebrates the law, God's gift to Israel. The two parts, which superficially have little to do with each other, are actually a celebration of the fact that God created the world in and through wisdom as expressed in the law.

The part of the psalm that we are using gives a series of synonyms for the law and its goodness. It is interesting that there are only six references to the LORD in this section. That is unusual for the perfect number in the Bible is seven, and one would expect the psalmist to speak of the LORD seven times. The seventh reference to the LORD occurs at the end of the psalm where the law is "the words of my mouth and the meditation of my heart." The law is only perfect when it is interiorized.

℟. **Lord, you have the words of everlasting life.**

The law of the LORD is perfect,
  refreshing the soul;
the decree of the LORD is trustworthy,
  giving wisdom to the simple.

℟. **Lord, you have the words of everlasting life.**

The precepts of the LORD are right,
  rejoicing the heart;
the command of the LORD is clear,
  enlightening the eye.

℟. **Lord, you have the words of everlasting life.**

The fear of the LORD is pure,
  enduring forever;
the ordinances of the LORD are true,
  all of them just.

℟. **Lord, you have the words of everlasting life.**

They are more precious than gold,
  than a heap of purest gold;
sweeter also than syrup
  or honey from the comb.

℟. **Lord, you have the words of everlasting life.**

SEVENTH READING: Ezekiel 36:16-17a, 18-28

I shall sprinkle clean water upon you and I shall give you a new heart.

God had intended the covenant with Israel to be an eternal covenant, but the people of Israel had violated God's commandments so insolently that God allowed them to be punished for their iniquities. They deserved everything they received in being led into exile in Babylon.

A reading from the Book of the Prophet Ezekiel

The word of the LORD came to me, saying:
  Son of man, when the house of Israel lived in
    their land,
  they defiled it by their conduct and deeds.
Therefore I poured out my fury upon them
  because of the blood that they poured out on the
    ground,
  and because they defiled it with idols.

In this reading from the Book of the Prophet Ezekiel we hear that God was removing the punishment that he had allowed his people to suffer. Yet, this reading makes it clear that he is not relenting because they deserve his mercy.

If anything, their conduct had been worse since they were exiled. The very fact that they were led into exile had been a source of embarrassment to God for his name had been profaned among the pagans (for the pagans said that it was God's fault that his people had ended up this way).

Therefore, God would forgive his people and give them a new beginning. It could not simply be a continuation of what had been going on. It had to be a whole new start. The covenant that God had made with Israel had been degraded by Israel's sins. A new covenant was their only hope.

God would put a new heart and a new spirit within them. Henceforth they would no longer follow the law superficially; they would live it with great fervor because it had been interiorized.

We must remember that the rebirth that we are celebrating this evening is not due to anything that we have done. God is showing us an astounding mercy in allowing us to be reborn in his Spirit. Tonight we should be filled with a profound sense of gratitude and awe for God has been so gracious to us.

I scattered them among the nations,
　　dispersing them over foreign lands;
　　according to their conduct and deeds I judged them.
But when they came among the nations wherever
　　they came,
　　they served to profane my holy name,
　　because it was said of them: "These are the people
　　　　of the LORD,
　　yet they had to leave their land."
So I have relented because of my holy name
　　which the house of Israel profaned
　　among the nations where they came.
Therefore say to the house of Israel: Thus says the
　　Lord GOD:
　　Not for your sakes do I act, house of Israel,
　　but for the sake of my holy name,
　　which you profaned among the nations to which
　　　　you came.
I will prove the holiness of my great name, profaned
　　among the nations,
　　in whose midst you have profaned it.
Thus the nations shall know that I am the LORD,
　　says the Lord GOD,
　　when in their sight I prove my holiness through
　　　　you.
For I will take you away from among the nations,
　　gather you from all the foreign lands,
　　and bring you back to your own land.
I will sprinkle clean water upon you
　　to cleanse you from all your impurities,
　　and from all your idols I will cleanse you.
I will give you a new heart and place a new spirit
　　within you,
　　taking from your bodies your stony hearts
　　and giving you natural hearts.
I will put my spirit within you and make you live by
　　my statutes,
　　careful to observe my decrees.

We celebrate the new covenant that Jesus inaugurated with his death and resurrection.

Lect. No. 41

You shall live in the land I gave your fathers;
  you shall be my people, and I will be your God.

The word of the Lord.

RESPONSORIAL PSALM:

When Baptism is celebrated, responsorial psalm A is used; when Baptism is not celebrated, responsorial psalm B or C is used.

 Ps 42:3, 5; 43:3, 4 (℟.: 42:2)

Psalms 42 and 43 were probably originally written as one lamentation psalm. Here we use selected verses from the two psalms to add to the spirit of joy and desire for the things of the LORD.

This psalm was probably written by a priest or Levite. It speaks of the incredible joy that he felt when he celebrated the liturgy of the LORD. This was, for him, the greatest reward for all that he did. Its memory was all that gave him hope in times of suffering.

He even speaks of his desire for the LORD as being a thirst, like the deer that longs for running water. We have to remember that this was written in a highly arid climate, and water was the difference between life and death.

This evening we could say that our relationship with God is the difference for us between life that is meaningful and an existence that has no ultimate meaning.

Thus, as we either make or renew our baptismal promises, we vow ourselves to life in God.

When Baptism is celebrated

℟. **Like a deer that longs for running streams, my soul longs for you, my God.**

Athirst is my soul for God, the living God.
  When shall I go and behold the face of God?

℟. **Like a deer that longs for running streams, my soul longs for you, my God.**

I went with the throng
  and led them in procession to the house of God,
amid loud cries of joy and thanksgiving,
  with the multitude keeping festival.

℟. **Like a deer that longs for running streams, my soul longs for you, my God.**

Send forth your light and your fidelity;
  they shall lead me on
and bring me to your holy mountain,
  to your dwelling-place.

℟. **Like a deer that longs for running streams, my soul longs for you, my God.**

Then will I go in to the altar of God,
  the God of my gladness and joy;
then will I give you thanks upon the harp,
  O God, my God!

℟. **Like a deer that longs for running streams, my soul longs for you, my God.**

B

Isaiah 12:2-3, 4bcd, 5-6 (℟.: 3)

When Baptism is not celebrated

In our readings this evening we have celebrated our creation, our call, and our rebirth in the new covenant written upon our hearts and our spirits.

These are all ways that God has shown himself to be our savior. And God continues to be our savior for he continues to protect us from our enemies.

Therefore, we proclaim his name and glory before all the nations. This is especially important considering what we have just read: that our conduct often gives scandal and betrays our commitment to the covenant.

People know that we call ourselves Christian, but all too often we fail to live as such. We have to make our words and actions powerful witnesses to God's love and mercy. We have to become more of what we say we are: people whose every word and deed shows them to be followers of Christ.

℟. **You will draw water joyfully from the springs of salvation.**

God indeed is my savior;
    I am confident and unafraid.
My strength and my courage is the LORD,
    and he has been my savior.
With joy you will draw water
    at the fountain of salvation.

℟. **You will draw water joyfully from the springs of salvation.**

Give thanks to the LORD, acclaim his name;
    among the nations make known his deeds,
    proclaim how exalted is his name.

℟. **You will draw water joyfully from the springs of salvation.**

Sing praise to the LORD for his glorious achievement;
    let this be known throughout all the earth.
Shout with exultation, O city of Zion,
    for great in your midst
    is the Holy One of Israel!

℟. **You will draw water joyfully from the springs of salvation.**

C

Ps 51:12-13, 14-15, 18-19 (℟.: 12a)

When Baptism is not celebrated

Our last reading spoke about the rebirth that God offers us, for he places a new heart and a new spirit within us.

This psalm is a penitential psalm that speaks of the need for this rebirth. We cannot hope to turn from sin if we do

℟. **Create a clean heart in me, O God.**

A clean heart create for me, O God,
    and a steadfast spirit renew within me.
Cast me not out from your presence,
    and your Holy Spirit take not from me.

℟. **Create a clean heart in me, O God.**

not receive the grace to do so from God.

We, for our part, must admit our brokenness and need. We cannot be arrogant, pretending that we can do it all by ourselves. We have to have humble and contrite hearts.

In this psalm we also promise to be instruments of God's mercy, for we will share our insights into his mercy with those who do not yet know how much he loves them.

Give me back the joy of your salvation,
  and a willing spirit sustain in me.
I will teach transgressors your ways,
  and sinners shall return to you.

℟. **Create a clean heart in me, O God.**

For you are not pleased with sacrifices;
  should I offer a holocaust, you would not accept it.
My sacrifice, O God, is a contrite spirit;
  a heart contrite and humbled, O God, you will not spurn.

℟. **Create a clean heart in me, O God.**

Lect.
No. 41

EPISTLE: Romans 6:3-11

Christ, raised from the dead, dies no more.

When Jesus rose from the dead, he was not reanimated like Lazarus and the widow of Naim's son. They were brought back to life, but one day they would die anew. They were still subject to all of the limitations of this mortal existence.

That was not the case with Jesus. When he rose from the dead, he received a glorified body that no longer suffers from the limitations of this world. He will no longer die. He is so filled with the life of God that death no longer has any power over him.

When we were baptized, we died to this world in order to live with Christ. Saint Paul speaks of being crucified to this world. We have rejected our previous life-style in which we were slaves to sin. We have chosen to live Christ's life and love. But now we have to live in a manner that is consistent with this choice.

A reading from the Letter of Saint Paul to the Romans

Brothers and sisters:
  Are you unaware that we who were baptized into Christ Jesus
were baptized into his death?
We were indeed buried with him through baptism into death,
  so that, just as Christ was raised from the dead
  by the glory of the Father,
  we too might live in newness of life.

For if we have grown into union with him through a death like his,
  we shall also be united with him in the resurrection.
We know that our old self was crucified with him,
  so that our sinful body might be done away with,
  that we might no longer be in slavery to sin.
For a dead person has been absolved from sin.
If, then, we have died with Christ,
  we believe that we shall also live with him.

This means that we have to continue to live as if we are dead to sin. Saying yes to God also means saying no to those things that keep us from union with him. When we are weak and feel ourselves slipping back into our old ways, we must reach out to the one who has died so that we might live in him, Jesus our Lord.

We know that Christ, raised from the dead, dies no
    more;
    death no longer has power over him.
As to his death, he died to sin once and for all;
    as to his life, he lives for God.
Consequently, you too must think of yourselves as
    being dead to sin
    and living for God in Christ Jesus.

The word of the Lord.

| Lect. |
| No. 41 |

RESPONSORIAL PSALM: Ps 118:1-2, 16-17, 22-23

How could we possibly express our gratitude to someone who was willing to die for us? Words fail. And yet we cannot but try to thank God for his incredible mercy.

Therefore, we live to praise God. Every moment of our lives must be lived as a response to God's gift of life. Furthermore, God does not just give us life: God gives us life filled with meaning and love.

The third section of our Responsorial Psalm speaks of a stone rejected by the builders becoming the cornerstone. This reminds us of the stone that held the cross (for it was a stone left by the builders in a quarry) and also that we ourselves were once rejected but have now become part of God's building, the Church.

℟. **Alleluia, alleluia, alleluia.**

Give thanks to the LORD, for he is good,
    for his mercy endures forever.
Let the house of Israel say,
    "His mercy endures forever."

℟. **Alleluia, alleluia, alleluia.**

"The right hand of the LORD has struck with power;
    the right hand of the LORD is exalted.
I shall not die, but live,
    and declare the works of the LORD."

℟. **Alleluia, alleluia, alleluia.**

The stone which the builders rejected
    has become the cornerstone.
By the LORD has this been done;
    it is wonderful in our eyes.

℟. **Alleluia, alleluia, alleluia.**

PASTORAL REFLECTIONS

The word Alleluia means praise (Hallel) to Yahweh (ya).

Lect.
No. 41

GOSPEL: Luke 24:1-12

Why do you seek the Living One among the dead?

All of the accounts agree that the women went to the tomb very early on Sunday morning (from the description, after one could see light on the horizon but before one could see the sun).

They disagree on the number of women. Luke speaks of a number of women. This is typical of Luke, who always emphasizes the role of women in his Gospel.

Jesus had already risen when the women arrive. They must believe because of what others tell them (just as we must believe because of what we have heard from others).

This is why the account speaks of two men in dazzling garments. They are obviously angels, but it calls them "men" to remind us that we receive our faith through others.

All of the resurrection accounts in Luke speak of how this was all a fulfillment of what had been foretold in Scripture. Jesus was only fulfilling what had been ordained by the Father.

The fact that the disciples do not believe the account of the women seems to be a bit of a criticism of the disciples. God chose the women to be true proclaimers of the resurrection, but that was not enough for these men.

A reading from the holy Gospel according to Luke

At daybreak on the first day of the week the women who had come from Galilee with Jesus
took the spices they had prepared
and went to the tomb.
They found the stone rolled away from the tomb;
but when they entered,
they did not find the body of the Lord Jesus.
While they were puzzling over this, behold,
two men in dazzling garments appeared to them.
They were terrified and bowed their faces to the ground.
They said to them,
"Why do you seek the living one among the dead?
He is not here, but he has been raised.
Remember what he said to you while he was still in Galilee,
that the Son of Man must be handed over to sinners
and be crucified, and rise on the third day."
And they remembered his words.
Then they returned from the tomb
and announced all these things to the eleven
and to all the others.
The women were Mary Magdalene, Joanna, and Mary the mother of James;
the others who accompanied them also told this to the apostles,
but their story seemed like nonsense
and they did not believe them.
But Peter got up and ran to the tomb,
bent down, and saw the burial cloths alone;
then he went home amazed at what had happened.

The Gospel of the Lord.

March 31, 2013

EASTER SUNDAY OF

THE RESURRECTION OF THE LORD

Lect. No. 42 FIRST READING: Acts 10:34a, 37-43

We ate and drank with him after he rose from the dead.

Our First Reading is taken from the speech that Saint Peter gave when he was called to the house of Cornelius, a Roman centurion whom God had led to conversion.

The speech is a form of the "kerygma," the first preaching that the apostles would proclaim concerning the life and mission of Jesus. Unlike Saint Paul's version, which often centered exclusively on the death and resurrection of Jesus, this one includes many of the elements of Jesus' earthly mission.

This is what one would expect, given the fact that Paul only knew the resurrected Jesus while Peter followed Jesus during his public ministry.

In proclaiming this kerygma, Peter is fulfilling his mission, which we hear outlined in this reading: Jesus commissioned them to be his witnesses and to preach the Good News to the nations. They were to continue the work of the prophets to proclaim the Word of the Lord in word and deed.

A reading from the Acts of the Apostles

Peter proceeded to speak and said:
"You know what has happened all over Judea,
beginning in Galilee after the baptism
that John preached,
how God anointed Jesus of Nazareth
with the Holy Spirit and power.
He went about doing good
and healing all those oppressed by the devil,
for God was with him.
We are witnesses of all that he did
both in the country of the Jews and in Jerusalem.
They put him to death by hanging him on a tree.
This man God raised on the third day and granted
that he be visible,
not to all the people, but to us,
the witnesses chosen by God in advance,
who ate and drank with him after he rose from
the dead.
He commissioned us to preach to the people
and testify that he is the one appointed by God
as judge of the living and the dead.
To him all the prophets bear witness,
that everyone who believes in him
will receive forgiveness of sins through his name."

The word of the Lord.

Lect.
No. 42

RESPONSORIAL PSALM: Ps 118:1-2, 16-17, 22-23 (℟.: 24)

Psalm 118 speaks about power and mercy. These are not two ideas that we would naturally associate, but it gives us an important insight into what mercy really is.

We often think of mercy as something that is gentle and even weak. But true mercy is a strong and courageous virtue.

Mercy does not avoid the truth. It fully recognizes that there are difficulties and yet forgives. It loves the other into healing. Mercy always ends up upon the cross.

This is Gospel truth. The world tells us that we can force others to do what we want them to do. Therefore, we sometimes try to use force to bring them to conversion.

God, on the other hand, realizes that you cannot force love. The only way to bring people to true love is by loving them over and over again. They do not deserve that love, but they need it. This is true mercy.

The Lord Jesus, through his cross and resurrection, has destroyed the power of sin and death and brought us into his life. He has taken what the world would consider a defeat and turned it into a powerful victory. This is truly the day the Lord has made, and we are filled with joy.

℟. **This is the day the Lord has made; let us rejoice and be glad.**

or:

℟. **Alleluia.**

Give thanks to the Lord, for he is good,
   for his mercy endures forever.
Let the house of Israel say,
   "His mercy endures forever."

℟. **This is the day the Lord has made; let us rejoice and be glad.**

or:

℟. **Alleluia.**

"The right hand of the Lord has struck with power;
   the right hand of the Lord is exalted.
I shall not die, but live,
   and declare the works of the Lord."

℟. **This is the day the Lord has made; let us rejoice and be glad.**

or:

℟. **Alleluia.**

The stone which the builders rejected
   has become the cornerstone.
By the Lord has this been done;
   it is wonderful in our eyes.

℟. **This is the day the Lord has made; let us rejoice and be glad.**

or:

℟. **Alleluia.**

SECOND READING

Lect.
No. 42

A Colossians 3:1-4

Seek what is above, where Christ is.

In this passage from the Letter to the Colossians, we are reminded of the consequences of our Baptismal commitment that we renew today.

If we have died with Christ in order to rise with him, then we must live in a manner that is consistent with that choice.

The reward we will receive is that when Jesus returns at the end of time, we will share in his glory. We will live with him and in him for all eternity.

A reading from the Letter of Saint Paul
to the Colossians

Brothers and sisters:
If then you were raised with Christ, seek what is above,
where Christ is seated at the right hand of God.
Think of what is above, not of what is on earth.
For you have died, and your life is hidden with Christ in God.
When Christ your life appears,
then you too will appear with him in glory.

The word of the Lord.

OR: B 1 Corinthians 5:6b-8

Clear out the old yeast, so that you may become a fresh batch of dough.

Saint Paul uses Passover symbolism to talk about the choices that we must make as Christians. Part of the Passover ceremony is to throw out all traces of leavened products at the beginning of the festival of unleavened bread.

We have experienced a new Passover: the death and resurrection of Jesus. With him we have passed over from death to life. We must reject all the traces of death (e.g., sin, hate, etc.) that can still be found in our conduct. We must live for and in Jesus, our Lord and our all.

A reading from the first Letter of Saint Paul
to the Corinthians

Brothers and sisters:
Do you not know that a little yeast leavens all the dough?
Clear out the old yeast,
so that you may become a fresh batch of dough,
inasmuch as you are unleavened.
For our paschal lamb, Christ, has been sacrificed.
Therefore, let us celebrate the feast,
not with the old yeast, the yeast of malice and wickedness,
but with the unleavened bread of sincerity and truth.

The word of the Lord.

Lect. No. 42

SEQUENCE: *Victimae paschali laudes*

Sequences are ancient poems written to celebrate some of the major feasts of the liturgical year. This particular Sequence is filled with Easter symbolism. Jesus the Paschal Lamb is also the shepherd (many ancient churches in Europe have mosaics that depict a lamb in the center of a flock).

Jesus the sinless one redeems us from our sin. Life and death collide on the cross. Death thinks itself victorious, but it has been defeated by love that gives life eternal.

The second part of the Sequence creates a dialogue between the Sequence's narrator and Mary of Magdala. She is encouraged to give witness to what she had seen at the tomb.

We call upon the risen Christ, our victorious King, to have mercy on us.

Christians, to the Paschal Victim
    Offer your thankful praises!
A Lamb the sheep redeems;
    Christ, who only is sinless,
    Reconciles sinners to the Father.
Death and life have contended in that combat stupendous:
    The Prince of life, who died, reigns immortal.
Speak, Mary, declaring
    What you saw, wayfaring.
"The tomb of Christ, who is living,
    The glory of Jesus' resurrection;
Bright angels attesting,
    The shroud and napkin resting.
Yes, Christ my hope is arisen;
    To Galilee he goes before you."
Christ indeed from death is risen, our new life obtaining.
    Have mercy, victor King, ever reigning!
    Amen. Alleluia.

Lect. No. 42

ALLELUIA: cf. 1 Corinthians 5:7b-8a

For the first time in many weeks we proclaim the Alleluia Verse. We celebrate Jesus who is our Paschal Lamb and who died out of love for us.

℟. **Alleluia, alleluia.**

Christ, our paschal lamb, has been sacrificed;
let us then feast with joy in the Lord.

℟. **Alleluia, alleluia.**

PASTORAL REFLECTIONS

Christ is both the Lamb that is sacrificed and the priest who offers that sacrifice on the altar of the cross.

At an afternoon or evening Mass, another Gospel may be read: Luke 24:13-35, pp. 212-213.

The Gospel from the Easter Vigil, p. 206, may also be read in place of the following Gospel at any time of the day.

<table>
<tr><td>

Lect.
No. 42

</td><td>

GOSPEL: John 20:1-9

He had to rise from the dead.

</td></tr>
</table>

In the Gospel of John only one woman goes to the tomb on the morning of the resurrection: Mary of Magdala. She represents the Church who is seeking her savior. She is the first to give witness to the resurrection and is often called the proto-apostle.

She runs to Peter and the beloved disciple and announces that Jesus is no longer in the tomb (she has not yet encountered the risen Jesus and therefore does not yet understand what has happened).

Peter and the beloved disciple run to the tomb. The latter arrives first, but waits at the entrance until Peter can arrive. The beloved disciple arrived first because he was running with his heart (he deeply loved the savior). He waited to enter because love bows to authority (represented by Peter).

Peter enters and sees, while the beloved disciple enters, sees, and believes (his heart leads him to faith). The beloved disciple is not named for, at one level, he represents all of us. Today we all run to the tomb to give witness to the resurrection of Jesus, our Lord and our God, from the dead.

A reading from the holy Gospel according to John

On the first day of the week,
    Mary of Magdala came to the tomb early in the morning,
    while it was still dark,
    and saw the stone removed from the tomb.
So she ran and went to Simon Peter
    and to the other disciple whom Jesus loved, and told them,
    "They have taken the Lord from the tomb,
    and we don't know where they put him."
So Peter and the other disciple went out and came to the tomb.
They both ran, but the other disciple ran faster than Peter
    and arrived at the tomb first;
    he bent down and saw the burial cloths there, but did not go in.
When Simon Peter arrived after him,
    he went into the tomb and saw the burial cloths there,
    and the cloth that had covered his head,
    not with the burial cloths but rolled up in a separate place.
Then the other disciple also went in,
    the one who had arrived at the tomb first,
    and he saw and believed.
For they did not yet understand the Scripture
    that he had to rise from the dead.

The Gospel of the Lord.

GOSPEL: Luke 24:13-35

They recognized Jesus in the breaking of bread.

The Gospel of Luke is one of the most artistic Gospels in presenting the life and mission of Jesus. It often has symbolic scenes that are both incredibly beautiful and powerfully meaningful. This is especially true of the account of the resurrection.

Luke presents three resurrection narratives to speak of what happened when Jesus rose and what it means to us.

In the first scene, the women go to the tomb and see the empty grave and speak with the two angels ("men dressed in shining clothes"), but they do not see the risen Jesus.

Today we hear the second scene, the road to Emmaus. Here the two disciples encounter Jesus in the breaking of the bread (a symbol for the celebration of the Eucharist) and the explanation of the word (for the disciples' hearts burned inside of them when he explained Scripture).

The third scene presents Jesus who appears to his disciples in the flesh.

These three scenes are a paradigm for the Christian life. At first we hear about Jesus from others. Then we come to meet him in word and sacrament. Finally, as our faith grows, we meet him face to face.

Typical of Luke, all three accounts include an explanation of how all that happened to Jesus was in fulfillment of God's plan and had been foretold in the law and prophets.

A reading from the holy Gospel according to Luke

That very day, the first day of the week,
two of Jesus' disciples were going
    to a village seven miles from Jerusalem called Emmaus,
    and they were conversing about all the things that
        had occurred.
And it happened that while they were conversing and
        debating,
    Jesus himself drew near and walked with them,
    but their eyes were prevented from recognizing him.
He asked them,
    "What are you discussing as you walk along?"
They stopped, looking downcast.
One of them, named Cleopas, said to him in reply,
    "Are you the only visitor to Jerusalem
    who does not know of the things
    that have taken place there in these days?"
And he replied to them, "What sort of things?"
They said to him,
    "The things that happened to Jesus the Nazarene,
    who was a prophet mighty in deed and word
    before God and all the people,
    how our chief priests and rulers both handed him
        over
    to a sentence of death and crucified him.
But we were hoping that he would be the one to
        redeem Israel;
    and besides all this,
    it is now the third day since this took place.
Some women from our group, however, have astounded us:
    they were at the tomb early in the morning
    and did not find his body;
    they came back and reported
    that they had indeed seen a vision of angels
    who announced that he was alive.

The phrase, "the breaking of the bread," was a liturgical phrase in use at the end of the first century A.D. Thus, when early Christian readers would read this phrase in this story, they would immediately associate it with the celebration of the Eucharist.

We should notice in this account that Jesus seems to appear in two different places at the same time (for while he was speaking with the disciples on the road to Emmaus, he was also appearing to Simon Peter in Jerusalem). Our glorified body will not be subject to the limitations of this earthly body. We will not be limited by time and space. We will not suffer from illness or death. Even our emotions will be purified. Our love will not be tinged by jealousy or confusion. We will be able to love as God himself loves.

We should also notice that the disciples do not recognize Jesus until late in the story. In some resurrection narratives, the disciples immediately recognize Jesus. In others, he is not recognized (Emmaus, Mary of Magdala in the garden, and by the sea in John 21). Jesus' risen body (and ours) is a continuity of his earthly body, but it is also changed and glorified.

The disciples speak of how their hearts burned within them while Jesus explained Scripture along the way. Even before Jesus broke bread with them, he was present to them in the word of God.

As we celebrate the Eucharist today, we meet Jesus in both of these moments: the breaking of the word and the breaking of the bread.

Then some of those with us went to the tomb
and found things just as the women had described,
but him they did not see."
And he said to them, "Oh, how foolish you are!
How slow of heart to believe all that the prophets spoke!
Was it not necessary that the Christ should suffer these things
and enter into his glory?"
Then beginning with Moses and all the prophets,
he interpreted to them what referred to him
in all the Scriptures.
As they approached the village to which they were going,
he gave the impression that he was going on farther.
But they urged him, "Stay with us,
for it is nearly evening and the day is almost over."
So he went in to stay with them.
And it happened that, while he was with them at table,
he took bread, said the blessing,
broke it, and gave it to them.
With that their eyes were opened and they recognized him,
but he vanished from their sight.
Then they said to each other,
"Were not our hearts burning within us
while he spoke to us on the way and opened the Scriptures to us?"
So they set out at once and returned to Jerusalem
where they found gathered together
the eleven and those with them who were saying,
"The Lord has truly been raised and has appeared to Simon!"
Then the two recounted
what had taken place on the way
and how he was made known to them in the breaking of bread.

The Gospel of the Lord.

April 7, 2013

SECOND SUNDAY OF EASTER
(OR OF DIVINE MERCY)

Lect.
No. 45

FIRST READING: Acts 5:12-16

More than ever, believers in the Lord,
great numbers of men and women, were added to them.

The First Reading speaks of the success of the early mission of the apostles. Even though people were frightened by what the leaders of the Jews might do to those who listened to or joined the disciples, they nevertheless recognized that the Lord was working through them.

God would not allow humans to obstruct the spread of the Good News.

Note that the apostles continued to go to the temple to pray throughout the early days of the Church. As far as we can tell, they continued to pray there until right before its destruction by the Romans in 70 A.D.

They considered themselves to be Jews until they were expelled from the synagogues (probably in the mid 80's).

A reading from the Acts of the Apostles

Many signs and wonders were done among the people
　at the hands of the apostles.
They were all together in Solomon's portico.
None of the others dared to join them, but the people esteemed them.
Yet more than ever, believers in the Lord,
　great numbers of men and women, were added to them.
Thus they even carried the sick out into the streets
　and laid them on cots and mats
　so that when Peter came by,
　at least his shadow might fall on one or another of them.
A large number of people from the towns
　in the vicinity of Jerusalem also gathered,
　bringing the sick and those disturbed by unclean spirits,
　and they were all cured.

The word of the Lord.

PASTORAL REFLECTIONS

We see a continuity between the mission of Jesus and that of the apostles. They preach about Jesus and thus make him present in word and sacrament. It should therefore not be surprising that they could perform deeds of wonder that would bring people to faith.

It should make us ask whether these miracles were reserved to a particular time and place, or if they still continue in our days.

RESPONSORIAL PSALM: Ps 118:2-4, 13-15, 22-24 (℟.: 1)

The Responsorial Psalm reminds us that this is a time of mercy and gratitude (especially because this is Divine Mercy Sunday).

We celebrate the fact that Jesus took our sins upon himself and suffered and died for us. We did not deserve this, but God acted on our behalf and did for us what we could not do for ourselves.

He has conquered sin, and alienation, and even death. This fills us with an incredible sense of gratitude.

The last section of the psalm speaks of the stone that had been rejected by the builders. As we saw during Holy Week, the place where they fixed the cross on the hill of Golgotha was probably a stone that had been rejected by the builders of the walls of Jerusalem because it had a natural flaw in it (a crack in which the cross was placed).

When the followers of Jesus saw this, they remembered this verse from Psalm 118 and saw it fulfilled in what was happening.

They then also applied it to Jesus himself who was rejected, but who served as the foundation of a new edifice, the Kingdom of God, which is even now dawning in our midst.

℟. **Give thanks to the Lord for he is good, his love is everlasting.**

or:

℟. **Alleluia.**

Let the house of Israel say,
  "His mercy endures forever."
Let the house of Aaron say,
  "His mercy endures forever."
Let those who fear the LORD say,
  "His mercy endures forever."

℟. **Give thanks to the Lord for he is good, his love is everlasting.**

or:

℟. **Alleluia.**

I was hard pressed and was falling,
  but the LORD helped me.
My strength and my courage is the LORD,
  and he has been my savior.
The joyful shout of victory
  in the tents of the just:

℟. **Give thanks to the Lord for he is good, his love is everlasting.**

or:

℟. **Alleluia.**

The stone which the builders rejected
  has become the cornerstone.
By the LORD has this been done;
  it is wonderful in our eyes.
This is the day the LORD has made;
  let us be glad and rejoice in it.

℟. **Give thanks to the Lord for he is good, his love is everlasting.**

or:

℟. **Alleluia.**

SECOND READING: Revelation 1:9-11a, 12-13, 17-19

I was dead, but now I am alive forever and ever.

The Second Reading presents images taken from the beginning of the Book of Revelation.

John receives this vision on the Lord's Day, Sunday. The switch from worshiping God on the Sabbath to worshiping God on Sunday occurred very early in the history of the Church.

We encounter one who is like the Son of Man (Jesus). He is wearing an ankle-length robe with a gold sash (or breast-plate).

These are clothes that one would find on the high priest, for Jesus is our high priest.

The visionary reacts with fear, for he recognizes that he is in the presence of something very holy, something that is beyond his understanding.

Jesus calms him and speaks of how he once was dead and now he is alive forever (for the resurrection means that he has a glorified body, a body that is not subject to the limitations of this earthly body).

He has conquered death forever and offers us the gift of eternal life (he holds the keys to death).

A reading from the Book of Revelation

I, John, your brother, who share with you
　the distress, the kingdom, and the endurance we
　have in Jesus,
　found myself on the island called Patmos
　because I proclaimed God's word and gave testi-
　mony to Jesus.
I was caught up in spirit on the Lord's day
　and heard behind me a voice as loud as a trumpet,
　which said,
"Write on a scroll what you see."
Then I turned to see whose voice it was that spoke
　to me,
　and when I turned, I saw seven gold lampstands
　and in the midst of the lampstands one like a son
　of man,
　wearing an ankle-length robe, with a gold sash
　around his chest.

When I caught sight of him, I fell down at his feet as
　though dead.
He touched me with his right hand and said, "Do not
　be afraid.
I am the first and the last, the one who lives.
Once I was dead, but now I am alive forever and
　ever.
I hold the keys to death and the netherworld.
Write down, therefore, what you have seen,
　and what is happening, and what will happen af-
　terwards."

The word of the Lord.

The Alleluia Verse speaks of us. We have not seen the risen Jesus, we have not touched him with our hands. Yet we have believed in him because of what others have told us, and because we have experienced his love.

ALLELUIA: John 20:29

℟. **Alleluia, alleluia.**

You believe in me, Thomas, because you have seen me, says the Lord;
blessed are they who have not seen me, but still believe!

℟. **Alleluia, alleluia.**

Lect. No. 45

GOSPEL: John 20:19-31

Eight days later Jesus came and stood in their midst.

The Gospel presents two encounters with the risen Jesus.

In the first, Jesus appears to the disciples on the evening of Easter Sunday. He greets them with the phrase, "Peace be with you."

This peace, *Shalom* in Hebrew, is a peace that goes beyond an absence of turmoil.

It is a peace so profound that no one can steal it away from us.

Jesus also breathes on the disciples. When God created Adam, he breathed upon a lump of clay and made it into a living human being.

Something of God, God's own breath or Spirit, is inside of us. When we sin, we reject that breath of the Holy One.

A reading from the holy Gospel according to John

On the evening of that first day of the week,
when the doors were locked, where the disciples were,
for fear of the Jews,
Jesus came and stood in their midst
and said to them, "Peace be with you."
When he had said this, he showed them his hands and his side.
The disciples rejoiced when they saw the Lord.
Jesus said to them again, "Peace be with you.
As the Father has sent me, so I send you."
And when he had said this, he breathed on them and said to them,
"Receive the Holy Spirit.
Whose sins you forgive are forgiven them,
and whose sins you retain are retained."

Thomas, called Didymus, one of the Twelve,
was not with them when Jesus came.
So the other disciples said to him, "We have seen the Lord."

Now, Jesus is recreating us by placing that breath, the Spirit of God, back inside of us. That Spirit enables us to be instruments of the forgiveness of sins (for the Spirit is the love of God that fills us with God's mercy).

The second account concerns Thomas. He did not believe what the others had told him about Jesus. His story is a lesson to all of us who will not see the risen Jesus until we die and meet him face to face. In the meantime, we must trust and believe what others have told us about him.

There is also a dimension to the story that reminds us that Jesus truly did have a body after he had risen from the dead (for Thomas could touch him). An early heresy called Docetism tried to deny this.

Finally, at the end of today's Gospel we hear the stated purpose for the writing of the entire Gospel: that we believe that Jesus is the Son of God.

This belief is the source of our life, for when Jesus is part of our lives, we are truly alive.

But he said to them,
   "Unless I see the mark of the nails in his hands
   and put my finger into the nailmarks
   and put my hand into his side, I will not believe."

Now a week later his disciples were again inside
   and Thomas was with them.
Jesus came, although the doors were locked,
   and stood in their midst and said, "Peace be with you."
Then he said to Thomas, "Put your finger here and see my hands,
   and bring your hand and put it into my side,
   and do not be unbelieving, but believe."
Thomas answered and said to him, "My Lord and my God!"
Jesus said to him, "Have you come to believe because you have seen me?
Blessed are those who have not seen and have believed."

Now, Jesus did many other signs in the presence of his disciples
   that are not written in this book.
But these are written that you may come to believe
   that Jesus is the Christ, the Son of God,
   and that through this belief you may have life in his name.

The Gospel of the Lord.

PASTORAL REFLECTIONS

There are many things in our lives that we cannot see or measure, yet we believe that they exist. We have never seen a virus with our own eyes, yet we believe that viruses exist. We have never seen a gravity wave, but we believe that gravity exists (for we have seen the effects of gravity). We have never seen love in its pure form. We cannot measure it, but we believe that it exists. Likewise, Jesus challenges us to trust in the mysteries of our faith.

THIRD SUNDAY OF EASTER

Lect. No. 48 **FIRST READING: Acts 5:27-32, 40b-41**

We are witnesses of these words as is the Holy Spirit.

The First Readings of the Sundays after Easter are not taken from the Old Testament. They contain stories from the Acts of the Apostles and present the history of the early Church.

In today's passage, Peter and John are interrogated concerning their preaching (they had been ordered by the Sanhedrin not to preach in the name of Jesus). The apostles refused to be silenced, for they were being guided by the Holy Spirit.

The apostles do not view their trial as a setback. They use even this occasion to give a short version of the kerygma, the early preaching of the Church. They are using their own persecution as an opportunity to further their Gospel mission. In fact, the apostles rejoice that they were given the privilege of suffering for the Gospel.

This is a challenge to each of us, for we have to have the courage to give witness to our faith, no matter what the consequences might be.

A reading from the Acts of the Apostles

When the captain and the court officers had brought the apostles in
and made them stand before the Sanhedrin,
the high priest questioned them,
"We gave you strict orders, did we not,
to stop teaching in that name?
Yet you have filled Jerusalem with your teaching
and want to bring this man's blood upon us."
But Peter and the apostles said in reply,
"We must obey God rather than men.
The God of our ancestors raised Jesus,
though you had him killed by hanging him on a tree.
God exalted him at his right hand as leader and savior
to grant Israel repentance and forgiveness of sins.
We are witnesses of these things,
as is the Holy Spirit whom God has given to those who obey him."

The Sanhedrin ordered the apostles
to stop speaking in the name of Jesus, and dismissed them.
So they left the presence of the Sanhedrin,
rejoicing that they had been found worthy
to suffer dishonor for the sake of the name.

The word of the Lord.

Lect. No. 48

RESPONSORIAL PSALM: Ps 30:2, 4, 5-6, 11-12, 13 (℟.: 2a)

The Responsorial Psalm continues the theme found in the First Reading: that God can transform events that might be considered to be curses and make them into blessings.

It is interesting that the psalm does not say that God will do away with all of our difficulties. It is assumed that there will be moments of mourning and discouragement and that there will be moments when we suffer the consequences of our sins.

Our hope lies in the fact that God will soon deliver us from our grief, and will always be willing to forgive us our faults.

In these Easter weeks we celebrate the victory of life over death, of light over darkness. This is the reason for mentioning the dawn (the time of the day when Jesus rose from the dead). Yet, we still experience death (our own and the deaths of those whom we love).

We must walk through the dark valley (the difficulties and discouragements of life), but God will never ask us to face these things alone. His love will change our mourning into dancing. We will never be alone again.

℟. **I will praise you, Lord, for you have rescued me.**

or:

℟. **Alleluia.**

I will extol you, O LORD, for you drew me clear
   and did not let my enemies rejoice over me.
O LORD, you brought me up from the netherworld;
   you preserved me from among those going down
     into the pit.

℟. **I will praise you, Lord, for you have rescued me.**

or:

℟. **Alleluia.**

Sing praise to the LORD, you his faithful ones,
   and give thanks to his holy name.
For his anger lasts but a moment;
   a lifetime, his good will.
At nightfall, weeping enters in,
   but with the dawn, rejoicing.

℟. **I will praise you, Lord, for you have rescued me.**

or:

℟. **Alleluia.**

Hear, O LORD, and have pity on me;
   O LORD, be my helper.
You changed my mourning into dancing;
   O LORD, my God, forever will I give you thanks.

℟. **I will praise you, Lord, for you have rescued me.**

or:

℟. **Alleluia.**

Lect. No. 48

SECOND READING: Revelation 5:11-14

Worthy is the Lamb that was slain to receive power and riches.

The Second Reading contains a hymn to praise the Lamb who was slain. Jesus is the Lamb of God who has taken away the sins of the world. (This was a title that even John the Baptist used for him.)

Jesus was totally obedient to the will of the Father, and totally loving to us. For this, he should be praised by every creature in all of creation.

The author applies seven attributes to the Lamb. Seven is the perfect number, so this means that any good thing that we could possibly say should be said about the Lamb.

The one who sits upon the throne is God the Father. The elders represent salvation history, while the four living creatures represent the best and the brightest of creation.

A reading from the Book of Revelation

I, John, looked and heard the voices of many angels who surrounded the throne
    and the living creatures and the elders.
They were countless in number, and they cried out
        in a loud voice:
    "Worthy is the Lamb that was slain
        to receive power and riches, wisdom and
        strength,
        honor and glory and blessing."
Then I heard every creature in heaven and on earth
    and under the earth and in the sea,
    everything in the universe, cry out:
    "To the one who sits on the throne and to the
        Lamb
        be blessing and honor, glory and might,
        forever and ever."
The four living creatures answered, "Amen,"
    and the elders fell down and worshiped.

The word of the Lord.

Lect. No. 48

We celebrate Jesus as the victor over death, the creator of all that exists, and the compassion of God.

ALLELUIA

℟. **Alleluia, alleluia.**

Christ is risen, creator of all;
he has shown pity on all people.

℟. **Alleluia, alleluia.**

Lect. No. 48

GOSPEL: A Longer Form: John 21:1-19

*Jesus came and took the bread and gave it to them
and in like manner the fish.*

The Gospel of John places this account of the miraculous catch of fish after the resurrection.

The Gospel of Matthew, on the other hand, places it at the beginning of Jesus' ministry (where it leads to the call of Peter to be a fisher of men).

Throughout this account, the disciples do not recognize Jesus by sight. Even when they are standing alongside of him, they cannot recognize him (except by faith).

This reminds us that, with the resurrection, Jesus is the same and yet changed. He has a glorified body that is not subject to the limitations of our mortal bodies.

It would be odd to continue to fish after the sun had dawned. The water on the surface of the Sea of Galilee heats up quickly and the fish tend to swim toward the deeper water during the day.

It is the beloved disciple who recognizes Jesus. He is seeing him not with his eyes, but rather with his heart.

Peter, on the other hand, foolishly throws on his clothes and jumps in the water (there are constant negative comparisons between the beloved disciple and Peter throughout the Gospel).

A reading from the holy Gospel according to John

At that time, Jesus revealed himself again to his disciples at the Sea of Tiberias.
He revealed himself in this way.
Together were Simon Peter, Thomas called Didymus,
    Nathanael from Cana in Galilee,
    Zebedee's sons, and two others of his disciples.
Simon Peter said to them, "I am going fishing."
They said to him, "We also will come with you."
So they went out and got into the boat,
    but that night they caught nothing.
When it was already dawn, Jesus was standing on
    the shore;
    but the disciples did not realize that it was Jesus.
Jesus said to them, "Children, have you caught any-
    thing to eat?"
They answered him, "No."
So he said to them, "Cast the net over the right side
    of the boat
    and you will find something."
So they cast it, and were not able to pull it in
    because of the number of fish.
So the disciple whom Jesus loved said to Peter, "It is
    the Lord."
When Simon Peter heard that it was the Lord,
    he tucked in his garment, for he was lightly clad,
    and jumped into the sea.
The other disciples came in the boat,
    for they were not far from shore, only about a
    hundred yards,
    dragging the net with the fish.
When they climbed out on shore,
    they saw a charcoal fire with fish on it and bread.

Jesus serves the disciples fish and bread, reminiscent of the miraculous multiplication of fish and bread in chapter 6. The fish is central here because Jesus is making the disciples fishers of men (as well as the fact that Jesus, the bread of life, is standing in their midst).

This explains the significance of the one hundred and fifty-three fish. Some Greek philosophers believed that this was the number of species of fish in the world. This would mean that the disciples' catch would be universal.

Jesus then turns to Peter and asks whether he loves him. Jesus asks this question three times to remind Peter of his triple denial.

This is an opportunity to heal that terrible failure. It is also a reminder to Peter.

Jesus is asking him to care for his flock. Jesus is the Good Shepherd, and he is now asking Peter to take over that responsibility. He is making Peter his vicar.

But, while Jesus gives Peter this authority, he is reminding him that he is not perfect. Peter, like all of us, has feet of clay, and he will have to depend upon the strength of God.

Jesus twice asks Peter whether he loves him using the word "agape," which is a great and total love. Peter twice responds that he loves him using "phileo," which means that he is his friend.

Jesus said to them, "Bring some of the fish you just caught."

So Simon Peter went over and dragged the net ashore
    full of one hundred fifty-three large fish.

Even though there were so many, the net was not torn.

Jesus said to them, "Come, have breakfast."

And none of the disciples dared to ask him, "Who are you?"
    because they realized it was the Lord.

Jesus came over and took the bread and gave it to them,
    and in like manner the fish.

This was now the third time Jesus was revealed to his disciples
    after being raised from the dead.

When they had finished breakfast, Jesus said to Simon Peter,
    "Simon, son of John, do you love me more than these?"

Simon Peter answered him, "Yes, Lord, you know that I love you."

Jesus said to him, "Feed my lambs."

He then said to Simon Peter a second time,
    "Simon, son of John, do you love me?"

Simon Peter answered him, "Yes, Lord, you know that I love you."

Jesus said to him, "Tend my sheep."

Jesus said to him the third time,
    "Simon, son of John, do you love me?"

Peter was distressed that Jesus had said to him a third time,
    "Do you love me?" and he said to him,
    "Lord, you know everything; you know that I love you."

Jesus said to him, "Feed my sheep.

Finally, Jesus asks Peter whether he loves him using the word "phileo," and Peter responds using the same word.

Some scholars believe that this indicates that Peter was not capable of agape. He was a simple man, and friendship was the best he could do.

Jesus accepted this, for he only asks us to do that which we are capable of doing.

Amen, amen, I say to you, when you were younger,
    you used to dress yourself and go where you wanted;
    but when you grow old, you will stretch out your hands,
    and someone else will dress you
    and lead you where you do not want to go."
He said this signifying by what kind of death he would glorify God.
And when he had said this, he said to him, "Follow me."

The Gospel of the Lord.

Lect. No. 48

GOSPEL: ▣ B Shorter Form: John 21:1-14

Jesus came and took the bread and gave it to them
and in like manner the fish.

The Gospel of John places this account of the miraculous catch of fish after the resurrection.

The Gospel of Matthew, on the other hand, places it at the beginning of Jesus' ministry (where it leads to the call of Peter to be a fisher of men).

Throughout this account, the disciples do not recognize Jesus by sight. Even when they are standing alongside of him, they cannot recognize him (except by faith).

This reminds us that, with the resurrection, Jesus is the same and yet changed. He has a glorified body that is not subject to the limitations of our mortal bodies.

It would be odd to continue to fish after the sun had dawned. The water on the surface of the

A reading from the holy Gospel according to John

At that time, Jesus revealed himself to his disciples at the Sea of Tiberias.
He revealed himself in this way.
Together were Simon Peter, Thomas called Didymus,
    Nathanael from Cana in Galilee,
    Zebedee's sons, and two others of his disciples.
Simon Peter said to them, "I am going fishing."
They said to him, "We also will come with you."
So they went out and got into the boat,
    but that night they caught nothing.
When it was already dawn, Jesus was standing on the shore;
    but the disciples did not realize that it was Jesus.
Jesus said to them, "Children, have you caught anything to eat?"
They answered him, "No."
So he said to them, "Cast the net over the right side of the boat
    and you will find something."

Sea of Galilee heats up quickly and the fish tend to swim toward the deeper water during the day.

It is the beloved disciple who recognizes Jesus. He is seeing him not with his eyes, but rather with his heart.

Peter, on the other hand, foolishly throws on his clothes and jumps in the water (there are constant negative comparisons between the beloved disciple and Peter throughout the Gospel).

Jesus serves the disciples fish and bread, reminiscent of the miraculous multiplication of fish and bread in chapter 6.

The fish is central here because Jesus is making the disciples fishers of men (as well as the fact that Jesus, the bread of life, is standing in their midst).

This explains the significance of the one hundred and fifty-three fish. Some Greek philosophers believed that this was the number of species of fish in the world.

This would mean that the disciples' catch would be universal. This scene is similar to Acts 2 where Peter preaches to people from all over the world on Pentecost Sunday.

So they cast it, and were not able to pull it in
because of the number of fish.
So the disciple whom Jesus loved said to Peter, "It is the Lord."
When Simon Peter heard that it was the Lord,
he tucked in his garment, for he was lightly clad,
and jumped into the sea.
The other disciples came in the boat,
for they were not far from shore, only about a hundred yards,
dragging the net with the fish.
When they climbed out on shore,
they saw a charcoal fire with fish on it and bread.
Jesus said to them, "Bring some of the fish you just caught."
So Simon Peter went over and dragged the net ashore
full of one hundred fifty-three large fish.
Even though there were so many, the net was not torn.
Jesus said to them, "Come, have breakfast."
And none of the disciples dared to ask him, "Who are you?"
because they realized it was the Lord.
Jesus came over and took the bread and gave it to them,
and in like manner the fish.
This was now the third time Jesus was revealed to his disciples
after being raised from the dead.

The Gospel of the Lord.

PASTORAL REFLECTIONS

During the Old Latin Mass, the priest would say, "Ite, Missa est." This means that the people were sent to share the Good News. In the Eucharist, we are so filled with God's love that we feel called to go forth and share it with others.

April 21, 2013

FOURTH SUNDAY OF EASTER

Lect. No. 51 **FIRST READING: Acts 13:14, 43-52**

We now turn to the Gentiles.

The First Reading presents an example of how Saint Paul exercised his ministry throughout Asia Minor and Greece. He first entered the synagogue in whichever city he entered.

There he would preach to the Jews and the God-fearers of the city. (God-fearers were pagans who were sympathetic to the Jewish faith but did not observe the entire law.)

They would listen to Paul for a couple of weeks, but then they would become jealous and reject him.

Paul would then reach out to the pagans of the city. He would often preach to them in the marketplace where crowds would gather during the day.

This served to allow him to address large numbers of people at one time, but also to encounter people of the entire region (for they would come to market with their produce and hear Paul there).

The Gentiles were eager to listen to the kerygma and embrace the Good News. This infuriated the Jews from the synagogue who then incited people against the apostles.

Paul and his companions were inevitably expelled from

A reading from the Acts of the Apostles

Paul and Barnabas continued on from Perga and reached Antioch in Pisidia.
On the sabbath they entered the synagogue and
took their seats.
Many Jews and worshipers who were converts to Judaism
followed Paul and Barnabas, who spoke to them
and urged them to remain faithful to the grace of God.

On the following sabbath almost the whole city gathered
to hear the word of the Lord.
When the Jews saw the crowds, they were filled with jealousy
and with violent abuse contradicted what Paul said.
Both Paul and Barnabas spoke out boldly and said,
"It was necessary that the word of God be spoken to you first,
but since you reject it
and condemn yourselves as unworthy of eternal life,
we now turn to the Gentiles.
For so the Lord has commanded us,
I have made you a light to the Gentiles,
that you may be an instrument of salvation
to the ends of the earth."

The Gentiles were delighted when they heard this
and glorified the word of the Lord.

226

that city. Yet, they had planted the Gospel there and left a small Christian community.

Paul would continue to nourish those communities by writing letters of encouragement and instruction to them. These communities would then share those letters with their neighboring communities.

All of this filled the disciples with joy, for they realized that this was part of God's plan (which was a major theme in Luke's writings). Furthermore, they considered it a privilege to suffer for their faith (for they were then participating in the suffering of Christ).

All who were destined for eternal life came to believe,
> and the word of the Lord continued to spread
> through the whole region.
The Jews, however, incited the women of prominence who were worshipers
> and the leading men of the city,
> stirred up a persecution against Paul and Barnabas,
> and expelled them from their territory.
So they shook the dust from their feet in protest against them,
> and went to Iconium.
The disciples were filled with joy and the Holy Spirit.

The word of the Lord.

Lect. No. 51

RESPONSORIAL PSALM: Ps 100:1-2, 3, 5 (R̸.: 3c)

The Responsorial Psalm celebrates the fact that Jesus is our Good Shepherd and we are the sheep of his flock.

This is the theme that is contained in the Gospel today, but it is also found in the First Reading.

That passage from the Acts of the Apostles shows how Jesus sends his Spirit to guide us in our every action.

This fact fills us with joy. We are not left to struggle through life by our own devices.

We have a loving shepherd who will guide us with kindness and gentleness.

R̸. **We are his people, the sheep of his flock.**

or:

R̸. **Alleluia.**

Sing joyfully to the LORD, all you lands;
> serve the LORD with gladness;
> come before him with joyful song.

R̸. **We are his people, the sheep of his flock.**

or:

R̸. **Alleluia.**

Know that the LORD is God;
> he made us, his we are;
> his people, the flock he tends.

R̸. **We are his people, the sheep of his flock.**

or:

R̸. **Alleluia.**

There are no limitations to the goodness and love of God, for they extend to every nation upon the earth and every era of history. God's mercy is all powerful and eternal. God will always be faithful to his promises.

The LORD is good:

his kindness endures forever,

and his faithfulness, to all generations.

℞. **We are his people, the sheep of his flock.**

or:

℞. **Alleluia.**

Lect. No. 51

SECOND READING: Revelation 7:9, 14b-17

The Lamb will shepherd them and lead them to springs of life-giving water.

The Second Reading gives a vision of heaven. In the verses before this passage, one heard that the number of those going to heaven would be one hundred and forty-four thousand. This was twelve times twelve times one thousand.

The first twelve stands for the Old Israel, the second twelve for the New Israel. Thus, the one hundred and forty-four thousand is the old and new Israel, multiplied many times over (one thousand).

This is therefore not the number of people who are going to heaven, but rather their spiritual identity.

This same idea is presented in today's reading. The number going to heaven is numberless. They have been redeemed with the blood of the Lamb. They have given witness to their faith through their own suffering.

They will now enter into their peace (every tear will be wiped away).

A reading from the Book of Revelation

I, John, had a vision of a great multitude,
  which no one could count,
from every nation, race, people, and tongue.
They stood before the throne and before the Lamb,
  wearing white robes and holding palm branches
    in their hands.

Then one of the elders said to me,
  "These are the ones who have survived the time of
    great distress;
  they have washed their robes
and made them white in the blood of the Lamb.

  "For this reason they stand before God's throne
    and worship him day and night in his temple.
  The one who sits on the throne will shelter
    them.
  They will not hunger or thirst anymore,
    nor will the sun or any heat strike them.
  For the Lamb who is in the center of the throne
    will shepherd them
    and lead them to springs of life-giving water,
    and God will wipe away every tear from their
      eyes."

The word of the Lord.

Jesus is our Good Shepherd. He will never abandon his flock, but will be willing to give up his life for the sheep whom he loves.

Lect. No. 51

The Gospel is a short passage from Jesus' proclamation that he is the Good Shepherd. Jesus does not proclaim this on his own authority, but rather because the Father has appointed him to this role. The Gospel of John continuously repeats the theme that Jesus must obey the will of the Father (for he and the Father are one).

The will of the Father is to reveal to us how much God loves us. (This Gospel presents the cross as the most powerful example of that love.)

ALLELUIA: John 10:14

℟. **Alleluia, alleluia.**

I am the good shepherd, says the Lord;
I know my sheep, and mine know me.

℟. **Alleluia, alleluia.**

GOSPEL: John 10:27-30

I give my sheep eternal life.

A reading from the holy Gospel according to John

Jesus said:
"My sheep hear my voice;
   I know them, and they follow me.
I give them eternal life, and they shall never perish.
No one can take them out of my hand.
My Father, who has given them to me, is greater
      than all,
   and no one can take them out of the Father's
      hand.
The Father and I are one."

The Gospel of the Lord.

PASTORAL REFLECTIONS

Sheep are not the most intelligent of animals. They often graze on hillsides that are too steep and they fall over on their backs. Once they have fallen over, they cannot right themselves. If they were to be left there, they would die. Because of this, the shepherd has to keep a constant eye on the sheep lest they place themselves in danger.

April 28, 2013

FIFTH SUNDAY OF EASTER

Lect. No. 54

FIRST READING: Acts 14:21-27

*They called the Church together and reported
what God had done with them.*

The First Reading continues the accounts of the history of the early Church from the Acts of the Apostles.

In this passage, we hear of how the apostles strengthened Christians by exhorting them. They appointed elders in the community.

(Note, that in the earliest days of the Church, there were no titles such as bishops, priests, and deacons.)

Paul reminds the community that they must undergo many hardships in order to give witness to their faith.

Very few of us will ever be arrested for being Christians, but we will all have a price to pay if we truly give witness to our faith in word and deed.

Picture trying to be a true Christian at home, at work, at school, on the road, etc. St. Therese called this *white martyrdom,* a martyrdom of pin pricks.

The apostles continuously attribute all of their success to God. Again, this is essential to remember, for it is easy to be filled with pride when things go well. God is the source of every good thing.

A reading from the Acts of the Apostles

After Paul and Barnabas had proclaimed the good news
   to that city
   and made a considerable number of disciples,
   they returned to Lystra and to Iconium and to Antioch.
They strengthened the spirits of the disciples
   and exhorted them to persevere in the faith, saying,
   "It is necessary for us to undergo many hardships
   to enter the kingdom of God."
They appointed elders for them in each church and,
   with prayer and fasting, commended them to the Lord
   in whom they had put their faith.
Then they traveled through Pisidia and reached Pamphylia.
After proclaiming the word at Perga they went down to Attalia.
From there they sailed to Antioch,
   where they had been commended to the grace of God
   for the work they had now accomplished.
And when they arrived, they called the church together
   and reported what God had done with them
   and how he had opened the door of faith to the Gentiles.

The word of the Lord.

RESPONSORIAL PSALM: Ps 145:8-9, 10-11, 12-13 (℞.: cf. 1)

The Responsorial Psalm is a series of verses taken from Psalm 145. This psalm is a hymn of praise. It is an alphabetic psalm, with each verse of the psalm beginning with a successive letter of the Hebrew alphabet.

The verses used today speak of God's kingdom. The term "kingdom" should not be understood as a reality that exists in a particular time or place.

It is better understood as the reign of God (for it is more of a verb than a noun). It exists whenever and wherever God's law is obeyed and his love revealed.

There are a series of adjectives to describe the reign of God. Words such as gracious, merciful, and kindness abound.

God does not reign through terror and rage, but by conquering our hearts with his love. He is the king of our hearts.

This is not a message intended only for those who belong to the Old and New Israel. As we hear in the last section of this psalm, it is a message for all of the children of Adam (all members of the human race).

It is also a message that all should hear until the very end of time, for God's dominion endures through all generations.

℞. **I will praise your name for ever, my king and my God.**

or:

℞. **Alleluia.**

The LORD is gracious and merciful,
  slow to anger and of great kindness.
The LORD is good to all
  and compassionate toward all his works.

℞. **I will praise your name for ever, my king and my God.**

or:

℞. **Alleluia.**

Let all your works give you thanks, O LORD,
  and let your faithful ones bless you.
Let them discourse of the glory of your kingdom
  and speak of your might.

℞. **I will praise your name for ever, my king and my God.**

or:

℞. **Alleluia.**

Let them make known your might to the children of Adam,
  and the glorious splendor of your kingdom.
Your kingdom is a kingdom for all ages,
  and your dominion endures through all generations.

℞. **I will praise your name for ever, my king and my God.**

or:

℞. **Alleluia.**

SECOND READING: Revelation 21:1-5a

God will wipe every tear from their eyes.

The Second Reading is another passage taken from the Book of Revelation. This one describes what awaits us after our death.

There will be a new heavens and a new earth. That which taught us about God will continue in the world to come (but without the limitations that we knew in this world).

One of the other things that will not have limitations is our love. God has taught us the true meaning of love.

That love (God's love for us and our love for God and each other) will be perfected in the world to come.

Heaven, in fact, is not so much a particular time or place, as much as a relationship. We will be one with God and one with each other.

Lect. No. 54

Love is the basis and the totality of the law, for God is love, and when we are living in love, we are living in God and God in us.

A reading from the Book of Revelation

Then I, John, saw a new heaven and a new earth.
The former heaven and the former earth had passed away,
and the sea was no more.
I also saw the holy city, a new Jerusalem,
coming down out of heaven from God,
prepared as a bride adorned for her husband.
I heard a loud voice from the throne saying,
"Behold, God's dwelling is with the human race.
He will dwell with them and they will be his people
and God himself will always be with them as their God.
He will wipe every tear from their eyes,
and there shall be no more death or mourning,
wailing or pain,
for the old order has passed away."

The One who sat on the throne said,
"Behold, I make all things new."

The word of the Lord.

ALLELUIA: John 13:34

℟. **Alleluia, alleluia.**

I give you a new commandment, says the Lord:
love one another as I have loved you.

℟. **Alleluia, alleluia.**

Lect. No. 54

GOSPEL: John 13:31-33a, 34-35

I give you a new commandment: love one another.

The first part of today's Gospel speaks of the fact that Jesus has been glorified. The Gospel of John uses the word "glory" in an unusual manner.

In this Gospel it means to live in love, and Jesus has proven that he is the fullness of God's love in his willingness to die on the cross for us.

Now that we have learned this astounding lesson of love, we must live it. We do this by observing God's commandments.

We are God-like inasmuch as we love God and one another for God is love.

A reading from the holy Gospel according to John

When Judas had left them, Jesus said,
"Now is the Son of Man glorified, and God is glorified in him.
If God is glorified in him,
    God will also glorify him in himself,
    and God will glorify him at once.
My children, I will be with you only a little while longer.
I give you a new commandment: love one another.
As I have loved you, so you also should love one another.
This is how all will know that you are my disciples,
    if you have love for one another."

The Gospel of the Lord.

PASTORAL REFLECTIONS

This Gospel reminds us of our ultimate destiny: to share in the glory of God in heaven. When we hear that phrase, we often think in terms of the rewards that we will receive. But if Jesus is glorified on the cross, in that moment of the ultimate outpouring of love, then heaven will not be an eternal vacation. It will be an opportunity to love and serve and give of ourselves.

We know that this is true because even now we ask for the intercession of the saints. They are not selfishly concerned with their own comfort. They devote themselves to the service of God and ourselves.

When the Ascension of the Lord is celebrated the following Sunday, the Second Reading and Gospel from the Seventh Sunday of Easter, pp. 247-248, may be read on the Sixth Sunday of Easter.

May 5, 2013

SIXTH SUNDAY OF EASTER

FIRST READING: Acts 15:1-2, 22-29

*It is the decision of the Holy Spirit and of us
not to place on you any burden beyond these necessities.*

The Church has always been guided by the action of the Holy Spirit, but this does not mean that it was always easy to discern what the Spirit wants.

One of the most difficult problems in the early Church was to decide what Christ wanted of the first Gentile-Christians.

Baptism initiated pagans into the faith. But what were they becoming when they were baptized?

They were actually becoming Jews, for they were committing themselves to the Messiah whom the God of Israel had sent.

Now that they were Jews, how much of the Jewish faith should they observe? Should they be circumcised? Should they keep the dietary laws?

In order to discern God's will in this matter, the apostles (including Paul and Barnabas) gathered in Jerusalem. There are two accounts of this meeting, here and in Paul's Letter to the Galatians.

A reading from the Acts of the Apostles

Some who had come down from Judea were instructing the brothers,
"Unless you are circumcised according to the Mosaic practice,
you cannot be saved."
Because there arose no little dissension and debate
by Paul and Barnabas with them,
it was decided that Paul, Barnabas, and some of the others
should go up to Jerusalem to the apostles and elders about this question.

The apostles and elders, in agreement with the whole church,
decided to choose representatives
and to send them to Antioch with Paul and Barnabas.
The ones chosen were Judas, who was called Barsabbas,
and Silas, leaders among the brothers.
This is the letter delivered by them:

"The apostles and the elders, your brothers,
to the brothers in Antioch, Syria, and Cilicia
of Gentile origin: greetings.
Since we have heard that some of our number
who went out without any mandate from us
have upset you with their teachings

In both of these versions, the final decision was that the pagans should not be obligated to follow Jewish law. They were to live in the freedom of the children of God.

The major difference between these two accounts is the role of the apostles.

In Acts, it is the apostles James and Peter who lead the discussion and propose the compromise. In Galatians, it is Paul who does this.

Yet, in spite of the fact that this decision was reached through discussion and compromise, it was the Holy Spirit who was behind it. This is often how the Spirit acts, through normal human interaction.

and disturbed your peace of mind,
we have with one accord decided to choose representatives
and to send them to you along with our beloved Barnabas and Paul,
who have dedicated their lives to the name of our Lord Jesus Christ.
So we are sending Judas and Silas
who will also convey this same message by word of mouth:
'It is the decision of the Holy Spirit and of us
not to place on you any burden beyond these necessities,
namely, to abstain from meat sacrificed to idols,
from blood, from meats of strangled animals,
and from unlawful marriage.
If you keep free of these,
you will be doing what is right. Farewell.' "

The word of the Lord.

Lect. No. 57

RESPONSORIAL PSALM: Ps 67:2-3, 5, 6, 8 (℟.: 4)

Psalm 67 is a hymn of thanksgiving that is based upon the blessing of Aaron found in the Book of Numbers (6:24-26).

The psalm celebrates the fact that God has blessed Israel abundantly. Yet, it is not only Israel that should give thanks to the Lord.

The psalm calls upon all the nations on the earth to give praise to the Lord, for Yahweh is the God of all peoples.

The reason for this gratitude is the fact that God's blessing

℟. **O God, let all the nations praise you!**

or:

℟. **Alleluia.**

May God have pity on us and bless us;
    may he let his face shine upon us.
So may your way be known upon earth;
    among all nations, your salvation.

℟. **O God, let all the nations praise you!**

or:

℟. **Alleluia.**

May the nations be glad and exult
    because you rule the peoples in equity;
    the nations on the earth you guide.

upon Israel was only the beginning. God's blessing was a model of the way that God would now treat all the peoples upon the earth.

They were now all his chosen people, all his beloved.

We have seen this in the First Reading when we heard about the mission of the early Church to the pagans, to the very ends of the earth.

℟. **O God, let all the nations praise you!**

or:

℟. **Alleluia.**

May the peoples praise you, O God;
   may all the peoples praise you!
May God bless us,
   and may all the ends of the earth fear him!

℟. **O God, let all the nations praise you!**

or:

℟. **Alleluia.**

SECOND READING: Revelation 21:10-14, 22-23

The angel showed me the holy city coming down out of heaven.

The Second Reading is a continuation of the description of the heavenly Jerusalem. It is pictured as a city built out of precious stones.

Its beauty recalls the description of God the Father in chapter 4 of the Book of Revelation. We will be like God for we will see him as he is.

The twelve gates and the twelve courses of stones recall the twelve patriarchs and the twelve apostles who are the founders of the Old and the New Israel.

There is no temple in the city, for there is no place where God cannot be found.

When the veil of the temple was split at the moment of Jesus' death, the separation between God and the world was forever shattered.

A reading from the Book of Revelation

The angel took me in spirit to a great, high mountain
  and showed me the holy city Jerusalem
  coming down out of heaven from God.
It gleamed with the splendor of God.
Its radiance was like that of a precious stone,
   like jasper, clear as crystal.
It had a massive, high wall,
   with twelve gates where twelve angels were stationed
  and on which names were inscribed,
   the names of the twelve tribes of the Israelites.
There were three gates facing east,
   three north, three south, and three west.
The wall of the city had twelve courses of stones as
    its foundation,
   on which were inscribed the twelve names
   of the twelve apostles of the Lamb.

I saw no temple in the city
   for its temple is the Lord God almighty and the
    Lamb.

Likewise, there is no need of a sun or a moon, for the Lord himself is the light of the world. He is the true light in which there is no darkness.

The city had no need of sun or moon to shine on it,
    for the glory of God gave it light,
    and its lamp was the Lamb.

The word of the Lord.

It is not enough to say that we believe in God but then not do anything about it. We must keep God's word by living his commandments. This is the way that we will know that we are living in the truth.

ALLELUIA: John 14:23

℟. **Alleluia, alleluia.**

Whoever loves me will keep my word, says the Lord,
and my Father will love him and we will come to him.

℟. **Alleluia, alleluia.**

Lect. No. 57

GOSPEL: John 14:23-29

The Holy Spirit will teach you everything and remind you of all that I told you.

This is the last Sunday before the Ascension, and we are already preparing for the descent of the Holy Spirit. This is why the First Reading spoke of the action of the Holy Spirit through the discussions of the community, and the Gospel speaks of the coming of the Advocate.

The phrase used in the Gospel of John is the "Paraclete." This is an ambiguous phrase, for it could be translated as the advocate, the consoler, the counselor, etc.

One will find all of these translations, but one will also find the word in the original Greek since no individual English word can translate it well.

A reading from the holy Gospel according to John

Jesus said to his disciples:
"Whoever loves me will keep my word,
    and my Father will love him,
    and we will come to him and make our dwelling with him.
Whoever does not love me does not keep my words;
    yet the word you hear is not mine
    but that of the Father who sent me.

"I have told you this while I am with you.
The Advocate, the Holy Spirit,
    whom the Father will send in my name,
    will teach you everything
    and remind you of all that I told you.
Peace I leave with you; my peace I give to you.
Not as the world gives do I give it to you.
Do not let your hearts be troubled or afraid.

It was necessary for Jesus to ascend to the Father. This was the Father's will, and we should be filled with joy that Jesus was doing what the Father had requested of him (even if it is difficult for us to accept this). It means that we must not cling to Jesus as Mary Magdalene tried to do after the resurrection.

You heard me tell you,
   'I am going away and I will come back to you.'
If you loved me,
   you would rejoice that I am going to the Father;
   for the Father is greater than I.
And now I have told you this before it happens,
   so that when it happens you may believe."

The Gospel of the Lord.

PASTORAL REFLECTIONS

There are various functions for the Paraclete described in John's Gospel. In this passage, we hear that the Paraclete will remind us of what Jesus taught, for the disciples were incapable of remembering what was important on their own. The Paraclete would also teach the disciples, for they had not been able to learn all that was important right from the start.

The Spirit is also presented as an intercessor for Christians before the Father. The Spirit gives consolation to those who are suffering. (In fact, Paul states that a sign that one is filled with the Spirit is that one suffers with a spirit of joy.) The Spirit strengthens Christians.

Furthermore, the Spirit was always associated with the forgiveness of sins. The Spirit is God's love (which is why it is seen as a dove, a symbol of love in the Old Testament). God's love heals the wounds caused by our sins, for sins are acts of non-love.

In the dioceses of the United States where it has been approved, the following Mass of the Ascension of the Lord is celebrated on May 12, in place of the Mass of the Seventh Sunday of Easter that appears on p. 245. These readings are used at the Vigil Mass and at the Mass during the Day.

May 9, 2013

THE ASCENSION OF THE LORD

Lect. No. 58

FIRST READING: Acts 1:1-11

As the Apostles were looking on, Jesus was lifted up.

The First Reading begins with the dedication of the Acts of the Apostles to Theophilus. We do not know who Theophilus was.

He might be a royal official, or a rich patron, or the name might be symbolic (for "Theos" in Greek means "God" and "phileo" means "to love," so this book could be intended for those who love God: Christians).

The disciples ask Jesus whether it is time for the Kingdom of God. His answer is ambiguous, for the kingdom was dawning, but not in the manner that they expected.

They thought that the kingdom was going to be a political entity, but this was not what Jesus had come to establish. Jesus was the king who reigned in our hearts.

Acts gives an outline of the ministry of the early Church. It would begin in Judea, and then extend to Samaria, and finally reach to the ends of the earth.

This prediction was fulfilled when the Gospel reached Rome, which was the political ends of the earth.

A reading from the beginning of
the Acts of the Apostles

In the first book, Theophilus,
I dealt with all that Jesus did and taught
until the day he was taken up,
after giving instructions through the Holy Spirit
to the apostles whom he had chosen.
He presented himself alive to them
by many proofs after he had suffered,
appearing to them during forty days
and speaking about the kingdom of God.
While meeting with them,
he enjoined them not to depart from Jerusalem,
but to wait for "the promise of the Father
about which you have heard me speak;
for John baptized with water,
but in a few days you will be baptized with the
Holy Spirit."

When they had gathered together they asked him,
"Lord, are you at this time going to restore the
kingdom to Israel?"
He answered them, "It is not for you to know the
times or seasons
that the Father has established by his own authority.
But you will receive power when the Holy Spirit
comes upon you,
and you will be my witnesses in Jerusalem,
throughout Judea and Samaria,
and to the ends of the earth."

The last part of today's passage speaks of the ascension. Jesus is described as being lifted up into the clouds. We know that heaven is not necessarily above us, and hell is not necessarily below us. Above and below are earthly terms, and heaven and hell are realities beyond our understanding.

In any case, Jesus would certainly have ascended in such a way that his disciples could understand that Jesus was now with the Father (so for the sake of the disciples he probably actually did go up into the clouds).

Lect.
No. 58

When he had said this, as they were looking on,
  he was lifted up, and a cloud took him from their sight.
While they were looking intently at the sky as he was going,
  suddenly two men dressed in white garments stood beside them.
They said, "Men of Galilee,
  why are you standing there looking at the sky?
This Jesus who has been taken up from you into heaven
  will return in the same way as you have seen him going into heaven."

The word of the Lord.

RESPONSORIAL PSALM: Ps 47:2-3, 6-7, 8-9 (℟.: 6)

This psalm proclaims God as the king of the heavens and the earth. There are no nations upon the earth that are not part of his reign. Nothing can escape God's control.

The first section speaks of God the Most High. The Hebrew phrase that we translate as "Most High" is "El Elyon." Originally, this title meant God of the heights (for there was a shrine to Yahweh upon every hill top).

It eventually came to mean that God was beyond our understanding.

One must ask what it means for God to be our king. This seems to be an archaic title, especially in those countries that do not have a tradition of a monarchy.

℟. **God mounts his throne to shouts of joy: a blare of trumpets for the Lord.**

or:

℟. **Alleluia.**

All you peoples, clap your hands,
  shout to God with cries of gladness.
For the LORD, the Most High, the awesome,
  is the great king over all the earth.

℟. **God mounts his throne to shouts of joy: a blare of trumpets for the Lord.**

or:

℟. **Alleluia.**

God mounts his throne amid shouts of joy;
  the LORD, amid trumpet blasts.
Sing praise to God, sing praise;
  sing praise to our king, sing praise.

℟. **God mounts his throne to shouts of joy: a blare of trumpets for the Lord.**

or:

But even in our country we can easily understand that it means that God is to be the center of our lives, the source and the goal of all that we have and are.

Every decision that we make in our daily lives must be based upon what God's will is for us. He is not only the king of the world, he must also be the king of our hearts.

℟. **Alleluia.**

For king of all the earth is God;
    sing hymns of praise.
God reigns over the nations,
    God sits upon his holy throne.

℟. **God mounts his throne to shouts of joy: a blare of trumpets for the Lord.**

or:

℟. **Alleluia.**

Lect. No. 58

SECOND READING A : Ephesians 1:17-23

Christ has entered into heaven itself.

This reading speaks of two revelations. The first is that we will know God the Father. This is not knowing about God, but knowing God.

The second revelation is the glory to which God has called us. This is our hope and the meaning of our lives.

The latter part of the reading speaks of how the Father raised Jesus from the dead (for Jesus did not raise himself, he was raised by the Father).

He is enthroned and is above every principality, authority, power and dominion.

In the Greek world, that which was totally spiritual was considered to be superior to the material. The angels (here called principalities, etc.) were totally spiritual, while Jesus was both spiritual and material.

Some in the early Church thought he might be inferior to the spiritual beings.

A reading from the Letter of Saint Paul
to the Ephesians

Brothers and sisters:
    May the God of our Lord Jesus Christ, the Father
        of glory,
    give you a Spirit of wisdom and revelation
    resulting in knowledge of him.
May the eyes of your hearts be enlightened,
    that you may know what is the hope that belongs
        to his call,
    what are the riches of glory
    in his inheritance among the holy ones,
    and what is the surpassing greatness of his power
    for us who believe,
    in accord with the exercise of his great might:
    which he worked in Christ,
    raising him from the dead
    and seating him at his right hand in the heavens,
    far above every principality, authority, power, and
        dominion,
    and every name that is named
    not only in this age but also in the one to come.
And he put all things beneath his feet
    and gave him as head over all things to the
        church,

We see that this is rejected, for Jesus is above all creatures. Finally, we hear that the Church is a body, and Christ is the head of that body.

which is his body,
the fullness of the one who fills all things in every way.

The word of the Lord.

Lect. No. 58

OR: **B** Hebrews 9:24-28; 10:19-23

Christ has entered into heaven itself.

The Letter to the Hebrews presents two levels of reality. This is an idea drawn from Greek philosophy.

One level is the level of "forms." This level is perfect and unique. We might speak of it in terms of ideas (e.g., the idea of a book).

The second level is that of matter. On that level, there are many different expressions of the idea (e.g., individual books, none of which fully expresses what it means to be a book).

In the Old Testament, the sanctuary in the temple was at the level of matter. It was not perfect. The high priests were at the level of matter. They, too, were not perfect.

Jesus, on the other hand, is perfect. The sanctuary he entered was not made of stone—it was the sanctuary of heaven.

Jesus did not have to ask for forgiveness of his own sins, for he did not have any.

He did not have to perform sacrifice after sacrifice, for his one sacrifice on the cross was perfect. It perfectly washed us free from our sins.

A reading from the Letter to the Hebrews

Christ did not enter into a sanctuary made by hands,
a copy of the true one, but heaven itself,
that he might now appear before God on our behalf.
Not that he might offer himself repeatedly,
as the high priest enters each year into the sanctuary
with blood that is not his own;
if that were so, he would have had to suffer repeatedly
from the foundation of the world.
But now once for all he has appeared at the end of the ages
to take away sin by his sacrifice.
Just as it is appointed that men and women die once,
and after this the judgment, so also Christ,
offered once to take away the sins of many,
will appear a second time, not to take away sin
but to bring salvation to those who eagerly await him.

Therefore, brothers and sisters, since through the blood of Jesus
we have confidence of entrance into the sanctuary
by the new and living way he opened for us through the veil,

The reading closes with an exhortation that we accept and embrace the salvation that Jesus is offering us. It is not enough to believe that Jesus has done these things for us—we must do something about it by living our faith.

This switch from theory to application is typical of the Letter to the Hebrews, for knowledge should bring us to conversion.

that is, his flesh,

and since we have "a great priest over the house of God,"

let us approach with a sincere heart and in absolute trust,

with our hearts sprinkled clean from an evil conscience

and our bodies washed in pure water.

Let us hold unwaveringly to our confession that gives us hope,

for he who made the promise is trustworthy.

The word of the Lord.

Lect. No. 58

The Alleluia Verse contains the commission that Jesus gave to his disciples in the Gospel of Matthew. We are to continue Jesus' mission, but we will never have to do it alone, for he will be with us.

ALLELUIA: Matthew 28:19a, 20b

℞. **Alleluia, alleluia.**

Go and teach all nations, says the Lord;
I am with you always, until the end of the world.

℞. **Alleluia, alleluia.**

PASTORAL REFLECTIONS

There is a church in Germany that was severely damaged during World War II. Almost everything was destroyed except for the crucifix, and even that was damaged. It lost its arms. When the church was rebuilt, the damaged cross was hung up with the inscription, "I have no arms now; you are my arms."

Today we celebrate the Ascension. Jesus is, in a sense, leaving us alone to carry on his work. In this, he shows an incredible trust, for he is making us his coworkers.

Lect.
No. 58

GOSPEL: Luke 24:46-53

As he blessed them, he was taken up to heaven.

The Gospel gives the shorter version of the ascension of Jesus (the longer version is found in the Acts of the Apostles).

Jesus reminds the disciples that all that happened was what had been foretold. This agrees with Luke's emphasis that God had a plan, and Jesus' ministry was to fulfill that plan.

He then tells his disciples to remain in the city (Jerusalem) until they will have been clothed in power (until they will have received the gift of the Holy Spirit).

Jesus ascends into heaven from the Mount of Olives.

That mount was always associated with the end of time, and the events of Jesus' death, resurrection, ascension, and the descent of the Spirit were the dawning of the Kingdom of God.

A reading from the holy Gospel according to Luke

Jesus said to his disciples:
"Thus it is written that the Christ would suffer
and rise from the dead on the third day
and that repentance, for the forgiveness of sins,
would be preached in his name
to all the nations, beginning from Jerusalem.
You are witnesses of these things.
And behold I am sending the promise of my Father
upon you;
but stay in the city
until you are clothed with power from on high."

Then he led them out as far as Bethany,
raised his hands, and blessed them.
As he blessed them he parted from them
and was taken up to heaven.
They did him homage
and then returned to Jerusalem with great joy,
and they were continually in the temple praising
God.

The Gospel of the Lord.

PASTORAL REFLECTIONS

Why did Jesus have to leave us in the Ascension? Would it not have been easier if the Lord had remained here with us on the earth? Maybe we needed the distance, though, for if Jesus were always around, we would never learn to be mature enough to be the guides for our own morality. (It is almost like when a parent is over-protective and the children never learn to stand on their own feet.) God loves us so much that he gives us the space that we need to grow (even though this means that God faces the risk that we might say "no.")

In the dioceses of the United States where it has been approved, the Mass of the Ascension of the Lord that appears on p. 239 is celebrated today in place of the following Mass of the Seventh Sunday of Easter.

May 12, 2013

SEVENTH SUNDAY OF EASTER

Lect. No. 61

FIRST READING: Acts 7:55-60

I see the Son of Man standing at the right hand of God.

On this Sunday there is an emphasis upon the continuation of Jesus' ministry in the life of the Church.

The First Reading speaks of Stephen, the first martyr of the Church. He was filled with the Holy Spirit, and this gave him the courage to proclaim the truth.

Stephen, one of the first deacons, was arrested for his preaching. The leaders of the Jews were infuriated when Stephen spoke of seeing the Son of Man standing at the right hand of God.

This implied that Jesus was the Messiah, and they did not want to hear this.

Paul (here called Saul) is mentioned as being part of the plot. Only a couple of chapters later Paul would meet Jesus on the road to Damascus.

A reading from the Acts of the Apostles

Stephen, filled with the Holy Spirit,
  looked up intently to heaven and saw the glory
    of God
and Jesus standing at the right hand of God,
and Stephen said, "Behold, I see the heavens
    opened
and the Son of Man standing at the right hand of
    God."
But they cried out in a loud voice,
  covered their ears, and rushed upon him together.
They threw him out of the city, and began to stone
    him.
The witnesses laid down their cloaks
  at the feet of a young man named Saul.
As they were stoning Stephen, he called out,
  "Lord Jesus, receive my spirit."
Then he fell to his knees and cried out in a loud
    voice,
  "Lord, do not hold this sin against them";
and when he said this, he fell asleep.

The word of the Lord.

PASTORAL REFLECTIONS

The way that Luke phrased the account of the death of Stephen is loosely based upon his story of Jesus' own Passion, for when we suffer for the faith Jesus is suffering with us. We are never alone.

RESPONSORIAL PSALM: Ps 97:1-2, 6-7, 9 (℟.: 1a and 9a)

The Responsorial Psalm is a hymn of praise to God, the king. There is a Hasidic Jewish saying that if God is our king, then we are at fault, but if God is not our king, then we are at fault.

If God is our king, then we are at fault, for we often have not treated God as if he were our king.

If God is not our king, then we are at fault, for we have not made him our king.

The praise of God is similar to what we would expect to find in hymns that praised the kings of Israel (e.g., Psalm 45).

But God is not like the kings of the earth. He is truly a God of justice. He is filled with glory.

This particular hymn was written in a period when Israel practiced henotheism (the belief that there are many gods, but that Yahweh was the main God).

It was only later that Israel became monotheist (the belief that there is only one God).

This is why God is described as being exalted far above all the gods, and those gods fall prostrate before Yahweh.

℟. **The Lord is king, the most high over all the earth.**

or:

℟. **Alleluia.**

The LORD is king; let the earth rejoice;
  let the many islands be glad.
Justice and judgment are the foundation of his
  throne.

℟. **The Lord is king, the most high over all the earth.**

or:

℟. **Alleluia.**

The heavens proclaim his justice,
  and all peoples see his glory.
All gods are prostrate before him.

℟. **The Lord is king, the most high over all the earth.**

or:

℟. **Alleluia.**

You, O LORD, are the Most High over all the earth,
  exalted far above all gods.

℟. **The Lord is king, the most high over all the earth.**

or:

℟. **Alleluia.**

Lect. No. 61

SECOND READING: Revelation 22:12-14, 16-17, 20

Come, Lord Jesus!

The Second Reading continues the readings from the Book of Revelation we have seen over the past several weeks. This particular reading is the liturgical conclusion to the book.

The first part of this passage speaks of Jesus' return in glory. He identifies himself as the Alpha and the Omega. Alpha is the first and Omega the last letter of the Greek alphabet, and it means that Jesus is the source and the goal of all that exists.

Jesus also identifies himself as the root and offspring of David (for while he is a descendant of David, he also existed long before David did).

He is also the bright morning star. The morning star is Venus, who in Greek mythology was the goddess of victory. Jesus, like the morning star, rose before the dawn.

The Spirit and the bride (the Church) invite us to come and share in the goodness that God offers us.

A reading from the Book of Revelation

I, John, heard a voice saying to me:
"Behold, I am coming soon.
I bring with me the recompense I will give to each
   according to his deeds.
I am the Alpha and the Omega, the first and the last,
   the beginning and the end."

Blessed are they who wash their robes
   so as to have the right to the tree of life
   and enter the city through its gates.

"I, Jesus, sent my angel to give you this testimony
   for the churches.
I am the root and offspring of David,
   the bright morning star."

The Spirit and the bride say, "Come."
Let the hearer say, "Come."
Let the one who thirsts come forward,
   and the one who wants it receive the gift of life-
   giving water.

The one who gives this testimony says, "Yes, I am
   coming soon."
Amen! Come, Lord Jesus!

The word of the Lord.

Lect. No. 61

On this Sunday after the Ascension, we are reminded that Jesus has not abandoned us. He will always be with us and will guide us until the end of time.

ALLELUIA: cf. John 14:18

℟. **Alleluia, alleluia.**

I will not leave you orphans, says the Lord.
I will come back to you, and your hearts will rejoice.

℟. **Alleluia, alleluia.**

Lect.
No. 61

GOSPEL: John 17:20-26

That they may be brought to perfection as one!

The Gospel is a passage taken from the Last Supper Discourse in the Gospel of John.

In ancient literature, the last words of an important person were considered to be the most important teachings of that person's life.

This reading is a prayer for the community of believers. It was not intended so much for the disciples surrounding Jesus at the Last Supper as for those who would come later.

The main theme of the reading is that those who follow Jesus should be one, one with him and the Father and one with each other.

This is logical, for if they were truly disciples of Jesus, then they would live in his love and be bound to him and each other with as intimate a bond as that which unites him to the Father.

Remember that the Gospel of John redefines the word "glory." It is not magnificence or prestige; it is the outpouring of love. We are called to live in that love in this world and the next.

A reading from the holy Gospel according to John

Lifting up his eyes to heaven, Jesus prayed, saying:

"Holy Father, I pray not only for them,
  but also for those who will believe in me through
    their word,
  so that they may all be one,
  as you, Father, are in me and I in you,
  that they also may be in us,
  that the world may believe that you sent me.
And I have given them the glory you gave me,
  so that they may be one, as we are one,
  I in them and you in me,
  that they may be brought to perfection as one,
  that the world may know that you sent me,
  and that you loved them even as you loved me.
Father, they are your gift to me.
I wish that where I am they also may be with me,
  that they may see my glory that you gave me,
  because you loved me before the foundation of
    the world.
Righteous Father, the world also does not know you,
  but I know you, and they know that you sent me.
I made known to them your name and I will make it
    known,
  that the love with which you loved me
  may be in them and I in them."

The Gospel of the Lord.

PASTORAL REFLECTIONS

Jesus came into this world so that we would never be alone again. Sin causes alienation. Jesus heals the wounds of sin with his love so that we might enter into the life of the Trinity.

PENTECOST SUNDAY
AT THE VIGIL MASS

FIRST READING:

Lect. No. 62

A Genesis 11:1-9

*It was called Babel because there the Lord confused
the speech of all the world.*

Saint Luke describes the day of Pentecost as being a new creation. On the first day of creation, the Spirit of the LORD was breathed into a clump of mud and made it into a living being: Adam. Now that same Spirit was being breathed into the disciples, and they were becoming a new creation in Christ.

This new act of creation involves a healing of all the damage that had been done to the human race through the effects of sin.

The First Reading today offers an example of some of the damage that sin produced. It presents a story of the early days of humanity. It explains the origin of all of the different languages in the world.

The creation of many different languages was seen as a punishment for sin for it prevented people from communicating with each other. People had tried to build a tower to the heavens in an attempt to bring God down to earth. God confounds their attempts and prevents them from ever attempting this again.

As with all of the stories found in the early chapters of the Book of Genesis (1-11), this story is more of a parable than an historical account of the birth

A reading from the Book of Genesis

The whole world spoke the same language, using the same words.
While the people were migrating in the east,
    they came upon a valley in the land of Shinar and settled there.
They said to one another,
    "Come, let us mold bricks and harden them with fire."
They used bricks for stone, and bitumen for mortar.
Then they said, "Come, let us build ourselves a city
    and a tower with its top in the sky,
    and so make a name for ourselves;
    otherwise we shall be scattered all over the earth."

The LORD came down to see the city and the tower
    that the people had built.
Then the LORD said: "If now, while they are one people,
    all speaking the same language,
    they have started to do this,
    nothing will later stop them from doing whatever they presume to do.
Let us then go down there and confuse their language,
    so that one will not understand what another says."
Thus the LORD scattered them from there all over the earth,
    and they stopped building the city.
That is why it was called Babel,
    because there the LORD confused the speech of all the world.

of the various languages upon the earth. It was probably based upon a very ancient story that has now been lost.

In this reading we hear of a great theophany in which God encounters his people on Mount Sinai. The mountain was wrapped in smoke and fire. There was thunder and the mountain shook violently. (It is interesting to contrast this description with the story of how God appeared to Elijah the prophet in 1 Kings 19.)

This epiphany of the power of God occurred shortly after the people of Israel left Egypt. The LORD had delivered them from the hands of their enemies. The people knew that God had intervened in their history to make them his own people.

The LORD therefore invited his people into this covenant. He would be their God and they would be his people for all time. He asked them only that they keep the commandments he was giving them so that they might be holy and set apart in his name.

The feast of Pentecost is also a time for setting apart a people for God. In this case, the people being set apart is the Church, the Mystical Body of Christ. The commandment he hands on to them is that they are to love each other as Jesus has loved them.

Like the people of Israel, God now calls the people of the Church to be a kingdom of priests, a holy nation unto the Lord.

It was from that place that he scattered them all over the earth.

The word of the Lord.

OR: **B** Exodus 19:3-8a, 16-20b

The Lord came down upon Mount Sinai before all the people.

A reading from the Book of Exodus

Moses went up the mountain to God.
  Then the LORD called to him and said,
  "Thus shall you say to the house of Jacob;
  tell the Israelites:
  You have seen for yourselves how I treated the Egyptians
  and how I bore you up on eagle wings
  and brought you here to myself.
Therefore, if you hearken to my voice and keep my covenant,
  you shall be my special possession,
  dearer to me than all other people,
  though all the earth is mine.
You shall be to me a kingdom of priests, a holy nation.
That is what you must tell the Israelites."
So Moses went and summoned the elders of the people.
When he set before them
  all that the LORD had ordered him to tell them,
  the people all answered together,
  "Everything the LORD has said, we will do."

On the morning of the third day
  there were peals of thunder and lightning,
  and a heavy cloud over the mountain,
  and a very loud trumpet blast,
  so that all the people in the camp trembled.
But Moses led the people out of the camp to meet God,
  and they stationed themselves at the foot of the mountain.
Mount Sinai was all wrapped in smoke,
  for the LORD came down upon it in fire.

God does not always encounter his people on mountains that tremble or with great winds and tongues of fire. This does not mean that God is absent.

It simply means that God acts in many different ways, some miraculous and some everyday, to set apart a holy people to be his own.

Lect.
No. 62

The smoke rose from it as though from a furnace,
  and the whole mountain trembled violently.
The trumpet blast grew louder and louder, while Moses was speaking,
  and God answering him with thunder.

When the LORD came down to the top of Mount Sinai,
  he summoned Moses to the top of the mountain.

The word of the Lord.

OR: 🅲 Ezekiel 37:1-14

Dry bones of Israel, I will bring spirit into you, that you may come to life.

This passage was written by the Prophet Ezekiel while he was in exile in Babylon. This is one of the first passages that speaks of the resurrection of the dead.

It is probable that when the prophet spoke of these bones coming to life, he intended this as a prophecy of the resurrection of the people of Israel. They were a nation in exile and they were as good as dead. God would breathe his spirit back into them and would bring them back to life. He would heal the wounds caused by their sins.

Nevertheless, this passage makes sense only if the prophet also believed that God could bring individuals back to life. The experience of living in exile in Babylon had taught Ezekiel that there must be a reward after this life.

It is probable that this passage is based upon the beliefs of the Persian people. They were the nation to the east of Babylon. Many of the Persians practiced the cult of Zoroaster. In this religion, the dead were laid out in

A reading from the Book of the Prophet Ezekiel

The hand of the LORD came upon me,
  and he led me out in the spirit of the LORD
and set me in the center of the plain,
  which was now filled with bones.
He made me walk among the bones in every direction
  so that I saw how many they were on the surface of the plain.
How dry they were!
He asked me:
  Son of man, can these bones come to life?
I answered, "Lord GOD, you alone know that."
Then he said to me:
  Prophesy over these bones, and say to them:
  Dry bones, hear the word of the LORD!
Thus says the Lord GOD to these bones:
  See! I will bring spirit into you, that you may come to life.
I will put sinews upon you, make flesh grow over you,
  cover you with skin, and put spirit in you
  so that you may come to life and know that I am the LORD.
I, Ezekiel, prophesied as I had been told,
  and even as I was prophesying I heard a noise;
  it was a rattling as the bones came together, bone joining bone.

the fields until the birds of the air picked their bones dry. The people of this religion believed that these bones would be raised from the dead by a good god on the last day.

Thus, when Ezekiel spoke to these bones, he probably had this idea in mind. Of course, like many of the prophets of the Old Testament, he added his own particular Jewish ideas to the passage.

In the same way in which the LORD breathed his Spirit into these bones to make them living creatures, so also God sent his Spirit into us to allow us to become a living people. Before he sent his Spirit, we were as good as dead.

We were separated from each other by false divisions brought about by our sinfulness. We were not joined together like the bones of a living body, we were scattered like dried out bones.

Now God has made us a living body again. We are one in him. We are God's own people, and we will be his presence upon the earth.

But we must choose to live in God's love. That means making decisions to reject selfishness, which only brings death, and choosing to live in the freedom of God's own children.

> Lect.
> No. 62

I saw the sinews and the flesh come upon them,
　　and the skin cover them, but there was no spirit in them.
Then the LORD said to me:
　　Prophesy to the spirit, prophesy, son of man,
　　and say to the spirit: Thus says the Lord GOD:
　　From the four winds come, O spirit,
　　and breathe into these slain that they may come to life.
I prophesied as he told me, and the spirit came into them;
　　they came alive and stood upright, a vast army.
Then he said to me:
　　Son of man, these bones are the whole house of Israel.
They have been saying,
　　"Our bones are dried up,
　　our hope is lost, and we are cut off."
Therefore, prophesy and say to them: Thus says the Lord GOD:
　　O my people, I will open your graves
　　and have you rise from them,
　　and bring you back to the land of Israel.
Then you shall know that I am the LORD,
　　when I open your graves and have you rise from them,
　　O my people!
I will put my spirit in you that you may live,
　　and I will settle you upon your land;
　　thus you shall know that I am the LORD.
I have promised, and I will do it, says the LORD.

The word of the Lord.

OR: **D** Joel 3:1-5

I will pour out my spirit upon the servants and handmaids.

This reading from the Book of the Prophet Joel is probably one of the last parts of the Old Testament written. It belongs to

A reading from the Book of the Prophet Joel

Thus says the LORD:
　I will pour out my spirit upon all flesh.

the apocalyptic tradition of the Bible. In this tradition, authors speak of how bad things have become, and how only an intervention of the LORD can make it better. Most apocalyptic books also use imaginative imagery to convey the idea of the coming judgment.

The LORD's intervention would occur through an outpouring of the Holy Spirit of the LORD upon all peoples. The Spirit of God would give us a revelation of the hidden secrets of God.

The prophet speaks of the great marvels that would accompany this outpouring of the Spirit. The image of the Spirit appearing in tongues of fire is taken from this passage. Saint Peter, in fact, quoted this very passage in his discourse to the crowd on Pentecost Sunday.

Your sons and daughters shall prophesy,
　your old men shall dream dreams,
　your young men shall see visions;
even upon the servants and the handmaids,
　in those days, I will pour out my spirit.
And I will work wonders in the heavens and on the
　earth,
　blood, fire, and columns of smoke;
the sun will be turned to darkness,
　and the moon to blood,
at the coming of the day of the LORD,
　the great and terrible day.
Then everyone shall be rescued
　who calls on the name of the LORD;
for on Mount Zion there shall be a remnant,
　as the LORD has said,
and in Jerusalem survivors
　whom the LORD shall call.

The word of the Lord.

Lect. No. 62 **RESPONSORIAL PSALM: Ps 104:1-2, 24, 35, 27-28, 29, 30 (℟.: cf. 30)**

This Responsorial Psalm is a hymn of praise to the God of all creation. The greatest reason we have to praise God is that when he created, he sent his Spirit out into the world. Then, after we sinned and damaged creation, God sent forth his Spirit again on the day of Pentecost to renew the face of the earth. We are now a new creation.

We are not subject to many of the destructive effects of sin. We have been rescued from them by grace. God has clothed us with majesty and glory and robed us in light.

This is not to say that the renewal is totally completed, for

℟. **Lord, send out your Spirit, and renew the face of the earth.**

or:

℟. **Alleluia.**

Bless the LORD, O my soul!
　O LORD, my God, you are great indeed!
You are clothed with majesty and glory,
　robed in light as with a cloak.

℟. **Lord, send out your Spirit, and renew the face of the earth.**

or:

℟. **Alleluia.**

How manifold are your works, O LORD!
　In wisdom you have wrought them all—
the earth is full of your creatures;
　bless the LORD, O my soul! Alleluia.

we live in the dawning of the kingdom and not its fulfillment. We have received the Holy Spirit, which is God's down payment of the glory that awaits us, but we are also still waiting for the total fulfillment of all the promises Jesus made. Still, the kingdom has dawned and, if we look at things through the eyes of God, we will see his power at work in our midst.

We are totally dependent upon the generosity of God. As with all living creatures, if God withholds his breath, we cannot hope to survive. Likewise, if God withholds his Spirit, our spiritual life will perish. We will suffocate spiritually.

But if we trust in God and find our refuge in him, then we will not have to fear. God will provide his Spirit to renew our hearts. He never refuses his gift of the Spirit to those who ask for it in his name.

℟. **Lord, send out your Spirit, and renew the face of the earth.**

or:

℟. **Alleluia.**

Creatures all look to you
    to give them food in due time.
When you give it to them, they gather it;
    when you open your hand, they are filled with good things.

℟. **Lord, send out your Spirit, and renew the face of the earth.**

or:

℟. **Alleluia.**

If you take away their breath, they perish
    and return to their dust.
When you send forth your spirit, they are created,
    and you renew the face of the earth.

℟. **Lord, send out your Spirit, and renew the face of the earth.**

or:

℟. **Alleluia.**

Lect.
No. 62

SECOND READING: Romans 8:22-27

The Spirit intercedes with inexpressible groanings.

When God created the world, he breathed his Spirit into Adam and made him a living creature, a human being. We are not simply animals; we have something of God within us.

But when we sinned, we denied that presence. We chose to follow that which could not give life. Furthermore, our sinfulness alienated not only us, but also all of creation. All that exists was made to be good, but our sins have made creation ambiguous. That which should lead us to God all too often leads us to sin.

A reading from the Letter of Saint Paul
to the Romans

Brothers and sisters:
We know that all creation is groaning in labor pains even until now;
and not only that, but we ourselves,
who have the firstfruits of the Spirit,
we also groan within ourselves
as we wait for adoption, the redemption of our bodies.
For in hope we were saved.
Now hope that sees is not hope.

As an example, one might think of how often we misuse food. God created it to be good and useful, but we frequently eat too little or too much or the wrong thing.

We recognize the emptiness within us, and unfortunately we try to fill the void with sin and bad habits, etc, but none of it works. We are left feeling lonelier. The Spirit that Jesus breathed into his disciples fills the void. It reminds us of who we are, beloved children of God.

The Holy Spirit descended upon the apostles and Mary in the form of tongues of fire. We ask that same Spirit to inflame our hearts.

Lect.
No. 62

In this Gospel passage Jesus identifies himself as the source of living water. This is an image that was found in Ezekiel. The prophet was commanded to pass through a great river that flowed from the temple. The water became so deep that he could not pass through it. The river was a symbol for the acts of worship in the temple that were a source of grace.

Jesus now identifies himself as the true source of all grace. This was the water he offered to the Samaritan woman, and this is the water he gives to us.

For who hopes for what one sees?
But if we hope for what we do not see, we wait with
    endurance.

In the same way, the Spirit too comes to the aid of
    our weakness;
    for we do not know how to pray as we ought,
    but the Spirit himself intercedes with inexpress-
        ible groanings.
And the one who searches hearts
    knows what is the intention of the Spirit,
    because he intercedes for the holy ones
    according to God's will.

The word of the Lord.

ALLELUIA

R̹. **Alleluia, alleluia.**

Come, Holy Spirit, fill the hearts of the faithful
and kindle in them the fire of your love.

R̹. **Alleluia, alleluia.**

GOSPEL: John 7:37-39

Rivers of living water will flow.

A reading from the holy Gospel according to John

On the last and greatest day of the feast,
    Jesus stood up and exclaimed,
    "Let anyone who thirsts come to me and drink.
As Scripture says:
    *Rivers of living water will flow from within him
        who believes in me.*"

He said this in reference to the Spirit
    that those who came to believe in him were to receive.
There was, of course, no Spirit yet,
    because Jesus had not yet been glorified.

The Gospel of the Lord.

May 19, 2013

PENTECOST SUNDAY

AT THE MASS DURING THE DAY

 Lect. No. 63

FIRST READING: Acts 2:1-11

They were all filled with the Holy Spirit
and began to speak.

This account of the day of Pentecost in Acts is filled with symbolic meaning.

Pentecost was already a pilgrimage festival for the Jewish people. That would explain the large crowd of Jews from all over the world who were there when the Holy Spirit descended upon the apostles and Mary. The fact that they are from all the countries mentioned in the account is a foreshadowing of the fact that the Gospel would eventually spread to all those nations. This might, in fact, be a list of all the nations that had already received the Gospel when this book was written.

The strong wind is reminiscent of the Spirit of the Lord that hovered over the waters on the first day of creation. This was a new creation in which the people of God were being made into the Church, the Mystical Body of Christ.

The tongues of fire were a fulfillment of the prophecy of Joel that the Spirit would come upon God's people. We are no longer filled with loneliness and alienation and fear.

There was a healing of the confusion of languages in the fact that the apostles could speak in their own language and

A reading from the Acts of the Apostles

When the time for Pentecost was fulfilled,
they were all in one place together.
And suddenly there came from the sky
a noise like a strong driving wind,
and it filled the entire house in which they were.
Then there appeared to them tongues as of fire,
which parted and came to rest on each one of them.
And they were all filled with the Holy Spirit
and began to speak in different tongues,
as the Spirit enabled them to proclaim.

Now there were devout Jews from every nation under
heaven staying in Jerusalem.
At this sound, they gathered in a large crowd,
but they were confused
because each one heard them speaking in his own
language.
They were astounded, and in amazement they asked,
"Are not all these people who are speaking Galileans?
Then how does each of us hear them in his native language?
We are Parthians, Medes, and Elamites,
inhabitants of Mesopotamia, Judea and Cappadocia,
Pontus and Asia, Phrygia and Pamphylia,
Egypt and the districts of Libya near Cyrene,
as well as travelers from Rome,
both Jews and converts to Judaism, Cretans and
Arabs,

everyone could understand them. Although this is called the gift of tongues, it is different from the phenomenon described in 1 Corinthians 12—14.

yet we hear them speaking in our own tongues
of the mighty acts of God."

The word of the Lord.

Lect. No. 63

RESPONSORIAL PSALM: Ps 104:1, 24, 29-30, 31, 34 (℟.: cf. 30)

This is a hymn of praise for the God of creation. We praise God for he sent out his Spirit to create the world. After we sinned and damaged creation, God sent forth his Spirit again to renew the face of the earth. We are a new creation, not subject to the destructive effects of sin.

This is not to say that the renewal is totally complete, for we live in the dawning of the kingdom and not its fulfillment. We have already received the Holy Spirit, which is God's down payment of the glory that awaits us, but we are also still awaiting the total fulfillment of the promises Jesus made. Yet the kingdom has dawned and if we look at things through the eyes of Jesus, we will see God's power at work in our midst.

We are totally dependent upon the generosity of God. As with all living creatures, we cannot survive if he withholds his breath. Likewise, if God withholds his Spirit, our spiritual life will perish. We will suffocate spiritually.

But if we trust in Jesus and find all of our strength in God, then we will not have to fear. God will provide his Spirit to those who ask him for it in his name. God will give us life that is so profound that even death will not conquer it.

℟. **Lord, send out your Spirit, and renew the face of the earth.**

or:

℟. **Alleluia.**

Bless the LORD, O my soul!
  O LORD, my God, you are great indeed!
How manifold are your works, O LORD!
  the earth is full of your creatures;

℟. **Lord, send out your Spirit, and renew the face of the earth.**

or:

℟. **Alleluia.**

If you take away their breath, they perish
  and return to their dust.
When you send forth your spirit, they are created,
  and you renew the face of the earth.

℟. **Lord, send out your Spirit, and renew the face of the earth.**

or:

℟. **Alleluia.**

May the glory of the LORD endure forever;
  may the LORD be glad in his works!
Pleasing to him be my theme;
  I will be glad in the LORD.

℟. **Lord, send out your Spirit, and renew the face of the earth.**

or:

℟. **Alleluia.**

SECOND READING: **A** 1 Corinthians 12:3b-7, 12-13

In one Spirit we were all baptized into one body.

The community of Corinth suffered from some misunderstandings concerning the role of the Holy Spirit. They considered the gifts they had received to be signs of power that made them better than others.

Saint Paul attempts to correct their arrogance by teaching them that gifts are given for the common service. They are not for our own profit. Each person in the community has been given special gifts that complement the gifts given to others. We need each other to be complete.

Furthermore, the gifts of the Spirit should bring us closer together, not create divisions. Before our baptism, we were divided from each other and forced to live as competitors and even enemies. Now we are one body in Christ and we only seek to build up that body in love.

A reading from the first Letter of Saint Paul to the Corinthians

Brothers and sisters:
No one can say, "Jesus is Lord," except by the Holy Spirit.

There are different kinds of spiritual gifts but the same Spirit;
there are different forms of service but the same Lord;
there are different workings but the same God who produces all of them in everyone.
To each individual the manifestation of the Spirit is given for some benefit.

As a body is one though it has many parts,
and all the parts of the body, though many, are one body,
so also Christ.
For in one Spirit we were all baptized into one body,
whether Jews or Greeks, slaves or free persons,
and we were all given to drink of one Spirit.

The word of the Lord.

OR: **B** Romans 8:8-17

Those who are led by the Spirit of God are children of God.

Throughout the Letter to the Romans, Saint Paul contrasts the flesh and the spirit. The flesh is not our physical body. It is that part of us that drags us down, our earthiness that can lead us into sin.

Even though our physical bodies were created by God and are therefore good, they have been weakened by that fleshiness and they are easily led into sin.

A reading from the Letter of Saint Paul to the Romans

Brothers and sisters:
Those who are in the flesh cannot please God.
But you are not in the flesh;
on the contrary, you are in the spirit,
if only the Spirit of God dwells in you.
Whoever does not have the Spirit of Christ does not belong to him.
But if Christ is in you,

It is because of this weakness that we have to make painful choices and stick to them. Paul calls this being crucified to the world. We must learn to say "no" to those things that would drag us down. Otherwise, we will end up doing things that we really do not want to do.

It is the Spirit of God who gives us the strength to say "no." The Spirit teaches us how much God loves us. God is a loving parent, an "Abba." This word means "father," but it means much more than that. It is an affectionate term that we might translate as "dad." This is how much God loves us, that we could call God "dad."

It is this love that gives us the courage and strength to live according to the Spirit. It is difficult to say "no" to the temptations of the world. If we try to do it based upon our own self-control, we are bound to fail. If, however, we base our strength on the fact that God loves us, then we will be able to let go of those other things.

although the body is dead because of sin,
the spirit is alive because of righteousness.
If the Spirit of the one who raised Jesus from the dead dwells in you,
the one who raised Christ from the dead
will give life to your mortal bodies also,
through his Spirit that dwells in you.
Consequently, brothers and sisters,
we are not debtors to the flesh,
to live according to the flesh.
For if you live according to the flesh, you will die,
but if by the Spirit you put to death the deeds of the body,
you will live.

For those who are led by the Spirit of God are sons of God.
For you did not receive a spirit of slavery to fall back into fear,
but you received a Spirit of adoption,
through whom we cry, "Abba, Father!"
The Spirit himself bears witness with our spirit
that we are children of God,
and if children, then heirs,
heirs of God and joint heirs with Christ,
if only we suffer with him
so that we may also be glorified with him.

The word of the Lord.

Lect.
No. 63

SEQUENCE: *Veni, Sancte Spiritus*

This beautiful Sequence is a hymn that celebrates the Holy Spirit. It speaks of many of the attributes that we associate with the Spirit.

First of all, the Spirit is called a light divine. We do not know our way to God, but the Spirit illumines our thoughts and prayers.

The Spirit is a comforter. This is one of the meanings of the title "Paraclete."

Come, Holy Spirit, come!
And from your celestial home
Shed a ray of light divine!
Come, Father of the poor!
Come, source of all our store!
Come, within our bosoms shine.
You, of comforters the best;
You, the soul's most welcome guest;
Sweet refreshment here below;

We need to experience God's love that is communicated through the Holy Spirit. The Spirit is the love between the Father and the Son and between them and us.

The Spirit fills up the void in our heart. We long for fulfillment, yet so often we seek it in things that do not bring true joy and peace. The Spirit responds to our deepest aspirations.

We receive healing, both spiritual and physical, through the action of the Holy Spirit.

We also speak of the seven gifts that the Spirit has given us. Seven is the perfect number, and therefore these gifts are symbolic of the incredible multiplicity of gifts that the Spirit pours out upon us. They allow us to continue the work of God in the world.

We invite the Holy Spirit into our lives and our hearts. Without the love that the Spirit imparts, we cannot hope to live in God's love.

In our labor, rest most sweet;
Grateful coolness in the heat;
　Solace in the midst of woe.
O most blessed Light divine,
Shine within these hearts of yours,
　And our inmost being fill!
Where you are not, we have naught,
Nothing good in deed or thought,
　Nothing free from taint of ill.
Heal our wounds, our strength renew;
On our dryness pour your dew;
　Wash the stains of guilt away:
Bend the stubborn heart and will;
Melt the frozen, warm the chill;
　Guide the steps that go astray.
On the faithful, who adore
And confess you, evermore
　In your sevenfold gift descend;
Give them virtue's sure reward;
Give them your salvation, Lord;
　Give them joys that never end. Amen.
　Alleluia.

ALLELUIA

R̸. **Alleluia, alleluia.**

Come, Holy Spirit, fill the hearts of your faithful and kindle in them the fire of your love.

R̸. **Alleluia, alleluia.**

GOSPEL: ◼ John 20:19-23

As the Father sent me, so I send you: Receive the Holy Spirit.

A reading from the holy Gospel according to John

On the evening of that first day of the week,
　when the doors were locked, where the disciples
　were,
　for fear of the Jews,
　Jesus came and stood in their midst

Having heard the Acts version of the descent of the Holy Spirit, we now hear the version contained in the Gospel of John.

Jesus breathes upon the disciples to give them the gift of the Holy Spirit. This is in imitation of how God created Adam. God breathed his Spirit into Adam and he came to life. In this account, Jesus breathes his Holy Spirit into the disciples and they are given new life in him.

The gift of the Holy Spirit is also associated with the forgiveness of our sins. The Spirit is God's love and is so filled with mercy that it brings us pardon. The sin against the Spirit is to believe that our sins are unforgivable or to presume upon God's mercy by only pretending to be sorry for what we have done.

and said to them, "Peace be with you."
When he had said this, he showed them his hands
    and his side.
The disciples rejoiced when they saw the Lord.
Jesus said to them again, "Peace be with you.
As the Father has sent me, so I send you."
And when he had said this, he breathed on them
    and said to them,
    "Receive the Holy Spirit.
Whose sins you forgive are forgiven them,
    and whose sins you retain are retained."

The Gospel of the Lord.

Lect. No. 63

OR: **B** John 14:15-16, 23b-26

The Holy Spirit will teach you everything.

This passage is taken from the Last Supper Discourse in the Gospel of John. Jesus speaks about the "Paracletos." That word is sometimes translated "Advocate" as it is here, or at other times it is translated as "counselor," "consoler," "friend," etc. Jesus speaks of "another" Advocate, for he is the first Advocate.

This Gospel emphasizes the fact that our goal is to dwell with Jesus and the Father. We are called to establish a relationship that becomes our true home (wherever we might find ourselves.)

In this text we hear that the Spirit both reminds us of what Jesus taught and did and teaches us the meaning of that revelation.

A reading from the holy Gospel according to John

Jesus said to his disciples:
    "If you love me, you will keep my commandments.
And I will ask the Father,
    and he will give you another Advocate to be with you
      always.

"Whoever loves me will keep my word,
    and my Father will love him,
    and we will come to him and make our dwelling with
      him.
Those who do not love me do not keep my words;
    yet the word you hear is not mine
    but that of the Father who sent me.

"I have told you this while I am with you.
The Advocate, the Holy Spirit whom the Father will
    send in my name,
    will teach you everything
    and remind you of all that I told you."

The Gospel of the Lord.

If it is customary or obligatory for the faithful to attend Mass on the Monday or even the Tuesday after Pentecost, the readings from the Mass of Pentecost Sunday may be repeated or the readings of the Ritual Mass for Confirmation, nos. 764-768, may be used in their place.

MAY 26, 2013

THE MOST HOLY TRINITY

Lect. No. 166

FIRST READING: Proverbs 8:22-31

Before the earth was made, Wisdom was conceived.

The First Reading speaks of Wisdom. In the earliest days of Israel, wisdom was a collection of simple folk sayings that taught one how to live the good life.

This chapter was written later, after the Greeks had conquered the Middle East under Alexander the Great. The people began to think of God in Greek terms, that God was far removed from everyday events.

When this happened, the religious leaders realized that the people needed some way to know that God cared for them.

They spoke of intermediaries who brought us God's revelation and carried our prayers to God. These included God's glory, God's Spirit, and God's holiness. The greatest of these was Wisdom.

Today we hear a hymn of how she accompanied God on the day of creation and served him as an architect in his work.

The idea of Wisdom gave the Israelites many of the concepts that would help them understand the Trinity when that idea was revealed.

A reading from the Book of Proverbs

Thus says the wisdom of God:
"The LORD possessed me, the beginning of his ways,
   the forerunner of his prodigies of long ago;
from of old I was poured forth,
   at the first, before the earth.
When there were no depths I was brought forth,
   when there were no fountains or springs of water;
before the mountains were settled into place,
   before the hills, I was brought forth;
while as yet the earth and fields were not made,
   nor the first clods of the world.

"When the Lord established the heavens I was there,
   when he marked out the vault over the face of the deep;
when he made firm the skies above,
   when he fixed fast the foundations of the earth;
when he set for the sea its limit,
   so that the waters should not transgress his command;
then was I beside him as his craftsman,
   and I was his delight day by day,
playing before him all the while,
   playing on the surface of his earth;
   and I found delight in the human race."

The word of the Lord.

RESPONSORIAL PSALM: Ps 8:4-5, 6-7, 8-9 (℟.: 2a)

Psalm 8 is a hymn that speaks about the glory that God has shared with human beings.

God did not create us to be slaves who would respond to God's every whim. Rather, God has shared his glory and honor with us and made us little less than the angels.

When God created us, he breathed his Spirit into us. In other words, there is something of God inside each of us. We are not animals or fancy machines. We are created in God's image and likeness.

Yet, this also carries a responsibility. Dominion does not mean that we can abuse nature at will.

It means that we must treat it with sacred dignity, for it is the handiwork of God. We should celebrate nature and praise God with a childlike sense of wonder because of it.

℟. **O Lord, our God, how wonderful your name in all the earth!**

When I behold your heavens, the work of your fingers,
  the moon and the stars which you set in place—
what is man that you should be mindful of him,
  or the son of man that you should care for him?

℟. **O Lord, our God, how wonderful your name in all the earth!**

You have made him little less than the angels,
  and crowned him with glory and honor.
You have given him rule over the works of your hands,
  putting all things under his feet.

℟. **O Lord, our God, how wonderful your name in all the earth!**

All sheep and oxen,
  yes, and the beasts of the field,
the birds of the air, the fishes of the sea,
  and whatever swims the paths of the seas.

℟. **O Lord, our God, how wonderful your name in all the earth!**

PASTORAL REFLECTIONS

There is a Jewish saying that in front of every human being fly a host of archangels who proclaim, "Fall on your knees before the image of the living God." This saying and this psalm give us an indication of the incredible dignity with which God has created us. We were not created to be slaves (as many of the pagan creation stories proposed). We were created to be God's coworkers. This is why the words "glory" and "honor," which in the Old Testament are used for God alone, can also be used for human beings.

Lect.
No. 166

SECOND READING: Romans 5:1-5

To God, through Christ, in love poured out through the Holy Spirit.

The Second Reading speaks of our dignity. We have been justified through faith. Justification means that we are at peace with God.

Jesus gave us the opportunity to find that peace through his death on the cross and resurrection. We must trust in him (this is the meaning of the phrase "to have faith").

Yet, there is still suffering in our lives. Normally, suffering makes one feel abandoned.

This is not the case with us, for we have received the gift of the Holy Spirit and the Spirit fills us with joy when we suffer (for we realize that God's love can be seen in us when we suffer with trust).

A reading from the Letter of Saint Paul
to the Romans

Brothers and sisters:
Therefore, since we have been justified by faith,
we have peace with God through our Lord Jesus
    Christ,
through whom we have gained access by faith
to this grace in which we stand,
and we boast in hope of the glory of God.
Not only that, but we even boast of our afflictions,
    knowing that affliction produces endurance,
    and endurance, proven character,
    and proven character, hope,
    and hope does not disappoint,
    because the love of God has been poured out into
        our hearts
    through the Holy Spirit that has been given to us.

The word of the Lord.

Lect.
No. 166

ALLELUIA: cf. Revelation 1:8

The Alleluia Verse is a doxology (short hymn of praise) to the three persons of the Blessed Trinity, God who is Father, Son, and Holy Spirit.

℟. **Alleluia, alleluia.**

Glory to the Father, the Son, and the Holy Spirit;
to God who is, who was, and who is to come.

℟. **Alleluia, alleluia.**

PASTORAL REFLECTIONS

There are mysteries such as the Trinity that we will never fully understand. Our only proper response is awe and praise.

Lect. No. 166

GOSPEL: John 16:12-15

*Everything that the Father has is mine;
the Spirit will take from what is mine and declare it to you.*

The Gospel is another passage taken from the Last Supper Discourse in the Gospel of John.

It speaks of the role of the Holy Spirit (here called the Spirit of Truth but in other passages called the Paraclete) who would reveal the truth to the disciples (for there are truths about God and life that we cannot know through our own efforts).

Furthermore, the Spirit reveals these things because the Spirit is obedient to the Father, even as Jesus was obedient to the Father when he died on the cross.

There is no jealousy in the Trinity, but rather mutual respect and profound love.

A reading from the holy Gospel according to John

Jesus said to his disciples:
"I have much more to tell you, but you cannot bear it now.
But when he comes, the Spirit of truth,
    he will guide you to all truth.
He will not speak on his own,
    but he will speak what he hears,
    and will declare to you the things that are coming.
He will glorify me,
    because he will take from what is mine and declare it to you.
Everything that the Father has is mine;
    for this reason I told you that he will take from what is mine
    and declare it to you."

The Gospel of the Lord.

PASTORAL REFLECTIONS

The Trinity offers an alternative vision to how our human society can be structured. We often think in terms of competition. We might believe that if someone else profits in any way, then it must be stolen from me. This is called a zero based mentality in which there is only so much to go around and one must fight to maintain one's own portion.

The Trinity is a society based on cooperation and mutual respect. The Son willingly obeys the Father out of love, never feeling that this robs him of his dignity. The Father only wants what is good for the Son. The Spirit is that love which unites the Father and the Son and us. How much healthier our societies (families, parishes, clubs, etc.) would be if they were based on the relationship of the Trinity.

June 2, 2013

THE MOST HOLY BODY AND BLOOD OF CHRIST (CORPUS CHRISTI)

Lect. No. 169

FIRST READING: Genesis 14:18-20

Melchizedek brought out bread and wine.

The First Reading speaks of Melchizedek, a king and priest of the city of Salem. He was seen as one who prefigured Jesus.

Jesus, too, was a priest and king.

He, too, was the king of Jerusalem ("city of" is "jeru" in Hebrew—so the phrase "city of Salem" is actually "jeru-salem").

He, too, offered bread and wine at the Last Supper, just as Melchizedek did when he met Abraham.

A reading from the Book of Genesis

In those days, Melchizedek, king of Salem, brought
    out bread and wine,
    and being a priest of God Most High,
    he blessed Abram with these words:
"Blessed be Abram by God Most High,
    the creator of heaven and earth;
and blessed be God Most High,
    who delivered your foes into your hand."
Then Abram gave him a tenth of everything.

The word of the Lord.

Lect. No. 169

RESPONSORIAL PSALM: Ps 110:1, 2, 3, 4 (℟.: 4b)

The Responsorial Psalm is taken from Psalm 110, a royal psalm. It was written to commemorate the enthronement of a new king in Israel.

In ancient times, kings were also considered to be priests. Remember how David sacrificed animals when he brought the Ark of the Covenant into Jerusalem and how Solomon sacrificed animals when he dedicated the temple in Jerusalem.

The proclamation at the end of the psalm was intended for

℟. **You are a priest for ever, in the line of Melchizedek.**

The LORD said to my Lord: "Sit at my right hand
    till I make your enemies your footstool."

℟. **You are a priest for ever, in the line of Melchizedek.**

The scepter of your power the LORD will stretch
    forth from Zion:
"Rule in the midst of your enemies."

℟. **You are a priest for ever, in the line of Melchizedek.**

266

the new king, for like Melchizedek, the new king was both a priest and king.

This was also true of Jesus, who is king and priest (and also prophet).

In fact, it is even more true of Jesus, for he is a king forever.

It is also true of us, for in our Baptism we are given a share in Christ's dignity. In that sacrament we are given the dignity of priest, prophet, and king.

"Yours is princely power in the day of your birth, in holy splendor;
before the daystar, like the dew, I have begotten you."

℟. **You are a priest for ever, in the line of Melchizedek.**

The LORD has sworn, and he will not repent:
"You are a priest forever, according to the order of Melchizedek."

℟. **You are a priest for ever, in the line of Melchizedek.**

SECOND READING: 1 Corinthians 11:23-26

For as often as you eat and drink, you proclaim the death of the Lord.

The Second Reading contains the oldest written version of the institution of the Sacrament of the Eucharist. Saint Paul was writing this account to help the Corinthians understand the gravity of their sin in their failure to be charitable to the members of their community (for in the Eucharist we are in communion with God and also with our sisters and brothers).

Although this version is the oldest written form, it is actually more edited than the earlier version found in Mark and Matthew. We know this is true because of the repetition of "remembrance" and the phrase "cup is the new covenant in my blood," as opposed to cup of "my blood of the covenant."

A reading from the first Letter of Saint Paul to the Corinthians

Brothers and sisters:
I received from the Lord what I also handed on to you,
that the Lord Jesus, on the night he was handed over,
took bread, and, after he had given thanks,
broke it and said, "This is my body that is for you.
Do this in remembrance of me."
In the same way also the cup, after supper, saying,
"This cup is the new covenant in my blood.
Do this, as often as you drink it, in remembrance of me."
For as often as you eat this bread and drink the cup,
you proclaim the death of the Lord until he comes.

The word of the Lord.

Sequences are ancient hymns that were written to celebrate important feasts of the Church Year. This one celebrates the sacrament of the Holy Eucharist.

This sacrament and the love that Jesus has expressed to us through his life and his death are so incredibly profound that even if we were to praise him all of our lives, we could not begin to pay him the praise that he is due. Our act of praising him, in fact, is actually his greatest gift to us, for when we praise and thank him, we are fulfilling our greatest destiny.

Today we are especially grateful for his gift of the sacrament of his body and blood. Jesus, on Holy Thursday evening, took the bread and wine that were used as part of the Passover supper ritual, and he called them his body and his blood. In this act, he transformed the significance of these actions. We are not only celebrating the passing over of the Israelites during their exodus; we are also celebrating the passing over of Jesus from death into life.

Jesus, at the Last Supper, also commanded us to continue to do what he was doing. He said to do this in his memory. That is what we do when we take the bread and wine and call them the body and the blood of Christ. This is not simply a symbolic action; it is

SEQUENCE: *Lauda Sion*

The sequence Laud, O Zion (Lauda Sion), *or the shorter form beginning with the verse* Lo! the angel's food is given, *may be sung optionally before the Alleluia.*

Laud, O Zion, your salvation,
Laud with hymns of exultation,
Christ, your king and shepherd true:

Bring him all the praise you know,
He is more than you bestow.
Never can you reach his due.

Special theme for glad thanksgiving
Is the quick'ning and the living
Bread today before you set:

From his hands of old partaken,
As we know, by faith unshaken,
Where the Twelve at supper met.

Full and clear ring out your chanting,
Joy nor sweetest grace be wanting,
From your heart let praises burst:

For today the feast is holden,
When the institution olden
Of that supper was rehearsed.

Here the new law's new oblation,
By the new king's revelation,
Ends the form of ancient rite:

Now the new the old effaces,
Truth away the shadow chases,
Light dispels the gloom of night.

What he did at supper seated,
Christ ordained to be repeated,
His memorial ne'er to cease:

And his rule for guidance taking,
Bread and wine we hallow, making
Thus our sacrifice of peace.

an action that truly accomplishes what it says. The bread truly becomes the body of Christ and the wine truly becomes the blood of Christ.

This is not something that our senses can detect. We believe by faith, for we trust fully in the fidelity of God's words. This is ultimately what faith means, an assent of trust, an act of surrender to God's love.

But the miracle is even greater than this. Even though many people consume the bread become body of Jesus, Christ is not divided or diminished by this action.

Furthermore, Jesus' presence in this holy sacrament does not depend upon our worthiness. Whether we are good or bad, Jesus still presents himself to us. If we are good, then this sacrament serves to enhance our sanctification. If we have chosen to be evil, however, then participating in the Eucharist would be a horrible lie. We would be committing a sin against the sacrament of God's love.

The sequence closes by reiterating that no matter how many times the host is broken, it is still the body of Christ. Jesus is still present in this holy sacrament and he is still offering himself to us.

This the truth each Christian learns,
Bread into his flesh he turns,
   To his precious blood the wine:

Sight has fail'd, nor thought conceives,
But a dauntless faith believes,
   Resting on a pow'r divine.

Here beneath these signs are hidden
Priceless things to sense forbidden;
   Signs, not things are all we see:

Blood is poured and flesh is broken,
Yet in either wondrous token
   Christ entire we know to be.

Whoso of this food partakes,
Does not rend the Lord nor breaks;
   Christ is whole to all that taste:

Thousands are, as one, receivers,
One, as thousands of believers,
   Eats of him who cannot waste.

Bad and good the feast are sharing,
Of what divers dooms preparing,
   Endless death, or endless life.

Life to these, to those damnation,
See how like participation
   Is with unlike issues rife.

When the sacrament is broken,
Doubt not, but believe 'tis spoken,
   That each sever'd outward token
     doth the very whole contain.

Nought the precious gift divides,
Breaking but the sign betides
   Jesus still the same abides,
     still unbroken does remain.

Sequences are ancient hymns that were written to celebrate important feasts of the Church Year. This one celebrates the sacrament of the Holy Eucharist using a series of images of the Blessed Sacrament.

The first is of Isaac who was an only-beloved son who was almost sacrificed (like Jesus, the only-begotten Son of God who was sacrificed on the cross).

Jesus is also the new Paschal lamb. He died the very hour that the Paschal lambs were being slaughtered in the temple. Like those lambs, none of his bones were broken.

He is also manna, bread come down from heaven to satisfy the deepest hunger of his people.

Lect.
No. 169

The Alleluia Verse quotes the Discourse on the Bread of Life from the Gospel of John. Jesus speaks of himself as being the bread that will nourish us and satisfy our most profound need.

The shorter form of the sequence begins here.

Lo! the angel's food is given
  To the pilgrim who has striven;
    See the children's bread from heaven,
      which on dogs may not be spent.

Truth the ancient types fulfilling,
Isaac bound, a victim willing,
    Paschal lamb, its lifeblood spilling,
    manna to the fathers sent.

Very bread, good shepherd, tend us,
Jesu, of your love befriend us,
    You refresh us, you defend us,
    Your eternal goodness send us
In the land of life to see.

You who all things can and know,
Who on earth such food bestow,
    Grant us with your saints, though lowest,
    Where the heav'nly feast you show,
Fellow heirs and guests to be. Amen. Alleluia.

ALLELUIA: John 6:51

R⎟. **Alleluia, alleluia.**

I am the living bread that came down from heaven,
    says the Lord;
whoever eats this bread will live forever.

R⎟. **Alleluia, alleluia.**

PASTORAL REFLECTIONS

In John's Discourse on the Bread of Life in chapter 6, Jesus first presents himself as wisdom incarnate (for Lady Wisdom offered a meal of bread and wine that would provide those who ate of it with everlasting life). In verse 51 the discourse changes, though, for Jesus proclaims that the living bread that he offers us is his flesh. This reaffirms the doctrine that we call the "real presence," for we believe that the bread and wine truly become the body and blood of Christ.

Lect.
No. 169

GOSPEL: Luke 9:11b-17

They all ate and were satisfied.

A reading from the holy Gospel according to Luke

Jesus spoke to the crowds about the kingdom of God,
and he healed those who needed to be cured.
As the day was drawing to a close,
the Twelve approached him and said,
"Dismiss the crowd
so that they can go to the surrounding villages and farms
and find lodging and provisions;
for we are in a deserted place here."
He said to them, "Give them some food yourselves."
They replied, "Five loaves and two fish are all we have,
unless we ourselves go and buy food for all these people."
Now the men there numbered about five thousand.
Then he said to his disciples,
"Have them sit down in groups of about fifty."
They did so and made them all sit down.
Then taking the five loaves and the two fish,
and looking up to heaven,
he said the blessing over them, broke them,
and gave them to the disciples to set before the crowd.
They all ate and were satisfied.
And when the leftover fragments were picked up,
they filled twelve wicker baskets.

The Gospel of the Lord.

Jesus is portrayed as being compassionate throughout the Gospel of Luke.

We see this in the beginning of today's Gospel passage when he heals those who are ill, and also later when he nourishes the crowd of over five thousand (the verse speaks of five thousand men, for women and children were generally not counted).

There were five loaves and two fish. This makes seven items, and seven was the perfect number.

What was given to Jesus was already good (for this was all that the disciples had), but Jesus blesses it and multiplies its goodness.

There are a number of terms in this account that are eucharistic (e.g., took, blessed, broke, gave, etc.).

This miracle is presented as a predecessor to the institution of the Sacrament of the Eucharist.

The twelve baskets of fragments are for the twelve tribes of Israel. No one in Israel would be hungry (physically or spiritually).

PASTORAL REFLECTIONS

Corpus Christi Sunday has long been associated with a procession of the Blessed Sacrament around one's church and/or one's neighborhood.

June 9, 2013

TENTH SUNDAY IN ORDINARY TIME

Lect. No. 90

FIRST READING: 1 Kings 17:17-24

See! Your son is alive.

The story of the death and reanimation of the son of the widow of Zarephath is a parallel to the story of the raising to life of the son of the widow of Nain.

The widow of Zarephath had already seen the power of God working through Elijah in the fact that her food supply had been miraculously multiplied all throughout the ongoing famine.

Nevertheless, she fiercely challenges the prophet when her son dies. In Yiddish, this is called "chutzpah," a nerviness and insistence that will not accept "no" as an answer.

Elijah's prayer to God is equally filled with chutzpah. He accuses God of "killing" the widow's son. This attitude can be a reminder to us to pray with insistence and full trust.

God, in fact, listens to the prophet and gives the child the breath of life again. The prophet restores the child to his mother (much as Jesus would restore the son of the widow of Nain to his mother in today's Gospel).

A reading from the first Book of Kings

Elijah went to Zarephath of Sidon to the house of a widow.
The son of the mistress of the house fell sick,
    and his sickness grew more severe until he
        stopped breathing.
So she said to Elijah,
    "Why have you done this to me, O man of God?
Have you come to me to call attention to my guilt
    and to kill my son?"
Elijah said to her, "Give me your son."
Taking him from her lap, he carried the son to the
        upper room
    where he was staying, and put him on his bed.
Elijah called out to the LORD:
    "O LORD, my God,
    will you afflict even the widow with whom I am
        staying
    by killing her son?"
Then he stretched himself out upon the child three
        times
    and called out to the LORD:
    "O LORD, my God,
    let the life breath return to the body of this child."
The LORD heard the prayer of Elijah;
    the life breath returned to the child's body and he
        revived.
Taking the child, Elijah brought him down into the
        house
    from the upper room and gave him to his mother.

The woman responds by proclaiming that the prophet is truly a man of God from whose mouth the word of God comes forth (something that could be said of Jesus).

Elijah said to her, "See! Your son is alive."
The woman replied to Elijah,
    "Now indeed I know that you are a man of God.
The word of the LORD comes truly from your mouth."

| Lect. No. 90 | **RESPONSORIAL PSALM: Ps 30:2, 4, 5-6, 11, 12, 13 (℟.: 2a)** |

This psalm represents a thanksgiving for a deliverance. It is not clear what the psalmist was delivered from, only that the danger was quite serious (for the psalm speaks of being preserved from the pit, which is a way of saying "the underworld" or "sheol").

There is a subtle acknowledgment that whatever had happened might have been at least partially the fault of the psalmist. We hear about the Lord's anger. Yet, that anger, even if justified, is mercifully brief.

What follows is a time of rejoicing. We trust we will be delivered from all our difficulties because the Lord will surely have pity on us.

The word of the Lord.

℟. **I will praise you, LORD, for you have rescued me.**

I will extol you, O LORD, for you drew me clear
    and did not let my enemies rejoice over me.
O LORD, you brought me up from the nether world;
    you preserved me from among those going down
        into the pit.

℟. **I will praise you, LORD, for you have rescued me.**

Sing praise to the LORD, you his faithful ones,
    and give thanks to his holy name.
For his anger lasts but a moment;
    a lifetime, his good will.
At nightfall, weeping enters in,
    but with the dawn, rejoicing.

℟. **I will praise you, LORD, for you have rescued me.**

Hear, O LORD, and have pity on me;
    O LORD, be my helper.
You changed my mourning into dancing;
    O LORD, my God, forever will I give you thanks.

℟. **I will praise you, LORD, for you have rescued me.**

Lect.
No. 90

SECOND READING: Galatians 1:11-19

God revealed his Son to me, so that I might proclaim him to the Gentiles.

There is a very defensive tone in this passage. St. Paul had preached to the Galatians and then moved on. After he left, Jewish-Christian missionaries arrived and undercut his authority. They told the Galatians that Paul was anti-Jewish and was not even an apostle.

Paul argues that his apostolic authority comes directly from God. He did not depend upon the Twelve in Jerusalem for his call.

In fact, he was called before his birth. This particular verse is an allusion to the call of Jeremiah the prophet, the prophet to the nations. Far from rejecting Jewish ways, Paul was the fulfillment of the promise contained in that title, for he preached the Good News to the nations, the Gentiles.

While Paul does not specifically mention his encounter with Jesus on the road to Damascus, what he says is consistent with what is said about that call found in the Acts of the Apostles.

What is inconsistent is the fact that Paul solemnly swears that he had minimum contact with the Jerusalem community, while Acts implies a much more intimate relationship. This emphasizes the fact that Paul's call came directly from God and not through the apostles.

A reading from the Letter of Saint Paul
to the Galatians

I want you to know, brothers and sisters,
that the gospel preached by me is not of human
origin.
For I did not receive it from a human being, nor was
I taught it,
but it came through a revelation of Jesus Christ.

For you heard of my former way of life in Judaism,
how I persecuted the church of God beyond measure
and tried to destroy it, and progressed in Judaism
beyond many of my contemporaries among my
race,
since I was even more a zealot for my ancestral
traditions.
But when God, who from my mother's womb had
set me apart
and called me through his grace,
was pleased to reveal his Son to me,
so that I might proclaim him to the Gentiles,
I did not immediately consult flesh and blood,
nor did I go up to Jerusalem
to those who were apostles before me;
rather, I went into Arabia and then returned to
Damascus.

Then after three years I went up to Jerusalem
to confer with Cephas and remained with him for
fifteen days.
But I did not see any other of the apostles,
only James the brother of the Lord.

The word of the Lord.

Lect.
No. 90

One of the titles used for Jesus was "prophet," which literally means "one who speaks in God's name."

Lect.
No. 169

The story of the widow of Nain is ultimately one in which Jesus performs a miracle to show his compassion for someone who is facing difficulties.

This widow had lost her only son. In ancient times, that was a disaster. The only way that she could earn a living was to resort to gleaning, gathering the wheat, grapes and olives that the harvesters had left. This was, at best, a precarious existence. By raising her young son from the dead, Jesus was rescuing her from this fate.

Jesus did not resurrect the young man. He reanimated him. Resurrection means rising from the dead with a new and glorious body that would no longer suffer from death. Reanimation means coming back to life, but only for the present. He would die again sometime in the future.

ALLELUIA: Luke 7:16

℟. **Alleluia, alleluia.**

A great prophet has risen in our midst;
God has visited his people.

℟. **Alleluia, alleluia.**

GOSPEL: Luke 7:11-17

Young man, I tell you, arise!

A reading from the holy Gospel according to Luke

Jesus journeyed to a city called Nain,
and his disciples and a large crowd accompanied
him.
As he drew near to the gate of the city,
a man who had died was being carried out,
the only son of his mother, and she was a widow.
A large crowd from the city was with her.
When the Lord saw her,
he was moved with pity for her and said to her,
"Do not weep."
He stepped forward and touched the coffin;
at this the bearers halted,
and he said, "Young man, I tell you, arise!"
The dead man sat up and began to speak,
and Jesus gave him to his mother.
Fear seized them all, and they glorified God, exclaiming,
"A great prophet has arisen in our midst,"
and "God has visited his people."
This report about him spread through the whole of
Judea
and in all the surrounding region.

The Gospel of the Lord.

June 16, 2013

ELEVENTH SUNDAY IN ORDINARY TIME

Lect. No. 93 **FIRST READING: 2 Samuel 12:7-10, 13**

The Lord has forgiven your sin; you shall not die.

The main theme for today's liturgy is the forgiveness of sins.

This first reading begins with Nathan the prophet's condemnation of David. David had slept with Bathsheba, Uriah the Hittite's wife. He also arranged for Uriah's death, even though Uriah had been a faithful soldier. He then took Bathsheba into his palace as part of his harem.

David thought that he had gotten away with this, that it was all a secret, but Nathan the prophet knew about what he had done. Nathan confronted David by telling a parable about a man whose only lamb was stolen by another. He then accused David of being the man who had stolen the lamb (Bathsheba).

One must recognize one's sinfulness before one can obtain forgiveness (not because God does not want to forgive us, but rather because we must be open to the forgiveness that God is offering). This is why David's confession is so important.

A reading from the second Book of Samuel

Nathan said to David:
"Thus says the LORD God of Israel:
'I anointed you king of Israel.
I rescued you from the hand of Saul.
I gave you your lord's house and your lord's wives
    for your own.
I gave you the house of Israel and of Judah.
And if this were not enough, I could count up for
    you still more.
Why have you spurned the LORD and done evil in
    his sight?
You have cut down Uriah the Hittite with the sword;
  you took his wife as your own,
    and him you killed with the sword of the Am-
    monites.
Now, therefore, the sword shall never depart from
    your house,
  because you have despised me
  and have taken the wife of Uriah to be your wife.'"
Then David said to Nathan,
  "I have sinned against the LORD."
Nathan answered David:
  "The LORD on his part has forgiven your sin:
  you shall not die."

The word of the Lord.

Lect. No. 93

RESPONSORIAL PSALM: Ps 32:1-2, 5, 7, 11 (℞.: cf. 5c)

Sin is a rejection of God's love. One would expect that God's reaction to that betrayal would be anger and possibly even rejection. The irony is that God will not allow our infidelity to destroy his faithfulness to his promises. God remains faithful even if we do not.

This fidelity brings us forgiveness. In a sense, we end up better off after we have sinned than we were before because through the mercy that God shows us we come to understand the profundity of God's love for us.

God's forgiveness of our sins makes us want to be more faithful to God. Even if we were not willing to observe God's law before, we now feel an even greater obligation to love God as a response to his great mercy.

℞. **Lord, forgive the wrong I have done.**

Blessed is the one whose fault is taken away,
  whose sin is covered.
Blessed the man to whom the LORD imputes not guilt,
  in whose spirit there is no guile.

℞. **Lord, forgive the wrong I have done.**

I acknowledged my sin to you,
  my guilt I covered not.
I said, "I confess my faults to the LORD,"
  and you took away the guilt of my sin.

℞. **Lord, forgive the wrong I have done.**

You are my shelter; from distress you will preserve me;
  with glad cries of freedom you will ring me round.

℞. **Lord, forgive the wrong I have done.**

Be glad in the LORD and rejoice, you just;
  exult, all you upright of heart.

℞. **Lord, forgive the wrong I have done.**

Lect. No. 93

SECOND READING: Galatians 2:16, 19-21

I live, no longer I, but Christ lives in me.

Justification means to be at peace with God. We are justified not by what we do, but by what God has done for us. We cannot earn God's love, but we can trust in that love. This is what is meant by "faith," trusting in God's promise and embracing that love.

When Paul says that he died to the law, he is saying that he tried to observe that law in all

A reading from the Letter of Saint Paul to the Galatians

Brothers and sisters:
  We who know that a person is not justified by works of the law
but through faith in Jesus Christ,
even we have believed in Christ Jesus
that we may be justified by faith in Christ
and not by works of the law,
because by works of the law no one will be justified.

its prescriptions, but this only brought frustration. He could only accept God's love when he finally realized how impossible it was to be perfect or to force God to love us.

This love is not earned through our actions. It was given to us through the death and resurrection of Jesus.

For through the law I died to the law,
    that I might live for God.
I have been crucified with Christ;
    yet I live, no longer I, but Christ lives in me;
    insofar as I now live in the flesh,
    I live by faith in the Son of God
    who has loved me and given himself up for me.
I do not nullify the grace of God;
    for if justification comes through the law,
    then Christ died for nothing.

The word of the Lord.

Lect. No. 93

Jesus paid the price for our sins through his death on the cross. We did not deserve that love; it was freely given to us by God.

ALLELUIA: 1 John 4:10b

℟. **Alleluia, alleluia.**

God loved us and sent his Son
as expiation for our sins.
    ℟. **Alleluia, alleluia.**

Lect. No. 93

GOSPEL: A Longer Form: Luke 7:36—8:3

Her many sins have been forgiven her because she has shown great love.

The Pharisees taught that it was important to avoid contact with sinners. Sin was considered to be a type of contagion. If one associated with a sinner, then one participated in that person's guilt. This was especially true of eating with someone who was a sinner, for it was considered to be an especially intimate social action.

This sinful woman is not identified. Some traditions say that this was Mary Magdalene, but there is nothing in the text that would warrant that identification.

A reading from the holy Gospel according to Luke

A Pharisee invited Jesus to dine with him,
    and he entered the Pharisee's house and reclined at table.
Now there was a sinful woman in the city
    who learned that he was at table in the house of the Pharisee.
Bringing an alabaster flask of ointment,
    she stood behind him at his feet weeping
    and began to bathe his feet with her tears.
Then she wiped them with her hair,
    kissed them, and anointed them with the ointment.
When the Pharisee who had invited him saw this he
    said to himself,

Even though Simon had invited Jesus into his home, it is clear that he had not really invited him into his heart (and his hospitality). We hear him and his friends question whether Jesus is a prophet.

They assume that Jesus did not know who the woman was, but, in fact, Jesus received her precisely because of who she was and what she had done.

Later in the passage we hear that Simon had not offered Jesus the normal, expected hospitality of washing his feet.

Jesus challenges Simon and the others with the simple lesson that one who has been forgiven much will be most grateful.

God transforms a curse into a blessing. God uses our sinfulness as an opportunity to show us greater mercy.

We learn the true meaning of mercy when we are forgiven even though we don't deserve it. We cannot earn God's mercy and love; it is a free gift.

Jesus tells the woman that her faith has saved her.

In this Gospel, we are saved when Jesus enters into our lives, for that is when we experience his love.

The Gospel of Luke tends to treat women with more respect than the other Gospels. This is the only Gospel, for example, that names the women who fol-

"If this man were a prophet,
  he would know who and what sort of woman this
    is who is touching him,
  that she is a sinner."
Jesus said to him in reply,
  "Simon, I have something to say to you."
"Tell me, teacher," he said.
"Two people were in debt to a certain creditor;
  one owed five hundred days' wages and the other
    owed fifty.
Since they were unable to repay the debt, he forgave
    it for both.
Which of them will love him more?"
Simon said in reply,
  "The one, I suppose, whose larger debt was for-
    given."
He said to him, "You have judged rightly."

Then he turned to the woman and said to Simon,
  "Do you see this woman?
When I entered your house, you did not give me
    water for my feet,
  but she has bathed them with her tears
  and wiped them with her hair.
You did not give me a kiss,
  but she has not ceased kissing my feet since the
    time I entered.
You did not anoint my head with oil,
  but she anointed my feet with ointment.
So I tell you, her many sins have been forgiven
  because she has shown great love.
But the one to whom little is forgiven, loves little."
He said to her, "Your sins are forgiven."
The others at table said to themselves,
  "Who is this who even forgives sins?"
But he said to the woman,
  "Your faith has saved you; go in peace."

Afterward he journeyed from one town and village
    to another,

lowed Jesus before the Passion.

They are considered to be his disciples even during his lifetime. They generously served Jesus' and the disciples' needs (remember the importance of service in this Gospel—the one who serves is more important than the one who is being served).

preaching and proclaiming the good news of the
   kingdom of God.
Accompanying him were the Twelve
   and some women who had been cured of evil spirits and infirmities,
   Mary, called Magdalene, from whom seven demons had gone out,
   Joanna, the wife of Herod's steward Chuza,
   Susanna, and many others who provided for them out of their resources.

The Gospel of the Lord.

GOSPEL: B Shorter Form: Luke 7:36-50

Her many sins have been forgiven her because she has shown great love.

The Pharisees taught that it was important to avoid contact with sinners. Sin was considered to be a type of contagion. If one associated with a sinner, then one participated in that person's guilt. This was especially true of eating with someone who was a sinner, for it was considered to be an especially intimate social action.

This sinful woman is not identified. Some traditions say that this was Mary Magdalene, but there is nothing in the text that would warrant that identification.

Even though Simon had invited Jesus into his home, it is clear that he had not really invited him into his heart (and his hospitality). We hear him and his friends question whether Jesus is a prophet.

They assume that Jesus did not know who the woman was, but, in fact, Jesus received her

A reading from the holy Gospel according to Luke

A Pharisee invited Jesus to dine with him,
   and he entered the Pharisee's house and reclined at table.
Now there was a sinful woman in the city
   who learned that he was at table in the house of the Pharisee.
Bringing an alabaster flask of ointment,
   she stood behind him at his feet weeping
   and began to bathe his feet with her tears.
Then she wiped them with her hair,
   kissed them, and anointed them with the ointment.
When the Pharisee who had invited him saw this he
   said to himself,
   "If this man were a prophet,
   he would know who and what sort of woman this
     is who is touching him,
   that she is a sinner."
Jesus said to him in reply,
   "Simon, I have something to say to you."
"Tell me, teacher," he said.

precisely because of who she was and what she had done.

Later in the passage we hear that Simon had not offered Jesus the normal, expected hospitality of washing his feet.

Jesus challenges Simon and the others with the simple lesson that one who has been forgiven much will be most grateful.

God transforms a curse into a blessing. God uses our sinfulness as an opportunity to show us greater mercy.

We learn the true meaning of mercy when we are forgiven even though we don't deserve it. We cannot earn God's mercy and love; it is a free gift. Likewise, we should be as merciful with others.

Jesus tells the woman that her faith has saved her.

In this Gospel, we are saved when Jesus enters into our lives, for that is when we experience his love. We already are receiving our heavenly reward here on earth.

"Two people were in debt to a certain creditor;
   one owed five hundred days' wages and the other
      owed fifty.
Since they were unable to repay the debt, he forgave
   it for both.
Which of them will love him more?"
Simon said in reply,
   "The one, I suppose, whose larger debt was for-
      given."
He said to him, "You have judged rightly."

Then he turned to the woman and said to Simon,
   "Do you see this woman?
When I entered your house, you did not give me
      water for my feet,
   but she has bathed them with her tears
   and wiped them with her hair.
You did not give me a kiss,
   but she has not ceased kissing my feet since the
      time I entered.
You did not anoint my head with oil,
   but she anointed my feet with ointment.
So I tell you, her many sins have been forgiven
   because she has shown great love.
But the one to whom little is forgiven, loves little."
He said to her, "Your sins are forgiven."
The others at table said to themselves,
   "Who is this who even forgives sins?"
But he said to the woman,
   "Your faith has saved you; go in peace."

The Gospel of the Lord.

PASTORAL REFLECTIONS

There is a wonderful correlation between love and forgiveness in this Gospel. Sin is an act of hate in which we push away those who love us most (God, others, and even our own hearts). Love heals the wounds caused by sin.

June 23, 2013

TWELFTH SUNDAY IN ORDINARY TIME

Lect. No. 96 **FIRST READING: Zechariah 12:10-11; 13:1**

They shall look on him whom they have pierced.

The First Reading comes from one of the latter chapters of the Book of the Prophet Zechariah (which were probably a later addition). We do not know who the pierced figure in the reading was intended to be, but in light of Jesus' sufferings, it is obvious why early Christians identified it with Jesus.

This image is used today to tie it to the Gospel reading in which Jesus predicts his passion and death.

The mourning of Hadadrimmon might refer to a pagan practice of performing a lamentation while one would plant seeds in the soil (for, in a sense, the seed was dying so that it might give life). This is an image that Jesus himself used when he spoke of the wheat seed that had to die in order to produce fruit.

A reading from the Book of the Prophet Zechariah

Thus says the LORD:
I will pour out on the house of David
  and on the inhabitants of Jerusalem
  a spirit of grace and petition;
  and they shall look on him whom they have
    pierced,
  and they shall mourn for him as one mourns for
    an only son,
  and they shall grieve over him as one grieves over
    a firstborn.

On that day the mourning in Jerusalem shall be as
    great
  as the mourning of Hadadrimmon in the plain of
    Megiddo.

On that day there shall be open to the house of
    David
  and to the inhabitants of Jerusalem,
  a fountain to purify from sin and uncleanness.

The word of the Lord.

PASTORAL REFLECTIONS

The fountain that would purify the inhabitants of Jerusalem from their sin reminds us that we need God's grace to turn our lives around from our sinful ways. We cannot do it on our own.

Lect. No. 96

RESPONSORIAL PSALM: Ps 63:2, 3-4, 5-6, 8-9 (℟.: 2b)

The Gospel today gives a challenge that is daunting: to follow Jesus we must take up our crosses and follow him. The psalm balances this challenge by stating that we do not really have a choice.

Jesus is our only source of life and goodness. We cannot choose not to follow him. It would be like walking out into a dry and forbidding desert and dying of thirst.

Jesus is the only one who can satisfy the deepest desires of our hearts. We cling to him, for there is no meaning outside of him.

The second paragraph has an interesting combination of ideas. It speaks of power and glory in one line, and then of kindness and goodness in the next. The first pair of terms emphasizes the greatness of God, the second the gentleness and goodness of God.

℟. **My soul is thirsting for you, O Lord my God.**

O God, you are my God whom I seek;
　　for you my flesh pines and my soul thirsts
　　like the earth, parched, lifeless and without water.

℟. **My soul is thirsting for you, O Lord my God.**

Thus have I gazed toward you in the sanctuary
　　to see your power and your glory,
for your kindness is a greater good than life;
　　my lips shall glorify you.

℟. **My soul is thirsting for you, O Lord my God.**

Thus will I bless you while I live;
　　lifting up my hands, I will call upon your name.
As with the riches of a banquet shall my soul be satisfied,
　　and with exultant lips my mouth shall praise you.

℟. **My soul is thirsting for you, O Lord my God.**

You are my help,
　　and in the shadow of your wings I shout for joy.
My soul clings fast to you;
　　your right hand upholds me.

℟. **My soul is thirsting for you, O Lord my God.**

PASTORAL REFLECTIONS

Soren Kirkegaard, a 19th century Danish philosopher, said that the choice is not between belief and unbelief. It is actually between belief and despair.

Lect.
No. 96

SECOND READING: Galatians 3:26-29

All of you who were baptized have clothed yourselves with Christ.

This passage speaks of the fact that our Baptism has changed our character. We are clothed with Christ. When people look at us, they should see Christ.

This is why every distinction that one could make among people is actually superficial (Jew or Greek, etc.). None of these differences really matters when one speaks of salvation.

This does not mean that we are all the same, but it does mean that no matter who or what we are, we have become one with Christ in our Baptism.

A reading from the Letter of Saint Paul to the Galatians

Brothers and sisters:
Through faith you are all children of God in Christ Jesus.
For all of you who were baptized into Christ
 have clothed yourselves with Christ.
There is neither Jew nor Greek,
 there is neither slave nor free person,
 there is not male and female;
 for you are all one in Christ Jesus.
And if you belong to Christ,
 then you are Abraham's descendant,
 heirs according to the promise.

The word of the Lord.

Lect.
No. 96

ALLELUIA: John 10:27

℟. **Alleluia, alleluia.**

My sheep hear my voice, says the Lord;
I know them, and they follow me.
 ℟. **Alleluia, alleluia.**

The Alleluia Verse is a call to follow our shepherd. The Gospel will remind us that this means that we must follow him to the cross.

PASTORAL REFLECTIONS

The Holy Spirit gives different gifts and responsibilities to each of us. These do not make us better than others. Like distinctions or race or gender, they in themselves are not as important as our being one in Christ Jesus.

Lect.
No. 96

GOSPEL: Luke 9:18-24

You are the Christ of God. The Son of Man must suffer greatly.

Typical of the Gospel of Luke, this passage speaks of Jesus praying when something important is about to happen.

Peter proclaims Jesus to be the Christ (which means the Messiah). Jesus does not want this to be publicized, for the crowd would misunderstand his mission.

They would expect him to conquer the enemies of Israel, but he had come to conquer our true enemies (sin and fear) through his death on the cross. This is why he predicts his passion.

Jesus also invites his listeners to take up their crosses and follow him. Once we have experienced the overwhelming love of God through the death of Jesus on the cross and the forgiveness of our sins, we must be willing to share that love with others.

This will lead us to the cross, for we will have to die to ourselves in order to live for others (just as Jesus did).

A reading from the holy Gospel according to Luke

Once when Jesus was praying in solitude,
and the disciples were with him,
he asked them, "Who do the crowds say that I am?"

They said in reply, "John the Baptist;
others, Elijah;
still others, 'One of the ancient prophets has arisen.'"

Then he said to them, "But who do you say that I am?"

Peter said in reply, "The Christ of God."

He rebuked them
and directed them not to tell this to anyone.

He said, "The Son of Man must suffer greatly
and be rejected by the elders, the chief priests, and the scribes,
and be killed and on the third day be raised."

Then he said to all,
"If anyone wishes to come after me, he must deny himself
and take up his cross daily and follow me.

For whoever wishes to save his life will lose it,
but whoever loses his life for my sake will save it."

The Gospel of the Lord.

June 30, 2013

THIRTEENTH SUNDAY IN ORDINARY TIME

Lect. No. 99 **FIRST READING: 1 Kings 19:16b, 19-21**

Then Elisha left and followed Elijah as his attendant.

The First Reading introduces a theme continued in the Gospel. It speaks of the cost of discipleship, that one has to leave everything in order to follow the LORD.

This reading speaks of the call of Elisha, the successor of Elijah. The Prophet Elijah had gone to Mount Sinai and had encountered the presence of the LORD in the whispering breeze.

The LORD instructed Elijah about the future kings of Israel and Syria, and he also told Elijah that Elisha would be his successor.

But Elisha did not seem ready to leave all. The fact that there were twelve yoke of oxen means that his family was wealthy, and Elijah was asking him to renounce what he had.

Elisha renounces all he had by performing a sacrifice in which he slaughters the oxen and cooks their flesh with the wood of his plow (a clear sign that he was leaving his old life and beginning a new one).

A reading from the first Book of Kings

The LORD said to Elijah:
"You shall anoint Elisha, son of Shaphat of Abel-meholah,
as prophet to succeed you."

Elijah set out and came upon Elisha, son of Shaphat,
as he was plowing with twelve yoke of oxen;
he was following the twelfth.
Elijah went over to him and threw his cloak over him.
Elisha left the oxen, ran after Elijah, and said,
"Please, let me kiss my father and mother good-bye,
and I will follow you."
Elijah answered, "Go back!
Have I done anything to you?"
Elisha left him and, taking the yoke of oxen, slaughtered them;
he used the plowing equipment for fuel to boil their flesh,
and gave it to his people to eat.
Then Elisha left and followed Elijah as his attendant.

The word of the Lord.

RESPONSORIAL PSALM: Ps 16:1-2, 5, 7-8, 9-10, 11 (℟.: cf. 5a)

Psalm 16 is a psalm of trust in God. Trust is essential, for both the First Reading and the Gospel invited the disciples (and all of us) to leave everything we have to follow our God.

This means that we must surrender many of the things that have brought us security (or at least the illusion of security).

We all have things we hold on to, but we cannot grasp them and embrace God.

This could leave us feeling frightened and insecure. But God promises to be our refuge and our portion. Rather than living in fear, we will be filled with joy and surrounded by the delights of our God.

The night was considered to be a time of danger. It was the dawn when God would intervene and save us from the hands of our enemies.

But in this psalm even the night is safe, for God is always revealing his love for us.

℟. **You are my inheritance, O Lord.**

Keep me, O God, for in you I take refuge;
  I say to the LORD, "My Lord are you.
O LORD, my allotted portion and my cup,
  you it is who hold fast my lot."

℟. **You are my inheritance, O Lord.**

I bless the LORD who counsels me;
  even in the night my heart exhorts me.
I set the LORD ever before me;
  with him at my right hand I shall not be disturbed.

℟. **You are my inheritance, O Lord.**

Therefore my heart is glad and my soul rejoices,
  my body, too, abides in confidence
because you will not abandon my soul to the nether-
    world,
  nor will you suffer your faithful one to undergo
    corruption.

℟. **You are my inheritance, O Lord.**

You will show me the path to life,
  fullness of joys in your presence,
  the delights at your right hand forever.

℟. **You are my inheritance, O Lord.**

PASTORAL REFLECTIONS

What is it that God really has promised us? Will God always make things work out perfectly, or will God at times allow things to be difficult and messy? Will God always be there for us, and if so, what does that mean in everyday terms? Do I at times feel that God is not upholding his part of the bargain?

Lect. No. 99

SECOND READING: Galatians 5:1, 13-18

You were called for freedom.

Saint Paul wrote the communities of Galatia and warned them against the teachings of those who would have them follow the Jewish law.

He told them that if they committed themselves to that law, they would become slaves to it. God had not created us to be slaves. We were created to be free.

Yet, freedom does not mean that we can do anything we want. Sin is not freedom, it is another form of slavery (enslavement to our passions).

We think that we are doing what we really want to do, but we end up choosing things that leave us feeling worse about ourselves.

We must choose the freedom of the Spirit. When Paul speaks of the flesh, he is referring to that part of us that drags us down, our earthiness. Saint Augustine calls this our concupiscence.

We must reject it and choose true freedom, which means a choice of love.

A reading from the Letter of Saint Paul to the Galatians

Brothers and sisters:
For freedom Christ set us free;
    so stand firm and do not submit again to the yoke of slavery.

For you were called for freedom, brothers and sisters.
But do not use this freedom
    as an opportunity for the flesh;
    rather, serve one another through love.
For the whole law is fulfilled in one statement,
    namely, *You shall love your neighbor as yourself.*
But if you go on biting and devouring one another,
    beware that you are not consumed by one another.

I say, then: live by the Spirit
    and you will certainly not gratify the desire of the flesh.
For the flesh has desires against the Spirit,
    and the Spirit against the flesh;
    these are opposed to each other,
    so that you may not do what you want.
But if you are guided by the Spirit, you are not under the law.

The word of the Lord.

Lect. No. 99

ALLELUIA: 1 Samuel 3:9; John 6:68c

The Alleluia Verse repeats the words of Samuel, the last judge of Israel, as he responded to the call of God during the night.

℟. **Alleluia, alleluia.**

Speak, Lord, your servant is listening;
you have the words of everlasting life.

℟. **Alleluia, alleluia.**

GOSPEL: Luke 9:51-62

He resolutely determined to journey to Jerusalem. I will follow you wherever you go.

The Gospel contains three separate fragments from the Gospel of Luke.

The first one concerns the rejection of Jesus by the Samaritans and the disciples' response. James and John wanted to see them punished.

They thought that the ministry of Jesus was one that would establish an earthly reign. They were thinking in terms of power and prestige and not in terms of love and service.

However, Jesus had come to heal hearts and not to establish a kingdom. He had come to invite and not to punish.

In the second passage, we hear that Jesus has no dwelling place. Discipleship is a journey and we arrive at our destination only when we are fully with Jesus at the end of time.

All throughout the Old Testament, the people of Israel tried to find the fulfillment of the promise. They thought it might be the land, the holy city, the kingship, the temple. But the promise was more profound than that.

Finally, we hear that discipleship means leaving all that we have and trusting in God. What this surrender means is different for each of us, but each of us is still called to follow Jesus.

A reading from the holy Gospel according to Luke

When the days for Jesus' being taken up were fulfilled,
   he resolutely determined to journey to Jerusalem,
   and he sent messengers ahead of him.
On the way they entered a Samaritan village
   to prepare for his reception there,
   but they would not welcome him
   because the destination of his journey was Jerusalem.
When the disciples James and John saw this they asked,
   "Lord, do you want us to call down fire from heaven to consume them?"
Jesus turned and rebuked them, and they journeyed to another village.

As they were proceeding on their journey someone said to him,
   "I will follow you wherever you go."
Jesus answered him,
   "Foxes have dens and birds of the sky have nests,
   but the Son of Man has nowhere to rest his head."

And to another he said, "Follow me."
But he replied, "Lord, let me go first and bury my father."
But he answered him, "Let the dead bury their dead.
But you, go and proclaim the kingdom of God."
And another said, "I will follow you, Lord,
   but first let me say farewell to my family at home."
To him Jesus said, "No one who sets a hand to the plow
   and looks to what was left behind is fit for the kingdom of God."

The Gospel of the Lord.

July 7, 2013

FOURTEENTH SUNDAY IN ORDINARY TIME

Lect. No. 102   **FIRST READING: Isaiah 66:10-14c**

Behold, I will spread prosperity over her like a river.

The First Reading is a hymn to celebrate the blessings that the LORD would shower upon Jerusalem. We hear of the comfort that the LORD would give to his beloved people.

It would be a more compassionate relationship than one would expect between a mother and that mother's child. There is a tremendous warmth and intimacy in the symbolism.

Notice that the hymn is built upon parallelism, a common technique used in Hebrew poetry.

The author repeats things over and over again, using slightly different terms each time. Each repetition emphasizes the symbolism being presented.

There is not an immediate connection between the First Reading and the Gospel, except for the fact that the blessings that are described in the First Reading would be visited upon those who would hear the Good News from the disciples.

A reading from the Book of the Prophet Isaiah

Thus says the LORD:
Rejoice with Jerusalem and be glad because of her,
all you who love her;
exult, exult with her,
all you who were mourning over her!
Oh, that you may suck fully
of the milk of her comfort,
that you may nurse with delight
at her abundant breasts!
For thus says the LORD:
Lo, I will spread prosperity over Jerusalem like a river,
and the wealth of the nations like an overflowing torrent.
As nurslings, you shall be carried in her arms,
and fondled in her lap;
as a mother comforts her child,
so will I comfort you;
in Jerusalem you shall find your comfort.
When you see this, your heart shall rejoice
and your bodies flourish like the grass;
the LORD's power shall be known to his servants.

The word of the Lord.

Lect. No. 102

RESPONSORIAL PSALM: Ps 66:1-3, 4-5, 6-7, 16, 20 (℟.: 1)

Psalm 66 is a hymn of thanksgiving, both for what the LORD had done for the nation and for what he had done for the psalmist.

God is both a God who guides the great events of history and a God who is concerned with every individual.

It is interesting that, while the events of which the psalmist is speaking involve Israel, he calls upon all the nations of the earth to give praise to the LORD.

The reason is that they had witnessed the covenant that God had made with Israel, and they had also witnessed the ways that God had reached out to save Israel in her times of need (e.g., during the Exodus from Egypt).

But the nations can also rejoice for they are being invited into that covenant in the Gospel passage that we hear today.

℟. **Let all the earth cry out to God with joy.**

Shout joyfully to God, all the earth,
    sing praise to the glory of his name;
    proclaim his glorious praise.
Say to God, "How tremendous are your deeds!"

℟. **Let all the earth cry out to God with joy.**

"Let all on earth worship and sing praise to you,
    sing praise to your name!"
Come and see the works of God,
    his tremendous deeds among the children of Adam.

℟. **Let all the earth cry out to God with joy.**

He has changed the sea into dry land;
    through the river they passed on foot;
    therefore let us rejoice in him.
He rules by his might forever.

℟. **Let all the earth cry out to God with joy.**

Hear now, all you who fear God,
    while I declare what he has done for me.
Blessed be God who refused me not
    my prayer or his kindness!

℟. **Let all the earth cry out to God with joy.**

Lect. No. 102

SECOND READING: Galatians 6:14-18

I bear the marks of Jesus on my body.

The Second Reading speaks of how Saint Paul has chosen to follow the Lord with heart and soul. This meant not only saying "yes" to the Lord; it meant also rejecting all those things that would get in the way (this is what it means to be crucified to the world).

A reading from the Letter of Saint Paul
to the Galatians

Brothers and sisters:
    May I never boast except in the cross of our Lord
        Jesus Christ,
    through which the world has been crucified to me,
    and I to the world.

We are a new creation (for with the death and resurrection of Jesus, all things are made new). We cannot return to the old ways that just dragged us down.

When Paul says that he bears the brand marks of Jesus, he is using the Greek word "stigmata." This does not mean that he bore the wounds of Christ (as Saint Francis did). It probably refers to the scars of scourgings and beatings.

For neither does circumcision mean anything, nor
     does uncircumcision,
but only a new creation.
Peace and mercy be to all who follow this rule
     and to the Israel of God.

From now on, let no one make troubles for me;
     for I bear the marks of Jesus on my body.

The grace of our Lord Jesus Christ be with your
     spirit,
     brothers and sisters. Amen.

The word of the Lord.

Lect. No. 102

ALLELUIA: Colossians 3:15a, 16a

The Alleluia Verse speaks of the word of Christ that will transform us. It will bring us a peace that nothing can take away from us.

℟. **Alleluia, alleluia.**

Let the peace of Christ control your hearts;
let the word of Christ dwell in you richly.

℟. **Alleluia, alleluia.**

Lect. No. 102

GOSPEL: 🅰 Longer Form: Luke 10:1-12, 17-20

Your peace will rest on that person.

In the Gospel of Luke we hear about two different groups of followers of Jesus.

The first group is the apostles. There are only twelve of them (the same number as the patriarchs of Israel). When one of them betrays Jesus, he is replaced by another so that they would continue to have the proper number.

The other group is the seventy-two disciples. This would be the same number as the elders of Israel who were chosen

A reading from the holy Gospel according to Luke

At that time the Lord appointed seventy-two others whom he sent ahead of him in pairs
to every town and place he intended to visit.
He said to them,
     "The harvest is abundant but the laborers are few;
     so ask the master of the harvest
     to send out laborers for his harvest.
Go on your way;
     behold, I am sending you like lambs among wolves.
Carry no money bag, no sack, no sandals;
     and greet no one along the way.
Into whatever house you enter, first say,
     'Peace to this household.'

to help Moses to govern the people of Israel.

Jesus sends them out to proclaim the Good News.

They were to trust in the goodness of the Lord. They were not to make provisions for their own need, because the Lord would provide.

They were also to depend upon the generosity of those to whom they preached. It is important to remember that when we minister to others, we must also be vulnerable enough to let them minister to us.

Love means both serving others and allowing them to serve us.

If, however, the people would not accept their message, then they were to shake the dust off their feet.

We cannot force people to change, we can only invite them. Some will say yes, others will not.

The disciples return very successful and they are filled with joy. Jesus warns them not to be filled with pride.

They should not rejoice in what they accomplished as much as what the Lord has accomplished in them (through his love).

If a peaceful person lives there,
    your peace will rest on him;
    but if not, it will return to you.
Stay in the same house and eat and drink what is offered to you,
    for the laborer deserves his payment.
Do not move about from one house to another.
Whatever town you enter and they welcome you,
    eat what is set before you,
    cure the sick in it and say to them,
    'The kingdom of God is at hand for you.'
Whatever town you enter and they do not receive you,
    go out into the streets and say,
    'The dust of your town that clings to our feet,
    even that we shake off against you.'
Yet know this: the kingdom of God is at hand.
I tell you,
    it will be more tolerable for Sodom on that day than for that town."

The seventy-two returned rejoicing, and said,
    "Lord, even the demons are subject to us because of your name."
Jesus said, "I have observed Satan fall like lightning from the sky.
Behold, I have given you the power to 'tread upon serpents' and scorpions
    and upon the full force of the enemy and nothing will harm you.
Nevertheless, do not rejoice because the spirits are subject to you,
    but rejoice because your names are written in heaven."
The Gospel of the Lord.

PASTORAL REFLECTIONS

What does it mean to be a disciple of the Lord? How does that change the way I think and act?

Lect. No. 102

GOSPEL: Ⓑ Shorter Form: Luke 10:1-9

Your peace will rest on that person.

In the Gospel of Luke we hear about two different groups of followers of Jesus.

The first group is the apostles. There are only twelve of them (the same number as the patriarchs of Israel).

The other group is the seventy-two disciples. This would be the same number as the elders of Israel who were chosen to help Moses to govern the people of Israel.

Jesus sends them out to proclaim the Good News.

They were to trust in the goodness of the Lord. They were not to make provisions for their own need, because the Lord would provide.

They were also to depend upon the generosity of those to whom they preached. It is important to remember that when we minister to others, we must also be vulnerable enough to let them minister to us.

Love means both serving others and allowing them to serve us.

A reading from the holy Gospel according to Luke

At that time the Lord appointed seventy-two others whom he sent ahead of him in pairs
to every town and place he intended to visit.
He said to them,
 "The harvest is abundant but the laborers are few;
 so ask the master of the harvest
 to send out laborers for his harvest.
Go on your way;
 behold, I am sending you like lambs among wolves.
Carry no money bag, no sack, no sandals;
 and greet no one along the way.
Into whatever house you enter, first say,
 'Peace to this household.'
If a peaceful person lives there,
 your peace will rest on him;
 but if not, it will return to you.
Stay in the same house and eat and drink what is offered to you,
 for the laborer deserves his payment.
Do not move about from one house to another.
Whatever town you enter and they welcome you,
 eat what is set before you,
 cure the sick in it and say to them,
 'The kingdom of God is at hand for you.'"

The Gospel of the Lord.

PASTORAL REFLECTIONS

Why is it easier to volunteer to help others than to ask for help? Why is it essential to admit that we need others' help? Can we say that we are really loving if we serve and serve and serve, but do not let others serve us?

Lect. No. 105 **FIRST READING: Deuteronomy 30:10-14**

The word is very near to you: you have only to carry it out.

The law that God gave to Israel was a wonderful gift. Many of the pagan nations lived in fear for they did not know what their gods wanted.

Their gods were capricious and would condemn them for faults that the people might not even have known they were committing. Furthermore, the rules were constantly changing so they could never be at peace.

But the God of Israel had given his chosen people the law to guide them in the right paths. They would not have to seek wisdom in some far-off land.

It had been placed in their hearts and their mouths by the LORD himself. All that the people of Israel had to do was observe that law with integrity.

A reading from the Book of Deuteronomy

Moses said to the people:
"If only you would heed the voice of the LORD,
    your God,
and keep his commandments and statutes
that are written in this book of the law,
when you return to the LORD, your God,
with all your heart and all your soul.

"For this command that I enjoin on you today
    is not too mysterious and remote for you.
It is not up in the sky, that you should say,
    'Who will go up in the sky to get it for us
    and tell us of it, that we may carry it out?'
Nor is it across the sea, that you should say,
    'Who will cross the sea to get it for us
    and tell us of it, that we may carry it out?'
No, it is something very near to you,
    already in your mouths and in your hearts;
    you have only to carry it out."

The word of the Lord.

Lect. No. 105

▮ RESPONSORIAL PSALM:

Ps 69:14, 17, 30-31, 33-34, 36, 37 (℞.: cf. 33)

The Responsorial Psalm is a series of verses taken from an individual lamentation.

In this type of psalm, the psalmist calls out to God in a

℞. **Turn to the Lord in your need, and you will live.**

I pray to you, O LORD,
    for the time of your favor, O God!
In your great kindness answer me
    with your constant help.

time of distress, for God is the only one who can help.

The closing verses of almost every lamentation are called the *todah*.

In the *todah* the psalmist proclaims his trust in God, for he is absolutely sure that God will deliver him from all his difficulties.

It is interesting that this psalm speaks of how God will deliver us from our problems, while the Gospel reminds us that we are the ones who have to reach out to others who have difficulties, for anyone who is in need is our brother or sister.

As God has loved us, now we must share that love with all of God's children.

Answer me, O LORD, for bounteous is your kindness:
     in your great mercy turn toward me.

℟. **Turn to the Lord in your need, and you will live.**

I am afflicted and in pain;
     let your saving help, O God, protect me.
I will praise the name of God in song,
     and I will glorify him with thanksgiving.

℟. **Turn to the Lord in your need, and you will live.**

"See, you lowly ones, and be glad;
     you who seek God, may your hearts revive!
For the LORD hears the poor,
     and his own who are in bonds he spurns not."

℟. **Turn to the Lord in your need, and you will live.**

For God will save Zion
     and rebuild the cities of Judah.
The descendants of his servants shall inherit it,
     and those who love his name shall inhabit it.

℟. **Turn to the Lord in your need, and you will live.**

Lect. No. 105   **OR: 2 RESPONSORIAL PSALM: Ps 19:8, 9, 10, 11 (℟.: 9a)**

While the first option for the Responsorial Psalm emphasizes the second half of the Gospel where we hear the story of the Good Samaritan, the second portion centers on the first half of the Gospel passage that speaks about the law of the LORD.

This portion of Psalm 19 gives six synonyms for the law and speaks about how perfect and wondrous the law is. It is odd that only six synonyms are used, for one would expect the number seven since that is the perfect number.

℟. **Your words, Lord, are Spirit and life.**

The law of the LORD is perfect,
     refreshing the soul;
the decree of the LORD is trustworthy,
     giving wisdom to the simple.

℟. **Your words, Lord, are Spirit and life.**

The precepts of the LORD are right,
     rejoicing the heart;
the command of the LORD is clear,
     enlightening the eye.

℟. **Your words, Lord, are Spirit and life.**

The fear of the LORD is pure,
     enduring forever;

The seventh reference to the law of the Lord is actually found at the end of the psalm, in a verse that is not used today.

That verse speaks of how the law of the Lord should be on our lips (public witness) and in our hearts (interiorized). Then it will be perfect.

the ordinances of the LORD are true,
    all of them just.
    R̦. **Your words, Lord, are Spirit and life.**

They are more precious than gold,
    than a heap of purest gold;
sweeter also than syrup
    or honey from the comb.
    R̦. **Your words, Lord, are Spirit and life.**

Lect.
No. 105

SECOND READING: Colossians 1:15-20

All things were created through him and for him.

The Second Reading is a beautiful hymn that speaks about Christ. The early Church struggled to develop concepts that would explain who Jesus was.

Here it calls him an icon of the Father. Icons are not simply pictures, they are considered to be representations of the holy one.

The hymn also presents Jesus as the Wisdom of God. In the Old Testament Wisdom is an attribute of God.

It was the architect who assisted him at creation and the revelation of God's will.

Jesus is also the head of the Church and the firstborn from the dead. He brought about our justification with God through his death and resurrection, and he has provided us a way to live in that justification by giving us the Church.

A reading from the Letter of Saint Paul
to the Colossians

Christ Jesus is the image of the invisible God,
    the firstborn of all creation.
For in him were created all things in heaven and
        on earth,
    the visible and the invisible,
    whether thrones or dominions or principalities
        or powers;
    all things were created through him and for
        him.
He is before all things,
    and in him all things hold together.
He is the head of the body, the church.
He is the beginning, the firstborn from the dead,
    that in all things he himself might be preemi-
        nent.
For in him all the fullness was pleased to dwell,
    and through him to reconcile all things for him,
    making peace by the blood of his cross
    through him, whether those on earth or those in
        heaven.

The word of the Lord.

Lect. No. 105

The word of God is not a simple utterance. It is a communication of life and of love. This Alleluia Verse proclaims that it is filled with Spirit and life.

Lect. No. 105

The beginning of this Gospel passage centers on the question of what the greatest law is.

Saint Luke has made a few changes in the original version of the story so that it would be understood better by his pagan audience.

While Mark and Matthew have a Pharisee or scribe question Jesus, here it is a lawyer (for the pagan audience of this Gospel would identify better with lawyers). He also asks how to gain eternal life (not what the greatest law is).

The lawyer responds to Jesus that one must love God and neighbor. Here, typical of the Gospel of Luke, the question of neighbor becomes the central focus.

Jesus gives an extreme example to challenge his listener.

He speaks of a Good Samaritan who helps someone who had been robbed on the road from Jerusalem to Jericho. To this day, that particular road is difficult and dangerous.

ALLELUIA: cf. John 6:63c, 68c

℟. **Alleluia, alleluia.**

Your words, Lord, are Spirit and life;
you have the words of everlasting life.

℟. **Alleluia, alleluia.**

GOSPEL: Luke 10:25-37

Who is my neighbor?

A reading from the holy Gospel according to Luke

There was a scholar of the law who stood up to test Jesus and said,
  "Teacher, what must I do to inherit eternal life?"
Jesus said to him, "What is written in the law?
How do you read it?"
He said in reply,
  "*You shall love the Lord, your God,*
  with all your heart,
  with all your being,
  with all your strength,
  and with all your mind,
  and your neighbor as yourself."
He replied to him, "You have answered correctly;
  do this and you will live."

But because he wished to justify himself, he said to Jesus,
  "And who is my neighbor?"
Jesus replied,
  "A man fell victim to robbers
  as he went down from Jerusalem to Jericho.
They stripped and beat him and went off leaving him half-dead.
A priest happened to be going down that road,
  but when he saw him, he passed by on the opposite side.

One would have expected religious leaders to help the man, but they pass by the wounded man without coming to his assistance. It might be that they were afraid, or possibly they were concerned with becoming ritually impure. Whatever the reason, they passed by.

Then a Samaritan came along and helped the wounded man. Samaritans hated Jews and Jews hated Samaritans. Yet, it was this very man who reached out and showed charity to the wounded man.

In addition, he also showed an exaggerated charity that one would expect of a family member or a loved one, not a stranger.

Having given this powerful example, Jesus now asks the lawyer who the true neighbor of the story is. The man answers that it is the Samaritan, and Jesus tells him that he must therefore follow the Samaritan's example.

Likewise a Levite came to the place,
    and when he saw him, he passed by on the opposite side.
But a Samaritan traveler who came upon him
    was moved with compassion at the sight.
He approached the victim,
    poured oil and wine over his wounds and bandaged them.
Then he lifted him up on his own animal,
    took him to an inn, and cared for him.
The next day he took out two silver coins
    and gave them to the innkeeper with the instruction,
    'Take care of him.
If you spend more than what I have given you,
    I shall repay you on my way back.'
Which of these three, in your opinion,
    was neighbor to the robbers' victim?"
He answered, "The one who treated him with mercy."
Jesus said to him, "Go and do likewise."

The Gospel of the Lord.

PASTORAL REFLECTIONS

The Gospel of Luke has a tendency to tell beautiful stories that also contain a sting. The story of the Good Samaritan is an example of this. It is a beautiful story on its surface level, but then one realizes that the hero of the story is a Samaritan. It is difficult for us to understand how hated the Samaritans were to the Jews. It would be comparable to being told that a terrorist was the hero of a story and the example of what a Christian should be. Jesus and Luke realized that we sometimes have to be shocked in order to break through the tendency to hear but not to listen.

July 21, 2013

SIXTEENTH SUNDAY IN ORDINARY TIME

Lect. No. 108 **FIRST READING: Genesis 18:1-10a**

Lord, do not go on past your servant.

The main themes of today's readings are hospitality and the promise.

The First Reading tells of the hospitality that Abraham gave to three strangers and how their response was the fulfillment of the promise that God had made to him.

One can see strangers from a distance in the desert. Abraham saw these three strangers approaching his tent. In this passage, although they are described as three men, it appears as if they are God and two angels.

Later, in the Christian era, they would come to be understood as the three persons of the Holy Trinity.

Hospitality is essential in the desert. Lack of hospitality was a death sentence, and it was considered to be one of the greatest sins that one could commit. (It is, in fact, one of the reasons for the destruction of Sodom and Gomorrah.)

But the hospitality that Abraham shows the strangers is exaggerated. Abraham and Sarah prepare a sumptuous meal for the strangers.

A reading from the Book of Genesis

The LORD appeared to Abraham by the terebinth of Mamre,
as he sat in the entrance of his tent,
while the day was growing hot.
Looking up, Abraham saw three men standing nearby.
When he saw them, he ran from the entrance of the tent to greet them;
and bowing to the ground, he said:
"Sir, if I may ask you this favor,
please do not go on past your servant.
Let some water be brought, that you may bathe your feet,
and then rest yourselves under the tree.
Now that you have come this close to your servant,
let me bring you a little food, that you may refresh yourselves;
and afterward you may go on your way."
The men replied, "Very well, do as you have said."

Abraham hastened into the tent and told Sarah,
"Quick, three measures of fine flour! Knead it and make rolls."
He ran to the herd, picked out a tender, choice steer,
and gave it to a servant, who quickly prepared it.
Then Abraham got some curds and milk,
as well as the steer that had been prepared,
and set these before the three men;
and he waited on them under the tree while they ate.

As a response to Abraham's generosity, the three strangers predict that God's promise to Abraham and Sarah would be fulfilled.

They tell Abraham that he and Sarah will have a son by the next year.

They asked Abraham, "Where is your wife Sarah?"
He replied, "There in the tent."
One of them said, "I will surely return to you about
    this time next year,
  and Sarah will then have a son."

The word of the Lord.

Lect.
No. 108

RESPONSORIAL PSALM: Ps 15:2-3, 3-4, 5 (℟.: 1a)

The First Reading spoke of hospitality and welcoming God into one's home. The Gospel speaks of the same thing, for it presents the story of Martha and Mary and their hospitality toward Jesus.

The Responsorial Psalm asks who can be a host to the LORD.

The answer given is a standard wisdom teaching: the one who lives a moral, righteous life. Among those things that such a wise person will do is to speak the truth and not gossip.

The wise one will stay away from those who live sinful lives, and will praise and associate with those who live according to God's ways.

The wise one will also use money carefully, not making extravagant profits at another's expense and not selling justice.

℟. **He who does justice will live in the presence of the Lord.**

One who walks blamelessly and does justice;
  who thinks the truth in his heart
  and slanders not with his tongue.

℟. **He who does justice will live in the presence of the Lord.**

Who harms not his fellow man,
  nor takes up a reproach against his neighbor;
by whom the reprobate is despised,
  while he honors those who fear the LORD.

℟. **He who does justice will live in the presence of the Lord.**

Who lends not his money at usury
  and accepts no bribe against the innocent.
One who does these things
  shall never be disturbed.

℟. **He who does justice will live in the presence of the Lord.**

PASTORAL REFLECTIONS

What do I consider true hospitality? What is most difficult for me to share (e.g., money, talents, time)?

**Lect.
No. 108**

SECOND READING: Colossians 1:24-28

The mystery hidden from ages has now been manifested to his holy ones.

The Second Reading continues the selections from the Letter to the Colossians. The author speaks of filling up what is lacking in the sufferings of Christ. One might ask what could be lacking.

There is only one thing: to make Christ's suffering present and alive again in ourselves. By trusting when we suffer, we become Sacraments of the Passion of Christ.

We also hear about the mystery hidden from ages past. The word "mystery" does not mean a secret that is purposely hidden. It is much more than that.

We, as humans, cannot even begin to know the fullness of God's will; it is so far beyond us. Yet, this is what has been revealed in Christ.

In his death and resurrection, we have learned how much God loves us and the glory that he had prepared for us.

A reading from the Letter of Saint Paul
to the Colossians

Brothers and sisters:
Now I rejoice in my sufferings for your sake,
and in my flesh I am filling up
what is lacking in the afflictions of Christ
on behalf of his body, which is the church,
of which I am a minister
in accordance with God's stewardship given to me
to bring to completion for you the word of God,
the mystery hidden from ages and from generations past.
But now it has been manifested to his holy ones,
to whom God chose to make known the riches of the glory
of this mystery among the Gentiles;
it is Christ in you, the hope for glory.
It is he whom we proclaim,
admonishing everyone and teaching everyone with all wisdom,
that we may present everyone perfect in Christ.

The word of the Lord.

**Lect.
No. 108**

ALLELUIA: cf. Luke 8:15

The Alleluia Verse speaks of accepting the word of God. Our generous hearts will then be fertile soil that will produce a harvest of one hundredfold and more.

℟. **Alleluia, alleluia.**

Blessed are they who have kept the word with a generous heart
and yield a harvest through perseverance.

℟. **Alleluia, alleluia.**

GOSPEL: Luke 10:38-42

Martha welcomed him. Mary has chosen the better part.

The Gospel tells the story of Martha and Mary and their hospitality toward Jesus.

Martha seems to have been a person who could become overwhelmed with the tasks at hand. Mary seems to be above it all.

When Martha complains to Jesus in the hope that he will scold her sister for being lazy, Jesus responds that Mary had chosen the better part.

In our faith life, it is easy to concentrate on "what has to be done." We could easily make our Christian life into a series of tasks that have to be fulfilled.

But, ultimately, our Christian life must be based upon a loving relationship with the Lord. Then whatever we do will be a loving response to love received.

A reading from the holy Gospel according to Luke

Jesus entered a village
where a woman whose name was Martha welcomed him.
She had a sister named Mary
who sat beside the Lord at his feet listening to him speak.
Martha, burdened with much serving, came to him and said,
"Lord, do you not care
that my sister has left me by myself to do the serving?
Tell her to help me."
The Lord said to her in reply,
"Martha, Martha, you are anxious and worried about many things.
There is need of only one thing.
Mary has chosen the better part
and it will not be taken from her."

The Gospel of the Lord.

PASTORAL REFLECTIONS

Any form of ministry can easily degenerate into an attempt to complete a series of tasks rather than be of service to the people whom we are supposedly serving. We can be more concerned with the number of meals we serve at the soup kitchen than with treating each individual with dignity. We can be more concerned with the number of people in our religious education classes or in our RCIA program than with the fact that we should listen to where they are in their faith journey and what they need to learn. Jesus always took time for the individual and treated each person with sacred respect.

July 28, 2013

SEVENTEENTH SUNDAY IN ORDINARY TIME

Lect. No. 111 **FIRST READING: Genesis 18:20-32**

Let not my Lord grow angry if I speak.

The theme found in the First Reading and the Gospel is that of the power of prayer.

The backdrop of the First Reading is the destruction of the cities of Sodom and Gomorrah.

The two angels who had accompanied God on his visit to Abraham in last week's First Reading continued on the road toward those cities.

They experienced the hospitality of Lot and his family and the gross lack of hospitality on the part of the townsfolk.

This sin (remember the significance of the lack of hospitality in a desert culture) and the other sins of these cities were too much for God.

God announces his plan to destroy the cities to his friend Abraham. As they walk along, Abraham tries to convince God not to destroy the city.

He plays on God's conscience and reputation, asking whether God would destroy the innocent with the guilty.

This is typical of argumentation with God in the Old Testa-

A reading from the Book of Genesis

In those days, the LORD said: "The outcry against Sodom and Gomorrah is so great,
and their sin so grave,
that I must go down and see whether or not their actions
fully correspond to the cry against them that comes to me.
I mean to find out."

While Abraham's visitors walked on farther toward Sodom,
the LORD remained standing before Abraham.
Then Abraham drew nearer and said:
"Will you sweep away the innocent with the guilty?
Suppose there were fifty innocent people in the city;
would you wipe out the place, rather than spare it
for the sake of the fifty innocent people within it?
Far be it from you to do such a thing,
to make the innocent die with the guilty
so that the innocent and the guilty would be treated alike!
Should not the judge of all the world act with justice?"
The LORD replied,
"If I find fifty innocent people in the city of Sodom,
I will spare the whole place for their sake."
Abraham spoke up again:
"See how I am presuming to speak to my LORD,
though I am but dust and ashes!

304

ment. There is a Jewish saying that God dances when one of his creatures wins an argument with him.

This is a typical Hebrew dialogue between a sovereign and a subject. Abraham is always respectful, but also continues to push a little further each time they speak.

By the end of the dialogue, God has agreed that he will not destroy the city if even ten righteous men are found there. Ten is a significant number in Judaism, for that is the number that is needed to form an assembly of prayer.

Unfortunately, not even ten righteous men were found there.

God, however, did not destroy the innocent along with the guilty, for he saved Lot and his family by having them flee from the doomed city. God is always filled with love and mercy.

What if there are five less than fifty innocent people? Will you destroy the whole city because of those five?"

He answered, "I will not destroy it, if I find forty-five there."

But Abraham persisted, saying, "What if only forty are found there?"

He replied, "I will forbear doing it for the sake of the forty."

Then Abraham said, "Let not my Lord grow impatient if I go on.

What if only thirty are found there?"

He replied, "I will forbear doing it if I can find but thirty there."

Still Abraham went on,
  "Since I have thus dared to speak to my Lord,
  what if there are no more than twenty?"

The LORD answered, "I will not destroy it, for the sake of the twenty."

But he still persisted:
  "Please, let not my Lord grow angry if I speak up this last time.

What if there are at least ten there?"

He replied, "For the sake of those ten, I will not destroy it."

The word of the Lord.

| Lect. |
| No. 111 |

RESPONSORIAL PSALM: Ps 138:1-2, 2-3, 6-7, 7-8 (℟.: 3a)

The theme of the First Reading and the Gospel is prayer, and that theme is continued in the Responsorial Psalm. Psalm 138 is a thanksgiving, but the verses chosen for the psalm of today's Responsorial Psalm are those that speak about God's faithful response to our prayer and need.

℟. **Lord, on the day I called for help, you answered me.**

I will give thanks to you, O LORD, with all my heart,
  for you have heard the words of my mouth;
  in the presence of the angels I will sing your praise;
I will worship at your holy temple
  and give thanks to your name.

God answers our prayers with kindness and truth. Kindness means that God is compassionate in his dealings with us. Truth means that God is faithful to the promises that he has made.

God also answers the prayers of the poor and lowly. God is their last source of hope, for humans often discount them since they are powerless.

Yet, God does not look at us according to the opinions of human beings. God reaches out to those who most need him and fills them with his blessings.

Throughout the psalm, there are hints of Hebrew argumentation. God is told that his name is great above all things for he has answered our prayers.

The implication is that if he does not answer them, his name will not be as respected.

℟. **Lord, on the day I called for help, you answered me.**

Because of your kindness and your truth;
  for you have made great above all things
  your name and your promise.
When I called you answered me;
  you built up strength within me.

℟. **Lord, on the day I called for help, you answered me.**

The LORD is exalted, yet the lowly he sees,
  and the proud he knows from afar.
Though I walk amid distress, you preserve me;
  against the anger of my enemies you raise your hand.

℟. **Lord, on the day I called for help, you answered me.**

Your right hand saves me.
  The LORD will complete what he has done for me;
your kindness, O LORD, endures forever;
  forsake not the work of your hands.

℟. **Lord, on the day I called for help, you answered me.**

Lect.
No. 111

SECOND READING: Colossians 2:12-14

God has brought you to life along with Christ, having forgiven us all our transgressions.

The Second Reading uses Baptismal symbolism, speaking of how our Baptism is a process of dying and rising to life. We die to our old way of life. We have to give up the life of sin and self-indulgence in which we were involved. At the same time, Jesus offers us the possibility of living a new life that has true meaning, one that is filled with love.

A reading from the Letter of Saint Paul
to the Colossians

Brothers and sisters:
You were buried with him in baptism,
in which you were also raised with him
through faith in the power of God,
who raised him from the dead.
And even when you were dead
  in transgressions and the uncircumcision of your flesh,

There is also the symbolism of being bound and being free. In our old days, we were bound to sin (we could not free ourselves from it). Now, sin has been bound (nailed to the cross) so that we might be free. This does not mean that we can do whatever we want to, but rather it means that we have the freedom to choose love and life.

Lect.
No. 111

The Alleluia Verse reminds us of the incredible dignity with which God treats us. We are not slaves; we have been called to be children of a loving God.

Lect.
No. 111

The Gospel has a series of teachings on prayer.

It begins with Jesus instructing his disciples on how they should pray.

Notice that Jesus is praying when the disciples ask Jesus how they should pray.

This is typical of the Gospel of Luke, for Jesus is constantly praying. He does this so that he might discern the will of his Father and have the courage to fulfill it.

The version of the Our Father found in Luke is more primitive than that found in Matthew. This is a series of individual requests, while Matthew's version seems to be an organized prayer.

he brought you to life along with him,
having forgiven us all our transgressions;
obliterating the bond against us, with its legal claims,
which was opposed to us,
he also removed it from our midst, nailing it to the cross.

The word of the Lord.

ALLELUIA: Romans 8:15bc

℞. **Alleluia, alleluia.**

You have received a Spirit of adoption,
through which we cry, Abba, Father.

℞. **Alleluia, alleluia.**

GOSPEL: Luke 11:1-13

Ask and you will receive.

A reading from the holy Gospel according to Luke

Jesus was praying in a certain place, and when he had finished,
  one of his disciples said to him,
  "Lord, teach us to pray just as John taught his disciples."
He said to them, "When you pray, say:
  Father, hallowed be your name,
    your kingdom come.
    Give us each day our daily bread
    and forgive us our sins
    for we ourselves forgive everyone in debt to us,
    and do not subject us to the final test."

And he said to them, "Suppose one of you has a friend
  to whom he goes at midnight and says,
  'Friend, lend me three loaves of bread,

Matthew probably used the "Our Father" in use in the community when he was writing the Gospel, while Luke used what Jesus had actually said.

There are also subtle differences between the wording of Matthew and Luke.

Matthew has us ask for our bread this day, while Luke prays for the daily bread (day after day).

Matthew prays for forgiveness of debts while Luke speaks of sins.

Finally, Matthew prays for deliverance from the evil one, while Luke prays for deliverance from the final trial (the great test at the end of time).

Jesus continues to speak of prayer by giving examples of what earthly fathers would do if a friend or a child would ask for something.

God is a truly loving parent who will respond to our every need. Therefore, when we need something, we should not be afraid to ask.

for a friend of mine has arrived at my house from
  a journey
and I have nothing to offer him,'
and he says in reply from within,
'Do not bother me; the door has already been
  locked
and my children and I are already in bed.
I cannot get up to give you anything.'
I tell you,
  if he does not get up to give the visitor the loaves
  because of their friendship,
  he will get up to give him whatever he needs
  because of his persistence.

"And I tell you, ask and you will receive;
  seek and you will find;
  knock and the door will be opened to you.
For everyone who asks, receives;
  and the one who seeks, finds;
  and to the one who knocks, the door will be
    opened.
What father among you would hand his son a snake
  when he asks for a fish?
Or hand him a scorpion when he asks for an egg?
If you then, who are wicked,
  know how to give good gifts to your children,
  how much more will the Father in heaven
  give the Holy Spirit to those who ask him?"

The Gospel of the Lord.

PASTORAL REFLECTIONS

It is said that God will give the most loving answer possible to our prayers. Sometimes that means that God will physically heal us or grant us some favor. At other times it means that God will meet us on the cross. We would naturally prefer to receive a positive response to our prayers, but God, who sees reality from a different perspective, can see that it is sometimes better if we do not receive the things for which we prayed. God thinks in terms of long-term good, eternal good, and not short-term, immediately obvious good.

EIGHTEENTH SUNDAY IN ORDINARY TIME

Lect. No. 114

FIRST READING:
Ecclesiastes 1:2; 2:21-23

What profit comes to a man from all his toil?

The theme developed in the First Reading and the Gospel is the futility of seeking after riches. One might think that riches will bring one security, but they do not.

The First Reading is taken from the writings of Qoheleth. We do not know if this is the author's real name or symbolic (for it means "preacher" in Hebrew).

This is a wisdom book that rejects much of the commonly accepted opinions of the era in which it was written. The author argues that God's ways are unknowable, so we should live a virtuous life and do the best we can.

A reading from the Book of Ecclesiastes

Vanity of vanities, says Qoheleth,
  vanity of vanities! All things are vanity!

Here is one who has labored with wisdom and
    knowledge and skill,
  and yet to another who has not labored over it,
  he must leave property.
This also is vanity and a great misfortune.
For what profit comes to man from all the toil and
    anxiety of heart
  with which he has labored under the sun?
All his days sorrow and grief are his occupation;
  even at night his mind is not at rest.
This also is vanity.

The word of the Lord.

PASTORAL REFLECTIONS

Qoheleth reminds us that there is not just one way of looking at things. We often think that being holy means to be patient and happy all the time. Yet, there are saints who often expressed their anger and impatience. There were others who suffered from despair. Still others seem to have been a bit strange.

Qoheleth challenged the conventional wisdom of his day. He was a bit cynical and pessimistic, but this tended to balance out the overly optimistic teachers of wisdom whose pronouncements sounded good but did not respect the evidence of everyday life.

Lect.
No. 114 **RESPONSORIAL PSALM: Ps 90:3-4, 5-6, 12-13, 14, 17 (℟.: 1)**

The Responsorial Psalm is a series of verses taken from Psalm 90.

That psalm is a lamentation, but the verses used today give another impression. They emphasize the fragility of human life and the greatness of God.

The message developed is that if we are so weak and God is so great, then we must depend upon God and God will respond to our need.

The theme here agrees well with that of the First Reading and the Gospel. Those readings speak of the futility of trusting in our own resources, for our God is the only one who can respond to our need. It is especially foolish to trust in one's riches.

The psalm, on the other hand, starts with that premise: that we can do nothing on our own. We are like the grass that springs up in the morning and then withers by the evening.

This psalm presents this truth, and then tells God that it is up to him. If he does not provide his gracious care, then we will not have a chance.

This is why we call upon God to "prosper the work of our hands for us." He is the only one who can bring our works to completion.

℟. **If today you hear his voice, harden not your hearts.**

You turn man back to dust,
    saying, "Return, O children of men."
For a thousand years in your sight
    are as yesterday, now that it is past,
    or as a watch of the night.

℟. **If today you hear his voice, harden not your hearts.**

You make an end of them in their sleep;
    the next morning they are like the changing grass,
which at dawn springs up anew,
    but by evening wilts and fades.

℟. **If today you hear his voice, harden not your hearts.**

Teach us to number our days aright,
    that we may gain wisdom of heart.
Return, O LORD! How long?
    Have pity on your servants!

℟. **If today you hear his voice, harden not your hearts.**

Fill us at daybreak with your kindness,
    that we may shout for joy and gladness all our days.
And may the gracious care of the LORD our God be ours;
    prosper the work of our hands for us!
Prosper the work of our hands!

℟. **If today you hear his voice, harden not your hearts.**

Lect.
No. 114

SECOND READING: Colossians 3:1-5, 9-11

Seek what is above, where Christ is.

The Second Reading reminds us that when we became Christians, we had to reject certain practices that we might have done before.

We have died to those old ways, and we must live in Christ.

This does not mean that we have to become prudish and reject the goodness of the created world. Rather, we must temper our passions so that they do not cause us to misuse the good things of the world.

We must reject immorality, impurity, passion, evil desire, and greed. We cannot lie or gossip. We must make moral choices, even if it costs us dearly.

Finally, we must keep our minds on what is above. In other words, by thinking about God and heaven and the saints, we will be able to keep our everyday life in perspective and we will have the strength to choose what is good and moral and loving.

A reading from the Letter of Saint Paul
to the Colossians

Brothers and sisters:
If you were raised with Christ, seek what is above,
   where Christ is seated at the right hand of God.
Think of what is above, not of what is on earth.
For you have died,
   and your life is hidden with Christ in God.
When Christ your life appears,
   then you too will appear with him in glory.

Put to death, then, the parts of you that are earthly:
   immorality, impurity, passion, evil desire,
   and the greed that is idolatry.
Stop lying to one another,
   since you have taken off the old self with its practices
   and have put on the new self,
   which is being renewed, for knowledge,
   in the image of its creator.
Here there is not Greek and Jew,
   circumcision and uncircumcision,
   barbarian, Scythian, slave, free;
   but Christ is all and in all.

The word of the Lord.

Lect.
No. 114

ALLELUIA: Matthew 5:3

The Alleluia Verse contains the Beatitude that reminds us that we must seek humility so that we might see things from God's point of view.

℟. **Alleluia, alleluia.**

Blessed are the poor in spirit,
for theirs is the kingdom of heaven.

℟. **Alleluia, alleluia.**

Lect.
No. 114

GOSPEL: Luke 12:13-21

The things you have prepared, to whom will they belong?

Throughout the Gospel of Luke there are continuous warnings against the tendency to trust in one's riches.

This Gospel passage presents the poor and weak as the chosen of God.

The rich are all too often self-sufficient, so when Jesus comes into their lives, they feel as if they do not really need him. The poor, on the other hand, know that they are powerless, and they therefore reach out to the Lord with all their strength.

The brother at the beginning of this passage wants to use Jesus to promote his cause. He does not want to listen to Jesus or change his ways; he wants everyone else to do that.

Jesus challenges him by refusing to go along with his project. He warns him that his entire premise is foolish, for he is seeking security in things that are passing and fragile.

One should remember that "riches" are not only material possessions.

As we heard in the Alleluia Verse, one should be poor in spirit (and not arrogant or self-righteous), lest we begin to think that we do not constantly need the strength and love of God.

A reading from the holy Gospel according to Luke

Someone in the crowd said to Jesus,
"Teacher, tell my brother to share the inheritance
with me."
He replied to him,
"Friend, who appointed me as your judge and ar-
bitrator?"
Then he said to the crowd,
"Take care to guard against all greed,
for though one may be rich,
one's life does not consist of possessions."

Then he told them a parable.
"There was a rich man whose land produced a
bountiful harvest.
He asked himself, 'What shall I do,
for I do not have space to store my harvest?'
And he said, 'This is what I shall do:
I shall tear down my barns and build larger ones.
There I shall store all my grain and other goods
and I shall say to myself, "Now as for you,
you have so many good things stored up for many
years,
rest, eat, drink, be merry!"'
But God said to him,
'You fool, this night your life will be demanded of
you;
and the things you have prepared, to whom will
they belong?'
Thus will it be for all who store up treasure for
themselves
but are not rich in what matters to God."

The Gospel of the Lord.

NINETEENTH SUNDAY IN ORDINARY TIME

Lect. No. 117

FIRST READING: Wisdom 18:6-9

*Just as you punished our adversaries,
you glorified us whom you had summoned.*

The First Reading and the Gospel speak of placing our trust in God, even when we cannot immediately see the results of our actions.

The First Reading comes from the Book of Wisdom, and it presents the standard wisdom teaching that God rewards those who trust in him while he punishes those who do evil.

Specifically, the reading speaks of remembering the blessings that God gave his people at the Passover.

God was faithful to his people in the past. Thus we can trust that he will surely bless his people in the present as well.

A reading from the Book of Wisdom

The night of the passover was known beforehand to our fathers,
that, with sure knowledge of the oaths in which
they put their faith,
they might have courage.
Your people awaited the salvation of the just
and the destruction of their foes.
For when you punished our adversaries,
in this you glorified us whom you had summoned.
For in secret the holy children of the good were
offering sacrifice
and putting into effect with one accord the divine institution.

The word of the Lord.

Lect. No. 117

RESPONSORIAL PSALM: Ps 33:1, 12, 18-19, 20-22 (℟.: 12b)

The Responsorial Psalm continues the wisdom teaching that God will bless those who trust in him. It is fitting to praise God, not because we are obliged to, but rather because praising God is the most rewarding thing that we can do.

We always feel good when we praise a friend for what he or she has done.

℟. **Blessed the people the Lord has chosen to be his own.**

Exult, you just, in the LORD;
  praise from the upright is fitting.
Blessed the nation whose God is the LORD,
  the people he has chosen for his own inheritance.

℟. **Blessed the people the Lord has chosen to be his own.**

How much more should that be true of our relationship with God.

God has been wonderful to us and has blessed us in innumerable ways. We would be selfish and inconsiderate if we were not to acknowledge this.

Our words of praise have reminded us of our dependence upon God. We thus have confidence that he will respond to our every need.

See, the eyes of the LORD are upon those who fear him,
> upon those who hope for his kindness,
to deliver them from death
> and preserve them in spite of famine.

℟. **Blessed the people the Lord has chosen to be his own.**

Our soul waits for the LORD,
> who is our help and our shield.
May your kindness, O LORD, be upon us
> who have put our hope in you.

℟. **Blessed the people the Lord has chosen to be his own.**

Lect. No. 117

SECOND READING: **A** Longer Form: Hebrews 11:1-2, 8-19

Abraham looked forward to the city whose architect and maker is God.

This reading from the Letter to the Hebrews is a beautiful presentation on the meaning of faith.

Faith is not just an intellectual endeavor. Logic alone cannot bring us to the leap of faith.

Faith is an act of trust. The Creed that we profess every Sunday does not say, "We believe the following things about God." It says, "We believe in God."

In other words, we are telling God that we trust in him.

The author of this letter then uses various figures from the Old Testament as examples of faith. He first speaks of Abraham and Sarah. God called them to leave their homeland and travel to a land that they did not know.

A reading from the Letter to the Hebrews

Brothers and sisters:
> Faith is the realization of what is hoped for
and evidence of things not seen.
Because of it the ancients were well attested.

By faith Abraham obeyed when he was called to go out to a place
> that he was to receive as an inheritance;
> he went out, not knowing where he was to go.
By faith he sojourned in the promised land as in a foreign country,
> dwelling in tents with Isaac and Jacob, heirs of the same promise;
> for he was looking forward to the city with foundations,
> whose architect and maker is God.
By faith he received power to generate,
> even though he was past the normal age
> —and Sarah herself was sterile—

They left everything and trusted in the LORD. God promised them land and descendants. Yet, in their lifetime, they received very little of what had been promised. The only land they acquired was a small burial plot.

The only descendants that Abraham and Sarah had was their son Isaac. Yet, Abraham and Sarah trusted.

This is a reminder that we will not receive the full reward until after our death. In this life there will be disappointments and failures.

This does not mean that God does not love us. Rather, it is a call to keep the perspective that our true homeland is heaven.

If we want to know how much we might be tested in our faith, we should remember the story of Abraham's call to sacrifice Isaac.

This request did not make any sense, for as far as Abraham knew, Isaac would be the fulfillment of God's promise. Yet, Abraham risked everything and trusted in God when trust seemed totally impossible.

Sooner or later, each of us will face that test, and we can only pray that God will give us the wisdom and courage to trust.

for he thought that the one who had made the
promise was trustworthy.
So it was that there came forth from one man,
himself as good as dead,
descendants as numerous as the stars in the sky
and as countless as the sands on the seashore.

All these died in faith.
They did not receive what had been promised
but saw it and greeted it from afar
and acknowledged themselves to be strangers
and aliens on earth,
for those who speak thus show that they are seeking a homeland.
If they had been thinking of the land from which
they had come,
they would have had opportunity to return.
But now they desire a better homeland, a heavenly
one.
Therefore, God is not ashamed to be called their
God,
for he has prepared a city for them.

By faith Abraham, when put to the test, offered up
Isaac,
and he who had received the promises was ready
to offer his only son,
of whom it was said,
"Through Isaac descendants shall bear your
name."
He reasoned that God was able to raise even from
the dead,
and he received Isaac back as a symbol.

The word of the Lord.

SECOND READING: Shorter Form: Hebrews 11:1-2, 8-12

Abraham looked forward to the city whose architect and maker is God.

This reading from the Letter to the Hebrews is a beautiful presentation on the meaning of faith.

Faith is not just an intellectual endeavor. It is an act of trust.

The Creed that we profess every Sunday does not say, "We believe the following things about God." It says, "We believe in God."

In other words, we are telling God that we trust in him.

The author of this letter then uses various figures from the Old Testament as examples of faith. He first speaks of Abraham and Sarah.

God called them to leave their homeland and travel to a land that they did not know. They left everything and trusted in the Lord. God promised them land and descendants. Yet, in their lifetime, they received very little of what had been promised.

The only land they acquired was a small burial plot. The only descendants that Abraham and Sarah had was their son Isaac. Yet, Abraham and Sarah trusted.

A reading from the Letter to the Hebrews

Brothers and sisters:
Faith is the realization of what is hoped for
and evidence of things not seen.
Because of it the ancients were well attested.
By faith Abraham obeyed when he was called to go
    out to a place
  that he was to receive as an inheritance;
  he went out, not knowing where he was to go.
By faith he sojourned in the promised land as in a
    foreign country,
  dwelling in tents with Isaac and Jacob, heirs of
    the same promise;
  for he was looking forward to the city with foun-
    dations,
  whose architect and maker is God.
By faith he received power to generate,
  even though he was past the normal age
  —and Sarah herself was sterile—
  for he thought that the one who had made the
    promise was trustworthy.
 So it was that there came forth from one man,
  himself as good as dead,
  descendants as numerous as the stars in the sky
  and as countless as the sands on the seashore.

The word of the Lord.

PASTORAL REFLECTIONS

Who are some people in my experience whom I might call examples of faith? Who taught me to trust even when this sounded all but impossible?

Lect.
No. 117

We do not know how much time we have, and so we should spend each day as if it were our last. In that way we will be ready to greet the Lord when he returns in glory.

ALLELUIA: Matthew 24:42a, 44

℟. **Alleluia, alleluia.**

Stay awake and be ready!
For you do not know on what day the Son of Man will come.

℟. **Alleluia, alleluia.**

Lect.
No. 117

GOSPEL: **A** Longer Form: Luke 12:32-48

You also must be prepared.

The Gospel continues the theme of trusting in God and not in one's possessions. Jesus tells his followers that the Father has a kingdom prepared for those who leave all they have and follow him.

Again, this is an act of faith, trusting in things that cannot be seen. We have all experienced the futility of trying to be self-sufficient here on earth. We have all tried to depend upon our riches (whether material or spiritual). Jesus tells us that this is pointless.

The only treasure that remains is the treasure that we will receive in heaven.

He continues by teaching us to put this decision in an eschatological perspective. Eschatology means the end things, what we will expect in the world to come.

Throughout the Gospel of Luke we often hear that we have already started to receive the rewards of the world to come. We

A reading from the holy Gospel according to Luke

Jesus said to his disciples:
"Do not be afraid any longer, little flock,
    for your Father is pleased to give you the kingdom.
Sell your belongings and give alms.
Provide money bags for yourselves that do not wear out,
    an inexhaustible treasure in heaven
    that no thief can reach nor moth destroy.
For where your treasure is, there also will your heart be.

"Gird your loins and light your lamps
    and be like servants who await their master's return from a wedding,
    ready to open immediately when he comes and knocks.
Blessed are those servants
    whom the master finds vigilant on his arrival.
Amen, I say to you, he will gird himself,
    have them recline at table, and proceed to wait on them.
And should he come in the second or third watch
    and find them prepared in this way,
    blessed are those servants.

already have experienced salvation when we encounter and embrace Jesus. We do not have to wait until our death to be saved. He has already saved us from our sin and loneliness and self-sufficiency.

Yet, this is not all there is to it. Even if we have begun to experience the rewards of heaven, we have not yet experienced its fullness.

It is important to remember that there is a world to come. Sometimes that knowledge is the only thing that gives us the courage to do what is right.

We are often tempted beyond what we think we can bear.

We need to know that, while this world is good, there is something else that is worth the sacrifice that we will endure by saying no to what seems pleasurable today.

As is typical of the Gospel of Luke, we find that the example offered to present this teaching is that of serving a meal.

This passage closes with the saying that much will be required of that person to whom much is given.

Often we ask ourselves why we are always the ones who are expected to be charitable and make peace with the family.

The answer is that we can, and therefore it is expected of us. We have been gifted by God to be able to see the truth;

Be sure of this:
> if the master of the house had known the hour
> when the thief was coming,
> he would not have let his house be broken into.

You also must be prepared, for at an hour you do not expect,
> the Son of Man will come."

Then Peter said,
> "Lord, is this parable meant for us or for everyone?"

And the Lord replied,
> "Who, then, is the faithful and prudent steward
> whom the master will put in charge of his servants
> to distribute the food allowance at the proper time?

Blessed is that servant whom his master on arrival finds doing so.

Truly, I say to you, the master will put the servant in charge of all his property.

But if that servant says to himself,
> 'My master is delayed in coming,'
> and begins to beat the menservants and the maidservants,
> to eat and drink and get drunk,
> then that servant's master will come
> on an unexpected day and at an unknown hour
> and will punish the servant severely
> and assign him a place with the unfaithful.

That servant who knew his master's will
> but did not make preparations nor act in accord with his will
> shall be beaten severely;
> and the servant who was ignorant of his master's will
> but acted in a way deserving of a severe beating
> shall be beaten only lightly.

therefore we are expected to live in that truth.

The others might not have received that gift yet, so we cannot expect it of them. We can only do what we can do.

Much will be required of the person entrusted with much,

and still more will be demanded of the person entrusted with more."

The Gospel of the Lord.

GOSPEL: B Shorter Form: Luke 12:35-40

You also must be prepared.

This reading teaches us to make our decisions in an eschatological perspective. Eschatology means the end things, what we will expect in the world to come.

Luke often tells us that we have already started to receive those rewards. We experience salvation when we encounter and embrace Jesus. He has saved us from our sin and loneliness and self-sufficiency.

Yet, this is not all there is. It is important to remember that there is a world to come. Sometimes that knowledge is the only thing that gives us the courage to do what is right.

We are often tempted beyond what we think we can bear.

We need to know that, while this world is good, there is something else that is worth the sacrifice that we will endure by saying no to what seems pleasurable today.

A reading from the holy Gospel according to Luke

Jesus said to his disciples:
"Gird your loins and light your lamps
and be like servants who await their master's return from a wedding,
ready to open immediately when he comes and knocks.
Blessed are those servants
whom the master finds vigilant on his arrival.
Amen, I say to you, he will gird himself,
have them recline at table, and proceed to wait on them.
And should he come in the second or third watch
and find them prepared in this way,
blessed are those servants.
Be sure of this:
if the master of the house had known the hour
when the thief was coming,
he would not have let his house be broken into.
You also must be prepared, for at an hour you do not expect,
the Son of Man will come."

The Gospel of the Lord.

August 14, 2013

THE ASSUMPTION OF THE BLESSED VIRGIN MARY

AT THE VIGIL MASS

Lect. No. 621

FIRST READING:

1 Chronicles 15:3-4, 15-16; 16:1-2

They brought in the ark of God and set it within the tent which David had pitched for it.

The First Reading speaks of the day that King David brought the Ark of the Covenant into Jerusalem. He had recently conquered the city, and now he wanted to make it a focal point of the faith.

The first attempt to bring the Ark into the city ended in failure. One of the soldiers accompanying the Ark touched it. He was immediately struck dead, for he had touched a sacred object.

The Ark was left where it was until David saw that the Ark brought blessing to the owner of the property where it had been placed.

Notice that David performs sacrifices and gives blessings. In ancient Israel, the king was also considered to be a priest.

The reason that this reading was chosen for this feast is that Mary is the Ark of the New Covenant. She held the presence of the living God within her womb, even as the Ark was the place where God manifested his presence.

A reading from the first Book of Chronicles

David assembled all Israel in Jerusalem to bring the ark of the LORD
to the place that he had prepared for it.
David also called together the sons of Aaron and the Levites.

The Levites bore the ark of God on their shoulders with poles,
as Moses had ordained according to the word of the LORD.

David commanded the chiefs of the Levites
to appoint their kinsmen as chanters,
to play on musical instruments, harps, lyres, and cymbals,
to make a loud sound of rejoicing.

They brought in the ark of God and set it within the tent
which David had pitched for it.
Then they offered up burnt offerings and peace offerings to God.
When David had finished offering up the burnt offerings and peace offerings,
he blessed the people in the name of the LORD.

The word of the Lord.

Lect. No. 621

RESPONSORIAL PSALM: Ps 132:6-7, 9-10, 13-14 (℟.: 8)

This psalm seems to have been written for a liturgical feast. It celebrates the kingship of David and the day that he brought the Ark of the Covenant into Jerusalem.

The conquest of Jerusalem was a question of power politics. David saw that the city lay between the northern and the southern tribes. He conquered the city and made it his capital because he wanted to unite the tribes. He moved the Ark into the city so that pilgrims would be forced to enter the city periodically and see the grandeur of the palace that he had built. His political machinations were brilliant.

And yet the LORD used David's base political motives to reveal his mercy. He chose Zion (the mountain associated with the city Jerusalem) to be his dwelling place upon the earth.

℟. **Lord, go up to the place of your rest, you and the ark of your holiness.**

Behold, we heard of it in Ephrathah;
  we found it in the fields of Jaar.
Let us enter into his dwelling,
  let us worship at his footstool.

℟. **Lord, go up to the place of your rest, you and the ark of your holiness.**

May your priests be clothed with justice;
  let your faithful ones shout merrily for joy.
For the sake of David your servant,
  reject not the plea of your anointed.

℟. **Lord, go up to the place of your rest, you and the ark of your holiness.**

For the LORD has chosen Zion;
  he prefers her for his dwelling.
"Zion is my resting place forever;
  in her will I dwell, for I prefer her."

℟. **Lord, go up to the place of your rest, you and the ark of your holiness.**

Lect. No. 621

SECOND READING: 1 Corinthians 15:54b-57

God gave us the victory through Jesus Christ.

This passage is taken from the end of a consideration on the resurrection of the dead. Saint Paul wants the Corinthians to understand that we will all rise on the last day. Death is no longer victorious, for Christ has conquered death and sin.

Paul speaks of the power of sin being the law. Sin had entered the world and it was terrible. But the law made sin even more horrific. We thought that

A reading from the first Letter of Saint Paul to the Corinthians

Brothers and sisters:
    When that which is mortal clothes itself with immortality,
then the word that is written shall come about:
  Death is swallowed up in victory.
  Where, O death, is your victory?
  Where, O death, is your sting?

the law would liberate us from sin, but the best that it could do was point out how much we are sinners. It left us more frustrated than before, and therefore ready to accept Christ as our only true liberation from our slavery to sin.

This Beatitude speaks of those who listen to the word of God and make it part of their lives. Of all who ever lived, Mary did this most fully, for in her the word truly became incarnate.

When a woman cried out that Mary was blessed for she was the mother of Jesus, Jesus responded that the person is blessed who hears the word of God and observes it.

This is not downgrading Mary, for of all people who ever lived, she most successfully heard the word of God (e.g., in the invitation from the Archangel Gabriel to be the mother of the Son of God) and observed it.

The sting of death is sin,
  and the power of sin is the law.
But thanks be to God who gives us the victory
  through our Lord Jesus Christ.

The word of the Lord.

ALLELUIA: Luke 11:28

℟. **Alleluia, alleluia.**

Blessed are they who hear the word of God
and observe it.

℟. **Alleluia, alleluia.**

GOSPEL: Luke 11:27-28

Blessed is the womb that carried you!

A reading from the holy Gospel according to Luke

While Jesus was speaking,
  a woman from the crowd called out and said to him,
  "Blessed is the womb that carried you
  and the breasts at which you nursed."
He replied,
  "Rather, blessed are those
  who hear the word of God and observe it."

The Gospel of the Lord.

PASTORAL REFLECTIONS

The Assumption of the Blessed Virgin Mary into heaven foretells what will happen to all of us at the end of time, that we will be taken up into heaven body and soul. In the resurrection of the dead we receive a glorified body that will not be subject to the limitations of our present mortal body.

August 15, 2013
THE ASSUMPTION OF THE BLESSED VIRGIN MARY
AT THE MASS DURING THE DAY

Lect. No. 622

FIRST READING:
Revelation 11:19a; 12:1-6a, 10ab

A woman clothed with the sun, with the moon beneath her feet.

A reading from the Book of Revelation

God's temple in heaven was opened,
and the ark of his covenant could be seen in the temple.

A great sign appeared in the sky, a woman clothed with the sun,
with the moon beneath her feet,
and on her head a crown of twelve stars.
She was with child and wailed aloud in pain as she labored to give birth.
Then another sign appeared in the sky;
it was a huge red dragon, with seven heads and ten horns,
and on its heads were seven diadems.
Its tail swept away a third of the stars in the sky
and hurled them down to the earth.
Then the dragon stood before the woman about to give birth,
to devour her child when she gave birth.
She gave birth to a son, a male child,
destined to rule all the nations with an iron rod.
Her child was caught up to God and his throne.
The woman herself fled into the desert
where she had a place prepared by God.

Then I heard a loud voice in heaven say:
"Now have salvation and power come,
and the Kingdom of our God
and the authority of his Anointed One."

The word of the Lord.

The First Reading is taken from the Book of Revelation. On one level, it speaks of the birth of Jesus upon the earth. On another level, it presents an image of the Church making Christ present again each day.

Like the woman in this passage, Mary gave birth to a child who was immediately endangered by the evil one who wanted to devour him (this is probably a reference to the plot of King Herod to put the child to death). God protected the child and destroyed the power of the serpent. The image of this woman clothed with the sun, with the moon under her feet and wearing a crown of twelve stars, has become an image of the Immaculate Conception.

But in this account the woman also represents the Church. She is constantly being attacked by the forces of evil. Yet she makes Christ present in the world. This is especially true when she suffers for the sake of the Gospel.

It is appropriate that the image would stand both for Mary and for the Church. Mary is the model of the Church. She is the example of what the Church should be, for she made the word of God incarnate.

323

RESPONSORIAL PSALM: Ps 45:10, 11, 12, 16 (℟.: 10bc)

The Responsorial Psalm is taken from Psalm 45, a psalm written to celebrate the wedding feast of a king of Israel to his bride.

The queen stands at the right hand of the king in gold of Ophir. Gold of Ophir is a very precious form of gold. The queen at the right of the king is not his bride. His bride is the princess borne in before them. The queen is actually the queen mother.

Kings of Israel had many wives and none of them was the queen. The queen was the queen mother. One of her most important responsibilities was to prepare the wedding feast for her son. This is what she is doing at the right hand of the king.

The presence of Mary at the wedding feast of Cana is based upon this image. She is the queen mother who invites her son to his wedding, the cross.

℟. **The queen stands at your right hand, arrayed in gold.**

The queen takes her place at your right hand in gold of Ophir.

℟. **The queen stands at your right hand, arrayed in gold.**

Hear, O daughter, and see; turn your ear,
    forget your people and your father's house.

℟. **The queen stands at your right hand, arrayed in gold.**

So shall the king desire your beauty;
    for he is your lord.

℟. **The queen stands at your right hand, arrayed in gold.**

They are borne in with gladness and joy;
    they enter the palace of the king.

℟. **The queen stands at your right hand, arrayed in gold.**

Lect. No. 622

SECOND READING: 1 Corinthians 15:20-27

Christ, the firstfruits; then those who belong to him.

Jesus is described as being the firstfruits of those who have fallen asleep. The firstfruits are generally known for two things. First of all, they are known as being the best. Second, they are the promise of more that will shortly arrive. Jesus is the best of those who have been risen from the dead, and he is also a promise to us that we will one day rise from the dead to live with him in heaven.

A reading from the first Letter of Saint Paul
to the Corinthians

Brothers and sisters:
    Christ has been raised from the dead,
    the firstfruits of those who have fallen asleep.
For since death came through man,
    the resurrection of the dead came also through man.
For just as in Adam all die,
    so too in Christ shall all be brought to life,
    but each one in proper order:

Adam's sin brought death into the world. We are not sure if Paul means physical death or spiritual death. Whichever, we were left hopeless due to the power of sin.

With Jesus having risen from the dead, sin and death no longer have any power over us. Jesus has already risen, and on the last day we will all rise with him to share in his glory. That is when Jesus' defeat of his last enemy, death, will be made manifest, for we will live forever with him to share in his glory.

Lect.
No. 622

Christ the firstfruits;
then, at his coming, those who belong to Christ;
then comes the end,
when he hands over the Kingdom to his God and
   Father,
when he has destroyed every sovereignty
and every authority and power.
For he must reign until he has put all his enemies
   under his feet.
The last enemy to be destroyed is death,
   for "he subjected everything under his feet."

The word of the Lord.

ALLELUIA

Our Alleluia Verse celebrates the reason for this feast: that our Blessed Mother was taken up into heaven body and soul to share in God's glory forever.

Lect.
No. 622

℟. **Alleluia, alleluia.**

Mary is taken up to heaven;
a chorus of angels exults.

℟. **Alleluia, alleluia.**

GOSPEL: Luke 1:39-56

The Almighty has done great things for me: he has raised up the lowly.

The Gospel presents the story of the visitation of Mary to her cousin Elizabeth. The traditional site of Elizabeth's and Zechariah's house is Ein Karim, a small village not far outside of Jerusalem.

The child that Elizabeth is carrying gives witness to the presence of Jesus in their midst. The first person who ever recognized the presence of Jesus in the world was an unborn child. Typically, it is those whom society would evaluate as insignificant who are able to respond to God's call.

A reading from the holy Gospel according to Luke

Mary set out
and traveled to the hill country in haste
to a town of Judah,
   where she entered the house of Zechariah
   and greeted Elizabeth.
When Elizabeth heard Mary's greeting,
   the infant leaped in her womb,
   and Elizabeth, filled with the Holy Spirit,
   cried out in a loud voice and said,
   "Blessed are you among women,
   and blessed is the fruit of your womb.

Elizabeth is filled with the Holy Spirit and thus is able to greet Mary with the phrase that we still use in the "Hail Mary." The Holy Spirit is important throughout the writings of Saint Luke.

Mary is especially blessed for her trust in the words of the Lord. She was generous and willing to place herself at the disposition of God.

Mary responds to this remarkable greeting with the hymn that we call the "Magnificat." This hymn is largely based upon the hymn of Hannah in 1 Samuel 2 (with the verses of various psalms added).

This beautiful hymn expresses the feelings of the "anawim," the poor ones of Yahweh. In the time of Jesus, the poor were despised by the powers that be. Jesus portrayed the exact opposite judgment of the poor. He considered them to be the chosen of the Father.

Mary, in this hymn and throughout the Gospel of Luke, is portrayed as a representative of the "anawim." She was humble enough to respond lovingly to God's call to become the mother of his Son. When God called her, she replied that she was the servant of the Lord and that it should be done unto her according to his will.

And how does this happen to me,
    that the mother of my Lord should come to me?
For at the moment the sound of your greeting reached my ears,
    the infant in my womb leaped for joy.
Blessed are you who believed
    that what was spoken to you by the Lord
would be fulfilled."

And Mary said:
    "My soul proclaims the greatness of the Lord;
        my spirit rejoices in God my Savior
        for he has looked upon his lowly servant.
    From this day all generations will call me blessed:
        the Almighty has done great things for me,
        and holy is his Name.
        He has mercy on those who fear him
        in every generation.
    He has shown the strength of his arm,
        and has scattered the proud in their conceit.
    He has cast down the mighty from their thrones,
        and has lifted up the lowly.
    He has filled the hungry with good things,
        and the rich he has sent away empty.
    He has come to the help of his servant Israel
        for he has remembered his promise of mercy,
        the promise he made to our fathers,
        to Abraham and his children for ever."

Mary remained with her about three months
    and then returned to her home.

The Gospel of the Lord.

PASTORAL REFLECTIONS

This feast reminds us that there are two sources of revelation: Scripture and Tradition. Even though the Assumption of Mary is not found in the former, Scripture, it can be trusted for it is found in the sacred Tradition of the Church.

TWENTIETH SUNDAY IN ORDINARY TIME

Lect. No. 120

FIRST READING: Jeremiah 38:4-6, 8-10

A man of strife and contention to all the land.

These past Sundays we have heard about the need to trust in God and not in our own riches. This Sunday takes the theme one step further. If we hold on to God, then we will have to endure persecution.

The First Reading speaks of the persecution of the Prophet Jeremiah. God had called the prophet to warn Israel that their ways were decadent and they were bringing destruction upon their heads.

They refused to listen to him and they continued in their sins. Then, when the foretold destruction occurred, they blamed Jeremiah.

In this reading, we hear of a plot that the princes of Jerusalem hatched against him.

Jeremiah told the people of Jerusalem to surrender for their efforts were futile. Besides, what was happening to them was God's punishment upon them.

But they interpreted Jeremiah's words as sedition. They threw him into a cistern in an effort to kill him. Ironically, Ebed-melech, a foreigner, saved him.

A reading from the Book of the Prophet Jeremiah

In those days, the princes said to the king:
"Jeremiah ought to be put to death;
  he is demoralizing the soldiers who are left in this
    city,
  and all the people, by speaking such things to them;
  he is not interested in the welfare of our people,
  but in their ruin."
King Zedekiah answered: "He is in your power";
  for the king could do nothing with them.
And so they took Jeremiah
  and threw him into the cistern of Prince Malchiah,
  which was in the quarters of the guard,
  letting him down with ropes.
There was no water in the cistern, only mud,
  and Jeremiah sank into the mud.

Ebed-melech, a court official,
  went there from the palace and said to him:
  "My lord king,
  these men have been at fault
  in all they have done to the prophet Jeremiah,
  casting him into the cistern.
He will die of famine on the spot,
  for there is no more food in the city."
Then the king ordered Ebed-melech the Cushite
  to take three men along with him,
  and draw the prophet Jeremiah out of the cistern
    before he should die.

The word of the Lord.

327

Lect.
No. 120

RESPONSORIAL PSALM: Ps 40:2, 3, 4, 18 (℟.: 14b)

The Responsorial Psalm celebrates the fact that God delivers us from all of our difficulties.

This is especially significant today, for the First Reading and the Gospel speak of the fact that we will suffer if we give witness to the word of God in our lives.

When we are suffering, for whatever reason, the reaction is often depression or anger or frustration. We wonder why God is not doing anything to help us. We wonder, like the psalmist, when God will intervene (for we waited, waited for him).

This psalm reminds us to trust in God who will deliver us. He is our hope and our all.

The image of the pit of destruction and the mud of the swamp were often used as a symbol for death.

℟. **Lord, come to my aid!**

I have waited, waited for the LORD,
　and he stooped toward me.

℟. **Lord, come to my aid!**

The LORD heard my cry.
He drew me out of the pit of destruction,
　out of the mud of the swamp;
he set my feet upon a crag;
　he made firm my steps.

℟. **Lord, come to my aid!**

And he put a new song into my mouth,
　a hymn to our God.
Many shall look on in awe
　and trust in the LORD.

℟. **Lord, come to my aid!**

Though I am afflicted and poor,
　yet the LORD thinks of me.
You are my help and my deliverer;
　O my God, hold not back!

℟. **Lord, come to my aid!**

PASTORAL REFLECTIONS

We often feel that if we do the right thing, then God should make all work out for our benefit. Then, when things fall apart, we feel as if God is not upholding his part of the bargain. Jesus never promised his disciples wealth and worldly success; he promised them a cross through which they could express their love and trust of him.

SECOND READING: Hebrews 12:1-4

Let us persevere in running the race that lies before us.

The Letter to the Hebrews alternates between theological teachings and exhortation.

The theory is that if we really understood how much Jesus has done for us, then we would be willing to do what it takes to live in his love.

This reading begins with a reminder of all of those who have preceded us and have given that witness. The implied message is that we should be willing to do the same.

We also hear about Jesus who was willing to die out of love for us. This love should give us the strength to reject our temptations.

Those temptations have not yet called us to sacrifice as much as Jesus sacrificed when he died for us on the cross.

A reading from the Letter to the Hebrews

rothers and sisters:
Since we are surrounded by so great a cloud of witnesses,
let us rid ourselves of every burden and sin that clings to us
and persevere in running the race that lies before us
while keeping our eyes fixed on Jesus,
the leader and perfecter of faith.
For the sake of the joy that lay before him
he endured the cross, despising its shame,
and has taken his seat at the right of the throne of God.
Consider how he endured such opposition from sinners,
in order that you may not grow weary and lose heart.
In your struggle against sin
you have not yet resisted to the point of shedding blood.

The word of the Lord.

ALLELUIA: John 10:27

The Lord is our shepherd, and he will protect us against those who try to persecute us for giving witness to the love of the Lord.

℟. **Alleluia, alleluia.**

My sheep hear my voice, says the Lord;
I know them, and they follow me.

℟. **Alleluia, alleluia.**

Lect.
No. 120

GOSPEL: Luke 12:49-53

I have come not to establish peace, but rather division.

We are surprised when Jesus tells us that he came to bring division and not peace. This does not mean that Jesus wants us to fight others. Rather, if we try to live God's love, we will be rejected (often by those who are closest to us).

We have to remember that this passage was written in a time when members of the community were being persecuted for their faith.

Not many of us will face actual physical violence for giving witness to the faith, but there is always a price to pay.

Some will make fun of us, others will call us a fool, still others will take advantage of us. This is the price we pay for being a disciple.

A reading from the holy Gospel according to Luke

Jesus said to his disciples:
"I have come to set the earth on fire,
  and how I wish it were already blazing!
There is a baptism with which I must be baptized,
  and how great is my anguish until it is accomplished!
Do you think that I have come to establish peace on the earth?
No, I tell you, but rather division.
From now on a household of five will be divided,
  three against two and two against three;
  a father will be divided against his son
  and a son against his father,
  a mother against her daughter
  and a daughter against her mother,
  a mother-in-law against her daughter-in-law
  and a daughter-in-law against her mother-in-law."

The Gospel of the Lord.

PASTORAL REFLECTIONS

In the ancient world, family harmony was a sign of those who lived lives of virtue. Christians, in particular, tried to give a witness to the world of mutual respect and responsibilities within families. Yet, even this most important relationship is secondary to the call of discipleship, which might require one to make a choice between Christ and family.

TWENTY-FIRST SUNDAY IN ORDINARY TIME

Lect. No. 123

FIRST READING: Isaiah 66:18-21

They shall bring all your brothers and sisters from all the nations.

Throughout most of the Old Testament we are told that God would reach out to the people of Israel. The only reason that the Gentiles existed, it seems, is so that God could vent his rage against them.

There is even a verse that says, "As you have used us to show them your mercy, so now use them to show us your wrath."

This First Reading speaks of the opposite trend. In this passage, written shortly after the return of the exiles from Babylon, we hear of how God will reach out to all of the nations.

Yahweh is the only God who exists, and he is therefore the God of all peoples upon the earth.

God will bring them to his holy city and make them part of his holy people. They will even be invited to be priests and Levites, to serve God in the holiest places in the temple.

A reading from the Book of the Prophet Isaiah

Thus says the LORD:
I know their works and their thoughts,
and I come to gather nations of every language;
   they shall come and see my glory.
I will set a sign among them;
   from them I will send fugitives to the nations:
   to Tarshish, Put and Lud, Mosoch, Tubal and Javan,
   to the distant coastlands
   that have never heard of my fame, or seen my glory;
   and they shall proclaim my glory among the nations.
They shall bring all your brothers and sisters from all the nations
   as an offering to the LORD,
   on horses and in chariots, in carts, upon mules and dromedaries,
   to Jerusalem, my holy mountain, says the LORD,
   just as the Israelites bring their offering
   to the house of the LORD in clean vessels.
Some of these I will take as priests and Levites, says the LORD.

The word of the Lord.

Lect. No. 123

RESPONSORIAL PSALM: Ps 117:1, 2 (℟.: Mk 16:15)

The Responsorial Psalm continues the theme found in the First Reading and also in the Gospel, i.e., God reaches out to the nations of the earth.

Up to this time, only the people of Israel had experienced the kindness and fidelity of the LORD.

The word in Hebrew for kindness is *"hesed,"* and it means the love that God expresses in the covenant.

The word in Hebrew for fidelity is *"emet,"* and it means the truthfulness and loyalty that God shows by keeping his promises even when we do not.

℟. **Go out to all the world and tell the Good News.**

or:

℟. **Alleluia.**

Praise the LORD, all you nations;
  glorify him, all you peoples!

℟. **Go out to all the world and tell the Good News.**

or:

℟. **Alleluia.**

For steadfast is his kindness toward us,
  and the fidelity of the LORD endures forever.

℟. **Go out to all the world and tell the Good News.**

or:

℟. **Alleluia.**

PASTORAL REFLECTIONS

The Jewish people who heard today's readings (that from Isaiah and that proclaimed by Jesus) were severely challenged by what was being proclaimed. They thought they knew exactly what God wanted and who was living in God's favor and who was not. Hearing that the Gentiles were being called to be part of God's people would have left them disconcerted, but sometimes that is good. It can be good to be off balance a bit so that we can learn new things.

Who would we be hesitant to see among those who are called the chosen of God? Who would it be difficult to believe is a recipient of God's mercy and fidelity?

SECOND READING: Hebrews 12:5-7, 11-13

Those whom the Lord loves, he disciplines.

This passage from the Letter to the Hebrews speaks of the discipline that the Lord uses with us, just as a parent might discipline a child.

The parent does not punish the child because it makes the parent feel good, but rather because it is in the best interest of the child.

If a child is not punished, then it might not learn to distinguish between right and wrong. That would be a form of child abuse.

Obviously, our understanding of what punishment means today is significantly different from what would have been understood when this passage was written.

Nevertheless, it remains true that children need clear boundaries if they are to develop a balanced moral life.

A reading from the Letter to the Hebrews

Brothers and sisters,
You have forgotten the exhortation addressed to
    you as children:
"My son, do not disdain the discipline of the Lord
    or lose heart when reproved by him;
for whom the Lord loves, he disciplines;
    he scourges every son he acknowledges."
Endure your trials as "discipline";
    God treats you as sons.
For what "son" is there whom his father does not discipline?
At the time,
    all discipline seems a cause not for joy but for pain,
    yet later it brings the peaceful fruit of righteousness
    to those who are trained by it.

So strengthen your drooping hands and your weak
    knees.
Make straight paths for your feet,
    that what is lame may not be disjointed but healed.

The word of the Lord.

ALLELUIA: John 14:6

The Alleluia Verse reminds us that Jesus is the source of all life. We cannot come to the Father except through Jesus for he is the revelation of who God is.

℟. **Alleluia, alleluia.**

I am the way, the truth and the life, says the Lord;
no one comes to the Father, except through me.

℟. **Alleluia, alleluia.**

Lect.
No. 123

GOSPEL: Luke 13:22-30

They will come from east and west and recline at table in the kingdom of God.

The story begins with Jesus on his way to Jerusalem. This was the place of destiny, and Jesus is on his way to Jerusalem throughout most of the Gospel.

Yet, in spite of the fact that Jerusalem is the chosen city, the chosen people should be cautious. Jesus speaks of how many who would consider themselves to be chosen will find themselves excluded at the final judgment.

At the same time, many of those who were considered to be excluded (the Gentiles) will be part of the promise. They will be invited to recline at the table of the heavenly banquet.

We might ask what it means that the door to heaven is narrow. Jesus tends to speak in a Middle Eastern manner, which often says one thing in one verse and then the opposite in the next.

These sayings, although they contradict each other, were both considered to be true.

By saying that few would be saved, Jesus was emphasizing that entering the kingdom is not a question of belonging to a certain group of people.

It is a question of committing oneself to the kingdom, even if that costs all that one has.

A reading from the holy Gospel according to Luke

Jesus passed through towns and villages,
teaching as he went and making his way to Jerusalem.
Someone asked him,
"Lord, will only a few people be saved?"
He answered them,
"Strive to enter through the narrow gate,
for many, I tell you, will attempt to enter
but will not be strong enough.
After the master of the house has arisen and locked the door,
then will you stand outside knocking and saying,
'Lord, open the door for us.'
He will say to you in reply,
'I do not know where you are from.'
And you will say,
'We ate and drank in your company and you taught in our streets.'
Then he will say to you,
'I do not know where you are from.
Depart from me, all you evildoers!'
And there will be wailing and grinding of teeth
when you see Abraham, Isaac, and Jacob
and all the prophets in the kingdom of God
and you yourselves cast out.
And people will come from the east and the west
and from the north and the south
and will recline at table in the kingdom of God.
For behold, some are last who will be first,
and some are first who will be last."

The Gospel of the Lord.

September 1, 2013

TWENTY-SECOND SUNDAY IN ORDINARY TIME

Lect. No. 126 FIRST READING: Sirach 3:17-18, 20, 28-29

Humble yourself and you will find favor with God.

The First Reading comes from the Book of Sirach, a book of wisdom teachings. This passage deals with the interior attitude that one should have, one of humility. If one reaches beyond one's grasp, then one will surely be frustrated. If someone is arrogant and places self over others, then that person will be very lonely.

If, on the other hand, one walks about with a spirit of simplicity and humility, then one will be respected by others.

A reading from the Book of Sirach

My child, conduct your affairs with humility,
 and you will be loved more than a giver of gifts.
Humble yourself the more, the greater you are,
 and you will find favor with God.
What is too sublime for you, seek not,
 into things beyond your strength search not.
The mind of a sage appreciates proverbs,
 and an attentive ear is the joy of the wise.
Water quenches a flaming fire,
 and alms atone for sins.

The word of the Lord.

Lect. No. 126 RESPONSORIAL Psalm: Ps 68:4-5, 6-7, 10-11 (℟.: cf. 11b)

The Responsorial Psalm praises the LORD for his goodness to the psalmist and to the people of Israel.

This goodness is especially expressed in the way that the LORD treats the poor.

The widow and the orphan are the exemplars of those who have no one to stand up for them.

The LORD is also the one who provides a home for those who are homeless and who sets prisoners free.

℟. **God, in your goodness, you have made a home for the poor.**

The just rejoice and exult before God;
 they are glad and rejoice.
Sing to God, chant praise to his name,
 whose name is the LORD.

℟. **God, in your goodness, you have made a home for the poor.**

The father of orphans and the defender of widows
 is God in his holy dwelling.
God gives a home to the forsaken;
 he leads forth prisoners to prosperity.

335

There is no refuge except in God.

God even expresses his generosity in the way he bestows fertility upon the land.

Without rain, the land will languish. Without his blessing, the flocks will fail to flourish.

Thus, when we feel that the fields of our heart are dry and barren, we have to turn to God who will shower his love upon us.

℟. **God, in your goodness, you have made a home for the poor.**

A bountiful rain you showered down, O God, upon
   your inheritance;
you restored the land when it languished;
your flock settled in it;
   in your goodness, O God, you provided it for the
   needy.

℟. **God, in your goodness, you have made a home for the poor.**

SECOND READING: Hebrews 12:18-19, 22-24a

You have approached Mount Zion and the city of the living God.

Throughout the Letter to the Hebrews, the author has spoken of various things from the Old Testament and how Jesus replaced them.

In the Old Testament, there was an earthly sanctuary in the temple. Now, Jesus has entered into the heavenly sanctuary.

Previously there were many high priests and sacrifices; now there is one high priest, Jesus, and his one and eternal sacrifice on the cross. Before the blood of animals was offered; now the blood of the Lamb of God has been shed.

In this passage the author compares Mount Sinai and the Old Covenant made on that mountain with the heavenly Jerusalem and the New Covenant made in the blood of Jesus. The latter is so much greater than the earlier things that they cannot even be compared.

A reading from the Letter to the Hebrews

Brothers and sisters:
You have not approached that which could be
   touched
and a blazing fire and gloomy darkness
and storm and a trumpet blast
and a voice speaking words such that those who
   heard
begged that no message be further addressed to
   them.
No, you have approached Mount Zion
   and the city of the living God, the heavenly Jerusalem,
   and countless angels in festal gathering,
   and the assembly of the firstborn enrolled in
   heaven,
   and God the judge of all,
   and the spirits of the just made perfect,
   and Jesus, the mediator of a new covenant,
   and the sprinkled blood that speaks more elo-
   quently than that of Abel.

The word of the Lord.

Lect. No. 126

ALLELUIA: Matthew 11:29ab

The Alleluia Verse speaks of God's invitation to us: he invites us to take his yoke upon ourselves. We will not have to carry it alone, for he will carry it with us and we with him.

℟. **Alleluia, alleluia.**

Take my yoke upon you, says the Lord,
and learn from me, for I am meek and humble of
   heart.

℟. **Alleluia, alleluia.**

Lect. No. 126

GOSPEL: Luke 14:1, 7-14

Everyone who exalts himself will be humbled, everyone who humbles himself will be exalted.

The Gospel today has two passages that deal with banquets. This is not unusual, for Saint Luke often uses meals and food as a symbol of the way we interact with others. Even heaven is presented as being a heavenly banquet.

The first passage deals with the question of humility. Jesus observed how certain people entered the banquet hall and immediately gravitated toward the places of honor. He told his listeners it would have been better for them to seek more humble positions, and then they might be invited to more important places.

This passage asks us to consider how and why we do the things that we do. Do we do them for prestige, to be thought of as important or good or nice? Or do we do them as an expression of love?

The second passage continues this theme. It asks us whom we would invite to a meal. Will we invite those who can pay us

A reading from the holy Gospel according to Luke

On a sabbath Jesus went to dine
   at the home of one of the leading Pharisees,
   and the people there were observing him carefully.

He told a parable to those who had been invited,
   noticing how they were choosing the places of
    honor at the table.
"When you are invited by someone to a wedding
    banquet,
   do not recline at table in the place of honor.
A more distinguished guest than you may have been
    invited by him,
   and the host who invited both of you may ap-
    proach you and say,
   'Give your place to this man,'
   and then you would proceed with embarrassment
   to take the lowest place.
Rather, when you are invited,
   go and take the lowest place
   so that when the host comes to you he may say,
   'My friend, move up to a higher position.'
Then you will enjoy the esteem of your companions
    at the table.
For everyone who exalts himself will be humbled,
   but the one who humbles himself will be exalted."

back, or will we invite those who most need an expression of our love and generosity?

Whom do we make our friends: those with whom it is pleasant to share our time, or rather those who are lonely and need our company?

We know it is true Christian love when we reach out to help those who cannot pay us back in any way (and in fact, those who might respond to our generosity with an attempt to hurt us).

Then he said to the host who invited him,
    "When you hold a lunch or a dinner,
    do not invite your friends or your brothers
    or your relatives or your wealthy neighbors,
    in case they may invite you back and you have re-
        payment.
Rather, when you hold a banquet,
    invite the poor, the crippled, the lame, the blind;
    blessed indeed will you be because of their inabil-
        ity to repay you.
For you will be repaid at the resurrection of the
    righteous."

The Gospel of the Lord.

PASTORAL REFLECTIONS

Human beings rarely have only one layer of motivation. We might think that we are doing something for all the right motives, but there may be a mix of motives as to why we are doing those things. Some of those motives might be quite altruistic, others a bit selfish.

It is essential that we be brutally honest with ourselves concerning all of these motives. When we know them, we can deal with them and purify them. If, on the other hand, we try to kid ourselves into thinking that we are acting from a perfectly pure motivation, then our somewhat less generous motives will tend to blindside us. We will end up doing something (even the right thing) for the wrong reason.

September 8, 2013

TWENTY-THIRD SUNDAY IN ORDINARY TIME

Lect. No. 129

FIRST READING: Wisdom 9:13-18b

Who can conceive what the Lord intends?

A reading from the Book of Wisdom

Who can know God's counsel,
   or who can conceive what the LORD intends?
For the deliberations of mortals are timid,
   and unsure are our plans.
For the corruptible body burdens the soul
   and the earthen shelter weighs down the mind
      that has many concerns.
And scarce do we guess the things on earth,
   and what is within our grasp we find with diffi-
      culty;
   but when things are in heaven, who can search
      them out?
Or who ever knew your counsel, except you had
      given wisdom
   and sent your holy spirit from on high?
And thus were the paths of those on earth made
      straight.

The word of the Lord.

The theme of today's First Reading and Gospel is that God's ways are far beyond our ways. We cannot hope to know exactly what God wants for us.

Yet, God reveals his truth to us through wisdom. He breathes his Spirit into us to place the breath of truth into our heart.

This is the only way that we can make sense of our lives (for on our own we cannot even understand earthly things, let alone heavenly things).

But when God gives us this wisdom, we can make sense out of our lives. It was through his wisdom that God created the world. It is God's wisdom that teaches us his ways.

PASTORAL REFLECTIONS

The fact that God's ways are beyond our understanding does not mean that we cannot know anything. St. Augustine said that the mystery of our faith is like swimming in the ocean. We can never hope to know all of the water in the ocean. We can, however, swim around a bit and come to know more of the water.

This is what we do when we study about our faith. It is a mystery beyond our understanding. As we study it more and more, though, we come to realize what we can know and what we cannot. It fills us with a sense of awe and gratitude.

Lect. No. 129   **RESPONSORIAL PSALM: Ps 90:3-4, 5-6, 12-13, 14, 17 (℞.: 1)**

The Responsorial Psalm continues the theme of the wisdom of God and how his ways are far beyond our understanding.

The main theme is that God brings people to life and also brings people to death. We, as human beings, are nothing more than mud and breath.

If God takes back that breath, then we return to the earth. We are fragile, and God is so great.

Furthermore, God even looks at time differently. We count time day by day, but God knows things in eternity. A thousand years in his sight seem like a moment that passes without notice.

Yet, it is remarkable that God who sees all things and is above all things would nevertheless be concerned with every event that occurs upon the earth.

We therefore ask God to intervene and "prosper the work of our hands," for it is only in and through God that our lives are filled with peace.

℞. **In every age, O Lord, you have been our refuge.**

You turn man back to dust,
    saying, "Return, O children of men."
For a thousand years in your sight
    are as yesterday, now that it is past,
    or as a watch of the night.

℞. **In every age, O Lord, you have been our refuge.**

You make an end of them in their sleep;
    the next morning they are like the changing grass,
which at dawn springs up anew,
    but by evening wilts and fades.

℞. **In every age, O Lord, you have been our refuge.**

Teach us to number our days aright,
    that we may gain wisdom of heart.
Return, O Lord! How long?
    Have pity on your servants!

℞. **In every age, O Lord, you have been our refuge.**

Fill us at daybreak with your kindness,
    that we may shout for joy and gladness all our days.
And may the gracious care of the Lord our God be
        ours;
    prosper the work of our hands for us!
Prosper the work of our hands!

℞. **In every age, O Lord, you have been our refuge.**

PASTORAL REFLECTIONS

This psalm reminds us to open our hearts to the ways of the Lord. We can easily get so caught up in our everyday lives that we forget to explore its spiritual dimension. This psalm reveals that aspect of our lives and celebrates it.

SECOND READING: Philemon 9-10, 12-17

Receive him no longer as a slave but as a beloved brother.

Saint Paul's Letter to Philemon is the only letter that he wrote to an individual.

Paul was writing Philemon from prison. While he was there, one of Philemon's slaves, Onesimus, came to visit him (it seems as if he had run away from Philemon).

During his visit, Onesimus converted to the faith. Paul was now sending him back to Philemon.

Paul asks Philemon not to punish Onesimus. He makes a word play upon his name, saying that Onesimus was once worthless, but now he is worthy (which is the meaning of the name Onesimus).

He never exactly says that Onesimus should be set free (for Paul seems to accept slavery as an established institution), but he certainly hints that Philemon should do this as a favor to Paul.

A reading from the Letter of Saint Paul to Philemon

I, Paul, an old man,
    and now also a prisoner for Christ Jesus,
urge you on behalf of my child Onesimus,
    whose father I have become in my imprisonment;
I am sending him, that is, my own heart, back to you.
I should have liked to retain him for myself,
    so that he might serve me on your behalf
    in my imprisonment for the gospel,
    but I did not want to do anything without your consent,
    so that the good you do might not be forced but voluntary.
Perhaps this is why he was away from you for a while,
    that you might have him back forever,
    no longer as a slave
    but more than a slave, a brother,
    beloved especially to me, but even more so to you,
    as a man and in the Lord.
So if you regard me as a partner, welcome him as you would me.

The word of the Lord.

ALLELUIA: Psalm 119:135

The Alleluia Verse reminds us that one of the greatest gifts that God could give us is to teach us how to live our lives in the proper way.

℟. **Alleluia, alleluia.**

Let your face shine upon your servant;
and teach me your laws.

℟. **Alleluia, alleluia.**

GOSPEL: Luke 14:25-33

Anyone of you who does not renounce all possessions cannot be my disciple.

This passage gives an example of Gospel irony, that we must lose our lives in order to save them. We must leave everything that we have in order to gain the world.

This is not logical according to the standards of the world, but it is the wisdom of the Gospel.

The saying at the beginning of this passage is typical of the Middle Eastern way of speaking. Jesus tells his disciples that they must hate their parents to follow him.

This is his way of saying that we must love him more than we love others. He must be at the center of our lives.

It is clear that we must be careful how we interpret this saying (lest we interpret literally passages that were intended to be understood in a more symbolic manner).

The two examples given at the end of the passage speak of knowing what we are committing ourselves to when we make a decision (such as the decision to follow Jesus).

It will sooner or later cost us all that we have, but we will acquire more than we ever hoped to receive.

A reading from the holy Gospel according to Luke

Great crowds were traveling with Jesus, and he turned and addressed them,
"If anyone comes to me without hating his father and mother,
wife and children, brothers and sisters,
and even his own life,
he cannot be my disciple.
Whoever does not carry his own cross and come after me
cannot be my disciple.
Which of you wishing to construct a tower
does not first sit down and calculate the cost
to see if there is enough for its completion?
Otherwise, after laying the foundation
and finding himself unable to finish the work
the onlookers should laugh at him and say,
'This one began to build but did not have the resources to finish.'
Or what king marching into battle would not first sit down
and decide whether with ten thousand troops
he can successfully oppose another king
advancing upon him with twenty thousand troops?
But if not, while he is still far away,
he will send a delegation to ask for peace terms.
In the same way,
anyone of you who does not renounce all his possessions
cannot be my disciple."

The Gospel of the Lord.

TWENTY-FOURTH SUNDAY IN ORDINARY TIME

Lect. No. 132

FIRST READING: Exodus 32:7-11, 13-14

The Lord relented in the punishment he had threatened to inflict on his people.

The First Reading and the Gospel give two different examples of how God reacts to sin.

In the First Reading we hear of the episode that occurred when Moses went up Mount Sinai to meet the LORD.

The people who remained at the base of the mountain decided to take their gold jewelry and make a golden calf that they would worship.

God offers to destroy this people and to make a great people come from Moses. He calls them a stiff-necked people.

After everything that he had done in their behalf, they should not have doubted him for a second. Yet, they seemed to use every occasion to rebel against the LORD.

Moses implored God to have mercy upon his people. He reminded God of the history of God's relationship with them.

God had acted in Abraham's, Isaac's, and Jacob's behalf. He had promised his people the land and a great number of descendants.

How could God now go back on his promises?

A reading from the Book of Exodus

The LORD said to Moses,
"Go down at once to your people,
whom you brought out of the land of Egypt,
for they have become depraved.
They have soon turned aside from the way I pointed
out to them,
making for themselves a molten calf and worshiping it,
sacrificing to it and crying out,
'This is your God, O Israel,
who brought you out of the land of Egypt!'
I see how stiff-necked this people is," continued the
LORD to Moses.
"Let me alone, then,
that my wrath may blaze up against them to consume them.
Then I will make of you a great nation."

But Moses implored the LORD, his God, saying,
"Why, O LORD, should your wrath blaze up against
your own people,
whom you brought out of the land of Egypt
with such great power and with so strong a hand?
Remember your servants Abraham, Isaac, and Israel,
and how you swore to them by your own self, saying,
'I will make your descendants as numerous as the
stars in the sky;

Moses was reminding God that even if his people were not faithful, God is always faithful to his promises. God will never go back on his promises.

and all this land that I promised,
I will give your descendants as their perpetual heritage.' "
So the LORD relented in the punishment
he had threatened to inflict on his people.

The word of the Lord.

RESPONSORIAL PSALM: Ps 51:3-4, 12-13, 17, 19 (℟.: Lk 15:18)

Psalm 51 is a penitential psalm written to commemorate the day that David repented for his sin against God and against Uriah the Hittite.

The psalm reminds us that we cannot obtain forgiveness of sin by ourselves.

The only way that we can find forgiveness is to have a humble, contrite heart, for it is God who will renew us.

God gave us his Spirit when he created us. If God were to take that Spirit back, then we would return to the dust.

But if God breathes that Spirit into our hearts again, we will be renewed. We will be a new creation.

℟. **I will rise and go to my father.**

Have mercy on me, O God, in your goodness;
   in the greatness of your compassion wipe out my
      offense.
Thoroughly wash me from my guilt
   and of my sin cleanse me.

℟. **I will rise and go to my father.**

A clean heart create for me, O God,
   and a steadfast spirit renew within me.
Cast me not out from your presence,
   and your Holy Spirit take not from me.

℟. **I will rise and go to my father.**

O Lord, open my lips,
   and my mouth shall proclaim your praise.
My sacrifice, O God, is a contrite spirit;
   a heart contrite and humbled, O God, you will not
      spurn.

℟. **I will rise and go to my father.**

PASTORAL REFLECTIONS

What does God feel when we sin? Is God angry at us, or for us? The latter would mean that God interprets sin as a poison that is killing the spiritual life of his beloved children, and he hates it (the sin, not his children). It would be like a parent might feel concerning a child who is taking drugs. The parent hates the drugs, but continues to love the child.

Lect. No. 132

SECOND READING: 1 Timothy 1:12-17

Christ came to save sinners.

This Sunday is one of those rare occasions when the same theme is found in all three readings. They all deal with how God treats sinners.

The Second Reading speaks of how Saint Paul was a great sinner. He opposed the ways of the Lord when he persecuted Christians in the early days of the Church. He calls himself a blasphemer, persecutor, and arrogant man.

Instead of punishing Paul, God forgave him and used him as an instrument of his mercy. He was visible proof that Jesus came into the world to save sinners.

This is really the story of each one of us. We have been forgiven by the Lord. We should be willing to share our story with all who are willing to hear.

We are frequently ready to share the stories of our victories, but it is just as important to share the stories of our weaknesses (and how God worked through those weaknesses to show his strength).

A reading from the first Letter of Saint Paul to Timothy

Beloved:
I am grateful to him who has strengthened me,
   Christ Jesus our Lord,
because he considered me trustworthy
in appointing me to the ministry.
I was once a blasphemer and a persecutor and arrogant,
   but I have been mercifully treated
because I acted out of ignorance in my unbelief.
Indeed, the grace of our Lord has been abundant,
   along with the faith and love that are in Christ Jesus.
This saying is trustworthy and deserves full acceptance:
   Christ Jesus came into the world to save sinners.
Of these I am the foremost.
But for that reason I was mercifully treated,
   so that in me, as the foremost,
   Christ Jesus might display all his patience as an example
for those who would come to believe in him for everlasting life.
To the king of ages, incorruptible, invisible, the only God,
   honor and glory forever and ever. Amen.

The word of the Lord.

Lect. No. 132

ALLELUIA: 2 Corinthians 5:19

The Alleluia Verse continues the theme of reconciliation, that the mission of Jesus was to bring us healing from our sinful ways.

℟. **Alleluia, alleluia.**

God was reconciling the world to himself in Christ and entrusting to us the message of reconciliation.

℟. **Alleluia, alleluia.**

GOSPEL: 🅐 Longer Form: Luke 15:1-32

There will be great joy in heaven over one sinner who repents.

A reading from the holy Gospel according to Luke

Tax collectors and sinners were all drawing near
    to listen to Jesus,
  but the Pharisees and scribes began to complain,
    saying,
  "This man welcomes sinners and eats with them."
So to them he addressed this parable.
"What man among you having a hundred sheep and
      losing one of them
    would not leave the ninety-nine in the desert
    and go after the lost one until he finds it?
And when he does find it,
    he sets it on his shoulders with great joy
    and, upon his arrival home,
    he calls together his friends and neighbors and
      says to them,
    'Rejoice with me because I have found my lost
      sheep.'
I tell you, in just the same way
    there will be more joy in heaven over one sinner
      who repents
    than over ninety-nine righteous people
    who have no need of repentance.

"Or what woman having ten coins and losing one
    would not light a lamp and sweep the house,
    searching carefully until she finds it?
And when she does find it,
    she calls together her friends and neighbors
    and says to them,
    'Rejoice with me because I have found the coin
      that I lost.'
In just the same way, I tell you,
    there will be rejoicing among the angels of God
    over one sinner who repents."

The Gospel of Luke is a Gospel of compassion and the forgiveness of sins. The three parables in today's Gospel give clear evidence of this.

The Gospel begins with two short parables concerning God's attitude toward sinners. God is not out to get them. He is not sitting in heaven planning his revenge against those who have sinned.

Rather, he is actively seeking out those who have sinned so that he might offer them his forgiveness.

The first parable speaks of a shepherd leaving ninety-nine sheep in the wilderness so that the shepherd might seek out the one that is lost.

When that sheep is found, the shepherd responds with great joy.

This is remarkable. It means that Jesus' mission is not for those who are religious and righteous, but Jesus has come to reach out to those who are sinners and alienated.

The second parable is the female parallel to the first parable.

This is typical of Luke's Gospel, for often when a man's story is told, there is a woman's story told immediately afterward to balance it.

There is then a long parable that is one of the most memorable passages of the New Testament: the story of the prodigal son.

The story speaks of a father who had two sons. One of them, the younger son, asks his father for his inheritance so that he might use it immediately. Even before he does anything with the money, he has already rejected his father.

He was effectively telling his father that he was as good as dead for him, and that the only thing his father meant to him was what he could give him.

The son then goes out and squanders his money on dissolute living. He makes friends, but they are only fair weather friends (ironically, they were treating the son exactly the way he had treated his father).

When he is starving, he realizes his folly and decides to go back to the father and ask his forgiveness.

One might very well ask whether the son was really sorry for what he had done, or just sorry for having been caught. It seems as if he was ready to say anything that he might have to say to be received back by his father.

When he arrives back home, his father is waiting for him. He catches sight of the son from a distance and runs over to meet him.

Then he said,
  "A man had two sons, and the younger son said to
    his father,
  'Father give me the share of your estate that
    should come to me.'
So the father divided the property between them.
After a few days, the younger son collected all his
    belongings
  and set off to a distant country
  where he squandered his inheritance on a life of
    dissipation.
When he had freely spent everything,
  a severe famine struck that country,
  and he found himself in dire need.
So he hired himself out to one of the local citizens
  who sent him to his farm to tend the swine.
And he longed to eat his fill of the pods on which
    the swine fed,
  but nobody gave him any.
Coming to his senses he thought,
  'How many of my father's hired workers
  have more than enough food to eat,
  but here am I, dying from hunger.
I shall get up and go to my father and I shall say to
    him,
  "Father, I have sinned against heaven and against
    you.
I no longer deserve to be called your son;
  treat me as you would treat one of your hired
    workers."'
So he got up and went back to his father.
While he was still a long way off,
  his father caught sight of him,
  and was filled with compassion.
He ran to his son, embraced him and kissed him.
His son said to him,
  'Father, I have sinned against heaven and against
    you;

This was unusual for a father of that era. According to the law, he should have had his son put to death for he was considered to be an incorrigible son.

But even if he had not done this, he would never have been waiting for his son outside of his house. He would have been waiting inside, expecting his son to come and fall on his knees and beg him for his forgiveness.

This father only wants to forgive his son. He does not wait for his son's apology (possibly because he knows that his son's words would not be as honest as one would hope).

He forgives him totally and prepares a feast to celebrate his return.

The older son is angry that his father forgave his brother and prepared a feast in his honor. He will not even call him his "brother" when he speaks of him. He calls him "your son" and not "my brother."

Ironically, his attitude toward his father was scarcely different from that of the first son, for he was only thinking of what he could get out of him.

God only wants mercy. We have to ask ourselves whether we will be willing to celebrate if our worst enemy gets into heaven before us, or will we be like the older brother in this story who resents the fact that his brother "got away with it."

I no longer deserve to be called your son.'
But his father ordered his servants,
    'Quickly bring the finest robe and put it on him;
    put a ring on his finger and sandals on his feet.
Take the fattened calf and slaughter it.
Then let us celebrate with a feast,
    because this son of mine was dead, and has come
        to life again;
    he was lost, and has been found.'
Then the celebration began.
Now the older son had been out in the field
    and, on his way back, as he neared the house,
    he heard the sound of music and dancing.
He called one of the servants and asked what this
        might mean.
The servant said to him,
    'Your brother has returned
    and your father has slaughtered the fattened calf
    because he has him back safe and sound.'
He became angry,
    and when he refused to enter the house,
    his father came out and pleaded with him.
He said to his father in reply,
    'Look, all these years I served you
    and not once did I disobey your orders;
    yet you never gave me even a young goat to feast
        on with my friends.
But when your son returns,
    who swallowed up your property with prostitutes,
    for him you slaughter the fattened calf.'
He said to him,
    'My son, you are here with me always;
    everything I have is yours.
But now we must celebrate and rejoice,
    because your brother was dead and has come to
        life again;
    he was lost and has been found.'"

The Gospel of the Lord.

Lect.
No. 132

GOSPEL: B Shorter Form: Luke 15:1-10

There will be great joy in heaven over one sinner who repents.

The Gospel of Luke is a Gospel of compassion and the forgiveness of sins. The two parables in today's Gospel give clear evidence of this.

These two short parables deal with God's attitude toward those who are sinners. God is not out to get them. He is not sitting in heaven planning his revenge against those who have sinned.

Rather, he is actively seeking out those who have sinned so that he might offer them his forgiveness. God is always filled with mercy.

The first parable speaks of a shepherd leaving ninety-nine sheep in the wilderness so that he might seek out the one that is lost.

When that sheep is found, the shepherd responds with great joy. This is remarkable.

It means that Jesus' mission is not for those who are religious and righteous, but for those who are sinners and alienated.

The second parable is the female parallel to the first parable.

This is typical of Luke's Gospel, for often when a man's story is told, there is a woman's story told immediately afterward to balance it.

A reading from the holy Gospel according to Luke

Tax collectors and sinners were all drawing near to listen to Jesus,
   but the Pharisees and scribes began to complain, saying,
"This man welcomes sinners and eats with them."
So to them he addressed this parable.
"What man among you having a hundred sheep and losing one of them
   would not leave the ninety-nine in the desert
   and go after the lost one until he finds it?
And when he does find it,
   he sets it on his shoulders with great joy
   and, upon his arrival home,
   he calls together his friends and neighbors and says to them,
   'Rejoice with me because I have found my lost sheep.'
I tell you, in just the same way
   there will be more joy in heaven over one sinner who repents
   than over ninety-nine righteous people
   who have no need of repentance.

"Or what woman having ten coins and losing one
   would not light a lamp and sweep the house,
   searching carefully until she finds it?
And when she does find it,
   she calls together her friends and neighbors
   and says to them,
   'Rejoice with me because I have found the coin that I lost.'
In just the same way, I tell you,
   there will be rejoicing among the angels of God
   over one sinner who repents."

The Gospel of the Lord.

September 22, 2013

TWENTY-FIFTH SUNDAY IN ORDINARY TIME

Lect. No. 135

FIRST READING: Amos 8:4-7

Against those who buy the poor for money.

The Prophet Amos was ruthless in his denunciation of those who pretended to be religious and who nevertheless were dishonest in their daily lives.

They cheated whenever they bought and sold produce. They exploited the weakness of the poor. They resented the Sabbath, the day of the LORD, because they could not make a profit.

The connection between this reading and the Gospel is that if we say that we are believers, then we have to give witness to that faith in the way that we do business with others.

A reading from the Book of the Prophet Amos

Hear this, you who trample upon the needy
  and destroy the poor of the land!
"When will the new moon be over," you ask,
  "that we may sell our grain,
  and the sabbath, that we may display the wheat?
We will diminish the ephah,
  add to the shekel,
  and fix our scales for cheating!
We will buy the lowly for silver,
  and the poor for a pair of sandals;
  even the refuse of the wheat we will sell!"
The LORD has sworn by the pride of Jacob:
  Never will I forget a thing they have done!

The word of the Lord.

Lect. No. 135

RESPONSORIAL PSALM: Ps 113:1-2, 4-6, 7-8 (℟.:cf. 1a, 7b)

The Responsorial Psalm is a hymn of praise to the LORD who is king over all the earth.

This psalm is a reminder that we cannot hide our activities from God. We cannot pretend that we can do things that he does not see.

We must live in a manner that is consistent with what we say we are. We cannot say we are Christians and live in a way

℟. **Praise the Lord, who lifts up the poor.**

or:

℟. **Alleluia.**

Praise, you servants of the LORD,
  praise the name of the LORD.
Blessed be the name of the LORD
  both now and forever.

℟. **Praise the Lord, who lifts up the poor.**

or:

℟. **Alleluia.**

that might give scandal to others (especially if they were to know we are Christian).

This means that we must have a radical trust in the providence of God. We cannot pretend that it all depends upon our own efforts.

If we depend only on ourselves, then we will do whatever we can to succeed (often betraying the things we hold most precious, e.g., our family, our faith, etc.).

We have to be prudent in providing for ourselves and our family, and we have to remember to keep our priorities in perspective.

High above all nations is the LORD;
　above the heavens is his glory.
Who is like the LORD, our God, who is enthroned on high
　and looks upon the heavens and the earth below?

℟. **Praise the Lord, who lifts up the poor.**

or:

℟. **Alleluia.**

He raises up the lowly from the dust;
　from the dunghill he lifts up the poor
to seat them with princes,
　with the princes of his own people.

℟. **Praise the Lord, who lifts up the poor.**

or:

℟. **Alleluia.**

Lect.
No. 135

SECOND READING: 1 Timothy 2:1-8

Let prayers be offered for everyone to God who wills everyone to be saved.

The Second Reading contains a number of loosely connected ideas.

It begins with the idea that we should pray for everyone (for as we will shortly hear, God sent Jesus into the world to save all people).

We should especially pray for those who exercise authority in our society (for they have received that authority from God to lead us in the right paths, in "quiet and tranquil" lives).

The author then passes to a credal formula that he calls the truth: that there is one God and one mediator whom God sent into the world for our salvation.

A reading from the first Letter of Saint Paul
to Timothy

Beloved:
　First of all, I ask that supplications, prayers,
　petitions, and thanksgivings be offered for everyone,
　for kings and for all in authority,
　that we may lead a quiet and tranquil life
　in all devotion and dignity.
This is good and pleasing to God our savior,
　who wills everyone to be saved
　and to come to knowledge of the truth.
　　For there is one God.
　　There is also one mediator between God and men,
　　the man Christ Jesus,
　who gave himself as ransom for all.

God also appointed ministers to proclaim this message to the world, preachers and apostles, who will proclaim the truth to everyone everywhere.

Finally, we hear that Christians should dedicate themselves to prayer.

This was the testimony at the proper time.
For this I was appointed preacher and apostle
—I am speaking the truth, I am not lying—,
teacher of the Gentiles in faith and truth.

It is my wish, then, that in every place the men should pray,
lifting up holy hands, without anger or argument.

The word of the Lord.

The Alleluia Verse speaks of the Gospel value of choosing to be poor according to the standards of the world so that we might experience the riches of the Lord.

ALLELUIA: cf. 2 Corinthians 8:9

℟. **Alleluia, alleluia.**

Though our Lord Jesus Christ was rich, he became poor,
so that by his poverty you might become rich.

℟. **Alleluia, alleluia.**

Lect. No. 135

GOSPEL: 🅰 Longer Form: Luke 16:1-13

You cannot serve both God and mammon.

The parable contained in the Gospel today is a bit odd, for it almost seems as if it is promoting dishonesty.

It must be remembered that this entire passage falls under the understanding of the saying contained at the end of this passage: "No servant can serve two masters. . . . You cannot serve both God and mammon."

It is with this in mind that we can study the parable. It speaks of a steward who is in charge of the accounts of a rich man.

He finds out that he will be let go because he has been squandering the rich man's property. He is a bit desperate because he does not know what he will do to earn a living.

A reading from the holy Gospel according to Luke

Jesus said to his disciples,
"A rich man had a steward
who was reported to him for squandering his property.
He summoned him and said,
'What is this I hear about you?
Prepare a full account of your stewardship,
because you can no longer be my steward.'
The steward said to himself, 'What shall I do,
now that my master is taking the position of steward away from me?
I am not strong enough to dig and I am ashamed to beg.
I know what I shall do so that,
when I am removed from the stewardship,
they may welcome me into their homes.'

He therefore decides to approach his clients and to lessen the burden of what they owe his master.

This is probably not a case of him writing off something that these people actually borrowed. Rather, he seems to be lessening the exaggerated interest that they were being charged by his master.

He is therefore not really stealing anything from them. He is simply writing off a debt that their creditors probably should not have put upon them in the first place.

The point that Jesus makes with this story is that the worldly are more clever in their dealings than those committed to religion.

Sometimes we have to be a bit crafty in sharing the Gospel message. Elsewhere Jesus tells his disciples to be clever as serpents and innocent as doves. We have to say and do things that are an investment in the future (planting seeds of faith that we might not see germinate).

If we are totally committed to the Lord, then we will be willing to use all of our resources (money, property, talents, etc.) to serve the Gospel.

Everything that we have was given to us in trust so that it might be used for the good of all. Our wealth lies not in what we possess but in what we share.

He called in his master's debtors one by one.
To the first he said,
⠀'How much do you owe my master?'
He replied, 'One hundred measures of olive oil.'
He said to him, 'Here is your promissory note.
Sit down and quickly write one for fifty.'
Then to another the steward said, 'And you, how much do you owe?'
He replied, 'One hundred kors of wheat.'
The steward said to him, 'Here is your promissory note;
⠀write one for eighty.'
And the master commended that dishonest steward for acting prudently.

"For the children of this world
⠀are more prudent in dealing with their own generation
⠀than are the children of light.
I tell you, make friends for yourselves with dishonest wealth,
⠀so that when it fails, you will be welcomed into eternal dwellings.
The person who is trustworthy in very small matters
⠀is also trustworthy in great ones;
⠀and the person who is dishonest in very small matters
⠀is also dishonest in great ones.
If, therefore, you are not trustworthy with dishonest wealth,
⠀who will trust you with true wealth?
If you are not trustworthy with what belongs to another,
⠀who will give you what is yours?
No servant can serve two masters.
He will either hate one and love the other,
⠀or be devoted to one and despise the other.
You cannot serve both God and mammon."

The Gospel of the Lord.

GOSPEL: **B** Shorter Form: Luke 16:10-13

You cannot serve both God and mammon.

We cannot serve both God and mammon. We must place God at the center of our lives. If God is the center, then we will use whatever God has given us in the appropriate manner.

Earthly possessions are not really very important when one considers the glory that awaits us in heaven. Yet, if we cannot even deal with possessions in the proper manner, then how will we be able to deal with greater things?

If we are totally committed to the Lord, then we will be willing to use all of our resources (money, property, talents, etc.) to serve the Gospel.

Everything that we have was given to us in trust so that it might be used for the good of all.

A reading from the holy Gospel according to Luke

Jesus said to his disciples:
"The person who is trustworthy in very small matters
is also trustworthy in great ones;
and the person who is dishonest in very small matters
is also dishonest in great ones.
If, therefore, you are not trustworthy with dishonest wealth,
who will trust you with true wealth?
If you are not trustworthy with what belongs to another,
who will give you what is yours?
No servant can serve two masters.
He will either hate one and love the other,
or be devoted to one and despise the other.
You cannot serve both God and mammon."

The Gospel of the Lord.

PASTORAL REFLECTIONS

What type of image would describe our parish? Most often we run our parishes as holding operations. We try to keep everyone in the parish satisfied lest we lose them to another parish or religion. What would our parish life be like if we ran it like political campaigns are run? People running for political office would do almost anything to attain their goal. Would that we put that much of ourselves into our willingness to share our faith.

TWENTY-SIXTH SUNDAY IN ORDINARY TIME

Lect. No. 138

FIRST READING: Amos 6:1a, 4-7

Their wanton revelry shall be done away with.

This Sunday we hear another passage from the Book of the Prophet Amos. The prophet was vicious in his attacks on the decadence of the rich.

They treated themselves to sumptuous pastimes and wasted their resources while the poor died of starvation.

They drank wine from bowls and anointed themselves with oil while those who were defenseless had no one to protect them.

The rich always wanted to be considered the first people of their society. Amos tells them that they will be the first, the first to be carried off into exile when the time of punishment will arrive for Israel.

A reading from the Book of the Prophet Amos

Thus says the LORD the God of hosts:
    Woe to the complacent in Zion!
Lying upon beds of ivory,
    stretched comfortably on their couches,
they eat lambs taken from the flock,
    and calves from the stall!
Improvising to the music of the harp,
    like David, they devise their own accompaniment.
They drink wine from bowls
    and anoint themselves with the best oils;
    yet they are not made ill by the collapse of Joseph!
Therefore, now they shall be the first to go into exile,
    and their wanton revelry shall be done away with.

The word of the Lord.

Lect. No. 138

RESPONSORIAL PSALM: Ps 146:7, 8-9, 9-10 (℟.: 1b)

Psalm 146 is a hymn of praise and thanksgiving to the LORD who is good and loving and generous.

The way that God expresses this goodness is by being the refuge of those in need. He is a guarantor of justice for those who have no one to defend them.

℟. **Praise the Lord, my soul!**

or:

℟. **Alleluia.**

Blessed is he who keeps faith forever,
    secures justice for the oppressed,
    gives food to the hungry.
The LORD sets captives free.

This psalm uses the traditional images for the poor: captives, hungry, blind, strangers, widows, and orphans.

If we are faithful followers of God, we will reach out to those same people.

The measure of any society is how well it treats those who are the powerless. The measure for how much we are Christian is how much we act as Christ would have acted.

This is obviously a call to fight for social justice.

It is also a call to look around at those who surround us (our friends, our family, the people at work or school, etc.) and see how they are also among the weak and broken (for we all have our difficulties and needs).

℟. **Praise the Lord, my soul!**

or:

℟. **Alleluia.**

The LORD gives sight to the blind;
  the LORD raises up those who were bowed down.
The LORD loves the just;
  the LORD protects strangers.

℟. **Praise the Lord, my soul!**

or:

℟. **Alleluia.**

The fatherless and the widow he sustains,
  but the way of the wicked he thwarts.
The LORD shall reign forever;
  your God, O Zion, through all generations. Alleluia.

℟. **Praise the Lord, my soul!**

or:

℟. **Alleluia.**

| Lect. No. 138 |

SECOND READING: 1 Timothy 6:11-16

Keep the commandment until the appearance of the Lord Jesus Christ.

In this Second Reading taken from First Timothy we hear again about the need to be consistent in our lives. We have committed ourselves to the Lord in our Baptism, and we have reaffirmed that commitment every time that we have participated in the Sacraments.

We say that we want to be one with the Lord. We have to live what we say we are.

Pope John XXIII was once asked why there are so many

A reading from the first Letter of Saint Paul to Timothy

But you, man of God, pursue righteousness, devotion, faith, love, patience, and gentleness.
Compete well for the faith.
Lay hold of eternal life, to which you were called
  when you made the noble confession in the presence of many witnesses.
I charge you before God, who gives life to all things,
  and before Christ Jesus,
  who gave testimony under Pontius Pilate for the noble confession,

atheists in the world. His answer was that it is our fault. We often fail to be what we say we are.

Likewise, Gandhi was asked what he thought of the Gospels. He said that they were wonderful, and that someone should try to live them.

But if we try to live God's love to the fullest, then we will share in God's glory when we meet him on the Day of the LORD.

to keep the commandment without stain or reproach

until the appearance of our Lord Jesus Christ

that the blessed and only ruler

will make manifest at the proper time,

the King of kings and Lord of lords,

who alone has immortality, who dwells in unapproachable light,

and whom no human being has seen or can see.

To him be honor and eternal power. Amen.

The word of the Lord.

Lect. No. 138

The Alleluia Verse reminds us that earthly treasures are not what is important.

It is the love of God that really makes all the difference.

ALLELUIA: cf. 2 Corinthians 8:9

℟. **Alleluia, alleluia.**

Though our Lord Jesus Christ was rich, he became poor,

so that by his poverty you might become rich.

℟. **Alleluia, alleluia.**

Lect. No. 138

The Gospel presents the beautiful and challenging story of Lazarus and the rich man.

Lazarus was a common name in New Testament times. (It was a form of the name Eliezer.)

We should therefore not think that this is the same person as Lazarus, the brother of Mary and Martha.

The rich man is dressed in purple garments. Purple was very rare in ancient times, usually reserved for the royal

GOSPEL: Luke 16:19-31

You received what was good, Lazarus what was bad;
now he is comforted, whereas you are tormented.

A reading from the holy Gospel according to Luke

Jesus said to the Pharisees:
"There was a rich man who dressed in purple garments and fine linen

and dined sumptuously each day.

And lying at his door was a poor man named Lazarus, covered with sores,

who would gladly have eaten his fill of the scraps

that fell from the rich man's table.

Dogs even used to come and lick his sores.

When the poor man died,

he was carried away by angels to the bosom of Abraham.

family. This man, therefore, was incredibly rich.

Saint Luke typically describes the heartlessness of the rich man in terms of his not being willing to share his meal.

Lazarus did not even ask to sit at the rich man's table; he would have been satisfied with the smallest scraps from the table.

Yet, the rich man refused to share his beneficence with the poor man in any way.

Note that it is not that the rich man did anything wrong to the poor man. He simply did not do the good that he could have. This is what is called a sin of omission.

When the rich man dies, he is punished by being sent to hell. The poor man, on the other hand, is placed in the bosom of Abraham (a euphemism for heaven).

At the end of the story, we hear that God would not send any messengers to warn the brothers of the rich man. God told him that they already had the law and the prophets.

We should not expect to receive miraculous appearances or utterances. We already have all we need in Scripture.

The last line, "neither will they be persuaded if someone should rise from the dead," is obviously a reminder that Jesus has risen and that should be enough for us.

The rich man also died and was buried,
    and from the netherworld, where he was in torment,
    he raised his eyes and saw Abraham far off
    and Lazarus at his side.
And he cried out, 'Father Abraham, have pity on me.
Send Lazarus to dip the tip of his finger in water
    and cool my tongue,
    for I am suffering torment in these flames.'
Abraham replied,
    'My child, remember that you received
    what was good during your lifetime
    while Lazarus likewise received what was bad;
    but now he is comforted here, whereas you are
    tormented.
Moreover, between us and you a great chasm is established
    to prevent anyone from crossing who might wish
    to go
    from our side to yours or from your side to ours.'
He said, 'Then I beg you, father,
    send him to my father's house, for I have five
    brothers,
    so that he may warn them,
    lest they too come to this place of torment.'
But Abraham replied, 'They have Moses and the
    prophets.
Let them listen to them.'
He said, 'Oh no, father Abraham,
    but if someone from the dead goes to them, they
    will repent.'
Then Abraham said, 'If they will not listen to Moses
    and the prophets,
    neither will they be persuaded if someone should
    rise from the dead.'"

The Gospel of the Lord.

Lect. No. 141

FIRST READING: Habakkuk 1:2-3; 2:2-4

The just one, because of his faith, shall live.

It is not always easy to trust in the providence of the LORD, especially when things are not going well at all. This is what the Prophet Habakkuk proclaims in the First Reading.

We sit and we wait, but still we are surrounded with violence and confusion.

Habakkuk tells us that we must trust and remain hopeful. God has a plan that we cannot fully know or understand.

God has already prepared for that moment when he will intervene and cause his justice to dawn upon the earth. It is not for us to say that God should have done it this way or that, for God's ways are not our ways.

Faith means that we trust in his ways and wait for his time.

A reading from the Book of the Prophet Habakkuk

How long, O LORD? I cry for help
    but you do not listen!
I cry out to you, "Violence!"
    but you do not intervene.
Why do you let me see ruin;
    why must I look at misery?
Destruction and violence are before me;
    there is strife, and clamorous discord.
Then the LORD answered me and said:
    Write down the vision clearly upon the tablets,
    so that one can read it readily.
For the vision still has its time,
    presses on to fulfillment, and will not disappoint;
if it delays, wait for it,
    it will surely come, it will not be late.
The rash one has no integrity;
    but the just one, because of his faith, shall live.

The word of the Lord.

PASTORAL REFLECTIONS

Biblical authors long struggled with the mystery of suffering. Habakkuk's writings dealt with this question. He asked why people suffered for so long, why God would use evil people to punish his own chosen people, why he would allow them to become arrogant, etc. Even though Habakkuk shows promise in his willingness to ask these questions, it seems as if he settles for a somewhat simplistic answer: that we just do not understand God's ways because they are beyond us.

Lect.
No. 141

RESPONSORIAL PSALM: Ps 95:1-2, 6-7, 8-9 (℟.: 8)

The Responsorial Psalm continues the theme of keeping our trust in the ways of Almighty God.

God is our rock and our salvation. He has delivered us from our difficulties in the past, and he will intervene again when we most need him.

We should be filled with gratitude and sing our thanksgiving to God for all that he has done and will do for us.

The alternative is to rebel against God like the Israelites did when they tested him in the desert at Meribah and Massah. God had just liberated the people of Israel from their slavery in Egypt.

He performed wondrous deeds to set them free. He fed them and gave them water to drink. He protected them from all of their enemies.

They should have trusted in God, but they did not.

℟. **If today you hear his voice, harden not your hearts.**

Come, let us sing joyfully to the LORD;
  let us acclaim the Rock of our salvation.
Let us come into his presence with thanksgiving;
  let us joyfully sing psalms to him.

℟. **If today you hear his voice, harden not your hearts.**

Come, let us bow down in worship;
  let us kneel before the LORD who made us.
For he is our God,
  and we are the people he shepherds, the flock he guides.

℟. **If today you hear his voice, harden not your hearts.**

Oh, that today you would hear his voice:
  "Harden not your hearts as at Meribah,
  as in the day of Massah in the desert,
where your fathers tempted me;
  they tested me though they had seen my works."

℟. **If today you hear his voice, harden not your hearts.**

PASTORAL REFLECTIONS

When is it legitimate to question God's motives and how things are going, and when is this a symptom of a lack of faith? This is a difficult question that does not have a clear answer. There are times we must ask "why," and there are other times we must simply trust.

Lect. No. 141

SECOND READING: 2 Timothy 1:6-8, 13-14

Do not be ashamed of your testimony to our Lord.

This passage from the Second Letter to Timothy presents the need to give heroic witness to our faith.

The author speaks of the fact that Timothy had received an imposition of hands (probably referring to his ordination).

The Sacraments give us the gift of the Spirit, and that Spirit should provide the courage that we need to live our Christian witness.

This is true even if there is a cost to pay. The premise of the letter is that Paul is in prison, and Timothy also seems to have suffered for the faith.

Yet, this should not be viewed as a failure but rather as a privilege: to suffer for and with Christ.

A reading from the second Letter of Saint Paul to Timothy

Beloved:
I remind you to stir into flame
    the gift of God that you have through the imposition of my hands.
For God did not give us a spirit of cowardice
    but rather of power and love and self-control.
So do not be ashamed of your testimony to our Lord,
    nor of me, a prisoner for his sake;
    but bear your share of hardship for the gospel
    with the strength that comes from God.

Take as your norm the sound words that you heard from me,
    in the faith and love that are in Christ Jesus.
Guard this rich trust with the help of the Holy Spirit
    that dwells within us.

The word of the Lord.

Lect. No. 141

The word of God has been planted in our hearts by the Spirit and through the preaching and teaching of those who brought us to the faith.

ALLELUIA: 1 Peter 1:25

℟. **Alleluia, alleluia.**

The word of the Lord remains for ever.
This is the word that has been proclaimed to you.

℟. **Alleluia, alleluia.**

Lect. No. 141

GOSPEL: Luke 17:5-10

If you have faith!

A reading from the holy Gospel according to Luke

The apostles said to the Lord, "Increase our faith." The Lord replied,
"If you have faith the size of a mustard seed,
you would say to this mulberry tree,
'Be uprooted and planted in the sea,' and it would obey you.

"Who among you would say to your servant
who has just come in from plowing or tending sheep in the field,
'Come here immediately and take your place at table'?
Would he not rather say to him,
'Prepare something for me to eat.
Put on your apron and wait on me while I eat and drink.
You may eat and drink when I am finished'?
Is he grateful to that servant because he did what was commanded?
So should it be with you.
When you have done all you have been commanded,
say, 'We are unprofitable servants;
we have done what we were obliged to do.'"

The Gospel of the Lord.

The Gospel begins with a saying concerning the need to have faith. Jesus tells his disciples that faith is incredibly powerful, for even if one had as much faith as a mustard seed (considered to be the smallest seed), then one would be able to uproot a great tree.

The second part of the passage speaks of the need for total dedication to the ways of God.

We sometimes feel that, if we do all the right things, then God owes us. We sometimes forget that the reward for being faithful to the Gospel is not that we will be lucky or healthy or successful.

The reward for serving God is the possibility to serve him, for the greatest gift that God has ever given us is the ability to give of ourselves to others (God and neighbor).

Through this, we become the most God-like that we could possibly be.

PASTORAL REFLECTIONS

Is it wrong to have moments of doubt? Faith is both a gift and a response. It seems as if some have received a greater measure of that gift and they do not have as many doubts as others have. God only asks each of us to respond as well as we can to the gift we have received (and not to be perfect).

Lect. No. 144

FIRST READING: 2 Kings 5:14-17

The First Reading speaks of Naaman, a Syrian (and therefore a pagan) who came to Israel to be healed of his leprosy. The Prophet Elisha ordered him to wash seven times in the Jordan.

At first Naaman refused to do this, for he thought that it was too insignificant an action to bring him healing. Then, however, he relented and washed and was healed.

Naaman's reaction was one of great gratitude. He offered a gift to the prophet (who would not accept it). He begged to be able to take two mule-loads of earth back to Syria so that he could worship the LORD on Israelite soil.

Naaman said that henceforth the God of Israel would be his own God, for he recognized what God had done for him and was filled with gratitude.

Naaman returned to the man of God and acknowledged the Lord.

A reading from the second Book of Kings

Naaman went down and plunged into the Jordan seven times
    at the word of Elisha, the man of God.
His flesh became again like the flesh of a little child,
    and he was clean of his leprosy.

Naaman returned with his whole retinue to the man of God.
On his arrival he stood before Elisha and said,
    "Now I know that there is no God in all the earth,
    except in Israel.
Please accept a gift from your servant."

Elisha replied, "As the LORD lives whom I serve, I
    will not take it";
    and despite Naaman's urging, he still refused.
Naaman said: "If you will not accept,
    please let me, your servant, have two mule-loads
      of earth,
    for I will no longer offer holocaust or sacrifice
    to any other god except to the LORD."

The word of the Lord.

PASTORAL REFLECTIONS

It sometimes takes an outsider to help us realize how blessed we are. We can so easily take things for granted while someone outside the situation can have a different perspective of what is happening. Naaman was able to be wildly grateful to God and his prophet while the Israelites failed to recognize that they had a powerful prophet in their midst.

RESPONSORIAL PSALM: Ps 98:1, 2-3, 3-4 (℟.: cf. 2b)

The Responsorial Psalm is a hymn of praise, the appropriate response that one should have toward God who has done wondrous things for us.

One should be willing to tell everyone upon the earth of all God's goodness. God's deeds are so great that even the pagan nations should praise him.

We sing a new song. There are two words in Hebrew for new. One means that which is not old, and the other means that which is radically new.

God often responds to our need in ways that we could not even imagine or hope for.

Yet, it is not always easy to be grateful. We like to think that we can do anything we want with our own talents.

It is an act of vulnerability to admit that, on our own, we could never have done what we have done.

℟. **The Lord has revealed to the nations his saving power.**

Sing to the Lord a new song,
  for he has done wondrous deeds;
his right hand has won victory for him,
  his holy arm.

℟. **The Lord has revealed to the nations his saving power.**

The Lord has made his salvation known:
  in the sight of the nations he has revealed his justice.
He has remembered his kindness and his faithfulness
  toward the house of Israel.

℟. **The Lord has revealed to the nations his saving power.**

All the ends of the earth have seen
  the salvation by our God.
Sing joyfully to the Lord, all you lands:
  break into song; sing praise.

℟. **The Lord has revealed to the nations his saving power.**

PASTORAL REFLECTIONS

All throughout the Old Testament the sea and land and sky stand as witnesses to God's covenant with Israel (and all too often to its infidelity). The "nations," on the other hand, were most often witnesses to God's wrath. Here they become witnesses to God's justice and mercy and his willingness to save the people of Israel. Even though they were not yet considered to be "God's people," they were called upon to praise God for his wondrous works (and in doing so they were foreshadowing that time when they would be the recipients of justice and mercy and salvation themselves).

Lect. No. 144

SECOND READING: 2 Timothy 2:8-13

If we persevere we shall also reign with Christ.

One of the questions that troubled the early Church was how was one to find meaning in the case of those who suffered for the faith.

If Jesus had risen from the dead and defeated the enemies of God, then should not his faith be triumphant? Why were the apostles thrown in jail and martyred?

In this letter we hear that Saint Paul's suffering is serving the spread of the Gospel. Paul even speaks in Philippians of how his imprisonment led to the possibility of preaching to the guards. The word of God cannot be chained.

The enemies of the faith cannot win, for the power of God will transform disasters into blessings, crosses into moments of resurrection.

That is why we hear the promise at the end of the reading that if we persevere, then we will reign with God in glory.

A reading from the second Letter of Saint Paul to Timothy

Beloved:
Remember Jesus Christ, raised from the dead, a descendant of David:
  such is my gospel, for which I am suffering,
  even to the point of chains, like a criminal.
But the word of God is not chained.
Therefore, I bear with everything for the sake of those who are chosen,
  so that they too may obtain the salvation that is in Christ Jesus,
  together with eternal glory.
This saying is trustworthy:
  If we have died with him
    we shall also live with him;
  if we persevere
    we shall also reign with him.
  But if we deny him
    he will deny us.
  If we are unfaithful
    he remains faithful,
    for he cannot deny himself.

The word of the Lord.

Lect. No. 144

ALLELUIA: 1 Thessalonians 5:18

The Alleluia Verse reminds us that it is our duty and our privilege to give thanks to the Lord in every circumstance in which we find ourselves.

℟. **Alleluia, alleluia.**

In all circumstances, give thanks,
for this is the will of God for you in Christ Jesus.

℟. **Alleluia, alleluia.**

Lect. No. 144

GOSPEL: Luke 17:11-19

None but this foreigner has returned to give thanks to God.

The Gospel presents an important lesson about gratitude.

Jesus entered a village and he healed ten men who were lepers. He ordered them to go to the priests to certify that they had been cleansed from their disease (for this was the prescription of the law).

But one of the men who had been healed returned and gave thanks to Jesus. The one who gave thanks was a Samaritan.

Remember, Samaritans were hated by the Jewish people. Even before the leprosy they would have been considered to be unclean by the Jewish leaders.

Yet, this humble Samaritan gave thanks to Jesus. He showed true gratitude (which should be the attitude that we all show toward the Lord for all the good things that he has done for us).

A reading from the holy Gospel according to Luke

As Jesus continued his journey to Jerusalem,
he traveled through Samaria and Galilee.
As he was entering a village, ten lepers met him.
They stood at a distance from him and raised their
   voices, saying,
   "Jesus, Master! Have pity on us!"
And when he saw them, he said,
   "Go show yourselves to the priests."
As they were going they were cleansed.
And one of them, realizing he had been healed,
   returned, glorifying God in a loud voice;
   and he fell at the feet of Jesus and thanked him.
He was a Samaritan.
Jesus said in reply,
   "Ten were cleansed, were they not?
Where are the other nine?
Has none but this foreigner returned to give thanks
   to God?"
Then he said to him, "Stand up and go;
   your faith has saved you."

The Gospel of the Lord.

PASTORAL REFLECTIONS

An experiment was recently performed at a shopping mall. Someone would hold open the door for a stranger passing through. As many as fifty people would go through the door before one of them would turn around to thank the person holding the door. A sense of gratitude is often lost when people develop a sense of entitlement, or they spend all their time thinking about what they don't have instead of being grateful for what they have. Gratitude is the ultimate cure for envy and resentment and a feeling that life is not fair.

Lect. No. 147 | **FIRST READING: Exodus 17:8-13**

As long as Moses kept his hands raised up, Israel had the better of the fight.

Earlier this year we had a Sunday dedicated to the importance of prayer (see p. 304). We heard that God would respond to our prayers with more love than our earthly fathers respond to our requests.

This Sunday we have another series of readings on the importance of prayer.

The First Reading speaks of Moses who makes intercession for his people.

The Israelites go into battle, and as long as Moses holds his hands up, the Israelites are successful. When he lets his hands fall, the Amalekites were successful.

Toward the end of the reading we hear that Aaron and Hur assist Moses to hold up his hands. This part of the story could provide us with insight into prayer: that we should ask others to pray with us.

Prayer is an act of trust and love, and asking others to pray with and for us is likewise an act of trust and love.

A reading from the Book of Exodus

In those days, Amalek came and waged war against Israel.
Moses, therefore, said to Joshua,
"Pick out certain men,
and tomorrow go out and engage Amalek in battle.
I will be standing on top of the hill
with the staff of God in my hand."
So Joshua did as Moses told him:
he engaged Amalek in battle
after Moses had climbed to the top of the hill with Aaron and Hur.
As long as Moses kept his hands raised up,
Israel had the better of the fight,
but when he let his hands rest,
Amalek had the better of the fight.
Moses' hands, however, grew tired;
so they put a rock in place for him to sit on.
Meanwhile Aaron and Hur supported his hands,
one on one side and one on the other,
so that his hands remained steady till sunset.
And Joshua mowed down Amalek and his people
with the edge of the sword.

The word of the Lord.

RESPONSORIAL PSALM: Ps 121:1-2, 3-4, 5-6, 7-8 (℟.: cf. 2)

The Responsorial Psalm is a psalm of trust in the LORD. It is an affirmation that God will always provide for his children and respond to their needs.

Does this mean that, if we have faith, nothing bad will ever happen to us? No, for there is an old saying that God always answers our prayers, but sometimes God's answer is, "No!"

Our vision is limited, for we view and judge reality according to what we know. God can see things that we cannot begin to understand.

God can see the end results of actions that are only beginning to happen. God, as a loving parent, might allow things to happen for which we can see no meaning.

Yet, good might come of these things (admittedly, it is often only in a very long-term perspective).

And so, God guards us from all evil. But God does not solve our every problem. He only promises that he will accompany us in whatever happens in our lives.

℟. **Our help is from the Lord, who made heaven and earth.**

I lift up my eyes toward the mountains;
  whence shall help come to me?
My help is from the LORD,
  who made heaven and earth.

℟. **Our help is from the Lord, who made heaven and earth.**

May he not suffer your foot to slip;
  may he slumber not who guards you:
indeed he neither slumbers nor sleeps,
  the guardian of Israel.

℟. **Our help is from the Lord, who made heaven and earth.**

The LORD is your guardian; the LORD is your shade;
  he is beside you at your right hand.
The sun shall not harm you by day,
  nor the moon by night.

℟. **Our help is from the Lord, who made heaven and earth.**

The LORD will guard you from all evil;
  he will guard your life.
The LORD will guard your coming and your going,
  both now and forever.

℟. **Our help is from the Lord, who made heaven and earth.**

Lect. No. 147

SECOND READING: 2 Timothy 3:14—4:2

One who belongs to God may be competent, equipped for every good work.

In the Second Reading we hear about the sources of information concerning our faith.

The first is Sacred Scripture. When the author of Second Timothy uses this term, he is referring to those series of writings that we call the Old Testament.

The writings of the New Testament were not called "Sacred Scripture" until much later, toward the end of the Second Century A.D.

The other source for our faith is the teaching of the apostles. Today we would call these teachings Tradition, for this is the series of teachings that have been passed down in and through the Church.

Thus, the two sources for our faith are Sacred Scripture and Tradition.

This passage closes with an exhortation to preach the word of God, whether it is convenient or inconvenient, easy or difficult.

Everything that happens to us should be one more opportunity for us to share God's love.

A reading from the second Letter of Saint Paul to Timothy

Beloved:
Remain faithful to what you have learned and believed,
because you know from whom you learned it,
and that from infancy you have known the sacred Scriptures,
which are capable of giving you wisdom for salvation
through faith in Christ Jesus.
All Scripture is inspired by God
and is useful for teaching, for refutation, for correction,
and for training in righteousness,
so that one who belongs to God may be competent,
equipped for every good work.

I charge you in the presence of God and of Christ Jesus,
who will judge the living and the dead,
and by his appearing and his kingly power:
proclaim the word;
be persistent whether it is convenient or inconvenient;
convince, reprimand, encourage through all patience and teaching.

The word of the Lord.

Lect. No. 147

The word of God is not simply an empty utterance of theory or pious platitudes. It is powerful, making real those things that it says.

Lect. No. 147

The parable in today's Gospel is about the need to pray with consistency.

Jesus speaks of a widow who demands her rights from an evil judge. (It is very odd that he would speak of an evil judge, for that is the person in the parable who symbolizes God the Father.) At first the judge does not give her what she wants, but she insists and insists until he finally gives in to her requests.

This means that we must ask for those things that we truly need from God. If we do not receive them immediately, we should continue to ask.

Do we change God's mind when we pray? A better way of describing the power of our prayer is that God trusts us so much that he invites us to join him in the decision-making process.

It is not that God decides everything or that we do. It is a union of the two (for God has called us to be his friends who assist him in his work of recreating this world in his image).

ALLELUIA: Hebrews 4:12

℟. **Alleluia, alleluia.**

The word of God is living and effective,
discerning reflections and thoughts of the heart.

℟. **Alleluia, alleluia.**

GOSPEL: Luke 18:1-8

God will secure the rights of his chosen ones who call out to him.

A reading from the holy Gospel according to Luke

Jesus told his disciples a parable
 about the necessity for them to pray always without becoming weary.
He said, "There was a judge in a certain town
 who neither feared God nor respected any human being.
And a widow in that town used to come to him and say,
 'Render a just decision for me against my adversary.'
For a long time the judge was unwilling, but eventually he thought,
 'While it is true that I neither fear God nor respect any human being,
 because this widow keeps bothering me
 I shall deliver a just decision for her
 lest she finally come and strike me.'"
The Lord said, "Pay attention to what the dishonest judge says.
Will not God then secure the rights of his chosen ones who call out to him day and night?
Will he be slow to answer them?
I tell you, he will see to it that justice is done for them speedily.
But when the Son of Man comes, will he find faith on earth?"

The Gospel of the Lord.

THIRTIETH SUNDAY IN ORDINARY TIME

Lect. No. 150 **FIRST READING: Sirach 35:12-14, 16-18**

The prayer of the lowly pierces the clouds.

Once again we hear that God's ways are not like our ways. While we tend to show partiality to those who are rich and powerful, God reaches out and embraces those who are weak and powerless.

They are the chosen ones of God, for they recognize that they cannot survive without his intervention.

The First Reading from the Book of Sirach speaks of this option for the poor and weak. God hears their prayers and responds to their needs. We hear that the "prayer of the lowly pierces the clouds; it does not rest till it reaches its goal."

A reading from the Book of Sirach

The LORD is a God of justice,
who knows no favorites.
Though not unduly partial toward the weak,
yet he hears the cry of the oppressed.
The LORD is not deaf to the wail of the orphan,
nor to the widow when she pours out her complaint.
The one who serves God willingly is heard;
his petition reaches the heavens.
The prayer of the lowly pierces the clouds;
it does not rest till it reaches its goal,
nor will it withdraw till the Most High responds,
judges justly and affirms the right,
and the LORD will not delay.

The word of the Lord.

Lect. No. 150 **RESPONSORIAL PSALM: Ps 34:2-3, 17-18, 19, 23 (℞.: 7a)**

The Responsorial Psalm continues the theme found in the First Reading.

God hears the cry of the poor. He answers the appeal of those in distress.

He searches the hearts of all and rewards the just and punishes those who do evil. For this we praise God.

℞. **The Lord hears the cry of the poor.**

I will bless the LORD at all times;
his praise shall be ever in my mouth.
Let my soul glory in the LORD;
the lowly will hear me and be glad.

℞. **The Lord hears the cry of the poor.**

The LORD confronts the evildoers,
to destroy remembrance of them from the earth.

It is good for us to know that there is another way to look at reality (from that which we experience every day of our lives).

It is good to know that there is someone who can guarantee true justice.

And so we find our refuge in God. We place all our hope in him.

When the just cry out, the LORD hears them,
  and from all their distress he rescues them.

℟. **The Lord hears the cry of the poor.**

The LORD is close to the brokenhearted;
  and those who are crushed in spirit he saves.
The LORD redeems the lives of his servants;
  no one incurs guilt who takes refuge in him.

℟. **The Lord hears the cry of the poor.**

SECOND READING: 2 Timothy 4:6-8, 16-18

From now on, the crown of righteousness awaits me.

The premise of the Second Letter to Timothy is that Saint Paul is writing Timothy while he is in prison facing the possibility of a death sentence. We cannot be absolutely sure that Paul wrote it (for many scholars believe that he did not).

Nevertheless, there is a beauty in the attitude expressed: that Paul views his life as a libation. He speaks of his ministry and his life as a sacrifice poured out to obtain the salvation of those to whom he preached.

Even when no one stood by him to defend him, Paul believed that God would never abandon him. There are many moments in our life when we are sure that no one could possibly understand what is happening to us.

It is at such moments that Paul's words can be a great consolation to us.

A reading from the second Letter of Saint Paul to Timothy

Beloved:
  I am already being poured out like a libation,
  and the time of my departure is at hand.
I have competed well; I have finished the race;
  I have kept the faith.
From now on the crown of righteousness awaits me,
  which the Lord, the just judge,
  will award to me on that day, and not only to me,
  but to all who have longed for his appearance.

At my first defense no one appeared on my behalf,
  but everyone deserted me.
May it not be held against them!
But the Lord stood by me and gave me strength,
  so that through me the proclamation might be
    completed
  and all the Gentiles might hear it.
And I was rescued from the lion's mouth.
The Lord will rescue me from every evil threat
  and will bring me safe to his heavenly kingdom.
To him be glory forever and ever. Amen.

The word of the Lord.

Lect.
No. 150

ALLELUIA: 2 Corinthians 5:19

The Alleluia Verse speaks of God's beneficence toward the world, and the fact that we have been entrusted with the proclamation of that goodness.

℟. **Alleluia, alleluia.**

God was reconciling the world to himself in Christ, and entrusting to us the message of salvation.

℟. **Alleluia, alleluia.**

Lect.
No. 150

GOSPEL: Luke 18:9-14

The tax collector, not the Pharisee, went home justified.

The Gospel presents a parable concerning righteousness in the eyes of God.

Jesus tells of two men, one a Pharisee and the other a tax collector. The Pharisees were a group of dedicated Jewish laymen who attempted to practice the law as fully as possible.

They even "built a fence around the law," meaning that they took the law to its widest possible extent to be sure that they observed the smallest part of the law.

This made this particular Pharisee feel good about himself. He had become self-righteous and felt that he was doing God a favor in all that he did.

The tax collector had the opposite attitude. Tax collecting was an unclean profession. He knew he was a sinner, so he approached God with humility.

He was forgiven while the Pharisee was not (for the Pharisee did not even feel that he needed forgiveness).

A reading from the holy Gospel according to Luke

Jesus addressed this parable
to those who were convinced of their own righteousness
and despised everyone else.
"Two people went up to the temple area to pray;
one was a Pharisee and the other was a tax collector.
The Pharisee took up his position and spoke this prayer to himself,
'O God, I thank you that I am not like the rest of humanity—
greedy, dishonest, adulterous—or even like this tax collector.
I fast twice a week, and I pay tithes on my whole income.'
But the tax collector stood off at a distance
and would not even raise his eyes to heaven
but beat his breast and prayed,
'O God, be merciful to me a sinner.'
I tell you, the latter went home justified, not the former;
for whoever exalts himself will be humbled,
and the one who humbles himself will be exalted."

The Gospel of the Lord.

November 1, 2013

ALL SAINTS

Lect. No. 667 **FIRST READING: Revelation 7:2-4, 9-14**

*I had a vision of a great multitude, which no one could count,
from every nation, race, people, and tongue.*

We hear about how the chosen ones were to be marked with the seal of the living God upon their foreheads. In the Book of the Prophet Ezekiel this mark was the Hebrew letter "tau," the first letter of the word "Torah," which means "the law." All faithful Jews were to be observers of the law to the deepest part of their being.

In the New Testament, the elect are to be sealed with the Greek letter "tau," which looks like the modern "T." It is a symbol for the cross, for all of Christ's brothers and sisters are to be sealed with the sign of the cross.

We hear that there are one hundred and forty-four thousand to be sealed. Some Christian sects argue that this is the number of people who will be going to heaven.

This is a misunderstanding of the symbolism of the Book of Revelation. In this book, that which we see is the superficial meaning, while that which we hear is the spiritual significance.

John saw a crowd without number from every nation and race and people and tongue. These are the people who are going to heaven. They are numberless.

A reading from the Book of Revelation

I, John, saw another angel come up from the East,
holding the seal of the living God.
He cried out in a loud voice to the four angels
who were given power to damage the land and
the sea,
"Do not damage the land or the sea or the trees
until we put the seal on the foreheads of the servants of our God."
I heard the number of those who had been marked
with the seal,
one hundred and forty-four thousand marked
from every tribe of the children of Israel.

After this I had a vision of a great multitude,
which no one could count,
from every nation, race, people, and tongue.
They stood before the throne and before the Lamb,
wearing white robes and holding palm branches
in their hands.
They cried out in a loud voice:
"Salvation comes from our God, who is seated on
the throne,
and from the Lamb."
All the angels stood around the throne
and around the elders and the four living creatures.
They prostrated themselves before the throne,
worshiped God, and exclaimed:
"Amen. Blessing and glory, wisdom and thanksgiving,

But John also heard that they were one hundred and forty-four thousand. This number is twelve times twelve times one thousand. Twelve stands for the twelve patriarchs of the Old Testament. Twelve also stands for the twelve apostles. One thousand stands for a very large number.

Thus, one hundred and forty-four thousand means the Old and New Israel. The number is their spiritual identity, not the actual number of those going to heaven.

honor, power, and might
 be to our God forever and ever. Amen."
Then one of the elders spoke up and said to me,
 "Who are these wearing white robes, and where
  did they come from?"
I said to him, "My lord, you are the one who knows."
He said to me,
 "These are the ones who have survived the time of
  great distress;
 they have washed their robes
 and made them white in the Blood of the Lamb."

The word of the Lord.

RESPONSORIAL PSALM: Ps 24:1bc-2, 3-4ab, 5-6 (℟.: cf. 6)

Psalm 24 is a wisdom psalm that was probably used for pilgrimages to the temple. Wisdom literature speaks of how to live the good life, a life pleasing to the LORD.

This psalm asks who can ascend the mountain of the LORD, the mountain leading to Jerusalem and its temple. Only that person whose hands are sinless and whose heart is clean can participate in the worship of the LORD.

This does not mean that we must be perfect to belong to God's holy people. All of us are sinners, but we must make an effort to convert and change our ways. This is a lifetime project and we will not be totally perfect until the last day. But in the meantime, we commit ourselves to service of God and our brothers and sisters. This is the way that we will be those who seek "the face of the God of Jacob."

℟. **Lord, this is the people that longs to see your face.**

The LORD'S are the earth and its fullness;
 the world and those who dwell in it.
For he founded it upon the seas
 and established it upon the rivers.

℟. **Lord, this is the people that longs to see your face.**

Who can ascend the mountain of the LORD?
 or who may stand in his holy place?
One whose hands are sinless, whose heart is clean,
 who desires not what is vain.

℟. **Lord, this is the people that longs to see your face.**

He shall receive a blessing from the LORD,
 a reward from God his savior.
Such is the race that seeks for him,
 that seeks the face of the God of Jacob.

℟. **Lord, this is the people that longs to see your face.**

Lect.
No. 667

SECOND READING: 1 John 3:1-3

We shall see God as he is.

A reading from the first Letter of Saint John

The First Letter of John is a masterful treatise on the love of God. It is here, in fact, that we hear the phrase that God is love.

God has demonstrated how much he loves us by the fact that we are called children of God. God does not call us slaves; God calls us his friends and even his beloved children.

This does not mean that everyone will love us. The world hated Jesus because it could not embrace Jesus and his message. It wanted selfishness, and Jesus preached love and sacrifice.

We are already God's children. What we shall be in the future cannot even be imagined, for it will be a participation in the glory of God.

Beloved:
See what love the Father has bestowed on us
  that we may be called the children of God.
Yet so we are.
The reason the world does not know us
  is that it did not know him.
Beloved, we are God's children now;
  what we shall be has not yet been revealed.
We do know that when it is revealed we shall be like him,
  for we shall see him as he is.
Everyone who has this hope based on him makes himself pure,
  as he is pure.

The word of the Lord.

Lect.
No. 667

ALLELUIA: Matthew 11:28

The Lord Jesus offers to be our refuge when life becomes a burden to us. He is the source of peace for our hearts, and our only true joy. Only in him will we find true rest.

℟. **Alleluia, alleluia.**

Come to me, all you who labor and are burdened,
and I will give you rest, says the Lord.

℟. **Alleluia, alleluia.**

Lect.
No. 667

GOSPEL: Matthew 5:1-12a

Rejoice and be glad, for your reward will be great in heaven.

A reading from the holy Gospel according
to Matthew

Today's Gospel presents the Beatitudes from the Gospel of Matthew. In Matthew's Gospel, Jesus is the new Moses. He is the founder of the New Israel, the Church. Like Moses who climbed Mount Sinai to receive the law, Jesus climbed a moun-

When Jesus saw the crowds, he went up the mountain,
  and after he had sat down, his disciples came to him.

tain in order to give the new law to the New Israel (the Sermon on the Mount).

Unlike the ten commandments of the old law, the Beatitudes are not a series of do's and don'ts. They are a call to generosity. One no longer asks what one can do before it becomes a sin. One must ask what one can do to become a better Christian.

The poor in spirit are those who are not proud (unlike the Pharisees). Those who hunger and thirst for righteousness are the Christians. They were unjustly thrown out of the synagogue for their profession of faith in Jesus. Likewise, they are persecuted for the sake of the kingdom.

Those who are clean of heart are those whose every thought is of God. If one's every thought is of God, then one will see signs of God's presence everywhere (for creation is a gift from God). One will judge everything that one sees to be a sign of God's goodness and generosity.

He began to teach them, saying:

"Blessed are the poor in spirit,
for theirs is the Kingdom of heaven.
Blessed are they who mourn,
for they will be comforted.
Blessed are the meek,
for they will inherit the land.
Blessed are they who hunger and thirst for righteousness,
for they will be satisfied.
Blessed are the merciful,
for they will be shown mercy.
Blessed are the clean of heart,
for they will see God.
Blessed are the peacemakers,
for they will be called children of God.
Blessed are they who are persecuted for the sake of righteousness,
for theirs is the Kingdom of heaven.
Blessed are you when they insult you and persecute you
and utter every kind of evil against you falsely because of me.
Rejoice and be glad,
for your reward will be great in heaven."

The Gospel of the Lord.

PASTORAL REFLECTIONS

Today's feast offers an excellent opportunity to consider those people in our lives who taught us the meaning of sanctity. Very few of us will ever meet someone who will one day be canonized, but we all meet people who lovingly respond to God's call. This is why Saint Paul called the members of the Christian communities "saints," for he realized that there are many saints all around us.

November 3, 2013

THIRTY-FIRST SUNDAY IN ORDINARY TIME

Lect. No. 153 **FIRST READING: Wisdom 11:22—12:2**

You have mercy on all because you love all things that are.

The theme of today's readings is that God is always ready to forgive our sins.

The First Reading comes from the Book of Wisdom, one of the last books of the Old Testament to be written.

This book shows the heavy influence of Greek culture for it was written after the conquests of Alexander the Great.

This particular passage emphasizes the grandeur of God. The "whole universe is as a grain from a balance." God is above all things.

This is consistent with Greek philosophy. It taught that God was the uncreated creator, far removed from everything that exists.

But the author then goes on to speak of how compassionate God is toward those who need his mercy.

This is the opposite of Greek theology. The gods of the Greek philosophers never got involved in the everyday affairs of humans.

A reading from the Book of Wisdom

Before the LORD the whole universe is as a grain from a balance
or a drop of morning dew come down upon the earth.
But you have mercy on all, because you can do all things;
and you overlook people's sins that they may repent.
For you love all things that are
and loathe nothing that you have made;
for what you hated, you would not have fashioned.
And how could a thing remain, unless you willed it;
or be preserved, had it not been called forth by you?
But you spare all things, because they are yours,
O LORD and lover of souls,
for your imperishable spirit is in all things!
Therefore you rebuke offenders little by little,
warn them and remind them of the sins they are committing,
that they may abandon their wickedness and believe in you, O LORD!

The word of the Lord.

RESPONSORIAL PSALM: Ps 145:1-2, 8-9, 10-11, 13-14 (℟.: cf. 1)

The Responsorial Psalm is a hymn of praise to God who is good and compassionate. He is gracious and merciful and slow to anger.

Sometimes it is difficult to reconcile this picture of a merciful God with the image of an angry God in the Old Testament.

One possible explanation is that God was not angry at us; God was angry at our sin.

God viewed sin as something that was destructive to his beloved children. It was a poison that robbed his children of their vitality. He hated sin. Yet, he still loved his children.

Unfortunately, our response to the anger was confusion. We thought that God was angry with us, but God was angry at what we were doing.

God is not capricious and vindictive. God is "faithful in all his words and holy in all his works."

Even when we are not faithful, God is faithful to us. Even when we turn our backs on God, God will be compassionate to us.

℟. **I will praise your name for ever, my king and my God.**

I will extol you, O my God and King,
  and I will bless your name forever and ever.
Every day will I bless you,
  and I will praise your name forever and ever.

℟. **I will praise your name for ever, my king and my God.**

The LORD is gracious and merciful,
  slow to anger and of great kindness.
The LORD is good to all
  and compassionate toward all his works.

℟. **I will praise your name for ever, my king and my God.**

Let all your works give you thanks, O LORD,
  and let your faithful ones bless you.
Let them discourse of the glory of your kingdom
  and speak of your might.

℟. **I will praise your name for ever, my king and my God.**

The LORD is faithful in all his words
  and holy in all his works.
The LORD lifts up all who are falling
  and raises up all who are bowed down.

℟. **I will praise your name for ever, my king and my God.**

Lect.
No. 153

SECOND READING: 2 Thessalonians 1:11—2:2

May the name of Christ be glorified in you and you in him.

The Second Reading begins with a prayer from the Second Letter to the Thessalonians.

The first part of this passage speaks of God's role and our role in sanctification. We cannot hope to be faithful to God if God does not send his grace into our hearts.

But, at the same time, we are responsible to do our best to respond to that grace. It is not that God directs our choices like puppets and a puppeteer, nor are we totally independent. We and God form a partnership.

The second part of the passage speaks of the end of the world. The author reminds the community that they should be careful about reports that the world is coming to an end, for there were bound to be many false predictions.

This warning is as important today as it was in the early Church.

A reading from the second Letter of Saint Paul to the Thessalonians

Brothers and sisters:
We always pray for you,
that our God may make you worthy of his calling
and powerfully bring to fulfillment every good purpose
and every effort of faith,
that the name of our Lord Jesus may be glorified in you,
and you in him,
in accord with the grace of our God and Lord Jesus Christ.

We ask you, brothers and sisters,
with regard to the coming of our Lord Jesus Christ
and our assembling with him,
not to be shaken out of your minds suddenly, or to be alarmed
either by a "spirit," or by an oral statement,
or by a letter allegedly from us
to the effect that the day of the Lord is at hand.

The word of the Lord.

Lect.
No. 153

The Alleluia Verse reminds us of God's benevolence, that he sent Jesus into the world not to condemn it but rather to save it (something we see in the readings this Sunday).

ALLELUIA: John 3:16

℟. **Alleluia, alleluia.**

God so loved the world that he gave his only Son,
so that everyone who believes in him might have eternal life.

℟. **Alleluia, alleluia.**

Lect. No. 153

GOSPEL: Luke 19:1-10

The Son of Man has come to seek and to save what was lost.

The Gospel presents the story of an encounter between Jesus and a tax collector.

Tax collectors were hated in Israel at the time of Jesus. Israel was a poor country, and the tax collectors took money that was sorely needed.

There was also the fact that they were considered to be collaborators of the occupying Roman army.

Furthermore, the system of taxation led to dishonesty. A tax collector would pay up front to collect taxes in a particular area, and then all that he collected was considered to be his. There was no incentive to be honest.

Zacchaeus was a tax collector who was probably as dishonest as the others. Yet, he desired to see Jesus. He took a risk by climbing a tree to catch sight of him.

Jesus invites him down and tells Zacchaeus that he will eat with him that very night. He proclaims that salvation had come to his house.

In Luke's Gospel, we are saved the minute we meet Jesus (and not when we die), for he gives us the love that heals us from the wounds of our sins.

A reading from the holy Gospel according to Luke

At that time, Jesus came to Jericho and intended to pass through the town.
Now a man there named Zacchaeus,
    who was a chief tax collector and also a wealthy man,
    was seeking to see who Jesus was;
    but he could not see him because of the crowd,
    for he was short in stature.
So he ran ahead and climbed a sycamore tree in order to see Jesus,
    who was about to pass that way.
When he reached the place, Jesus looked up and said,
    "Zacchaeus, come down quickly,
    for today I must stay at your house."
And he came down quickly and received him with joy.
When they all saw this, they began to grumble, saying,
    "He has gone to stay at the house of a sinner."
But Zacchaeus stood there and said to the Lord,
    "Behold, half of my possessions, Lord, I shall give to the poor,
    and if I have extorted anything from anyone
    I shall repay it four times over."
And Jesus said to him,
    "Today salvation has come to this house
    because this man too is a descendant of Abraham.
For the Son of Man has come to seek
    and to save what was lost."

The Gospel of the Lord.

November 10, 2013

THIRTY-SECOND SUNDAY IN ORDINARY TIME

Lect. No. 156 **FIRST READING: 2 Maccabees 7:1-2, 9-14**

The King of the world will raise us up to live again forever.

We are now approaching the end of the Church Year. For that reason, the themes of the Sunday readings turn more and more to the last things (the end of time, the resurrection from the dead, etc.).

Today's theme is the resurrection from the dead.

The First Reading is the powerful account of a mother and seven sons who were arrested during a persecution of the Jews.

The emperor of Syria, Antiochus Epiphanes, wanted to unify his extensive empire by ordering all peoples to give up their local religious practices and to adopt the Greek way of life.

Many peoples did this, but the Jewish people rebelled against such tyranny.

The Maccabees were a family that led the rebellion (hence this book is named after them).

There were many martyrs. People who circumcised their babies or who refused to eat pork were put to death.

This account shows the heroism of a mother and her seven sons. It is significant that they speak of the fact that God

A reading from the second Book of Maccabees

It happened that seven brothers with their mother were arrested
and tortured with whips and scourges by the king,
to force them to eat pork in violation of God's law.
One of the brothers, speaking for the others, said:
"What do you expect to achieve by questioning us?
We are ready to die rather than transgress the laws of our ancestors."

At the point of death he said:
"You accursed fiend, you are depriving us of this present life,
but the King of the world will raise us up to live again forever.
It is for his laws that we are dying."

After him the third suffered their cruel sport.
He put out his tongue at once when told to do so,
and bravely held out his hands, as he spoke these noble words:
"It was from Heaven that I received these;
for the sake of his laws I disdain them;
from him I hope to receive them again."
Even the king and his attendants marveled at the young man's courage,
because he regarded his sufferings as nothing.

After he had died,
they tortured and maltreated the fourth brother in the same way.

would reward them for their fidelity even after they died.

This means that they believed in the resurrection of the dead (a concept that only arose late in the history of Old Testament times).

When he was near death, he said,

"It is my choice to die at the hands of men
with the hope God gives of being raised up by
   him;
but for you, there will be no resurrection to life."

The word of the Lord.

Lect. No. 156

RESPONSORIAL PSALM: Ps 17:1, 5-6, 8, 15 (℞.: 15b)

The Responsorial Psalm is a lamentation. In this type of psalm the psalmist calls upon the LORD to deliver him from the hands of his enemies.

He is sure that God will intervene in his behalf for he feels that he has been steadfast to the LORD's ways.

God will certainly stand by those who are just. He will certainly punish those who choose the path of evil.

In the last section, the psalmist speaks of finding refuge under the shadow of God's wings. He is probably speaking of the wings of the cherubim that were placed on top of the Ark of the Covenant.

This was where God appeared to his people, and it was considered to be a place of safety.

℞. **Lord, when your glory appears, my joy will be full.**

Hear, O LORD, a just suit;
   attend to my outcry;
   hearken to my prayer from lips without deceit.

℞. **Lord, when your glory appears, my joy will be full.**

My steps have been steadfast in your paths,
   my feet have not faltered.
I call upon you, for you will answer me, O God;
   incline your ear to me; hear my word.

℞. **Lord, when your glory appears, my joy will be full.**

Keep me as the apple of your eye,
   hide me in the shadow of your wings.
But I in justice shall behold your face;
   on waking I shall be content in your presence.

℞. **Lord, when your glory appears, my joy will be full.**

PASTORAL REFLECTIONS

Sometimes telling our difficulties to God or to a friend can make it easier to carry our crosses. Rather than feeling that we don't want to burden others with our troubles, we should be vulnerable enough to invite them into our sufferings.

Lect. No. 156

SECOND READING: 2 Thessalonians 2:16—3:5

May the Lord encourage your hearts and strengthen them in every good deed and word.

This passage taken from Second Thessalonians is an admonition to continue to grow in the faith.

The word of God had been preached to this community, and they knew what was right and just. Now they had to live it.

Furthermore, the author asks for prayers so that the word of the Lord might be accepted as readily by others as it was by the Thessalonians. It is God who was behind this success.

Yet, there are some who could not accept that word. Sometimes it is a question of sinful rejection; at other times it might be that they have not yet received the gift of faith. God calls each of us in God's own time.

The author returns to the theme of endurance. Very few of us will be called to give witness to the faith as martyrs, but each one of us is called to give an everyday witness in the ordinary, common events of life.

A reading from the second Letter of Saint Paul to the Thessalonians

Brothers and sisters:
May our Lord Jesus Christ himself and God our Father,
who has loved us and given us everlasting encouragement
and good hope through his grace,
encourage your hearts and strengthen them in every good deed and word.

Finally, brothers and sisters, pray for us,
so that the word of the Lord may speed forward and be glorified,
as it did among you,
and that we may be delivered from perverse and wicked people,
for not all have faith.
But the Lord is faithful;
he will strengthen you and guard you from the evil one.
We are confident of you in the Lord that what we instruct you,
you are doing and will continue to do.
May the Lord direct your hearts to the love of God and to the endurance of Christ.

The word of the Lord.

Lect. No. 156

ALLELUIA: Revelation 1:5a, 6b

The theme of today's readings is the resurrection from the dead. Jesus is the firstborn from the dead, the forerunner of what we all shall experience.

℟. **Alleluia, alleluia.**

Jesus Christ is the firstborn of the dead;
to him be glory and power, forever and ever.

℟. **Alleluia, alleluia.**

Lect. No. 156

GOSPEL: Longer Form: Luke 20:27-38

He is not God of the dead, but of the living.

The Gospel speaks of the resurrection from the dead.

The Sadducees were a very conservative religious group in Israel. They were members of the royal family and the high priesthood.

They accepted only the first five books of the Bible as normative. They did not accept the idea of the resurrection from the dead (as the Pharisees did).

Therefore, they tried to trap Jesus by bringing up a case of a woman who had seven husbands. When a man died without an heir, the widow was to marry the next of kin. This woman married seven brothers in a row.

They asked Jesus whose wife she would be in the resurrection.

One problem with this question was that they spoke of the woman as if she were a piece of property. They were asking who owned her in heaven. Jesus responded that it was not like that in heaven.

We do not belong to one another in heaven. The love of heaven is not exclusive (for we will be able to love everyone with God's own love). It is a love for all without limit.

A reading from the holy Gospel according to Luke

Some Sadducees, those who deny that there is a resurrection,
came forward and put this question to Jesus, saying,
"Teacher, Moses wrote for us,
If someone's brother dies leaving a wife but no child,
his brother must take the wife
and raise up descendants for his brother.
Now there were seven brothers;
the first married a woman but died childless.
Then the second and the third married her,
and likewise all the seven died childless.
Finally the woman also died.
Now at the resurrection whose wife will that woman be?
For all seven had been married to her."
Jesus said to them,
"The children of this age marry and remarry;
but those who are deemed worthy to attain to the coming age
and to the resurrection of the dead
neither marry nor are given in marriage.
They can no longer die,
for they are like angels;
and they are the children of God
because they are the ones who will rise.
That the dead will rise
even Moses made known in the passage about the bush,
when he called out 'Lord,'
the God of Abraham, the God of Isaac, and the God of Jacob;

At the end of this passage, Jesus uses a rabbinic argument to challenge the Sadducees' rejection of the resurrection from the dead.

and he is not God of the dead, but of the living, for to him all are alive."

The Gospel of the Lord.

GOSPEL: **B** Shorter Form: Luke 20:27, 34-38

He is not God of the dead, but of the living.

The Sadducees did not accept the resurrection from the dead (as the Pharisees did). Therefore, they tried to trap Jesus by bringing up a case of a woman who had seven husbands.

When a man died without an heir, the widow was to marry the next of kin. This woman married seven brothers in a row.

They asked Jesus whose wife would she be in the resurrection.

One problem with this question was that they were asking who owned her in heaven. Jesus responded that it was not like that in heaven.

We do not belong to one another in heaven. The love of heaven is not exclusive (saying we can only love one and not another). It is a love for all without limit.

Toward the end, Jesus uses a rabbinic, scriptural argument to challenge the Sadducees' rejection of the resurrection from the dead.

A reading from the holy Gospel according to Luke

Some Sadducees, those who deny that there is a resurrection,
came forward.

Jesus said to them,
"The children of this age marry and remarry;
but those who are deemed worthy to attain to the coming age
and to the resurrection of the dead
neither marry nor are given in marriage.
They can no longer die,
for they are like angels;
and they are the children of God
because they are the ones who will rise.
That the dead will rise
even Moses made known in the passage about the bush,
when he called out 'Lord,'
the God of Abraham, the God of Isaac, and the God of Jacob;
and he is not God of the dead, but of the living,
for to him all are alive."

The Gospel of the Lord.

THIRTY-THIRD SUNDAY IN ORDINARY TIME

Lect. No. 159

The readings this Sunday speak of the end of the world.

The First Reading from the Book of the Prophet Malachi speaks of the Day of Judgment that would dawn upon the earth.

This was called the Day of the LORD. It was a day when God would punish those who did evil and would reward those who had been faithful to the ways of the LORD.

FIRST READING: Malachi 3:19-20a

The sun of justice will shine on you.

A reading from the Book of the Prophet Malachi

Lo, the day is coming, blazing like an oven,
    when all the proud and all evildoers will be
    stubble,
and the day that is coming will set them on fire,
    leaving them neither root nor branch,
    says the LORD of hosts.
But for you who fear my name, there will arise
    the sun of justice with its healing rays.

The word of the Lord.

Lect. No. 159

RESPONSORIAL PSALM: Ps 98:5-6, 7-8, 9 (℟.: cf. 9)

The idea of the Day of the LORD was that God was coming into the world to establish a reign of justice.

This is why the Responsorial Psalm emphasizes that God is the king of all. Since God is king, then it is only logical that he would come to establish his reign.

Furthermore, God is the LORD both of creation (which is why the rivers should clap their hands and the mountains shout with them for joy) and of the people who live upon the earth (for he will rule the world with justice and the peoples with equity).

℟. **The Lord comes to rule the earth with justice.**

Sing praise to the LORD with the harp,
    with the harp and melodious song.
With trumpets and the sound of the horn
    sing joyfully before the King, the LORD.

℟. **The Lord comes to rule the earth with justice.**

Let the sea and what fills it resound,
    the world and those who dwell in it;
let the rivers clap their hands,
    the mountains shout with them for joy.

℟. **The Lord comes to rule the earth with justice.**

Before the LORD, for he comes,
    for he comes to rule the earth;
he will rule the world with justice
    and the peoples with equity.

℟. **The Lord comes to rule the earth with justice.**

Lect. No. 159

SECOND READING: 2 Thessalonians 3:7-12

If anyone is unwilling to work, neither should that one eat.

The First Reading and the Gospel emphasize that the end of the world is at hand. The Second Reading teaches us that this does not mean that we should abandon our daily efforts to live the Gospel.

We cannot stop working, thinking that someone else will look out for us. We cannot become busybodies, getting involved with other people's business. We should live a quiet, gentle life-style, a life-style that will be a good example to anyone who might see us.

Work was an especially important idea to Paul. Wherever he went, he attempted to earn his own living with his own hands. He did not depend upon the generosity of those to whom he was preaching.

Likewise, he was concerned that some in the community might presume upon the generosity of others by depending on them for their sustenance.

A reading from the second Letter of Saint Paul to the Thessalonians

Brothers and sisters:
You know how one must imitate us.
For we did not act in a disorderly way among you,
    nor did we eat food received free from anyone.
On the contrary, in toil and drudgery, night and day
    we worked, so as not to burden any of you.
Not that we do not have the right.
Rather, we wanted to present ourselves as a model
        for you,
    so that you might imitate us.
In fact, when we were with you,
    we instructed you that if anyone was unwilling to
        work,
    neither should that one eat.
We hear that some are conducting themselves
        among you in a disorderly way,
    by not keeping busy but minding the business of
        others.
Such people we instruct and urge in the Lord Jesus
        Christ to work quietly
    and to eat their own food.

The word of the Lord.

Lect. No. 159

We are living in the end times, for Jesus' resurrection from the dead was the dawning of the end times. We are living on borrowed time.

ALLELUIA: Luke 21:28

℟. **Alleluia, alleluia.**

Stand erect and raise your heads
because your redemption is at hand.

℟. **Alleluia, alleluia.**

GOSPEL: Luke 21:5-19

By your perseverance you will secure your lives.

The Gospel presents a teaching about the end of the world.

Jesus is sitting on the Mount of Olives when he presents this teaching (for this Mount was always associated with the end of times).

The disciples are looking out over the temple, which was a magnificent structure.

Jesus speaks to them of the day when not one stone would be left upon another. (Remember that this passage was written after the destruction of the temple in 70 A.D.)

The disciples ask about when this would happen. The word for "time" used here is "kairos."

There are two words for time in Greek. "Chronos" simply means time, while "kairos" means the appointed or chosen time.

Jesus warns the disciples that many things would have to occur before the end. Even rumors of wars and insurrections would not signal the end.

In other words, he seems to be telling them that the end was not something that would happen in the near future.

The end of the passage talks about the persecution that would occur before the end.

A reading from the holy Gospel according to Luke

While some people were speaking about
    how the temple was adorned with costly stones
        and votive offerings,
Jesus said, "All that you see here—
the days will come when there will not be left
a stone upon another stone that will not be
    thrown down."

Then they asked him,
    "Teacher, when will this happen?
And what sign will there be when all these things
    are about to happen?"
He answered,
"See that you not be deceived,
    for many will come in my name, saying,
    'I am he,' and 'The time has come.'
Do not follow them!
When you hear of wars and insurrections,
    do not be terrified; for such things must happen
        first,
    but it will not immediately be the end."
Then he said to them,
    "Nation will rise against nation, and kingdom
        against kingdom.
There will be powerful earthquakes, famines, and
    plagues
    from place to place;
    and awesome sights and mighty signs will come
        from the sky.

"Before all this happens, however,
    they will seize and persecute you,
    they will hand you over to the synagogues and to
        prisons,

Jesus tells the disciples not to prepare their defense, for God would give them what they were to say when the time came. They were to trust that God would deliver them from all of their difficulties.

"To deliver" does not mean that God would make it all better. Many of them would still die as martyrs.

Yet, even if they were martyred, God would hold them in his heart and love. Their perseverance would secure their lives (not necessarily their earthly lives, but certainly their lives in the world to come).

and they will have you led before kings and governors
because of my name.
It will lead to your giving testimony.
Remember, you are not to prepare your defense beforehand,
for I myself shall give you a wisdom in speaking
that all your adversaries will be powerless to resist or refute.
You will even be handed over by parents, brothers, relatives, and friends,
and they will put some of you to death.
You will be hated by all because of my name,
but not a hair on your head will be destroyed.
By your perseverance you will secure your lives."

The Gospel of the Lord.

PASTORAL REFLECTIONS

We have to be careful how we interpret passages written with the apocalyptic style of literature. Interpreting them literally would be to expect a person to look just like an artist such as Picasso had depicted her. The apocalyptic form of literature uses certain stock images and colors that are intended to be symbolic.

The most important element of apocalyptic literature is that the present evil age is coming to an end through a powerful intervention from God. The life, death, and resurrection of Jesus was understood by many early Christians to be that intervention.

November 24, 2013

Last Sunday in Ordinary Time

OUR LORD JESUS CHRIST, KING OF THE UNIVERSE

Lect. No. 162

FIRST READING: 2 Samuel 5:1-3

They anointed David king of Israel.

In the early days after the death of Saul, the ten tribes of the north had a son of Saul as their king, while the two southern tribes had David.

After the death of Saul's son, all of the tribes of Israel proclaimed David as their king.

David was to be their shepherd. God was the shepherd of Israel, and David was now being made God's vicar upon the earth.

That is why the king of Israel was proclaimed to be the Son of God on the day of his enthronement.

A reading from the second Book of Samuel

In those days, all the tribes of Israel came to David in Hebron and said:
"Here we are, your bone and your flesh.
In days past, when Saul was our king,
    it was you who led the Israelites out and brought them back.
And the LORD said to you,
    'You shall shepherd my people Israel
    and shall be commander of Israel.'"
When all the elders of Israel came to David in Hebron,
    King David made an agreement with them there before the LORD,
    and they anointed him king of Israel.

The word of the Lord.

PASTORAL REFLECTIONS

Many Old Testament authors were ambivalent when it came to the idea of having kings. During the time of the judges, God had been Israel's king. Wanting another king seemed to be a rejection of God's leadership. The prophet Samuel warned the Israelites that their kings would lord it over them and take advantage of them.

That is why the image of the shepherd was so important. The shepherd was to be a benevolent leader who cared for those who were powerless. The shepherd risked his life to protect those who were in danger.

Jesus used the image of the shepherd to describe his own kingship. He was not an authoritarian leader. He was as gentle and caring as a shepherd is with his sheep.

RESPONSORIAL PSALM: Ps 122:1-2, 3-4, 4-5 (℟.: cf. 1)

The Responsorial Psalm is a Song of Zion, a song that would have been proclaimed as pilgrims climbed up the mount to arrive in the holy city of Jerusalem.

The first place that the pilgrim would visit was the temple, for this was the place where God dwelt upon the earth.

This was a place of blessing and peace. For Jewish people, it was their second home.

As Christians, we live in hope to dwell in our heavenly Jerusalem. That is our home, for while we live "in" this world, we are not "of" the world.

℟. **Let us go rejoicing to the house of the Lord.**

I rejoiced because they said to me,
    "We will go up to the house of the LORD."
And now we have set foot
    within your gates, O Jerusalem.

℟. **Let us go rejoicing to the house of the Lord.**

Jerusalem, built as a city
    with compact unity.
To it the tribes go up,
    the tribes of the LORD.

℟. **Let us go rejoicing to the house of the Lord.**

According to the decree for Israel,
    to give thanks to the name of the LORD.
In it are set up judgment seats,
    seats for the house of David.

℟. **Let us go rejoicing to the house of the Lord.**

Lect. No. 162

SECOND READING: Colossians 1:12-20

He transferred us to the kingdom of his beloved Son.

The Second Reading is a beautiful hymn that speaks about Christ.

The early Church struggled to develop concepts to understand who Jesus was. Here it calls him an icon of the Father.

Icons are not simply pictures. They are considered to be representations of the holy one.

Jesus is thus the visible manifestation of the invisible glory of God.

A reading from the Letter of Saint Paul
to the Colossians

Brothers and sisters:
    Let us give thanks to the Father,
    who has made you fit to share
    in the inheritance of the holy ones in light.
He delivered us from the power of darkness
    and transferred us to the kingdom of his beloved
        Son,
    in whom we have redemption, the forgiveness of
        sins.

He is the image of the invisible God,
    the firstborn of all creation.

The hymn also presents Jesus as the Wisdom of God. In the Old Testament Wisdom was an attribute of God. It was the architect who assisted him at creation and the revelation of God's will.

All things are under Jesus' dominion. In Greek philosophy, that which was spiritual was superior to that which was material.

Was Jesus inferior to the angels? This hymn tells us that everything, visible and invisible, is under his care.

Jesus is also the head of the Church and the firstborn from the dead. As the firstborn, he is both the first of those who would rise from the dead and the best.

He brought about our justification with God through his death and resurrection, and he has provided us a way to live in that justification by giving us the Church.

| Lect. |
| No. 162 |

The Alleluia Verse speaks of the kingship of Jesus, for he inherited the throne of David his ancestor. He is the Messiah, the one who comes in the name of the Lord.

For in him were created all things in heaven
   and on earth,
   the visible and the invisible,
   whether thrones or dominions or principalities or powers;
   all things were created through him and for him.
He is before all things,
   and in him all things hold together.
He is the head of the body, the church.
He is the beginning, the firstborn from the dead,
   that in all things he himself might be preeminent.
For in him all the fullness was pleased to dwell,
   and through him to reconcile all things for him,
   making peace by the blood of his cross
   through him, whether those on earth or those in heaven.

The word of the Lord.

ALLELUIA: Mark 11:9, 10

℟. **Alleluia, alleluia.**

Blessed is he who comes in the name of the Lord!
Blessed is the kingdom of our father David that is to come!

℟. **Alleluia, alleluia.**

PASTORAL REFLECTIONS

Those who were anointed as kings of Israel did not heed God's call as they should have. This is why we needed a Messiah, an anointed one like Jesus, who would proclaim the kingdom of God in word and deed.

Lect. No. 162

GOSPEL: Luke 23:35-43

Lord, remember me when you come into your kingdom.

On the Solemnity of Our Lord Jesus Christ, King of the Universe, we acknowledge Jesus as king. Yet, he is the king who does not sit upon a throne but rather hangs from a cross.

He does not wear a crown of gold, but rather a crown of thorns. Thus, Jesus is most a king when he is dying upon the cross.

The crowds mock Jesus with titles such as the "chosen one of God," "the Christ of God," and the "King of the Jews." All of these are true titles, but this would only be understood when Jesus had risen from the dead.

They call upon Jesus to save himself as he had saved others. The irony is that he was saving others in the very act of not saving himself.

This is the only Gospel that speaks of the good thief who defends Jesus. Again, this is typical of the Gospel of Luke, for Jesus had come to save those who were lost and most needed his love.

He forgives the good thief and invites him to be with him in paradise.

A reading from the holy Gospel according to Luke

The rulers sneered at Jesus and said,
  "He saved others, let him save himself
  if he is the chosen one, the Christ of God."
Even the soldiers jeered at him.
As they approached to offer him wine they called out,
  "If you are King of the Jews, save yourself."
Above him there was an inscription that read,
  "This is the King of the Jews."

Now one of the criminals hanging there reviled Jesus, saying,
  "Are you not the Christ?
Save yourself and us."
The other, however, rebuking him, said in reply,
  "Have you no fear of God,
  for you are subject to the same condemnation?
And indeed, we have been condemned justly,
  for the sentence we received corresponds to our crimes,
  but this man has done nothing criminal."
Then he said,
  "Jesus, remember me when you come into your kingdom."
He replied to him,
  "Amen, I say to you,
  today you will be with me in Paradise."

The Gospel of the Lord.

APPENDIX 1: INTRODUCTION TO THE BOOKS OF THE BIBLE THAT ARE READ IN THE THREE-YEAR CYCLE

GENESIS

The first book of the Bible tells of the history of the world in its earliest stages (the Primordial History) and during the period of the Patriarchs up to the time that the people of Israel went down to Egypt to escape the great drought during the days of Joseph.

The first eleven chapters contain stories that are not strictly historical in the sense of being a day-to-day account of the early history of the world. These chapters nevertheless contain important truths about the early days of humanity.

God created us out of love and called us to live in obedience to his commands. We, in the person of Adam and Eve, sinned against God and were punished for our disobedience. Sin grew in the world until God sent his punishment in the form of a great flood.

Beginning with chapter 12, we hear of the history of Abraham and Sarah, Isaac and Rebekah, Jacob and his wives and children, especially Joseph. These stories seem to contain more historic information than the earlier chapters. Some of the customs mentioned in the stories, for example, have been dated back to the period in which the Patriarchs were said to have lived.

It is believed that the information contained in this book comes from three major sources.

The first source is the Yahwist source. It was written during the reigns of David and Solomon (c. 950 B.C.) in the southern part of Israel. It emphasizes the role of the monarchy and the importance of Judah and his tribe in salvation history. This source is called the Yahwist source because it often refers to God by the name Yahweh.

The second source is the Elohist source. This dates to around 850 B.C. and was written in the north of Israel. It emphasizes the importance of prophets and the Sinai covenant. Because the kings of the north were often unfaithful to the ways of the Lord, kings are not seen as laudable figures.

The third source is the Priestly source. It was written during the exile in Babylon (587-539 B.C.). It emphasizes the importance of law and tradition. This source tends to be very accurate in measurements of time and space.

The book achieved its present form sometime around the Babylonian exile (c. 587-539 B.C.).

EXODUS

This book tells of the miraculous events that surrounded the exodus of the people of Israel from their slavery in Egypt. It begins with the infancy of Moses and ends with a description of the construction of the objects of cult that Israel was to use when it worshiped the Lord.

The same sources that appear in the Book of Genesis are also found in this book. This would explain why certain events are sometimes described twice in slightly different circumstances (for the two versions were derived from different sources).

This book contains one version of the ten commandments (20:1-7; the other version is found in the Book of Deuteronomy 5:6-21). The law is seen as a gift from God, for it instructs Israel on how it can follow the ways of the Lord and be faithful to their covenant.

The hymn that the community sings to celebrate its escape from the forces of Pharaoh in Exodus 15 is actually a very ancient hymn. Scholars believe the grammar and vocabulary of the hymn show it to date to the actual time of the exodus. Thus, this is one of the earliest parts of the Bible to have been written.

It is also in this book that God reveals his name, YHWH (i.e., Yahweh), to Moses (3:14). It is said that this name means "I am who I am." It has been interpreted by some rabbis as meaning, "I am who I am for you, who I have always been for you, who I will always be for you." (In modern Bibles LORD in capital letters stands for the name of God, because the Jews never pronounced it.)

LEVITICUS

This is the third of the five books of the Pentateuch. Its name is derived from the word "Levite," for most of the material contained in the book is Levitical law. Unlike Genesis, Exodus, and Numbers, which are amalgamations of various sources, this book is almost entirely derived from the Priestly source written during the Babylonian Exile (587-539 B.C.).

The people of Israel were living in exile, and the priestly authors felt that they needed to define the obligations of the law in a clear manner so that the Israelites would not lose their cultural identity while living in a foreign land. Among the topics presented are laws concerning sacrifice, the priesthood of Aaron and his descendants, cleanliness and uncleanness, the ritual for the day of atonement, votive offerings, and the law of holiness.

NUMBERS

The Book of Numbers continues the story of Israel during the period in which they dwelt in the desert for forty years while they were being purified by the Lord so that they might enter the promised land.

It is composed of the same sources that we saw in Genesis and Exodus.

It obtained its name from the fact that Israel took a census of those who were with them in the desert. The number of men who left Egypt is cited as being over 600,000, most probably an exaggerated number.

It also contains many instructions for worship and other community actions.

Important episodes include the first attempt to enter the promised land (which failed because of the fear of the people and their lack of trust in the providence of the Lord), Balaam's curse upon Israel (which actually turns out to be a blessing), the choice of the seventy-two elders to assist Moses in governing the people of Israel, and instructions for the division of the promised land when Israel would conquer it.

DEUTERONOMY

Deuteronomy means "the second law." A scroll of the law was discovered by King Josiah when he was reforming the temple cult. It is not known whether the book is ancient and had been lost in the temple during a period of decline in the faith of Israel or whether it was placed in the temple to be found at that time.

Its teachings represent a reform of the way that Israel practiced its religion. Previous to its promulgation, there were shrines to the Lord upon most of the heights of the land. Many of these shrines were dedicated both to Yahweh and to Baal, the pagan god of fertility. The main reform of this book was that it established that one could only worship the Lord with sacrifices in the temple in Jerusalem.

There is an extensive series of legislation throughout the book, including another version of the ten commandments (one version is found in Exodus). Many of the laws are aimed at the pagan practices that had entered into the faith of Israel. The *She'ma Israel*, the profession of faith of the Jewish people, is contained in 6:4ff.

The book closes with Moses designating Joshua as his successor and then dying. He was buried by God on Mount Nebo. These chapters might have originally been in another of the books of the Pentateuch, and were then attached to the end of this particular book.

The school that produced this book is called the Deuteronomist school. They not only wrote this book of law but also edited many of the other books that had been written previous to this period. Their tendency was to write history as it should have happened, and not as it necessarily happened. Thus, they describe the conquest of the holy land as a series of spectacular successes against pagan armies (e.g., Joshua) as opposed to a slow infiltration of tribes into a land where they faced bitter opposition (e.g., Judges).

JOSHUA

The Book of Joshua is the sixth Book of the Old Testament, named after the successor of Moses, who led the Israelites into Canaan. The book contains a systematic account of the conquest of the promised land. Its purpose is to demonstrate God's fidelity in giving the Israelites the land he had promised them for an inheritance. It includes: (1) the conquest of Canaan; (2) division of the land; and (3) return of the Trans-jordanian tribes and Joshua's farewell. Like the first five Books of the Bible, Joshua was built up by a long and complex process of editing traditional materials.

Although the victories of Joshua are an action of God, they also call for the active collaboration and faith of his people.

FIRST SAMUEL

First Samuel describes the history of Israel from the end of the period of Judges until the time when Saul and his sons die in battle against the Philistines.

The book opens with the story of the birth of Samuel, the last and greatest of the judges. Judges were charismatic leaders who exercised executive, legislative, judicial, and even priestly power. Chapter 2 presents the hymn that Hannah chanted to celebrate the birth of her son Samuel. This hymn was used as the basis of Mary's hymn in the Gospel of Luke.

The early part of the book describes some of the disasters that Israel suffered in this period. The people became frightened and they asked for a king. God and Samuel chose Saul, a Benjaminite, as the king of Israel. There are two judgments concerning Israel's request (each judgment derives from a different source). One judgment is that the request is understandable, but the other is that the people of Israel were subtly rejecting God, their true king, by requesting a human king.

Saul displeased God, and Samuel had to choose another king who was more pleasing to God. He chose David and anointed him. The latter chapters of this book speak of the growing enmity between Saul and David based upon Saul's jealousy.

SECOND SAMUEL

Second Samuel describes the history of Israel from the death of Samuel until the end of the reign of David (his death is described at the beginning of First Kings). The book begins with David's mourning for the death of King Saul and especially for his son and David's friend Jonathan.

David accedes to the throne of the southern tribes while Ishbaal, one of Saul's sons, becomes king of the ten northern tribes. At the end of a long civil war, David is proclaimed king of the united tribes. He conquers Jerusalem, makes it his capital, and moves the ark of the covenant there.

The rest of the book is a history of David's deeds and even misdeeds. While he is spectacularly successful in political terms, his personal and family life are another matter. He sins against the LORD by committing adultery with Bathsheba, the wife of Uriah the Hittite, and by conducting a census of Israel implying that they were his possession. He witnessed the death of his son Amnon who raped his daughter Tamar, and of another son Absalom, who rose up in rebellion against David.

FIRST KINGS

The First Book of Kings describes the period of history that began with the death of David and the succession of Solomon as king until the days of King Jehoshaphat of Judah and of King Ahaziah of Israel.

The book opens with the twelve tribes forming a united kingdom. After the death of Solomon, however, King Rehoboam acted foolishly and alienated the ten northern tribes, which seceded and formed their own kingdom, Israel. The southern kingdom was henceforth known as Judah.

The early chapters describe the successes of Solomon, e.g., his construction of the temple in Jerusalem and massive cities and fortifications throughout the land. They also speak of his sinfulness, for he built shrines to the pagan gods of his many wives.

The latter chapters speak of the prophetic career of Elijah. He led Israel away from syncretism to greater fidelity in the Lord. He condemned King Ahab and his wife Jezebel for their religious errors and their social conduct (e.g., robbing the field of Naboth the Jezreelite by having him killed).

In chapter 18 we hear about the contest on Mount Carmel between Elijah and the priests of Baal to determine who was the true God in Israel. In chapter 19 we hear of Elijah's encounter with God on Mount Sinai when he met him not in earthquake or fire or wind as Moses had when he received the law, but in the gentle breeze. The meaning of this passage is that God does not always act in a miraculous, spectacular fashion, but rather he often brings about his will in ordinary, everyday events.

SECOND KINGS

The Second Book of Kings tells the history of the kingdoms of Israel and Judah from the days of Elijah and Elisha until the time of the Babylonian exile.

The early chapters of the book speak of the ascent of Elijah into heaven on a fiery chariot and the ministry of Elisha. The account of Elisha resembles the story of a famous miracle worker.

Much of the book is a chronicle of the infidelity of the kings of both kingdoms and how God visited his judgment upon them through the hands of pagan kings.

In 722 B.C. the northern kingdom of Israel was annihilated and its nobility carried off into exile in Assyria. In 587 B.C. the same fate befell the citizens of the southern kingdom of Judah (although they, at least, returned from exile in Babylon).

One of the high points of the book is the accession of King Josiah to the throne of Judah and his reform of the religion of his people (during which the Book of Deuteronomy was discovered and promulgated).

The book also reports the period of Kings Ahaz and Hezekiah. These were two kings who reigned during much of the prophetic career of Isaiah.

FIRST CHRONICLES

The First Book of Chronicles outlines the history of Israel from the creation of Adam until the construction of the temple in Jerusalem. Much of the information contained in this book is also contained in the Books of Samuel and the Books of Kings. It was probably produced by the Deuteronomist school, which tended to tell history as it should have happened and not necessarily as it happened. Thus, its story of King David excludes all of the more scandalous material concerning his adultery, the scandals in his family, etc.

SECOND CHRONICLES

Like First Chronicles, this book is a Deuteronomist revision of the information contained in the First and Second Books of Kings. It begins with the accession of Solomon to the throne and closes with the decree of Cyrus permitting the Jewish people to return from exile in Babylon (c. 539 B.C.). Typical of this school of literature, an idealized view of Israel's history is presented. Solomon is portrayed as being one of the greatest kings of Israel, second only to David. His role in constructing the temple of God in Jerusalem is strongly emphasized.

The history of the kings of the north is all but ignored (for this school considered those kings to be faithless and deceitful), while that of the kings of Judah is presented in greater detail.

NEHEMIAH

Nehemiah was a Jewish official of the Persian emperor who was appointed governor of Judah around 445 B.C. The book named after him speaks of the actions of the prophet and Ezra (a priest). Nehemiah arrived in Jerusalem at a time when the Jewish nation was demoralized and drifting. He rebuilt the walls of the city. He reestablished Jewish law as the law of the land. He promoted social justice (e.g., giving loans with no interest). He ordered those who had married foreign wives to send them away (in his days, this was seen as a purification of the religion of Israel).

JOB

The Book of Job presents an extended reflection upon the problem of pain and suffering. Satan (who is presented as being God's district attorney) convinces God to withdraw his beneficence from Job to see whether Job would curse the LORD. No matter how much Job suffers, he refuses to curse God. Yet he acknowledges that what he was suffering was unjust.

The theory that sin is the cause of all suffering is strongly rejected. Job expresses his anger at the injustice that he was experiencing, even challenging God to explain why he would allow these things to happen.

The saying, "the patience of Job," is a bit misleading. He is patient for two chapters, and then rants and raves against God for more than thirty chapters. In the end, God appears and puts Job to the test. Job realizes that he does not understand all things, and that he must respond to all trials with trust in God.

PSALMS

The Book of Psalms is a collection of 150 psalms written during a period of almost 1,000 years, and it has become the Prayer Book of the Church. They are divided into five books of psalms, each ending with a doxology. The numbers assigned to the psalms are different in the original Hebrew version and the Greek translation. Although many of them are attributed to great historic figures such as David, they were actually dedicated to those people and not written by them.

The psalms are poetry and many demonstrate the most common attribute of Hebrew poetry (parallelism). A large number of the words used in the psalms are *hapax legomena* (words used only once in the Bible).

There are several identifiable literary genres in the psalms. A large number of the psalms are individual or communal lamentations. There are also hymns, royal psalms, hymns of trust, wisdom psalms, thanksgivings, historic psalms, penitential psalms, etc.

PROVERBS

The Book of Proverbs is really two different books written at very different periods of Israel's history.

The older portion of the book is that beginning with chapter 10 and running to the end of the book. It is a series of folk sayings on how to live the good life. It was written to instruct the young on how they could live in the ways of the Lord and receive God's blessings.

This portion is very similar to wisdom books of neighboring cultures (especially Egypt). Some of the sayings, in fact, seem to have been borrowed from those cultures.

The first nine chapters of the book are much more Greek in tone. They must have been written after the conquest of Alexander the Great, so they probably date to the third century B.C. or later. They speak of wisdom as a personalized attribute of God, lady wisdom. The reason for this presentation is that Jewish people adopted the Greek idea that God was totally removed from our experience, that he was the uncreated creator who never had anything to do with his creation. They thus spoke of some of God's attributes as mediators to communicate God's will to us. Among those attributes were God's glory, holiness, spirit, and wisdom.

Wisdom calls to the foolish to instruct them in the ways of the Lord. She offers to nourish them, giving them bread and wine (this idea is used symbolically in the Discourse on the Bread of Life in John 6). She tells them that if they embrace her knowledge, they will receive everlasting life.

ECCLESIASTES

In addition to its Greek name ("Ecclesiastes"), this book is also known by its Hebrew name, Qoheleth. It is a wisdom book written late in the Old Testament period (c. 250 B.C.). The name of the author is uncertain, for the word Qoheleth could be symbolic since it means "the preacher." The book speaks of the impossibility of discerning God's will. God has a plan (for there is a season for everything), but we cannot adequately know it. Thus, it is best to live a reasonably virtuous life. Do not work too much or too little, nor eat too much or too little, etc. Everything else is a chasing after wind.

Rabbis argued about whether to accept this book into the canon or not for quite some time because of its cynicism. Yet this book serves as a good corrective for the overly optimistic attitude of other wisdom literature.

WISDOM

The Book of Wisdom is one of the younger books of the Old Testament. It displays many signs of having been written during the period in which Greek culture heavily influenced Judaism. Because it was only written in Greek, it was not accepted into the Hebrew Bible and is not found in Protestant Bibles as well.

Wisdom is personified as a spirit that is totally pure. We hear of how King Solomon prayed for and received the gift of wisdom in order to rule the people of Israel in the ways of the Lord.

We hear how the evil would be punished for their iniquity and the good would receive an eternal reward. This is one of the few books of the Old Testament that speak about our destiny in the afterlife as being one that is filled with joy.

The latter part of the book gives a panorama of the history of Israel and explains how wisdom was present in each of those stages. One interesting teaching contained in this section is that the plagues of Egypt involved many animals because the people of Egypt had worshiped animals. There is a rabbinic teaching that as the sin, so the punishment.

SIRACH

The Book of Sirach is one of the wisdom books of literature of the Old Testament. It is included in Catholic Bibles but is not found in Protestant Bibles because until recently we only possessed the Greek version of this book (and Protestants follow the rabbis' definition of the Old Testament, that only those books written in Hebrew or Aramaic were acceptable).

The premise of the book is that it was written by Jesus Sirach and translated into Greek by his grandson. Some manuscripts of portions of the original Hebrew text have been found in Qumran and Egypt.

Typical of wisdom literature, the book contains a series of instructions on how to live the good life. The reader is advised to follow the path of virtue. There are instructions for almost every dimension of individual, family, and community life.

The hymn to wisdom in chapter 24 shows heavy Greek influence. It speaks of wisdom who was an architect helping God create the world. Wisdom visited the people of Israel and pitched her tent among them (an image used in the prologue of the Gospel of John when it speaks of the incarnation).

The book closes with a series of accounts of the deeds of the great men of Israel and a hymn of thanksgiving to the Lord.

ISAIAH

The Book of Isaiah is actually a combination of the prophecies of three different prophets (or schools of prophecy).

The first part of the book, from chapter 1 to 39, is attributed to Isaiah the prophet who ministered to the southern kingdom of Judah from around 740 B.C. until sometime after 700 B.C.

His major theme was that God was holy, and we were called to live in that holiness. That meant that we had to exhibit a lifestyle that was consistent with the holiness of God.

The first chapters of the book are similar to those of the Prophet Amos. Isaiah admonishes the people to live social justice and to care for the poor, for this is what the holiness of God demands.

From chapters 7 to 11 we hear various episodes and oracles that shaped Isaiah's understanding of the coming Messiah. At first Isaiah hoped for a new king who would be better than the old king (remember, all of the kings of Judah and Israel were considered to be the anointed of the Lord and thus each one of them was a messiah). Eventually, he stopped hoping for a better king and he began to speak of a coming era in which God would intervene through one particular Messiah. This era would be filled with peace and justice. Even nature would experience this, for animals that were natural enemies such as the lion and the lamb could lie down together in peace.

Much of the rest of his prophecy is a series of oracles against nations that had attacked Judah or against his own people for their infidelity.

The second part of the book runs from chapter 40 to 55. This was written during the exile in Babylon (587-539 B.C.) and is attributed to an anonymous author called Deutero-Isaiah. It is a book of consolation. God promises Israel that it will be wondrously restored.

This section of the book also contains four poems called the songs of the suffering servant of Yahweh. They speak about a mysterious figure who will bring salvation to Israel and also to the Gentiles. He will be meek and gentle. He will suffer for our sins and die for us, but the Lord will raise him from the dead.

The third section of the book runs from chapter 56 to 66. It was written after the exile. The people thought that when they returned to Israel all would be well, but it did not turn out that way. This prophecy encourages them and admonishes them to convert their ways. Chapter 58 speaks of fasting, telling the people that God does not want us to get involved in empty rituals. He wants us to transform the way we live with him and each other.

JEREMIAH

Of all of the prophets of the Old Testament, Jeremiah is the one who is said to have best foreshadowed Jesus. The reason for this is his heroic suffering for the sake of the message that God had given him to share with his people. He called them to conversion and warned them of the consequences of their actions, but they refused to listen to him. Then, when they suffered the consequences of their own choices, they blamed Jeremiah for what was happening to them. He was beaten, saw his writings burned by the king, was thrown into a cistern to die, and eventually died while being dragged down to Egypt.

Jeremiah preached during one of the most turbulent periods of the history of the kingdom of Judah. One king was following another with fearful rapidity. The people of Judah and their kings were at one moment subjects of Egypt, at the next of Babylon.

Early in Jeremiah's career he witnessed the finding of the Book of Deuteronomy in the temple. This book contained a new law that outlawed all shrines of the Lord in the land with the exception of the temple in Jerusalem. His own family lost their livelihood for they were a family of priests at a shrine to the north of Jerusalem. Yet Jeremiah rejoiced and embraced the reform.

But it brought him only trouble. He speaks in a series of poems of his feelings of abandonment by the Lord (these are called his Confessions, e.g., 20:7-18). Yet he felt that he could not run away from his responsibility to proclaim God's word, so he continued to preach.

In chapter 31 Jeremiah speaks of a new covenant that the Lord will make with the people of Israel. This covenant will not be written upon tablets of stone; it will be written upon their hearts.

Jeremiah also spoke of individual responsibility for sin. We will not be punished for the sins of our ancestors, but rather for our own sins.

Jeremiah's ministry ended shortly after the destruction of Jerusalem and the deportation of most of the nobility to Babylon. During the siege he had told the king and the people to surrender to the Babylonians and receive their punishment for God had sent this chastisement. Because he told the people to surrender and not fight, the princes of the land accused him of sedition and punished him. When the city was conquered, he was not mistreated by the Babylonians. Shortly after the conquest someone assassinated the Babylonian governor, and

Jeremiah was forced to accompany those who were fleeing to Egypt to avoid the coming punishment. He died along the way.

BARUCH

The Book of Baruch was purported to have been written by Baruch, the secretary to Jeremiah, during the Babylonian exile. Because the only version of the book extant is written in Greek, it was not included in the Hebrew or Protestant Old Testaments.

It begins with an appeal for the people to turn back to wisdom, which would lead them to the Lord. The law of God is seen as wisdom incarnate.

There are also some songs of lamentation and a purported letter of Jeremiah to the exiles in Babylon.

EZEKIEL

Ezekiel was the only major prophet to prophesy outside of Israel (for he prophesied while he lived in exile in Babylon). Because of this, it was quite some time before his book was accepted by the elders of the Jewish community. His book is filled with extraordinary visions, oracles, and prophetic actions.

Ezekiel was a priest carried away into exile during the first partial exile of 597 B.C. For the next ten years he preached to the exiles and to the community that still resided in Jerusalem. After the second exile of 587 B.C., he continued his ministry addressing himself to the old and new exiles with whom he lived.

His book begins with the account of a theophany, the appearance of the Lord in the form of a fiery chariot.

He performed a number of symbolic actions to draw the attention of his audience to the serious nature of their situation. They refused to listen and change their ways.

In the latter part of the book, we hear of the restoration that the Lord will bring upon

Israel. The temple would be rebuilt and purified (he describes its dimensions in great detail toward the end of the book). That which was dead in them would be filled with life (the meaning of the story of the valley filled with dry bones in chapter 37). The temple would become the source of grace and divine love that will renew the land (the story of the river flowing from the altar in the temple and running out into the entire land in chapter 47). God would give his people hearts of flesh to replace their hearts of stone (chapter 36).

DANIEL

Although this book was attributed to a prophet named Daniel during the period of the Babylonian exile, it was actually written during the period of persecution at the time of the Maccabees (c. 175 B.C.). (We know this because many of the historic details contained in this book are incorrect.)

The first half of the book is a series of stories set during the Babylonian period that are intended to be parables concerning the need to give witness to the faith. The second half of the book is apocalyptic in style and speaks of the eventual triumph of the people of God over every adversity.

Chapters 13 and 14 (the story of Susanna and Bel and the Dragon) were written only in Greek (as well as part of chapter 3, the hymn of the three young men in the furnace). They are thus not accepted by Protestant churches, while they are part of the canon accepted by Catholic and Orthodox churches.

HOSEA

Hosea was a minor prophet from the northern kingdom of Israel (c. 750 B.C.). He was married to a woman named Gomer who was unfaithful. No matter how much she strayed, he continued to love her. He even allowed himself to be made a fool of in order to try to win her back.

Hosea realized that his relationship with Gomer paralleled God's relationship with Israel. God had made a covenant with Israel and had blessed his people with prosperity, but God's people had strayed and worshiped false gods. The prophet also used the image of God being a loving parent and Israel being a disobedient child who refused to be corrected, or who even refused to be born when the time had come.

The book has suffered from a considerable amount of editorial reordering of material. This has made it difficult to understand the meaning of certain passages.

JOEL

The Book of Joel is one of the most apocalyptic books in the Old Testament. It speaks about the coming judgment of the Day of the Lord. The enemies of the Lord will be punished while those faithful to his covenant will be rewarded.

This book speaks about a coming outpouring of the Spirit of the Lord upon the whole nation. This passage is quoted by Peter on the day of Pentecost to explain what was happening to those who had received the gift of the Holy Spirit that day.

AMOS

Amos was one of the minor prophets (c. 750 B.C.). He was from the southern kingdom of Judah, but his mission was to the people of the north. Amos speaks of himself as being a herdsman and a dresser of sycamore trees (which probably indicates a relatively poor person).

He was not a professional prophet, and most of his message seems to have come from his observations of the world rather than through special revelations. He calls Israel to task for allowing social injustice in which the poor were oppressed while the rich lived in luxury.

JONAH

While the Book of Jonah is said to be a prophetic book, it is most probably a parable written during the post-exilic period (after 539 B.C.). It speaks of a prophet named Jonah who is called by God to proclaim the destruction of the pagan city of Nineveh for its sins. Jonah at first refuses because he fears that the Ninevites might repent and thus avoid the punishment that they deserve.

He tries to flee on a ship, but it runs into a storm. He is eventually thrown overboard and swallowed by a large fish, which spews him up on shore. He preaches repentance to the Ninevites, and they immediately begin a period of penance. God withholds his punishment, and Jonah is very depressed for what he feared had come true. God speaks to him of how all people are his own, and how he loves and cares for them all.

Many scholars believe that this was a parable written to speak of the fact that Yahweh was the God of all nations. Israel had been swallowed by a large fish (Babylon), and now they were being called to recognize the fact that God was concerned for everyone (for if there is only one God, then God is the God of all peoples).

MICAH

Micah was a minor prophet in the middle of the eighth century B.C. He came from the small town of Moresheth-Gath. He fostered small town values and fought the corruption of army officials and court officials from Jerusalem. He opposed social injustice and oppression. He, like Amos, condemned a formal liturgical life that did not result in a transformation of one's conduct. He speaks of the destruction of the dynasty ruling in Jerusalem and the rise of a new dynasty from the descendants of David living in Bethlehem. This prophecy would later be seen to foretell the birthplace of the Messiah.

HABAKKUK

Habakkuk was one of the minor prophets, and his book was written at the end of the seventh century B.C. The prophet questions why God allows his people to suffer. Why does God allow one pagan nation (Assyria) to be punished by another pagan nation (Babylon), for that second pagan nation only becomes arrogant? The prophet eventually concludes that God will right all things in God's own time. Chapter 3 of the book is a hymn of praise for God who will save his people.

ZEPHANIAH

The Book of Zephaniah is one of the books of the minor prophets. It gives a series of oracles against the people of the nations surrounding Israel and against the people of Israel itself. They will all be punished on the Day of the Lord. It describes that day as a day of woe and of distress.

Yet, the book closes with a hymn of praise of the Lord. Both the people of Israel and even the people of the nations would turn to the Lord and pray to him alone. All the dispersed will be gathered together and healed by the Lord.

ZECHARIAH

The Book of Zechariah is actually produced in two stages. The first part dates to the period shortly after the Jewish people had returned from their exile in Babylon. It is a series of warnings that they should walk in the ways of the Lord, but it also speaks of encouragement and hope. This continues through the first eight chapters of the book.

The second section of the book is a series of judgments and oracles that were written much later (some probably dating to the Greek period, after 330 B.C.). The most important passage for us is that which speaks of the entrance of the Messiah into the city of Jerusalem. He is described as riding a donkey, the colt of an ass (9:9). The humble manner in which he entered the city was intended to be contrasted with the arrogance of all of the kings and generals who had conquered Jerusalem and had entered it riding on great chargers. The Messiah would be a ruler who would restore peace to the land. This passage was fulfilled when Jesus entered the city of Jerusalem on Palm Sunday riding on a donkey.

MALACHI

Malachi is believed to be the last of the prophets. He was a minor prophet. We are not sure whether this is actually the author's name, for the word Malachi means "my messenger," so it might be more of a title than a proper name.

He complains especially that the Jewish people have not been faithful to their covenant responsibilities. Their priests offer inferior sacrifices, men divorce the wives of their youth, etc. There will be a coming judgment when God will reward the good and punish the evil.

The book closes with a promise of the return of Elijah to prepare for the Day of the Lord. This was fulfilled in the ministry of John the Baptist who performed Elijah's mission in New Testament times.

GOSPEL OF MATTHEW

Matthew is the longest and the most Jewish of the Gospels. It has numerous quotations from the Old Testament to show how Jesus fulfilled the law and the prophets and numerous references to Jewish customs all throughout.

Ancient tradition speaks of it being the first Gospel written. This is why it is always listed as the first Gospel in the list of the four. This tradition also speaks of it having been written in Aramaic.

Modern scholarship calls this into question. It is obvious that Matthew copied much of his material from Mark and not vice versa (for Mark is short and ungrammatical and Matthew is longer and better organized).

Furthermore, these same scholars have determined that the Greek version of the Gospel that we now possess is not a translation from another language. Rather, the Gospel was originally written in Greek.

We can still sustain the ancient tradition if we propose that Matthew, the tax collector, wrote part of today's Gospel of Matthew. Then, some decades later, a second author took that book, combined it with material from Mark and other sources, and produced the Gospel of Matthew as we know it today. This second author kept the original name of the Gospel of Matthew, because this name showed that the Gospel had apostolic authority.

This second author was probably a converted Pharisee (for there are so many quotes from the Old Testament throughout the Gospel). He probably wrote around 80 A.D. as a response to a persecution that his community was suffering. It was about this time that Christians were definitively excluded from the synagogue.

This was a response to the destruction of the temple. Jewish authorities felt that without the binding force of the temple, they could no longer afford the luxury of allowing several different versions of their faith to co-exist. Christians were shunned, and sometimes murdered for their faith. They were told that they had rejected the God of Israel and would burn in hell forever.

This second Matthew told Christians that they were not cut off from Israel. They were, in fact, the true Israel, while the Jews who had not accepted Jesus were a false Israel for they had not accepted the Messiah whom Yahweh had sent.

Second Matthew combined the material of the Gospel into sections of narrative (action) and discourse (teaching). He produced five major sections of teaching to mirror the first five books of the Old Testament that Jews called the Torah.

He presented Jesus as the new Moses for the new Israel. Like Moses, Jesus was endangered as a child by an evil king. Like him he fasted for forty days. Like him, he climbed a mountain where he presented a new law (the Sermon on the Mount).

Throughout the Gospel there is a polemic against the leaders of the Jews, especially the Pharisees. This is because they were the ones who had excluded Christians from the synagogues. Furthermore, there are refutations of lies spread about Jesus by the leaders of the Jews, e.g., the resurrection scene. Jesus also uses the Pharisees as an example of what the apostles should not be in their exercise of authority.

This Gospel contains more parables than Mark. Many of them speak about the coming judgment and how people must choose to live in the path of the Lord.

GOSPEL OF MARK

The Gospel of Mark is probably the first Gospel written. It is believed that it was written in Rome around the year 70 A.D. It was written by John Mark, a disciple who accompanied Paul and Barnabas on one missionary journey (but departed from their company before the journey was finished). John Mark eventually traveled to Rome and became a disciple of Peter.

The Gospel presents the story of Jesus in a straightforward manner with little embellishment. If one were to compare it to a modern medium, one might speak of it as the home movies of Jesus' ministry. The writing style is poor. Stories are often pasted together with little transition or connection.

Mark presents Jesus as the Messiah who is most of all the Son of Man. Every time that someone is prepared to proclaim Jesus as the Messiah, Jesus silences him. Rather, he says that he is the Son of Man. This title is derived from two Old Testament sources: Daniel 7 where the Son of Man would receive power and authority and dominion, and the Songs of the Suffering Servant in Isaiah where the servant of the Lord would suffer in order to expiate our sins.

The disciples of Jesus and his own family do not fully understand his mission until after the resurrection. Three times Jesus predicts his passion (chapters 8, 9, and 10), and three times the disciples respond inappropriately because they understand his role of being Messiah in terms of power and not in terms of service.

Even the resurrection scene presents this message. The shorter ending (ends at 16:8) speaks of the women hearing about the resurrection but not seeing Jesus themselves. This was most probably the original ending to the Gospel. Mark's message, especially to the Church of Rome that was undergoing persecution, was that one does not see the risen Jesus until one has died with him.

There are relatively few parables in the Gospel (only chapter 4, the parables on the kingdom). There is a further chapter of teaching in chapter 13, which speaks about the coming apocalyptic era when God will judge the earth.

Many of the expressions heard and the scenes portrayed show Jesus as embarrassingly human. The other Synoptic Gospels, Matthew and Luke, tend to modify that material to show Jesus as more dignified and more divine.

GOSPEL OF LUKE

We believe that the Gospel of Luke was written around 80-85 A.D. Tradition holds that it was written by Luke, a Gentile convert and disciple of Paul. He is also traditionally said to have been a physician. All of this is credible considering the content and the style of the Gospel.

Like the Gospel of Matthew, Luke begins with the story of the infancy of Jesus. There are actually a pair of annunciation and birth stories: that of John the Baptist, which is miraculous, and that of Jesus, which is even more astounding.

Throughout Luke's Gospel Jesus reaches out to the poorest of the poor, the "anawim."

This phrase means the poor ones of Yahweh. Jewish authorities in the time of Jesus looked with disdain upon the poor for they did not study or observe the law. Jesus, on the other hand, considered them the chosen of God. They could not rely upon their own resources, so they had to rely upon the grace of God to survive. This made them ready to accept the message of God whenever it was addressed to them, and especially when it came in the person of Jesus.

The poor in this Gospel are those who are physically poor, but also those who are spiritually poor or excluded from society for any reason. Thus, Jesus reaches out to sinners, to foreigners, to women, etc. The first to hear of his birth were the shepherds (this was not an honorable occupation at the time of the birth of Jesus) and the last was the good thief on the cross.

Jesus invited these people to experience salvation. Salvation is a present reality, for the minute we meet Jesus and encounter his love, we are already saved.

Jesus speaks of how God reaches out to the sinner and rejoices when that person turns from sin. Many of the parables that are specific to this Gospel are centered on that theme.

For Luke, the city of Jerusalem holds a special importance for it is the holy city where God's will would be manifested in the death and resurrection of Jesus. Thus, the Gospel begins in Jerusalem, and Jesus is on journey toward Jerusalem for most of the Gospel (from 9:51). Then in the Acts of the Apostles, the Gospel message spreads from Jerusalem (the spiritual center of the world) to Rome (the political center of the world).

This is also the Gospel of prayer. The other Synoptic Gospels speak of Jesus praying a couple of times, but this Gospel tells of eleven episodes in which he prayed. The purpose of Jesus' prayer was to discern the will of the Father so that he might be obedient to it. One of the ways that Jesus saves us is that he teaches how we can be obedient to the will of God so that the disobedience of the first sin might be repaired. Jesus also speaks of praying for those things that are needed with insistence (e.g., the parable of the widow who insists upon her rights from the judge).

GOSPEL OF JOHN

John is the only Gospel that is not considered to be a Synoptic Gospel. The word synoptic means that one is seeing the story from one point of view. The Gospel of John sees the Jesus story from a very different point of view than the other Gospels.

There are fewer miracles in this Gospel and they are never called miracles. They are always signs that point to a greater reality, the depth of the Father's love for us.

This is why Jesus came to earth, to reveal to us how much God loves us. When we recognize this love, we can turn from our sins and experience the life of God, which is so profound that even death cannot affect it.

There is only one sin in this Gospel: not to believe Jesus is the Son of God. All other sins and commandments are derived from this.

Throughout the Gospel we see the beloved disciple who most perfectly follows the will of the Father by loving Jesus with a profound love. The other disciples of Jesus, and especially the apostles, do not succeed as well. Peter often appears in the same scenes as the beloved disciple, but he always falls short of that disciple's faith response.

The prologue, the beginning of the Gospel, is a beautiful poem that the author of this Gospel borrowed and adapted to speak of Jesus as one who pre-existed even before he was born in Bethlehem. He is the word through whom the world was created, and the wisdom that instructed the people of Israel.

The Last Supper Discourse is an extended collection of teachings that instruct the community on the relationship between the

Father and Jesus, between them and the disciples, and on who the Paraclete is, etc.

The beautiful bread of life discourse lies at the very heart of the Gospel. It is not the mid-way point in terms of material, but it is the fourth of seven signs that appear in the Gospel. The Eucharist was the central Sacrament for this community and the very meaning of who they were as a community. In this discourse we hear that the bread of life is the very flesh of Jesus. The word flesh is the same word that is used in the prologue to say that the Word became human. Thus, the author is stating that whatever Jesus became in the incarnation, that is what the Eucharist is.

At the Last Supper Jesus further instructs the disciples upon the meaning of the Eucharist when he washes their feet. Eucharist is also Jesus serving us and we being called to serve each other.

Many of the scenes throughout the Gospel are written in symbolic language and can be understood fully only when one understands the key to the symbolic interpretation. For example, the abundance of wine at the wedding feast of Cana is due to the fact that Jesus was preparing his own messianic banquet where he would marry the Church.

There are a number of characters who appear only in this Gospel, e.g., Nathanael and Nicodemus. There are also characters whom we know only by a title and not by their name, e.g., the Samaritan woman at the well, the man born blind, etc.

This is the only Gospel that most emphasizes the divinity of Jesus. He knows all things. He is in control of everything from beginning to end. He is the pre-existent Word of God. When people ask him who he is, he often responds with a phrase that begins, "I am," in order to mirror the name Yahweh. Even when he is being arrested and he inquires whom his would-be captors are seeking and they respond, "Jesus of Nazareth," Jesus simply answers, "I am." This response causes them to fall on the ground, for they are in the presence of the living God.

ACTS OF THE APOSTLES

The Acts of the Apostles is the second volume of a two-volume work written by Luke. The first volume was the Gospel of Luke and this told of the ministry of Jesus while he resided in this world in the flesh. The second volume tells of the ministry of Jesus that the Spirit of God guided through the actions of the apostles.

The first part of the book emphasizes the actions of Peter and the other apostles who resided in Jerusalem, and the latter part of the book centers on the missionary journeys of Paul.

In the first chapter we hear Jesus tell the apostles that they must give witness to the Gospel in Jerusalem, in Judea, and in Samaria, and to the ends of the earth. This list serves as a short table of contents for Acts. We hear how the Gospel began in Jerusalem (the religious center of the world) and in the last chapters we hear how the Gospel reaches the ends of the earth (Rome, the political center of the world).

It is absolutely clear that all missionary activities are guided by the Holy Spirit. It is the Spirit who gives the apostles the courage to first proclaim the Gospel message on the day of Pentecost. It is the Spirit who leads them to accept Cornelius into the community. The Spirit guides Paul wherever he goes, etc.

The book does not close with the martyrdom of Paul in Rome. Many have asked why. The most obvious reason is that this book is not about Paul. It is about the preaching of the Good News, and when that teaching reached Rome, the narrative was complete.

Some of the details of the book are questionable historically. We know this because they contradict what Paul says in his own letters. It is possible that Luke did not have a full account of all that happened, and whenever he ran short of material, he still provided a story. Nevertheless, the majority of details in the book are at least credible, and sometimes even affirmed by what is found in Paul's letters.

Luke shows a tremendous prejudice toward order and comradeship within the community. He deemphasizes difficulties and speaks of the harmony of the early Christian community (2:43-47 and 4:32-37). He was trying to win converts from among the Gentiles, and so he tried to show them the community in its best light. Even he, though, cannot ignore the difficulties in chapter 6, which led to the naming of the seven Greek-speaking disciples to do the work of the diaconate, and the confusion over what obligations the Gentile converts had toward the law of Israel (chapter 15).

ROMANS

The Letter to the Romans is one of Paul's last, if not his last letter. He was writing to a community that he had not founded and that he had never visited.

Paul was planning to visit Jerusalem within the near future. He was carrying the proceeds of a collection that he had made in Greece and Asia Minor to help the poor of the mother Church. Yet he was worried, for many rumors had been spread about his teachings and especially about his attitude toward Judaism.

Therefore, he wrote to the community at Rome to explain his teaching concerning faith and salvation. The reasoning was that, since that community had been founded by missionaries from Jerusalem, they could communicate to that Church that Paul was really not teaching things contrary to the faith.

There is an overall Jewish tenor to the letter from its first words. Paul speaks of Jesus being a fulfillment of the promises of the prophets and having descended according to the flesh from King David.

Throughout the first chapters he argues that we are all worthy of God's condemna-

tion, both Jew and Gentile. We have all sinned, and we are all subject to the wrath of God. But God has responded to our plight with incredible mercy. God, through the death and resurrection of his Son, has ransomed us from sin and called us into the liberty of the children of God.

Later in the letter he speaks of the fate of those Jews who had not yet converted. Paul says that they are subject to disobedience for a good reason, for they have been removed from the tree of the people of God for a while so that the Gentiles who believed in Jesus might be grafted on to that tree. His future hope was that the Jews would then become jealous and would themselves accept Jesus.

Paul also speaks of the proper attitude toward civil authorities. They have received their commission from the Lord, so they should be respected and obeyed.

The letter closes with a long list of people who are to be greeted. Scholars have often wondered where this list originated, for Paul did not know the members of this community. It is now believed that this might be part of a covering letter for a copy of the Letter to the Romans that Paul sent to another community (possibly Ephesus, for many of the people mentioned are associated with that region).

FIRST CORINTHIANS

The First Letter to the Corinthians was a letter written to a community that was deeply troubled by divisions and heretical tendencies.

When Paul arrived in Corinth, he was only one of many preachers proclaiming a new religion from the East. Most of the other religions had ecstatic tendencies in which the believer would seek to be possessed by the spirits of the gods. From the tenor of this letter, it would seem that some in the community interpreted Paul's message in this same manner.

They claimed that they had received a special revelation from the Holy Spirit that was superior to any human teaching. This led to factionalism in the community, for one group felt itself superior to the others. It led to problems of sexual immorality, for the adherents of this belief either practiced an attitude that they were spiritual creatures and it did not matter what they did in the flesh (licentiousness) or stated that they were spiritual creatures and they should never have anything to do with the flesh (absolute abstemiousness).

There were difficulties concerning the eating of meat offered to idols. Most meat sold in the markets had previously been offered to pagan idols. Could a Christian eat it? The response that the problem makers gave was that since the pagan god did not really exist, they could do whatever they wanted. Paul responded that while that was true, they might be giving poor example, especially to those whose consciences were weak.

There were problems in the celebration of the Lord's Supper. At this time the entire Passover meal was celebrated at the Eucharist, but some in the community had little to eat while others had too much. Paul spoke to them of the fact that the Eucharist is communion both with Jesus and with each other. By not practicing charity, they were sinning against the Eucharist.

There were problems with speaking in tongues, a practice in which one allows the Holy Spirit to speak through oneself. Unfortunately, some vaunted their ability to speak in tongues, even disrupting services in the community. Paul gave clear instructions on how this gift should be used.

Finally, there were some who denied the bodily resurrection. They wanted to be entirely spiritual, so they rejected the idea that they would regain their body at the resurrection. Paul responded that if Jesus did not rise from the dead, then we are the most pitiable of creatures.

An important teaching is found in chapter 3, verses 10-15. This is one of the few places in the New Testament where there is a teaching on the existence of Purgatory.

SECOND CORINTHIANS

The Second Letter to the Corinthians is a continuation of the discussion begun in First Corinthians. The first nine chapters are an attempt by Paul to reconcile with the community. He felt that the difficulties had gone on long enough, and those who had been responsible for the problems had repented from their evil ways.

The last four chapters are an angry denunciation of the troublemakers.

Scholars now believe that the last four chapters were actually a letter written before the first nine chapters. In those nine chapters, in fact, he refers to an earlier angry letter, which could well be the last chapters of what is now Second Corinthians. Because the letters were copied from papyri to scrolls, it is possible that a scribe simply made a mistake in the order of the chapters and inverted them. This makes even more sense when one considers the fact that toward the end of the first nine chapters Paul asks the Corinthians to be generous in a collection that he is gathering for the community in Jerusalem. It would be very odd to ask for money and then berate the community for four chapters.

There is even a fragment toward the end of chapter six and the beginning of chapter seven (6:14—7:1) that scholars believe might be from a letter that preceded the present First Letter to the Corinthians. In First Corinthians Paul speaks of an earlier correspondence in which he had given them rules concerning how they should interact with nonbelievers. The verses mentioned above do not fit in their present context and speak of the very things that Paul said he spoke of in that first letter.

This would mean that Second Corinthians is actually composed of fragments of at least three letters. It also means that Paul had to write at least four letters to this community to address their difficulties, an indication of how deeply ingrained they were. Saint Clement of Rome, the fourth Pope, wrote them again toward the end of the first century to discuss the exact same difficulties that Paul addressed all throughout his Corinthians correspondence.

The most beautiful image presented in this letter is that in which Paul speaks of the ministers of the Gospel being earthen vessels that contain a great treasure, the Gospel message they are sharing.

GALATIANS

The Letter to the Galatians was one of the most difficult letters Paul wrote. He was writing to a community that had fallen into error, and throughout the letter there is a sense of anger and fear.

Galatians, unlike Paul's other letters, is not addressed to one community. Galatia was a region, and Paul was writing to all of the small Christian communities dispersed throughout that region.

He had preached the Gospel to them, and many had converted to the faith. The vast majority of those who converted were pagans.

Sometime later, a group of Jewish-Christian missionaries arrived from Jerusalem. They undercut Paul's teaching by saying that Paul had preached an "easy" Gospel to them. Paul had told them that it was not necessary to be circumcised or to follow Jewish law after they had been baptized. Remember that when one was baptized, one was really becoming a Jew who believed in the Messiah whom Yahweh had sent. They said that Paul had only tried to buy their favor.

Many in the community favored adopting Jewish ways. Paul wrote them to admonish them severely. He told them that they were liberated from their sins not by Jewish customs, but by the death and resurrection of Jesus. Their sins had already been washed away in their Baptism. If they adopted Jewish ways, it meant that they did not suffi-

ciently trust in this message and that they did not have faith.

Paul adopted a very Jewish way of presenting this message. It is called Midrash, a type of rabbinic argumentation. In Midrash, one takes a verse from Scripture and combines it with a similar verse from another place to produce a third meaning. This is not often used today, especially in Christian circles, but in Paul's day it was accepted as the proper way to argue Jewish questions.

Paul also gives an account of the "Council of Jerusalem," a meeting between Paul (and his disciples) and the apostles that occurred in Jerusalem sometime during the middle to the late 40's. At that meeting, they reached the decision that pagans did not have to follow Jewish law if they converted to Christianity.

EPHESIANS

Colossians and Ephesians are two letters that are related (for they have many expressions in common). They are both attributed to Paul, but it is possible that he did not write either. There are phrases and situations described in the letters that cause some scholars to doubt their Pauline origin.

The author begins the letter with a hymn that praises Jesus and that proclaims that all existing things are to be put under Christ's headship in the fullness of time. As in Colossians, even heavenly powers are said to be subject to the authority of Jesus.

Paul's other letters speak of the fact that there is no importance if one is Jew or Gentile; this letter goes further and says that Jews and Gentiles have been made into one people through the death and resurrection of Christ.

Ephesians presents a developed theology of the Church as the body of Christ. In the course of his discussion on the Church, Paul speaks of the union of Christ and the Church in terms of something that is as intimate as the marriage union between a husband and a wife. This is a much more positive portrait of marriage than we find in Paul's other letters where marriage is something that must be done to avoid sin.

Much of the second part of the letter is an exhortation to live according to the values that give witness to the love of God in daily life. Christians are to combat vice and the powers of evil and live a totally blameless life. As in Colossians, there is an instruction on proper conduct within families and between slaves and masters, although this particular version is more elaborate.

PHILIPPIANS

The Letter to the Philippians is one of Paul's last and most intimate letters. He is writing from prison, and the fact that he faced possible death colors many of the thoughts he includes in this communication. He speaks of the necessity to make peace in the community. He tells the community that he does not know whether he will live or die, but that it does not make all that much difference because if he lives, he will preach and work for the Lord, but if he dies he will be with the Lord. He speaks about his conversion and how he changed his way of looking at things. The very things that he had previously considered most important were now considered to be rubbish in light of knowing and loving the Lord.

Chapter 2 contains a beautiful hymn that speaks of Jesus and his humility. Jesus, who was in the form of God (this means that he was God), gave up the prerogatives of his state to serve us by dying on the cross. God responded to this sacrifice by proclaiming him Lord of all of creation.

COLOSSIANS

Colossians and Ephesians are two letters that are related (for many expressions are in common). They are both attributed to Paul, but it is possible that he did not write either. There are expressions and situations described in the letters that cause some scholars to doubt their Pauline origin.

This letter's author speaks of Jesus in whom the fullness of divinity dwells. He is the visible likeness of the invisible God. All creatures, even those that are spiritual, are subject to him. This is important, for Greek philosophy taught that the more spiritual a creature was, the more it resembled God. Angels were totally spiritual creatures, while Jesus was incarnate. Some thought that this meant that the angels were superior to Jesus. This letter insists on Christians not worshiping angels, and on the fact that Jesus is far superior to them. Some types of behavior are condemned that seem to have originated in Jewish practices.

The letter closes with an instruction on how members of families and the community should treat one another and also with some information about Paul's travels and ministry. It is interesting that Mark is spoken of in positive terms, for Acts had spoken of a rift between Mark and Paul after he abandoned Paul on a missionary journey.

FIRST THESSALONIANS

The First Letter to the Thessalonians is most probably the first letter that Paul wrote. He was writing to a community that was very successful in turning from their previous errors to the truth of the Gospel. Paul even speaks of the faith of the Thessalonians being famous throughout the entire world.

This is actually one of the problems that Paul had to address. They were so successful that they started to become boastful, thinking that they had arrived at success through their own efforts. He writes an extensive thanksgiving (the entire first three chapters of this letter) to remind them that their success is a gift from the Lord.

In these chapters he speaks of the rapport that exists among the missionaries, the community, and God. The relationship between the missionaries and the Thessalonians is critical, for they learned about their faith through them. Yet the missionaries could never have preached if the Lord had not called them and given them the courage to proclaim the Gospel, and the Thessalonians could never have accepted their message if the Spirit of the Lord had not prompted their hearts to listen to the missionaries and interpret their message as the word of God. Our faith has both a horizontal and a vertical dimension.

The last chapters speak of the end times. Paul teaches in chapter 4 that on the last day those who have died will rise from the dead to be with the Lord, while those who are still alive will not have to die. They will be "caught up into the clouds." This particular expression should not be interpreted literally. It was simply Paul's way of expressing the fact that they would be with the Lord in heaven.

Finally, the last chapter talks about when the return of the Lord would occur (we do not know, so we should always be ready) and how we must combat against evil with the armor of the virtues.

SECOND THESSALONIANS

Second Thessalonians is one of the letters attributed to St. Paul. Many modern scholars doubt this attribution because of the dissimilarities in language and theology between it and First Thessalonians. Eschatology is one of the major themes of the letter. Paul warns the community not to be fooled by those who claim to foretell the end of the world. He also speaks of a mysterious figure whom he calls "the liar."

FIRST TIMOTHY

This is one of the Pastoral Epistles. The authorship is in doubt, for though it purports to have been written by St. Paul, its language and theology is different from that found in Paul's authentic letters.

This letter contains a warning concerning the false teachers who were troubling the community. There are a number of pastoral recommendations (e.g., present-ing the attributes of bishops and deacons, outlining proper relationships within families, etc.). Many of the teachings are based upon Stoic ideas concerning the proper ways to do things. The author of this letter was very concerned with giving good witness in whatever one did.

SECOND TIMOTHY

Second Timothy is one of the Pastoral Epistles. It is supposedly sent to Timothy, a convert whose father was pagan but whose mother was Jewish. Paul had him circumcised because he was technically Jewish since one obtained one's Jewishness through the mother.

This letter is purported to be Paul's last instruction to Timothy before he was martyred (it is doubtful that Paul actually wrote this letter). He wants to encourage him and instruct him that his own and Timothy's sufferings are a share in the suffering of Christ.

Paul speaks of the need to give witness, especially in what he calls the end times. He also warns Timothy concerning certain individuals who were spreading heresy.

This is one of the few writings in the Bible that speak of inspiration of these sacred texts (3:14-17).

TITUS

The Letter to Titus is one of the three Pastoral letters. It is attributed to Paul, although many scholars believe that it was probably written by one of his disciples. Titus, the recipient, was a pagan who was baptized by Paul. He accompanied Paul to the Council of Jerusalem. At the time he received this letter, he was a bishop and organizer of the Church in Crete.

The letter speaks of the qualifications that leaders of the Church should possess. It gives instructions on the proper way for Christians to act in family and in the community. It warns the reader not to become involved in silly arguments about questions of faith.

PHILEMON

This is the only undisputed letter of St. Paul to be written to an individual. Paul writes to Philemon, asking him to welcome his returning slave Onesimus. That slave had been with Paul in prison and had converted to the faith. Although Paul does not specifically ask for the release of the slave, he seems to imply this course of action.

HEBREWS

Paul's Letter to the Hebrews is not written by Paul, it is not a letter, and it is not intended for the Hebrews.

This treatise was written by an anonymous author in the middle of the first century A.D. The author is a Jewish-Christian who was trying to convince a community of Jewish-Christians that they could abandon many of their old Jewish ways because Jesus was their high priest.

The argumentation is strange to us, and is based upon Greek philosophy and Jewish Midrash interpretations. The main theme drawn from Greek philosophy is that of form and matter. A form is the ideal representation of an object, while the matter is the concrete representation of that thing. The form is perfect, for it represents all exemplars of a particular thing, while matter is imperfect for it represents only the one thing that it is (e.g., the idea of a book versus a real book).

Jesus was the "form" while all the other priests of the Old Testament were the "matter." Jesus was one and perfect. The priests of the Old Testament were imperfect, and they therefore had to be many.

The Jewish Midrash argument is that if one can say something that is true about a lesser creature, then one can say that it is much more true about a greater creature. The rabbis often spoke of how kings were this or that, and how the king of kings, Yahweh, was so much greater. The author of this treatise speaks of the worship of the Old Testament and how it was this or that, while the worship inaugurated by Jesus was far superior.

The "letter" closes with an admonition to live with greater faith and obedience to God the Father. Faith is described as being assurance about the things hoped for and conviction about the things not seen.

JAMES

The Letter of James is attributed to James, the brother (cousin) of the Lord Jesus.

The central argument of the letter is that we must live our commitment of faith in the Lord in our everyday lives. We cannot say we have faith and then treat the poor with disdain or ignore their need.

The letter speaks of the blessedness of those who undergo trials and therefore whose faith is proven real.

James warns against using the tongue to create divisions within the community. He speaks of it as a small organ in the body, yet one that can cause the greatest of difficulties.

He condemns arrogance and boasting, presumption and avarice. Toward the end of the letter he speaks of those who are ill and who should seek an anointing from the elders of the community (the Scriptural basis for the Sacrament of Anointing).

FIRST PETER

Some scholars question whether First Peter was written by the prince of the apostles, but there are no convincing arguments that would make us reject Peter's authorship.

The letter speaks of the dignity that has been conferred upon us Christians through the Sacrament of Baptism. We have been made a holy race chosen by the Lord, a royal priesthood. We must live that holiness by choosing a virtuous life.

We are to live an ordered life-style, obeying the proper authorities. Our families should be examples of virtue lived out on an everyday basis.

Peter exhorts the reader not to become discouraged by suffering, for Christ himself suffered. He also says that it would be better to suffer unjustly (when we do not deserve it) than to be punished for what we have done.

In chapter 3 Peter speaks of how Jesus preached to the souls of those who had died and invited them into heaven. This is the Scriptural basis for our belief that Jesus descended into the underworld after his death to invite into heaven all of those who had never heard of him.

Peter closes the letter by charging the leaders of the Church to be honest and gentle in their care of the flock. He also encourages younger men to obey their elders with humility.

SECOND PETER

While the author of this letter claims to be Peter the Apostle, it is almost surely written by an anonymous author (most probably a Hellenistic Jew). The major theme of the letter is that the delay of the parousia does not mean that it will not occur. Some heretical movements proclaimed that there would be no final judgment. The author uses his claim of apostolic authority to show that both the second coming and the final judgment are revealed truth.

The letter was probably written at the end of the first century A.D. or the beginning of the second century. It was accepted into the canon at a relatively late date (the 4th century A.D.). Even in the earliest days of the Church its authorship was an open question.

FIRST JOHN

Ironically, the First Letter of John is not a letter. This becomes clear when one observes that it does not have the formal opening and closing that one would expect in a Greek letter, nor does it speak of what is going on in either the writer's or recipients' life as one would expect to see in a letter.

It is a treatise written sometime after the publication of the Gospel of John. Because that Gospel portrayed Jesus as totally divine, knowing and controlling everything all throughout his ministry, it was a bit suspect by the early Christian community. They were being assailed by a heresy called Docetism, which denied the humanity of Jesus. Some thought that this Gospel was suspiciously similar to the Docetist teachings.

Thus, the author of this letter emphasizes the humanity of Jesus. The prologue to the letter mirrors the prologue to the Gospel of John, but while the Gospel's prologue spoke of the Word that existed forever in the presence of God, the letter's prologue speaks of the Word of God that became so incarnate that we observed it, spoke with it, touched it, etc.

The other major point that this letter makes is that one must observe the commandments if one wants to be called a disciple of Jesus. The Gospel of John taught that there was really only one commandment: to believe that Jesus was the only-begotten Son of God. The theory was that if one believed this, one would live a life compatible with that belief. It was what Saint Augustine said when he taught us that we should love God and do what we would.

The problem was that some members of the community did what they wanted, which was not always moral. When they were questioned on it, they would proclaim that they were living in the freedom of the Sons of God and that they were anointed by the Holy Spirit, so no one should be questioning their conduct.

This letter calls them liars, for one cannot sin and still live in the light. By sinning, one has already chosen the darkness. Furthermore, if one loves God, one must love God's children, one's own brothers and sisters in the community.

The letter also defines God as love, and it states that if anyone wants to live in God, that person must live in love. It gives an important observation by stating that it is not that we have loved God first. God has loved us first and taught us the true meaning of love. We can only respond to this incredible generosity on the part of God.

BOOK OF REVELATION

The Book of Revelation is the only apocalyptic book to be part of the New Testament. Between 200 B.C. and 200 A.D., several apocalyptic books were written in Jewish and Christian communities. They all have certain things in common.

All apocalyptic books speak of two world eras: the present evil era and the coming age when God will reign upon the earth. This is their major difference with prophetic books. Prophetic books call people to conversion, for if they convert, God might remit their punishment. In apocalyptic books, things have progressed too far. There must be a cataclysmic change to purify the world from its perfidy.

Apocalyptic books also have extensive symbolism. Colors, numbers, animals, clothing, battles between angels and the forces of evil, etc., are all part of their symbolic matrix.

For example, numbers are important throughout most of these books. Ten stands for a fairly large amount, but seven stands for perfection (for ancient peoples believed that there were seven planets, and thus to say seven was to say the entire universe). Therefore, in their thinking, seven designated a number that was larger than ten. One thousand was considered an indefinite sum but a very large number.

Twelve symbolized both the number of the tribes of Israel and the number of the apostles. Thus, twelve times twelve times one thousand, or one hundred and forty-four thousand, stood for the Old and the New Israel, which the Lord had blessed with incredible fecundity (the meaning of the 1,000).

The Book of Revelation is not so much about when the end times will occur. Rather, it is a call to witness while one awaits the end times (remember the word witness in Greek is "martureo," for many will be called to martyrdom in order to give witness to the Gospel).

The forces of evil will combat the forces of good throughout history. Jesus defeated those forces on the cross, and we share in that victory every time we take up our cross in order to die with Jesus so that we might live with him forever.

APPENDIX 2: THE RESPONSORIAL PSALM*

In his final recorded appearance to the apostles before his Ascension, Jesus spoke of what was written about him in "the Law, the Prophets, and the Psalms" (Luke 24:44). Hence, the Church has always indicated, especially through the Liturgy, that there is a history of Christ in the Psalms.

Each Sunday in the Responsorial Psalm at Mass, the liturgical assembly is invited to read a page of this history. In doing so, every one of us can discern some aspect of Jesus and hear his voice on a matter of importance to us.

However, in order for this result to be attained we must participate fully, consciously, and actively in the Responsorial Psalm, which occurs after the First Reading in the Liturgy of the Word.

Liturgists tell us that the Responsorial Psalm together with the Alleluia Acclamation before the Gospel is the most important part of the people in the Proper of the Mass for it functions as a kind of commentary on the Scriptures just proclaimed. It draws the soul to arrive at the interpretation of the Reading intended by the Church.

Indeed, the Responsorial Psalm is the only psalm used at Mass for its own sake rather than to accompany an action. It is the Word of God. That is why the Church insists that it may never be replaced by a nonbiblical text.

However, it is evident that in many cases, the people do not even know what is happening as the Responsorial Psalm goes flitting by during the celebration. This is even truer when the Responsorial Psalm is sung by the cantor with only a Refrain relegated to the people.

What is needed is to make information available to all about the function of this part of Mass, so that they will be able to take advantage of the music and the words to enter into the theme of response. The following observations may be of help in this respect.

CANTICLE OF THE COVENANT

Throughout the history of the Church, which is the people of God (in figure in the Old Testament and in fulfillment in the New), we find a pattern. God "speaks" to his people by accomplishing wondrous deeds for them. The people respond by celebrating these wondrous deeds.

God guides the people of the Exodus across the Red Sea. Miriam, following the lead of Moses her brother, celebrates the Lord who has cast horse and rider into the sea (Exodus 15:1, 21).

God delivers Hannah from her sterility by giving her a son, Samuel. Hannah responds by celebrating the Lord who enables a sterile woman to give birth (1 Samuel 2:5).

God delivers Tobit from blindness. Tobit responds by celebrating the Lord who lets his light rise over Jerusalem as well as in the hearts of his people (Tobit 13:11).

In New Testament times, God blesses Mary's virginity by letting her become the Mother of Jesus. Mary responds by glorifying the Lord and exulting in God her Savior, in Jesus whom she is bearing (Luke 1:46-55).

In accord with these examples, the Responsorial Psalm plays a similar role in the liturgical celebration. The Word proclaimed recalls God's wondrous deeds of old. The assembly celebrates these wondrous deeds and actualizes them in the celebration. It responds to the God of these wonders with the Responsorial Psalm.

The Word proclaimed is the word of the Covenant. The Responsorial Psalm is the canticle of the Covenant. It prepares for the Covenant, and asks God to keep us in it.

THE PSALTER: THE CHRISTIAN PRAYER BOOK

In order to sing the Responsorial Psalm well, we should get to know something about the Book of Psalms or Psalter. It has become the book of Christian prayer, the compendium of the entire biblical message.

According to St. Thomas Aquinas, the Psalter—in contrast to the other biblical writings—"embraces in its universality the matter of all of theology. The reason why this biblical book is the one most used in the Church is that it contains in itself all Scripture. Its characteristic note is to restate, under the form of praise, all that the other biblical books express by way of narrative, exhortation, and discussion.

"The purpose of the Psalter is to make people pray, to elevate souls to God through contemplation of his infinite majesty, through meditation on the excellence of eternal happiness, and through communion in the holiness of God and the efficacious imitation of his perfection" (*Exposition on the Psalms of David*).

The Psalms have been called with good reason "a school of Christian prayer." These sacred songs cover a wide range of human experiences; they bring out our strengths and weaknesses, faith and wonderment, joys and sorrows.

The Psalms also show forth the prophesied glory of Jesus: for it is only in Christ that their full significance is revealed. The noted Bible scholar Joseph Gelineau has written that Jesus "personally described himself as the Lord whom God seated at his right hand (Psalm 110 - Matthew 22:44); as the

*Reprinted with permission from *Active Participation at Mass* by Anthony M. Buono, pp. 65-72, © 1994 by Alba House.

stone rejected by the builders which became the head of the corner (Psalm 118 - Matthew 21:42); as he who comes, blessed in the name of the Lord (Psalm 118 - Matthew 23:39); he personally applied to himself on the cross the appeal of the persecuted psalmist (Psalm 22 - Matthew 27:46) and his prayer of trust (Psalm 31 - Luke 23:46)."

Thus, the Psalms set forth Christ's lowly coming to earth, then his kingly and priestly power, and finally his beneficent labors and the shedding of his Blood for our redemption. So Christological are they that they have rightly been termed "the Gospel according to the Holy Spirit." It is the Holy Spirit who inserted in them indisputable references to the life of Christ.

POETIC QUALITIES OF THE PSALMS

The Psalms are among the world's best poetry. We all know "The Lord Is My Shepherd," but there are a host of others among the 150 Psalms that are just as classical.

The poetry of the Psalms contains rhythm, which is the recurrence of accented or unaccented syllables at regular intervals. But its outstanding trait is parallelism, which consists in the equal distribution or balance of thought in the various lines of each verse.

Synonymous parallelism is the repetition of the same thought with equivalent expressions:

"He who is throned in heaven laughs;
the Lord derides them."

Antithetic parallelism expresses a thought by contrast with an opposite:

"For the Lord watches over the way of the just,
but the way of the wicked vanishes."

Synthetic parallelism occurs when a second line completes the thought of the first by giving a comparison:

"When I call out to the Lord,
he answers me from his holy mountain,
when I lie down in sleep,
I wake again, for the Lord sustains me."

By paying attention to the poetic aspect of the Psalms, we will be able to recite or sing the Responsorial Psalm with more understanding and greater participation.

PRAYING THE RESPONSORIAL PSALM

The Psalms are not readings or prose prayers, even though on occasion they may be recited as readings. In Hebrew they were called "Songs of praise" and in Greek *Psalmoi*, that is, "Songs to be sung to the lyre." All the Psalms have a musical quality that dictates the correct way of delivering them.

Even when a Psalm is recited and not sung, its delivery must still be governed by its musical char-

acter. A Psalm presents a text to the minds of those singing it and listening to it, but it aims at moving their hearts.

In order to pray the Psalms with understanding, we must meditate on them verse by verse, with our hearts ready to respond in the way the Holy Spirit desires. As the one who inspired the Psalmists, the Holy Spirit is always present to those who in faith and love are ready to receive his grace.

Indeed, the singing of the Responsorial Psalm expresses the reverence that is due to God's majesty. But it should also be the expression of a joyful spirit and a loving heart, in keeping with its character as sacred poetry and inspired song and above all in keeping with the freedom of the children of God.

The Responsorial Psalm is a different prayer from one composed by the Church. The inspired Psalmist often addresses the people as he recalls the history of God's people; sometimes he addresses creation; and at other times he even introduces a dialogue between God and the people.

In praying the Psalm we should open our hearts to the different attitudes that may be expressed, which vary with the type of writing to which it belongs (Psalms of Grief or Trust or Gratitude and the like). Although the Psalms originated many centuries ago in the East, they express accurately the pain and hope, the unhappiness and trust, of every people and every age and country, and celebrate especially faith in God, revelation, and redemption.

In the words of another renowned Scripture scholar, Andre Choracqui, "We were born with this book [of Psalms] in our very bones. A small book; 150 poems; 150 steps between death and life; 150 mirrors of our rebellions and our loyalties, of our agonies and our resurrections."

The Psalms have great power to raise minds to God, to inspire devotion, to evoke gratitude in favorable times, and to bring consolation and strength in sad times. They constitute an inexhaustible treasury of prayers for every occasion and mood in a format that is true to the whole tradition of the History of Salvation.

Thus, we should strive to pray the Responsorial Psalm with the best of intentions both at home and at Mass. It will then become for us an opportunity to rediscover our own humanity, in its anguish, its rebellion, its violence, and its reconciliation as well.

It will become for us an opportunity to rediscover more broadly the whole of history, for example, those men and women who also struggle, who suffer, who cry out, who hope, and who pray in the four corners of the earth.

Finally, it will become for us an opportunity to encounter Christ mysteriously present in the heart of this humankind in which we find ourselves.

APPENDIX 3: GLOSSARY AND PRONUNCIATION GUIDE

For purposes of pronunciation, a simple system of phonetic spelling has been devised and included in parentheses for every entry defined. The **accented syllable** is indicated by **capital letters,** and the pronunciation for the letters is as follows.

uh = a, e, i, o, u unaccented (the Schwa)	**o** = odd (short)	**yoo** = use, unite (accented, long)
a = hat	**oh** = no	**uhr** = further
ah = father	**oi** = noise, joy	**ch** = church
ai = aisle, ice	**ow** = cow	**sh** = shame, wish
aw = awful, for	**oo** = boot	**zh** = vision
ay = ape, care	**u** = foot, book (accented, long)	**g** = get
e = get (short)	**uh** = culture, cut (accented, short)	**j** = judge
ee = eve	**yuh** = nature (unaccented, short)	**k** = cow, key
i = pit (short)		**kw** = quick
		w = witch

Aaron (AR-uhn; ER-uhn). Brother of Moses and the first high priest of Israel (Ex 6:20; 28:1ff).

Abba (AB-uh; ah-BAH). Aramaic word for "father" or "dad" used by Jesus of his Father (Mk 14:36).

Abelmoholah (ay-buhl-mi-HOH-luh). A city on the Jordan river and the residence of Elisha the prophet (1 Kgs 19:16).

Abiathar (uh-BAI-uh-thuh). Son of the priest Ahimelech (1 Sm 22:20) and himself a priest of David (2 Sm 8:17). He is mentioned by Jesus in the discussion with the Pharisees concerning the apostles' picking grain on the sabbath (Mk 2:26).

Abijah (uh-BAI-juh). Son and successor of Rehoboam (1 Chr 3:10) and ancestor of Jesus (Mt 1:7).

Abilene (ab-uh-LEEN; -LEE-nee). A district ruled by Lysanias (Lk 3:1) at the time of Jesus that lay to the northwest of Damascus.

Abishai (uh-BAI-shi). A brother of Joab, he accompanied David during his flight from Saul (1 Sm 26:6ff) and from Absalom (2 Sm 16:9).

Abiud (uh-BAI-uhd). An ancestor of Jesus (Mt 1:13).

Abner (AB-nuhr). A commander of the army of Saul (1 Sm 17:55; 26:7). He first sided with a son of Saul, Ishbaal, after the death of Saul. He eventually betrayed him and furthered the cause of David among the tribes of the north.

Abraham (AY-bruh-ham). Founder of the Hebrew nation and father of the people of God (Gn 11:26ff; 17:4f, etc.). Originally called Abram (Gn 11:26), he received the name Abraham at the time of God's covenant with him (Gn 17:4).

Abram (AY-bruhm). *See* **Abraham.**

Achaia (uh-KAI-uh). Roman province comprising the central part of modern Greece (Acts 18:12, 27).

Achim (AY-kim). An ancestor of Jesus (Mt 1:14).

Acts of the Apostles (aks uhv thee uh-POS-uhlz). The book that continues the Gospel of Luke with a history of the primitive Church.

Adam (AD-uhm). The first man (Gn 2:8), who was placed in the garden of Eden (Gn 2:15) but disobeyed God and was expelled from the garden (Gn 3:23).

Advocate (AD-vuh-kut). See *Paraclete.*

Ahaz (AY-haz). Son and successor of King Jotham of Judah (2 Kgs 15:38) and father of Hezekiah (2 Kgs 16:20). It was to him that Isaiah prophesied that the Messiah would be Emmanuel, God with us (Is 7:14).

Alexander (al-ig-ZAN-duhr). Son of Simon of Cyrene and brother of Rufus (Mk 15:21).

Alpha (AL-fuh). First letter of the Greek alphabet. Used with "omega," the last letter, it signifies completeness, as "from A to Z." God is termed the Alpha and Omega, the First and the Last, the Beginning and the End (Rv 1:8), as is also Christ (Rv 22:13).

Alphaeus (al-FEE-uhs). Father of James the Less (Mt 10:3; Acts 1:13).

Amalek (AM-uh-lek). Eponymous founder of a nomadic tribe that dwelt in the Negeb (Gn 36:12). The Amalekites fought with the Israelites during their time in the Sinai (Ex 17:8ff). They also fought various battles against Israel, often in alliance with Israel's enemies.

Amaziah (am-uh-ZAI-uh). A priest at Bethel at the time of the Prophet Amos (Am 7:12).

Amminadab (uh-MIN-uh-dab). Father of Nahshon (Nm 1:7), father-in-law of Aaron (Ex 6:23), and an ancestor of Jesus (Mt 1:4).

Amos (AY-muhs). The third of the 12 minor prophets of the Old Testament, who proclaimed the need for social justice in people's relationships with each other. One of the ancestors of Jesus (Mt 1:10) bears the name Amos, but—as the NAB indicates in a footnote—a better reading is "Amon."

Amoz (AY-muhz). Father of the Prophet Isaiah (Is 2:1).

Ancient One (AYN-chuhnt won). A new translation for the more traditional "Ancient of Days," it is a name of God taken from apocalyptic writings that appears three times in Daniel (7:9, 13, 22).

Andrew (AN-droo). Brother of Peter (Jn 1:40) and one of the twelve apostles (Mt 10:2).

Anna (AN-uh). The aged prophetess who spoke of the coming redemption at Jesus' presentation in the temple (Lk 2:36ff).

Annas (AN-uhs). High priest of Jerusalem (6-15 A.D.), whose office passed to his sons and his son-in-law Caiaphas (Jn 18:13). He was involved in the trials of Jesus (Jn 18:13ff).

Antioch (AN-tee-ok). Name of two cities. Antioch on the Orontes River was the capital of Syria where the disciples of Jesus were first called "Christians" (Acts 11:19-26). Antioch in Pisidia on the border with Phrygia was one of the first cities in which Paul preached (Acts 13:14ff).

Apollos (uh-POL-uhs). An educated Christian Jew from Alexandria, who preached in Ephesus and in Corinth (Acts 18:24—19:1).

Arabia (uh-RAY-bee-uh). Northern part of the peninsula between the Red Sea and the Persian Gulf (Is 21:13) or the entire peninsula (Neh 2:19).

Arabs (AR-uhbz). Inhabitants of Arabia, some of whom were in Jerusalem on the day of Pentecost (Acts 2:11).

Aramean (ar-uh-MEE-uhn). A member of a nomadic people from northern Syria and southern Babylon.

Archelaus (ar-kuh-LAY-uhs). Son of Herod the Great, who became the ruler of Judea, Samaria, and Idumea upon his father's death in 4 B.C.-6 A.D. and was deposed in 6 A.D. (Mt 2:22).

Arimathea (ar-i-muh-THEE-uh). A town in Judah that was the birthplace of Joseph of Arimathea, who buried Jesus in his own tomb (Mk 15:43).

Asaph (AY-saf). A person's name, e.g., a cantor in the temple under David and Solomon to whom Psalms 50 and 73—83 are attributed.

Asher (ASH-uhr). Name of one of the twelve tribes of Israel and of its Patriarch, who was the eighth son of Jacob (Gn 49:20). Anna was from this tribe (Lk 2:36).

Asia (AY-zhuh). The Roman province of Asia, which included only the western third of what is now Asia Minor. Ephesus was its capital and it was evangelized by Paul on his 3rd missionary journey (Acts 18—21).

Attalia (at-uh-LAI-uh). A seaport on the coast of Pamphylia (Asia Minor).

Augustus (uh-GUS-tuhs). Emperor of Rome from 31 B.C. to 14 A.D., during whose reign Jesus was born (Lk 2:1).

Azor (AY-zawr). An ancestor of Jesus (Mt 1:13f).

Baal (BAY-uhl). The chief god of the Phoenicians and Canaanites, worshiped as the god of crops, flocks, and fertility—even by some Israelites (1 Kgs 16:31-33).

Baal-shalishah (BAY-uhl SHAHL-uh-shuh). A place in Ephraim from which bread and corn were brought to Elisha when he was at Gilgal (2 Kgs 3:42-44).

Babel (BAY-buhl). The place where the ancients built a tower to the heavens in arrogance before God (Gn 11:9).

Babylon (BAB-uh-luhn). A city on the Euphrates and the capital of the Babylonian Empire to which the Israelites were exiled in 597 and 587 B.C. (2 Chr 36:20; Ps 137:1). In the New Testament, the name was used as a synonym for Rome (1 Pt 5:13; Rv 14:8; 17:5). *See* **Babylonian Exile.**

Babylonian Exile (ba-buh-LOH-nee-uhn EK-sai-uhl). The period in Jewish history from the carrying away of the people to Babylon in 597 and 587 to their return in 538 B.C. (Mt 1:11).

Barabbas (buh-RAB-uhs). A prisoner whom Pilate released in place of Jesus (Mk 15:6-15).

Barsabbas (bahr-SAB-uhs). Name of two men: (1) Joseph Barsabbas, also called Justus, who was one of the candidates to succeed Judas Iscariot as an apostle (Acts 1:23). (2) The surname of Judas, the prophet, who was sent to Antioch together with Barnabas, Paul, and Silas to communicate the decisions of the Council of Jerusalem to the community there (Acts 15:22-32).

Bartholomew (bahr-THOL-uh-myoo). One of the twelve apostles (Mk 3:18).

Bartimaeus (bahr-tuh-MEE-uhs). A blind beggar from Jericho who was cured by Jesus (Mk 10:46-52).

Baruch (BA-ruhk; buh-ROOk). The prophet Jeremiah's secretary, to whom is ascribed the third of the 18 Prophetic Books of the Old Testament.

Beautiful Gate (bee-YOO-tuh-fuhl gayt). Possibly a gate on the eastern side of the temple where Peter and John healed a paralytic (Acts 3:1-11).

Beelzebul (bee-EL-zee-buhl). Name of the god of Canaan, who in the New Testament is referred to as the prince of demons (Mk 3:22).

Bethany (BETH-uh-nee). A village on the eastern slope of the Mount of Olives (Lk 10:38; Jn 11:1, 18).

Bethlehem (BETH-li-hem). The birthplace of Jesus, a village 4.5 miles south of Jerusalem (Lk 2:4-7).

Bethphage (BETH-fuh-jee). A village east of Bethany mentioned in connection with Jesus' triumphal entry into Jerusalem (Mk 11:1).

Bethsaida (beth-SAY-uh-duh; -SAI-duh). A town on the northern shore of the Sea of Galilee (later called Julia) that was the home of Andrew, Peter, and Philip (Jn 1:44; 12:21).

Boaz (BOH-az). Husband of Ruth (Ru 4:13) and ancestor of Jesus (Mt 1:5f).

Caesar (SEE-zuhr). Surname of Julius Caesar, given from the 1st century onward to the Roman emperors (Lk 2:1; 3:1).

Caesarea (sez-uh-REE-uh). Name of various cities. (1) Caesarea Philippi, a town where Jesus prepared his disciples for his approaching sufferings and death and Peter made his famous confession of Christ's divinity (Mk 8:27). (2) A town where the converted Paul was sent to escape the Hellenists who tried to kill him (Acts 9:30).

Caiaphas (KAY-uh-fuhs; KAI-yuh-fuhs). High priest (18-36 A.D.) and head of the Sanhedrin during the trial of Jesus (Mt 26:57).

Cana (KAY-nuh). Village of Galilee, located north of Nazareth, and site of Jesus' first miracle (Jn 2:1-11).

Canaan (KAY-nuhn). One of the old names for Palestine, the land of the Canaanites who were dispossessed by the Israelites.

Capernaum (kuh-PUHR-nay-uhm). A town on the northwestern shore of the Sea of Galilee where Jesus made his headquarters during his Galilean ministry (Mk 2:1).

Cappadocia (kap-uh-DO-shee-uh). A province in eastern Asia Minor (Acts 2:9).

Carbuncles (KAHR-bun-kuhlz). As used in the Bible, something bright and glittering, possibly rubies or emeralds (Is 54:12).

Carmel (KAHR-mel). A mountain chain and ancient site of worship, often lauded for its beauty (Is 35:2).

Carnelians (kahr-NEL-yuhnz). Hard sparkling reddish quartz used in jewelry (Is 54:11).

Cephas (SEE-fuhs). The name given by Jesus to the apostle Peter (Jn 1:42).

Chaldeans (kal-DEE-uhnz). Members of an Eastern Aramean tribe that beginning in 1100 B.C. invaded Babylon. They are termed ancestors of the Israelites (Jdt 5:6) as a result of the tradition that Abraham came from Ur of the Chaldees (Gn 11:28). In exile the Israelites became servants of the "king of the Chaldeans" (2 Chr 36:20).

Cherubim (CHER-uh-bim). In the Old Testament, these were superhuman beings whose nature was not made explicit. They were regarded as the porters who carry God (Ps 18:11; 80:2) and were a sign of his power, for he was enthroned on the cherubim (1 Sm 4:4; 2 Kgs 19:15). In Christian tradition, they are identified as the second of the nine choirs of angels.

Chloe (KLOH-ee). A woman whose people informed Paul of factions in the Corinthian community (1 Cor 1:11).

Chronicles (KRON-i-kulz). Fifth and sixth of the 17 Historical Books of the Old Testament.

Cilicia (suh-LISH-ee-uh). A region that lay along the southeastern coast of Asia Minor.

Cleopas (KLEE-oh-puhs). One of the disciples with whom Jesus walked on the way to Emmaus and broke bread (Lk 24:18).

Clopas (KLOH-puhs). The husband of Mary of Clopas (Jn 19:25).

Colossians (kuh-LOSH-uhnz). People of Colossae in Phrygia to whom Paul wrote one of the Letters of the New Testament.

Corinth (KOR-inth). Capital of the province of Achaia, and an extremely commercial city, which Paul made the center of his activity in Greece (Acts 18:11).

Corinthians (kuh-RIN-thee-uhnz). Christians of Corinth to whom Paul wrote two of the Letters of the New Testament.

Cornelius (kawr-NEEL-yuhs). A Roman centurion from Caesarea who was baptized by Peter (Acts 10f), showing that the Church was open to pagans as well as Jews.

Cretans (KREE-tans). Inhabitants of Crete, an island in the Mediterranean forming a natural bridge between Europe and Asia Minor, some of whom were in Jerusalem on the day of Pentecost (Acts 2:11).

Cush (koosh). Ethiopia (modern day Sudan).

Cyrene (sai-REEN). A Greek colony in northern Africa, with a large population of Greek-speaking Jews. Many of them were in Jerusalem on the day of Pentecost (Acts 2:10).

Cyrus (SAI-ruhs). Founder of the Persian world empire, who in October 539 B.C. overthrew the Babylonian king, Nabonidus, and allowed the Jews to return from their exile (2 Chr 36:22f). He is termed God's anointed by Isaiah (Is 45:1).

Daniel (DAN-yuhl). An ancient figure of wisdom who is attributed to be the author of the Book of Daniel (which although placed in the time of the Babylonian exile was actually written much later during the time of the Maccabees). He is called the last of the 4 major prophets of the Old Testament.

David (DAY-vid). Second and greatest King of Israel and an ancestor of Jesus (Mt 1:6).

Decapolis (di-KAP-uh-lis). A federation of 10 Greek cities in Palestine mostly east of the Jordan, through which Jesus passed during his public ministry (Mk 5:20; 7:31).

Deuteronomy (doo-tuh-RON-uh-mee). Fifth and last Book of the Pentateuch.

Diadem (DAI-uh-dem). A crown or royal headband (Is 62:3).

Didymus (DID-i-muhs). Greek form of the name Thomas (the apostle), which signifies "twin" (Jn 11:16; 20:24; 21:2).

Dromedaries (DROM-uh-der-eez). Camels with unusual speed and trained for riding (Is 60:6).

Ebed-melech (ee-bid-MEE-lik). An Ethiopian eunuch who saved Jeremiah the prophet from a cistern into which he had been thrown (Jer 38:7ff).

Ecclesiastes (i-klees-ee-AS-tees). Fourth of the 7 Wisdom Books of the Old Testament.

Eden (EE-duhn). Place where God planted a garden in which he put Adam and Eve (Gn 2:8).

Egypt (EE-juhpt). A country northeast of Africa often in contact with Israel. Egyptian Jews were in Jerusalem on the day of Pentecost (Acts 2:10).

Elamites (EE-luh-maits). Inhabitants of Elam, east of Babylon (Gn 10:22; 14:1ff), some of whom were in Jerusalem on the day of Pentecost (Acts 2:9).

Eldad (EL-dad). One who prophesied in the Israelite camp in the wilderness (Nm 11:26ff).

Eleazar (el-ee-AYZ-uhr). An ancestor of Joseph, the husband of Mary (Mt 1:15).

Eli (EE-lai). A priest of Shiloh (1 Sm 1:9) who judged Israel forty years (1 Sm 4:18). He spoke to Hannah (1 Sm 1:12ff), and it was to him that the child Samuel was brought (1 Sm 1:28; 2:11; 3:1-10).

Eli, Eli [or: Eloi, Eloi], Lema Sabachthani (AY-lee, AY-lee, LAY-muh, sa-BAK-thuh-nee). The English transliteration of a Greek phrase (Mt 27:46; Mk 15:34), which is in turn the transliteration of the Hebrew (or Aramaic) version of Ps 22:1: "My God, my God, why have you abandoned me?"

Eliab (i-LEE-uhb). Eldest son of Jesse and brother of David who presented a commanding appearance (1 Sm 16:6).

Eliakim (i-LAI-uh-kim). Son of Hilkiah and successor to Shebna as King Hezekiah's majordomo (Is 22:20ff).

Elijah (i-LAI-juh). A prophet during the reigns of Ahab and Jezebel in the northern kingdom (1 Kgs 17:1-16).

Elisha (i-LAI-shuh). A prophet in the northern kingdom in the second half of the 9th century B.C. (2 Kgs 4:8-16).

Eliud (i-LAI-uhd). An ancestor of Jesus (Mt 1:14f).

Elizabeth (i-LIZ-uh-buhth). Wife of Zechariah, mother of John the Baptist, and relative of the Virgin Mary (Lk 1:5-57).

Emmanuel (i-MAN-yoo-uhl). Symbolic name meaning "God is with us" given by Isaiah to the child whose birth he foretold (Is 7:14) and which is applied to Jesus (Mt 1:23).

Emmaus (i-MAY-uhs). The town 7 miles from Jerusalem to which two disciples walked on the day of the resurrection accompanied by Jesus (Lk 24:13-35).

Ephah (EE-fuh). A measurement of weight (1 Sm 1:24); also the name of a son of Midian (Gn 25:4) and eponymous ancestor of a tribe (Is 60:6).

Ephesians (i-FEE-shuhnz). Inhabitants of Ephesus in Asia Minor to whom Paul wrote one of the Letters of the New Testament.

Ephphathah (EF-uh-thuh). An Aramaic word, meaning "Be opened," that was uttered by Jesus as he was healing a deaf man (Mk 7:34).

Ephraim (EE-free-uhm). One of the twelve tribes of Israel, which became the principal tribe of the northern kingdom (Jer 31:9; Zec 9:10).

Ephrathah (EF-ruh-thuh). Ancient name of Bethlehem or the district around it (Mi 5:1).

Esther (ES-tuhr). Eleventh of the 13 Historical Books of the Old Testament.

Euphrates (yoo-FRAY-teez). A large river that runs from Armenia to the Persian Gulf. It and the Tigris form the two boundaries of Mesopotamia. It also forms one of the boundaries of the widest extent of the borders of Israel.

Eve (EEV). The first woman whom God placed in the garden of Eden (Gn 2:22).

Exodus (EK-suh-duhs). The deliverance of the Israelites from Egypt by God's mighty hand; also, the second Book of the Pentateuch that narrates the story of this great event.

Expiation (ek-spee-AY-shuhn). A translation of the Hebrew word for pardon or suppression of sin. Jesus is called "an expiation" because he assumes pardon of all sins (Rom 3:25).

Ezekiel (i-ZEE-kee-uhl). Third of the 4 major prophets who prophesied in exile during the Babylonian Captivity in the 6th century B.C.

Ezra (EZ-ruh). Priest and scribe who is the main character of the seventh of the 13 Historical Books of the Old Testament.

Feast of Unleavened Bread (feest uhv uhn-LEV-uhnd bred). A feast of spring and renewal celebrating the founding event of the people of God: the deliverance from bondage by the Exodus from Egypt (Lv 23:4-8; Mk 14:1, 12). Each family reenacted the first Passover by eating the Passover meal.

Gabbatha (GAB-uh-thuh). A district in Jerusalem where Pilate's official residence was located (Jn 19:13).

Gabriel (GAY-bree-uhl). An angel who interpreted the vision of Daniel (Dn 8:15ff) and told him of the seventy weeks (Dn 9:22ff). He also announced the birth of John the Baptist to Zechariah (Lk 1:11ff) and that of Jesus to Mary (Lk 1:26ff). In Christian tradition he is known as an archangel, the eighth of the nine choirs of angels.

Galatians (guh-LAY-shuhnz). The inhabitants of Galatia, a Roman province in central Asia, to whom Paul addressed one of the Letters of the New Testament.

Galileans (gal-uh-LEE-uhnz). Inhabitants of Galilee (Lk 13:1).

Galilee (GAL-uh-lee). The region west of the Sea of Galilee and the Jordan, where Jesus was reared and began preaching (Mk 1:14).

Gehazi (gi-HAY-zee). Servant of the prophet Elisha (2 Kgs 4:8ff).

Gehenna (gi-HEN-uh). Place of punishment after death or after the Last Judgment (Mt 10:28).

Genesis (JEN-uh-sis). First Book of the Pentateuch.

Gennasaret (gi-NES-uh-ret). *See* **Sea of Galilee.**

Gentiles (JEN-tailz). Among the Jews it meant either foreign nations (Acts 7:45) or pagans, i.e., polytheists or idolaters who did not worship Yahweh (Mt 4:15; Lk 2:32).

Gethsemane (geth-SEM-uh-nee). A garden on the Mount of Olives, which was the scene of Christ's agony and betrayal (Mt 26:36-56).

Gibeon (GIB-ee-uhn). Hivite city north of Jerusalem that was a cult center and a royal shrine until Solomon's reign (1 Kgs 3:4-15).

Gilgal (GIL-gal). A site near Jericho associated with Joshua's renewal of the covenant (Jos 4:19f) and the site of Saul's installation as king (1 Sm 10:8).

Golgotha (GOL-guh-thuh). Aramaic name ("Place of the Skull") for a little hill northwest of Jerusalem where Jesus was crucified (Mt 27:33).

Gomorrah (guh-MAWR-uh). One of the cities destroyed by God because of its immorality (Gn 19:1ff). It became a symbol for God's judgment upon the sinful.

Greeks (greekz). Name that identified the inhabitants of Greece but also referred to a specific culture: Hellenism (cf. 1 Cor 1:22).

Habakkuk (HAB-uh-kuk). Eighth of the 12 minor prophets of the Old Testament.

Haggai (HAG-ai). Tenth of the 12 minor prophets of the Old Testament.

Hannah (HAN-uh). The mother of Samuel, the last judge of Israel (1 Sm 1—2).

Hebrews (HEE-brooz). Last of the Letters of the New Testament.

Hebron (HEE-bruhn). A city in the hill country of Judah, this was the city from which David reigned for seven years before he was made king of the united kingdom of the northern and southern tribes of Israel (2 Sm 2:11).

Hellenists (HEL-uh-nists). Jews from outside Palestine who took Greek as their primary language and adopted Greek ideas and practices (Acts 6:1).

Herod (HER-uhd). The Herodian family, which though Jewish in religion was Idumean in origin. Herod "the Great" was appointed by Rome as King of Judea in 40 B.C. He slaughtered the infants at Bethlehem (Mt 2:16). **Archelaus (ahr-kuh-LAY-uhs)** was ethnarch of Judea 4 B.C. to 6 A.D. **Antipas (AN-tee-pahs)** was tetrarch of Galilee and Perea until 39 A.D. He married his brother's wife Herodias and beheaded John the Baptist. **Philip (FIL-uhp)**, tetrarch of Trachonitis, was a mild man. His grandson, Herod **Agrippa (uh-GRIP-uh) I**, was king of all Palestine from 41 to 44 A.D. and put James to death (Acts 12:2). His son, Agrippa II, ruled in Trachonitis until 100 A.D. The latter heard Paul's defense (Acts 25:23ff).

Herodians (hi-ROH-dee-unz). Partisans and courtiers of the reigning dynasty of the Herods. Although they were Jews in religion, their spirit was Gentile. They conspired with their enemies, the Pharisees, against Jesus (Mt 22:16).

Hezekiah (hez-uh-KAI-uh). Son and successor of Ahaz as King of Judah for 29 years (2 Kgs 18—20), who reformed the worship (2 Kgs 18:4ff) and was an ancestor of Jesus (Mt 1:9f).

Hezron (HEZ-ruhn). An ancestor of Jesus (Mt 1:3).

Hilkiah (hil-KAI-uh). The father of Eliakim (Is 22:20). Name of six other persons (mostly priests) in Israel.

Holocausts (HAHL-oh-kosts). In the ancient sacrifices only the blood and certain parts of the victim were offered to God; the rest was divided among the priest and faithful who had offered it (Lv 7:11-21). A holocaust (from the Greek "wholly burnt") was a sacrifice in which an entire animal except its hide was consumed in the fire on the altar, with the primary purpose of rendering glory to God (Lv 1:1ff).

Horeb (HAWR-eb). The mountain at which Moses received his commission (Ex 3:1) and to which Elijah fled (1 Kgs 19:9).

Hosanna (hoh-ZAH-nuh). Hebrew expression signifying "May God save," used in the course of Jewish feasts (Ps 118:25f). It served as an acclamation during Jesus' entrance into Jerusalem, in the sense of "Long live," and it is always chanted during the course of the Liturgy (Mt 21:9).

Hosea (hoh-ZAY-uh). Third of the 12 minor prophets of the Old Testament, who spoke of his difficult rela-

tionship with his wife as being parallel to the relationship between God and the people of Israel.

Hur (huhr). A contemporary of Moses who, along with Aaron, helped hold Moses' arms upright during Israel's battle with Amalek (Ex 17:10ff).

Iconium (i-KOH-nee-uhm). A city in Asia Minor visited by Paul (Acts 13:51—14:6, 21).

Isaac (AI-zik). Son of Abraham (Gn 17:19), whose immolation ordered by God, then prevented, prefigures the sacrifice of Christ (Gn 22).

Isaiah (ai-SAY-uh). First of the 4 major prophets of the Old Testament, who prophesied especially about the Passion of our Lord. Isaiah was a great prophet of Israel from 740 to 700 B.C. Chapters 40 to 55 of the Book named after him were probably written much later during the Babylonian Exile (587-539 B.C.) and chapters 56 to 66 after the exile.

Iscariot (is KAR-ee-uht). Surname of Judas, the apostle who betrayed Jesus (Mt 26:14).

Isles (ailz). Dry land as opposed to water (Is 42:15), but its extended meaning was one of the farthest regions of the earth (Ps 72:10; Is 41:5).

Israel (IZ-ray-uhl). Name given by God to Jacob, the son of Isaac (Gn 32:29). Also used for his descendants, the twelve tribes of the Hebrews, and later the ten northern tribes led by Ephraim, as well as of the Church (the new Israel: Gal 6:16).

Israelites (IZ-ray-uh-laits). People of Israel (Acts 10:36).

Ituraea (i-TYOO-ree-uh). A region northwest of Palestine beyond the Jordan ruled by Herod Philip (Lk 3:1).

Jaar (JAY-uhr). Another name for Kiriath-jearim, one of the Canaanite towns and a center of Baal worship, where the Ark remained for a few generations (Ps 132:6).

Jacob (JAY-kuhb). Son of Isaac and Rebekah and twin brother of Esau, whose birthright he took (Gn 25). He was renamed Israel by God (Gn 32:29). The name also refers to the father of Joseph, foster father of Jesus (Mt 1:16).

Jairus (JAI-ruhs). The synagogue-ruler whose daughter Jesus raised from the dead (Mk 5:22; 8:41).

James (jaymz). Name of three persons: (1) the apostle James ("the less"), son of Alphaeus (Mt 10:3); (2) the apostle James ("the greater"), son of Zebedee and brother of John the apostle who died as a martyr during the persecution of Herod Agrippa (Acts 12:2); (3) James, the "brother of the Lord," probably the son of Mary of Clopas, who was the first bishop of Jerusalem, martyred in 62, and presumed author of one of the Letters of the New Testament (Gal 1:19; Mt 13:55).

Javan (JAY-vuhn). A name that stands for the cities on the west coast of Asia Minor (Is 66:19; Ez 27:13).

Jechoniah (jek-uh-NAI-uh). A variant of Jehoiachin, son of Jehoiakim, grandson of Josiah (1 Chr 3:15, 17), and ancestor of Jesus (Mt 1:11f).

Jehoshaphat (ji-HOSH-uh-fat). Son and successor of Asaph as King of Judah for 25 years (1 Kgs 22:42) and ancestor of Jesus (Mt 1:8).

Jeremiah (jer-uh-MAI-uh). Second of the 4 major prophets, who prefigures the Messiah mainly by his personal sufferings.

Jericho (JER-uh-koh). An ancient city at the southern end of the Jordan Valley, also called the City of Palms (Dt 34:3), which was miraculously captured by Joshua as the opening wedge of his battle to take Canaan (Jos 6). It was also the site of Jesus' healing of the blind Bartimaeus (Mk 10:46).

Jerusalem (ji-ROO-suh-luhm). Capital of Israel, conquered by David (also called City of David), known as the city of God (Heb 12:22; Rv 3:12) and the Holy City (Mt 4:5; 27:53). The Church is the new Jerusalem and the image of the Heavenly Jerusalem (Gal 4:26; Rv 21:1—22:5).

Jesse (JES-ee). The Father of David (Is 11:1) and an ancestor of Jesus (Mt 1:6).

Jesu (JAY-zoo). Diminutive and familiar form of Jesus.

Jesus (JEE-zuhs). The personal name of the Son of God made man, which means: "The Lord is salvation" or "Savior," and denotes his mission: to save humans from death and sin and make them once more children of God and heirs of heaven.

Jethro (JETH-roh). The father-in-law of Moses (Ex 3:1), he is also called

Reuel (Ex 2:18) and Hobab (Nm 10:29). He was a priest of Midian.

Joanna (joh-AN-uh). A woman who helped to support Jesus and his followers (Lk 8:2) and who went to the tomb on Easter Sunday (Lk 24:10).

Job (johb). First of the 7 Wisdom Books of the Old Testament.

Joel (JOH-uhl). Second of the 12 minor prophets of the Old Testament.

John (jon). Son of Zebedee and brother of James the Greater who became an apostle and wrote the last of the 4 Gospels; three of the Catholic Letters are also attributed to him. Another John is the author of the Book of Revelation.

John the Baptist (jon thuh BAP-tist). Son of Zechariah and Elizabeth (Lk 1:5ff), who was Christ's precursor.

Jonah (JOH-nuh). Fifth of the 12 minor prophets of the Old Testament, whose book serves as a parable reminding Israel that God is Lord of all peoples upon the earth.

Joram (JAWR-uhm). Son and successor of Jehoshaphat as King of Judah (1 Kgs 22:51) and an ancestor of Jesus (Mt 1:8). Also called Jehoram.

Jordan (JAWR-duhn). The largest river in Palestine, which played a large part in the history of Israel and the early public life of Christ (Mt 3:13-17).

Joseph (JOH-sif). Son of Jacob and Rachel (Gn 30:24). He is regarded by the Church as a figure of Joseph, the "just man," who was the spouse of the Virgin Mary and foster father of Christ (Mt 1:18ff).

Joses (JOH-siz). Cousin of Jesus (Mk 6:3—called Joseph in Mt 13:55). Son of Mary (Mk 15:40, 47), wife of Clopas (Jn 19:25—called Joseph in Mt 27:56).

Joshua (JOSH-yoo-uh). First of the 3 books that follow the Pentateuch.

Josiah (joh-SAI-uh). Son and successor of Amon as King of Judah (2 Kgs 21:24), who reformed religion and repaired the temple, and was an ancestor of Jesus (Mt 1:10f).

Jotham (JOH-thuhm). King of Judah in the time of Isaiah (2 Kgs 15:32) and an ancestor of Jesus (Mt 1:9).

Judah (JOO-duh). Son of Jacob (Gn 29:35) and ancestor of the tribe of Israel whose capital was Jerusalem. After the schism of the 10 northern tribes it became the Kingdom of Judah or Judea. He was an ancestor of Jesus (Mt 1:3).

Judas (JOO-duhs). Name of five persons: (1) Judas (Jude Thaddeus) the apostle (Lk 6:16; Mt 10:3); (2) Judas, a "brother of the Lord," and presumed author of the "Letter of Jude" (Mk 6:3); (3) Judas, surnamed Barsabbas, sent by the apostles to Antioch (Acts 15:22, 32); (4) Judas Iscariot, who betrayed Jesus (Mt 10:4); (5) Judas of Damascus at whose house Paul lodged after his conversion (Acts 9:11).

Jude (jood). *See* **Judas: 2.**

Judea (joo-DEE-uh). The most southern part of the three districts of Palestine west of the Jordan. Together with Samaria and Idumea it formed the Roman province of Judea with its capital at Jerusalem.

Judean (joo-DEE-uhn). Adjectival form of Judea.

Judges (JUHJ-iz). Second of the 3 books that follow the Pentateuch.

Judith (JOO-dith). Tenth of the 13 Historical Books of the Old Testament.

Justus (JUHS-tuhs). Surname of Joseph Barsabbas (Acts 1:23).

Kidron (KAI-druhn). Valley along the east side of Jerusalem that joins the Valley of Hinnom and extends 20 miles to the Dead Sea.

Kings (kings). Third and fourth of the 13 Historical Books of the Old Testament.

Kor (also spelled cor) (kor). An indeterminate large weight measure.

Lamb of God (lam uhv god). A title of Jesus to show that he bears the sins of mankind and offers himself as a sacrificial lamb, prefigured by the paschal lamb through whose blood the Israelites were saved from their Egyptian bondage (Jn 1:29).

Lamentations (lam-en-TAY-shuhnz). Third of the 18 Prophetic Books of the Old Testament.

Law (law). Primarily the ten commandments that God gave to the chosen people, which were concerned mostly with external obedience. The new law was instituted by Christ and is based on charity (which sums up the ten commandments). It requires both internal and external obedience.

Lazarus (LAZ-uhr-uhs). Brother of Martha and Mary (Jn 11:5). He was raised from the dead by Jesus (Jn 11:43ff) and was present at the supper in his honor (Jn 12:2). This is also the name of the poor man in the parable of Lazarus and the rich man who would not assist him (Lk 16:20ff).

Lebanon (LEB-uh-nuhn). Mountainous chain north of Palestine, heavily wooded and known especially for its cedars (Jgs 9:15; Is 35:2).

Levi (LEE-vai). Name of two persons. (1) The son of Jacob and Leah (Gn 29:34), who gave his name to a tribe of Israel (Mal 2:4). (2) The tax collector who became an apostle and is called Matthew (Mt 9:9ff), the eventual author of the first Gospel.

Levites (LEE-vaits). Members of the tribe of Levi, who assisted the priests in temple worship. In the parable of the Good Samaritan the Levite failed to help his neighbor (Lk 10:32).

Leviticus (li-VIT-i-kuhs). Third Book of the Pentateuch.

Libya (LIB-ee-uh). Ancient Greek name for northern Africa west of Egypt, which has Cyrene as one of its cities (Acts 2:10).

Lord (lawrd). Originally a title that signified nothing more than "sir." From the 3rd century B.C. onward, the Jews replaced the ineffable name "Yahweh" with "Adonai" (Lord) in reading the Bible. Applied to Jesus by the first Christians, the name "Lord" was thus equivalent to an affirmation of his divinity (Acts 2:36).

Lud (luhd). The name for two separate regions, one in Asia Minor (Is 66:19; probably Lydia) and one in Africa (Jer 46:9; Ez 30:5).

Luke (look). Companion of Paul and author of the third Gospel and the Acts of the Apostles.

Lyre (LAI-uhr). A string musical instrument used to praise the Lord (Ps 81:3).

Lysanias (li-SAY-nee-uhs). Tetrarch of Abilene (Lk 3:1), a small region in Lebanon.

Lystra (LIS-truh). A city in Lycaonia (Asia Minor) where Paul and Barnabas were mistaken for Zeus and Hermes (Acts 14:6-18).

Maccabees (MAK-uh-beez). Twelfth and thirteenth of the 13 Historical Books of the Old Testament.

Macedonia (mas-uh-DOH-nee-uh). A Roman province north of Greece in the Balkans that was visited by Paul (1 Thes 1:7).

Magdala (MAG-duh-luh). A town on the northwest shore of the Sea of Galilee, 3 miles north of Tiberias (Mt 15:39), home of Mary Magdalene (Jn 19:25).

Magdalene (MAG-duh-luhn). Alternate surname of Mary of Magdala, who followed the body of Jesus to the grave (Mt 27:61) and was the first to learn of the resurrection (Mt 28:1-8).

Malachi (MAL-uh-kai). Last of the 12 minor prophets of the Old Testament.

Malchiah (mal-KAI-uh). A prince who owned the cistern into which Jeremiah was thrown in an assassination attempt. He was rescued by Ebed-melech (Jer 38:6ff).

Malchus (MAL-kuhs). A servant of the high priest whose ear Peter cut off with a sword (Jn 18:10).

Mammon (MAM-uhn). A word derived from the Aramaic *mamona,* meaning property, both in the New Testament and in rabbinic writings.

Mamre (MAM-ree). A site near Hebron. It was marked off with an ancient oak tree and was probably a sanctuary.

Man (man). In the eyes of the Jews, a being dependent on God for his life. The Christian has two selves within him: the "old self," drawn to evil, made up of body and soul; and the "new self" created by the Holy Spirit, who must triumph over sin (Rom 6:6).

Manna (MAN-uh). Food miraculously supplied by God to the Israelites during their 40 years in the desert (Nm 11:9), a type of the Eucharist—the Bread from heaven (Jn 6:31ff).

Mark (mahrk). Companion of Paul and author of the second Gospel.

Martha (MAHR-thuh). Sister of Mary (Lk 10:38) and Lazarus (Jn 11:1).

Mary (MAY-ree). The Virgin, mother of Jesus (Mt 1:18ff; Lk 2:6). Mary was also the name of the mother of James and Joses (Mt 27:56), who was present at the crucifixion and at the burial of Jesus (Mt 27:61) as well as on the morning of the resurrection (Mt 28:1). She seems to be the same as Mary the wife of Clopas (Jn 19:25). This is also the name of the sister of Martha and Lazarus (Lk 10:38; Jn 11:1) and of the woman from Magdala who was a follower of Jesus (*see* **Magdalene**).

Massah (MAS-uh). Name given to the site of the rock in Horeb from which Moses drew water for the rebellious Israelites (Ex 17:1-7; Ps 95:8f). The name is coupled with Meribah (Dt 33:8).

Matthan (MATH-an). Grandfather of Joseph, Mary's husband (Mt 1:15).

Matthew (MATH-yoo). One of the twelve apostles identified with Levi, son of Alphaeus, and a tax collector (Mt 9:9; Mk 2:14). He is regarded as the author of the Gospel that bears his name.

Matthias (muh-THAI-uhs). The disciple chosen by lot to replace Judas Iscariot (Acts 1:24ff).

Medad (MEE-dad). One who prophesied in the Israelite camp in the wilderness (Nm 11:26ff).

Medes (meedz). Inhabitants of the land of Media, some of whom were in Jerusalem on the day of Pentecost (Acts 2:9).

Melchizedek (mel-KIZ-uh-dek). King of Salem and priest of God who offered bread and wine as a sacrifice in thanksgiving for Abraham's victory (Gn 14:18-20). The Church sees therein the figure of the sacrifice of Jesus, "a priest forever according to the order of Melchizedek" (Ps 110:4; Heb 5:6, 10; 6:20; 7:11, 17).

Meribah (MER-i-buh). Hebrew word signifying "the (place of the) quarreling" that served to designate the same site as Massah (Ex 17:7).

Mesopotamia (mes-uh-puh-TAY-mee-uh). The area between the Tigris and the Euphrates rivers, some of whose inhabitants were in Jerusalem on the day of Pentecost (Acts 2:9). It is Iraq today.

Messiah (muh-SAI-uh). A Hebrew word signifying "one who has been anointed." The kings of Israel were anointed in the name of God (1 Sm 9:16). The term Messiah later was used to designate a "future king" who would make all things new (Dn 9:25-26). This son of David, expected by the Jewish nation, was the Messiah par excellence (Mk 10:47-48), a term that has been rendered in Greek by *Christos.* This was a common name that ultimately became a title for Jesus the Savior (Rm 1:1).

Micah (MAI-kuh). Sixth of the 12 minor prophets of the Old Testament.

Midian (MID-ee-uhn). Son of Abraham by Keturah (Gn 25:1-6), whose descendants became a tribe of nomads and merchants called Midianites (Nm 31:1-12, 32-34).

Moriah (muh-RAI-uh). The place where Abraham was told to offer up Isaac (Gn 22:2).

Moses (MOH-zis). The leader and lawgiver of the Israelites, who successfully brought them out of Egypt (Ex 12:50) through the desert (Ex 19ff), to the shores of the Jordan. On Mount Sinai he received the law, which contained the ethical teaching (Rom 5:12ff).

Mosoch (MOH-sok). An area believed to be in the vicinity of Armenia.

Mount of Olives (mount uhv OL-uhvz). A mountain with three summits east of Jerusalem. Gethsemane is on its lower slope. It is closely associated with the life of Jesus (Mk 11:1; 14:26). *See also* **Olivet.**

Myrrh (mir). An odorous resin (Mt 2:11).

Naaman (NAY-uh-muhn). A general of the king of Damascus who was healed of his leprosy by Elisha (2 Kgs 5).

Nahshon (NAH-shon). The son of Amminadab (1 Chr 2:10, 11) and ancestor of Jesus (Mt 1:4).

Nahum (NAY-huhm). Seventh of the 12 minor prophets of the Old Testament.

Name (naym). Identical with the person it designates. The name of God indicates God himself and all his perfections. "To act in the name" of someone means to participate in the reality (and its power) expressed by this name. Change of vocation also requires a new name (e.g., Peter).

Naphtali (NAF-tuh-lee). One of Jacob's sons (Gn 46:24), who gave his name to one of the twelve tribes (Jos 19:32-39) that later formed part of Galilee.

Nathan (NAY-thuhn). (1) Son of David by Bathsheba (2 Sm 5:13) and an ancestor of Jesus (Lk 3:31). (2) A prophet who dissuaded David from building the temple and promised him a sure succession (2 Sm 7:1ff), and who rebuked him when he sinned (2 Sm 12:1ff).

Nazarene (NAZ-uh-reen). A word derived from Nazareth, the hometown of Christ. He was often called a Nazarene (Mt 2:23). Another form of the name is "Nazorean."

Nazareth (NAZ-uh-rith). A town in low Galilee, which is the hometown of Mary and Joseph, mother and foster father of Jesus (Lk 1:26; 2:4) and where Jesus spent his early life (Mt 2:23).

Nazirite (NAZ-uh-rait). One who is set apart for service of the LORD by a vow. Nazirites were not to cut their hair, nor drink wine, nor partake of any fruit of the vine.

Nazorean (naz-uh-REE-uhn). An alternate form of "Nazarene" (Mt 2:23).

Nehemiah (nee-huh-MAI-uh). Cupbearer of the Persian King Cyrus, who helped to reestablish the Jewish commonwealth after the Babylonian exile and is the main character of the eighth of the 13 Historical Books of the Old Testament.

Neighbor (NAY-buhr). Jesus declares that one's neighbor is every person, even one belonging to a hostile group (Lk 10:29-37).

Ner (nuhr). The father of Abner, the commander of the army of King Saul of Israel (1 Sm 26:5).

Netherworld (NETH-uhr-wuhrld). The ancient concept of the abode of the dead (in Hebrew: "sheol"), which supposed no activity or lofty emotion among the deceased, who were pictured as surrounded by the darkness of oblivion (Ps 16:10).

Nicanor (nai-KAY-nuhr). One of the seven deacons of the Church at Jerusalem (Acts 6:5).

Nicholas (NIK-uh-luhs). A convert to Judaism from Antioch who became one of the seven deacons of the Church at Jerusalem (Acts 6:5).

Nicodemus (nik-uh-DEE-muhs). Greek name borne by an influential member of the Sanhedrin, who came to Jesus by night and later interceded for him when the plot was hatched that ended in his death (Jn 3:1-10; 7:50f).

Nineveh (NIN-uh-vuh). The later capital of Assyria, the great city on the Upper Tigris, whose inhabitants repented at the preaching of the Prophet Jonah (Jon 3:1ff).

Noah (NOH-uh). Patriarch who with his family was saved in the Ark from the Flood (Gn 6ff).

Nun (nuhn). Father of Joshua (Nm 11:28).

Obadiah (oh-buh-DAI-uh). Fourth of the 12 minor prophets of the Old Testament.

Obed (OH-bid). Son of Boaz and Ruth (Ru 4:17) and an ancestor of Jesus (Mt 1:5f).

Olivet (OL-i-vet). Alternative name for the Mount of Olives (Acts 1:12).

Omega (oh-MEG-uh). Last letter of the Greek alphabet. Used with "Alpha," it means the first and the last (Rv 1:8).

Ophir (OH-fuhr). A region on the coast of southern Arabia or eastern Africa—famous for its gold (Ps 45:10).

Pamphylia (pam-FIL-ee-uh). A small Roman province of southern Asia extending 75 miles along the Mediterranean coast and 30 miles inland to the Taurus mountains, some of whose inhabitants were in Jerusalem on the day of Pentecost (Acts 2:10).

Paraclete (PAR-uh-kleet). A word used in the Gospel of John for the Holy Spirit. It could be translated as "comforter," "consoler," "advocate," etc. The Paraclete will reveal that which the disciples could not understand (Jn 14:26; 16:13). He is the Spirit of Truth (Jn 14:16).

Parapet (PAR-uh-pet). The railing that one was to build on the edge of all roofs in Israel.

Parmenas (PAHR-muh-nuhs). One of the seven deacons of the Church at Jerusalem (Acts 6:5).

Parthians (PAHR-thee-uhnz). Inhabitants of the Parthian Empire to the east, known today as Iran, some of whom were in Jerusalem on the day of Pentecost (Acts 2:9).

Paschal (PAS-kuhl). An adjective referring to the Passover of the Old Testament and the Passover of the New (i.e., Easter).

Passover (PAS-oh-vuhr). Feast instituted to commemorate the departure from Egypt with the "passing over" of the angel of death and the crossing of the Red Sea (Dt 16:1-8). At this observance (Last Supper) Jesus instituted the Eucharist (Mt 26:26ff).

Patriarchs (PAY-tree-ahrks). Name given to those who founded the Hebrew race and nation. The New Testament applies it to Abraham (Heb 7:4), the sons of Jacob (Acts 7:8, 9), and David (Acts 2:29).

Pentateuch (PENT-uh-took). The first five Books of the Old Testament.

Pentecost (PEN-ti-kost). The Jewish feast, fifty days after Passover, that recalled the giving of the law and offered in thanks the firstfruits of the wheat harvest (Lv 23:15-22). At Pentecost the Holy Spirit came upon the apostles and the others gathered in the Upper Room (Acts 2:1ff), marking the birthday of the Church and inaugurating the Christian feast of Pentecost.

People of God (PEE-puhl uhv god). Term by which Israel is designated throughout the Bible. In its turn, Christianity is also called the People God claims for his own, but it rejects any kind of national particularism (1 Pt 2:9).

Perez (PEE-riz). Son of Judah by Tamar (Gn 28:29) and an ancestor of Jesus (Mt 1:3).

Perga (PURH-guh). A city in Pamphylia (Asia Minor). It was visited by Paul and Barnabas (Acts 13:13f).

Persians (PUHR-zhuhnz). Originally, a Median tribe that settled in Persia, east of the Persian Gulf, whose members are mentioned in 2 Chr 36:20). Scripture also mentions Cyrus the Great who released the captive Jews (Ezr 1:1); Darius, who confirmed the decree of Cyrus (Ezr 6:1), and Artaxerxes (Ezr 4:7; 7:1).

Peter (PEE-tuhr). One of the twelve apostles (Mt 10:2) and author of two of the seven Catholic Letters of the New Testament. His name was Simon, but he was surnamed Cephas (Jn 1:42) or its Greek equivalent Peter. He was made the first Pope of the Church by Jesus (Mt 16:16ff).

Phanuel (fuh-NYOO-uhl). Father of Anna (Lk 2:36).

Pharaoh (FAR-oh). Title of Egyptian rulers.

Pharisees (FAR-uh-seez). Jewish sect that sought the perfect expression of spiritual life through strict observance of the law and tradition alone. Some of its members were greatly at odds with Jesus (Jn 9:16, 22).

Philemon (fi-LEE-muhn). One of Paul's Letters of the New Testament.

Philip (FIL-ip). Name borne by the apostle from Bethsaida (Jn 1:43f); the deacon (Acts 6:5); the tetrarch, son of Herod the Great and Cleopatra (Lk 3:1); and Herod Philip, son of Herod the Great and Mariamme (Mt 14:3).

Philippi (fi-LIP-ai). City of Macedonia, named after Philip, father of Alexander the Great. It was evangelized by Paul (Acts 16:12ff).

Philippians (Fi-LIP-ee-uhnz). Inhabitants of Philippi to whom Paul wrote one of the Letters of the New Testament.

Phrygia (FRIJ-ee-uh). A province in southwest Asia Minor, where Paul preached on his 2nd and 3rd missionary journeys (Acts 16:6; 18:23), some of whose inhabitants were in Jerusalem on the day of Pentecost (Acts 2:10).

Pilate (PAI-luht). The fifth procurator or governmental representative of Rome in Palestine 26-36 A.D., who condemned Jesus to death (Jn 19:16).

Pisidia (pi-SID-ee-uh). One of the small Roman provinces in southern Asia Minor north of Pamphylia, visited by Paul on his 1st and 2nd missionary journeys (Acts 13:14-50; 14:21-24).

Pontius (PON-shuhs). First name of Pilate (Lk 3:1).

Pontus (PON-tuhs). A large province of northern Asia Minor located along the Black Sea, some of whose inhabitants were in Jerusalem on the day of Pentecost (Acts 2:9).

Poor (poor). Originally, a word with a purely economic and social meaning. Gradually, it took on the meaning of humble, modest, small, the little people often oppressed by the rich and powerful but who remained faithful to God (Am 2:6f). It was in this sense that Jesus said: "Blessed are you who are poor" (Lk 6:20).

Praetorium (pri-TAWR-ee-uhm). The residence of a Roman praetor, or his military headquarters, where he had his guard and held court. The procurators of Judea in the time of Christ had their praetorium at Caesarea, in the palace of Herod the Great (Acts 23:35). Tradition makes the fortress called Antonia the praetorium where Christ was tried (Mk 15:16).

Prochorus (PROK-uh-ruhs). One of the first seven deacons of the Church at Jerusalem (Acts 6:5).

Promise (PROM-uhs). A term of Greek origin that designates and interprets the meaning of all the previous prophetic history of the chosen people in their Messianic mission.

Prophets (PROF-its). Men chosen by God to speak in his name. They were the teachers and guardians of the religion of Israel, at times advisers to kings, defenders of the poor and oppressed, and heralds of the future Messiah and his kingdom.

Proverbs (PROV-uhrbs). Third of the 7 Wisdom Books of the Old Testament.

Psalms (sahmz). Second of the 7 Wisdom Books of the Old Testament.

Put (poot). A region most probably in Africa (Jer 46:9).

Qoheleth (koh-HEL-ith). The name of the author of the Book of Ecclesiastes. The name means "preacher," and this might be a symbolic name. His work is marked by cynicism and yet respect for the fact that the will of God is a mystery.

Quirinius (kwi-RIN-ee-uhs). Roman governor of Syria at the time of the birth of Jesus in Bethlehem (Lk 2:2).

Rabbi (RAB-ai). A title for the teachers of the law. It means "my master" (Mt 23:7-11; Jn 1:38) and was often applied to Christ.

Rahab (RAY-hab). A non-Jewish woman who played a large role in the capture of Jericho (Jos 2:1) and became the mother of Boaz, great-grandmother of King David and ancestor of Jesus (Mt 1:5).

Ram (ram). An ancestor of David (Ru 4:19) and of Jesus (Mt 1:4).

Raqa (RAH-kah). An Aramaic word probably meaning "fool," "imbecile," or "blockhead"—a term of abuse (Mt 5:22).

Redemption (ree-DEMP-shuhn). Deliverance procured by payment of a ransom. It refers to the deliverance of the human race from sin, its effects and punishments, by Jesus Christ, who by shedding his blood on the cross paid the price of our salvation (Rom 3:24). It was prefigured by the deliverance of Israel from bondage in Egypt and Babylonia.

Rehoboam (ree-huh-BOH-uhm). Son and successor of King Solomon (1 Kgs 11:43) and ancestor of Jesus (Mt 1:7).

Remnant (REM-nuhnt). An expression used by the prophets designating the survivors of great catastrophes (Gn 7:1f; Is 6:13) who will remain the depositories of the promise (Mi 4:6f) and help in the restoration (Is 37:31f).

Resurrection (res-uhr-REK-shuhn). The resurrection of Jesus, which became the fundamental historical fact, the principal witness of his divinity (1 Cor 15:4, 12). It is also the divine judgment that has ordered the defeat of death and pledges salvation and resurrection to the faithful (Rom 4:25; Col 2:12ff).

Revelation (rev-uh-LAY-shuhn). The only apocalyptic book of the New Testament. It speaks about the need to give witness to one's faith while one awaits the end of time.

River (RIV-uhr). A term that standing alone refers to the Euphrates River, the longest and most important river in Western Asia (Ps 72:8; Zec 9:10).

Romans (ROH-muhnz). One of Paul's Letters of the New Testament.

Rome (rohm). Capital of the Roman Empire, which like Babylon became a symbol of organized paganism and opposition to Christianity. The city also had a small Christian community from the forties onward. Both Peter and Paul were martyred there.

Rufus (ROO-fuhs). Son of Simon of Cyrene and brother of Alexander, mentioned during the way of the cross (Mk 15:21).

Ruth (rooth). A Moabite woman who married an Israelite, was widowed, and returned to Jerusalem with her mother-in-law, and became the ancestor of David and Jesus (Mt 1:5). Also, the last of the three books that follow the Pentateuch.

Sabbath (SAB-uhth). Seventh day of the week, consecrated to God, on which no work could be performed (Dt 5:12-15). Among Christians, the day after the sabbath gradually became the sabbath or first day in commemoration of the resurrection of Christ—hence "the Lord's day" (Jn 20:19ff; Acts 20:7).

Sadducees (SAD-joo-seez). A religious party of the Jews who were the nationalists of their day. They believed in God but rejected the oral traditions of their forefathers and denied the resurrection of human beings and the existence of angels. They opposed Jesus (Mt 22:23ff) and the apostolic Church (Acts 5:17).

Saints (saynts). A common Old Testament term to designate those who belong to God that was applied in the New Testament to those who believed in Christ. It occurs first in Acts 9:13 and is frequent in the writings of Paul.

Salem (SAY-luhm). The city ruled by Melchizedek (Gen 14:18), most probably a name for Jerusalem.

Salmon (SAL-muhn). Father of Boaz (called Salma in 1 Chr 2:11) and ancestor of Jesus (Mt 1:4).

Salome (suh-LOH-mee). One of the women present at the crucifixion of Jesus (Mt 15:40) and at the empty tomb (Mk 16:1).

Salvation (sal-VAY-shuhn). A term referring to the work of God on behalf of his people's deliverance (Ps 33:16f; Is 31:1; Hos 5:13—6:3) and then personal deliverance (Ps 51:14).

In the New Testament it means the work of spiritual deliverance—remission from sin (Lk 17:19) and the liberation from the servitude that sin brings to human beings (Mt 1:21; Lk 1:77; Acts 5:31).

Samaria (suh-MAYR-ee-uh). Capital of the kingdom of Israel after the schism of the ten tribes that was destroyed in 721 B.C. by Sargon (2 Kgs 18:9-12). It was rebuilt by Herod the Great and called Sebaste and Philip preached the Gospel there (Acts 8:5-9).

Samaritans (suh-MAYR-uh-tuhnz). Inhabitants of the central region of Palestine between Judea and Galilee who were a mixed race of Israelites and Assyrian colonists, and very hostile to the Jews at the time of Christ. Our Lord passed through their country more than once, and preached and worked miracles among the people. He also spoke well of them (Lk 10:30-37), defended them (Lk 9:51-56), and commanded that the Gospel be preached to them.

Samuel (SAM-yoo-uhl). The greatest of the Judges (1 Sm 7:15) and a prophet (1 Sm 9:9) instrumental in instituting the monarchy (1 Sm 9ff). The first two of the 13 Historical Books of the Old Testament are named after him.

Sanhedrin (san-HEE-druhn). Civil and religious council of the Jews, composed of 71 members and presided over by the high priest.

Sapphires (SAf-airz). Precious stones (Is 54:11).

Sarah (SAR-uh). Wife of Abraham who conceived in old age and gave him a son (Isaac) in accord with God's promise (Heb 11:11). Her name was changed by God from Sarai to Sarah (Gn 17:15).

Sarai (SAIR-ai). *See* **Sarah.**

Saraph (SAR-uhf). *See* **Seraph.**

Satan (SAY-tuhn). God's great adversary who seeks to destroy human beings (Mt 13:19, 28). This devil or prince of demons is a spirit completely given up to evil. By dying on the cross Christ crushed his power (Rv 20:1ff).

Saul (sawl). First King of the Israelites around 1020-1000 B.C. (1 Sm 10:17ff). This is also the Hebrew/Aramaic form of the name of the man

known as Paul (the Greco/Roman version), who became a great apostle of the Good News to the Gentiles (Acts 13:9).

Scribes (skraibz). Jews devoted to the study of the law (Mt 2:4; 17:10).

Scriptures (SKRIP-chuhrs). The inspired Books of the Old Testament, the work of the Holy Spirit, comprising the law, the prophets, and the writings (Foreword to the Book of Sirach). Christianity added its own writings: the Gospels and Letters of the New Testament (1 Tm 5:18; 2 Tm 3:16; 2 Pt 3:14-16).

Scythian (SITH-ee-uhn). A member of a nomadic people from central Asia.

Sea (see). A term that when standing alone refers to the Mediterranean Sea (Ps 80:12).

Sea of Galilee (see uhv GAL-uh-lee). A lake only 13 miles long and 8 miles wide, 60 miles north of Jerusalem, subject to sudden violent storms (Mt 8:24). Also called the Sea of Gennesaret (Lk 5:1) and the Sea of Tiberias (Jn 6:1).

Seba (SEE-buh). An unknown territory, possibly in Africa.

Seraph (SER-uhf). One of the choirs of angels who sing, "Holy, holy, holy" before the throne of God (Is 6). It is also a name for a poisonous serpent (Nm 21:8; Dt 8:15) but spelled "saraph" by the Lectionary text.

Servant (SUHR-vuhnt). An expression applied to the people of Israel within the framework of the covenant (Ex 7:16; Pss 69:37; 102:15) and the faithful in general (Ps 34:1). It became a Messianic title as the result of its use by Deutero-Isaiah in the so-called Servant of Yahweh Songs (Is 42:1-9; 49:1-13; 50:4-11; 52:13—53:12) and as such is applied to Jesus (Mt 12:18; Acts 3:13).

Shaphat (SHAY-fat). The father of Elisha the prophet (1 Kgs 19:16).

Sharon (SHAR-uhn). Coastal plain between Joppa and Mount Carmel, a plain proverbial for its fertility, pasture lands, and beauty (Is 35:2).

Shealtiel (shee-AL-tee-uhl). Father of Zerubbabel (Ezr 3:2) and an ancestor of Jesus (Mt 1:12).

Sheba (SHEE-buh). The kingdom of the Sabeans in southern Arabia, whose people are pictured as traders in precious stones and incense (Is 60:6).

Shebna (SHEB-nuh). Majordomo of King Hezekiah (Is 22:15ff).

Shekel (SHEK-uhl). A measure of precious metal. Each vendor would measure a given shekel against one's own sample shekel.

Shema Israel (shuh-MAH iz-RAY-uhl; -REE; IZ-ruhl). Ancient Jewish confession of faith recited daily by the pious. It is composed of three passages: Dt 6:4-9; 11:12-21; and Nm 15:37-41. The name comes from *Shema Yisrael* ("Hear, O Israel": Dt 6:4), the words with which the confession begins.

Shiloh (SHAI-loh). A sanctuary town in Israel and a site where the ark of the covenant was kept (1 Sm 4).

Shinar (SHAIN-ahr). Plain of Babylonia in which were located Babel, Erech, Accad, and Calneh (Gn 10:10) and where the Tower of Babel was built (Gn 11:1-9).

Shunem (SHOO-nuhm). A place in a very rich section of Palestine (2 Kgs 4:8), north of Jezreel and belonging to the tribe of Issachar (Jos 19:18).

Sidon (SAI-duhn). Phoenician port north of Tyre, on the Mediterranean (Mt 15:21). These two pagan cities served the evangelists as symbols of a corrupt civilization (Lk 10:13-15).

Silas (SAI-luhs). *See* **Silvanus.**

Siloam (sai-LOH-ahm). Pool situated south of the city of Jerusalem to which Jesus adverted in a talk about workmen killed there (Lk 13:4).

Silvanus (sil-VAY-nuhs). Also known as Silas, a Jerusalem Christian sent with Paul to Antioch (Acts 15:22ff) who later accompanied him on his 2nd missionary journey (Acts 15:40) and was imprisoned with him in Philippi (Acts 16:19ff).

Simeon (SIM-ee-uhn). Name of three persons: (1) the old man who received the child Jesus in his arms at the temple (Lk 2:25-35); (2) an influential member of the Christian community at Antioch (Acts 13:1); (3) Peter the apostle, according to his Hebrew name (Acts 15:14). (He is also called Simon.)

Simon (SAI-muhn). Name of several persons, including: (1) the father of Judas Iscariot (Jn 13:2); (2) the prince of the apostles, later called Peter or Simon Peter (Jn 20:1-9); (3) a Pharisee who entertained Jesus (Lk 7:40) and in whose house a woman anointed Jesus' feet.

Sinai (SAI-nai). A peninsula south of the Wilderness of Paran between the Gulf of Aqabah and Suez. Also applied to a wilderness (Ex 19:1), where Israel came after they left Egypt and to the mountain (Ex 19:20) where God gave Moses the law.

Sirach (SAI-ruhk). Last of the seven Wisdom Books of the Old Testament, whose author is Jesus, the son of Sirach (Sir 50:27).

Sodom (SOD-uhm). One of the cities destroyed by God because of their immorality (Gn 19:1ff). It became a symbol for God's judgment upon the sinful.

Solomon (SOL-uh-muhn). Son and successor of David, who was a pious king (1 Kgs 3:5, 7-12) but eventually lost much of the empire David had built up (1 Kgs 11:14ff) and led to discontent in Israel (1 Kgs 11:26ff). Also, an ancestor of Jesus (Mt 1:6).

Solomon's Portico (SOL-uh-mouhnz POR-ti-koh). A protected area in the outer court of the temple (Jn 10:23).

Son of Man (son uhv man). A Messianic title found in the Prophet Daniel (7:13f) and used by Jesus. It expresses Christ's twofold destiny of suffering (Mk 8:31) and of glory (Mk 8:38).

Song of Songs (song uhv songs). Fifth of the 7 Wisdom Books of the Old Testament.

Sosthenes (SOS-thuh-nees). An associate of Paul in the First Letter to the Corinthians (1:1).

Stephen (STEE-vuhn). One of the seven deacons of the Church at Jerusalem (Acts 6:5) and the first martyr for Christ, who—like his Master—prayed for his executioners (Acts 7:60).

Sychar (SAI-kahr). Village of Samaria located near Jacob's well, where Jesus encountered the Samaritan woman (Jn 4:5).

Synagogue (SIN-uh-gog). A place where the Jews gathered on the sabbath to listen to the explanations of the Scriptures. Each locality had one in which Jesus prayed and studied (Lk 4:20).

Syria (SIR-ee-uh). The region between Asia Minor to the north and Palestine to the south, whose chief cities were Damascus and Antioch. A Roman province to which Palestine was subordinated (Lk 2:2).

Talitha Koum (TAHL-uh-thuh koom). An Aramaic phrase meaning "Little girl, I say to you, arise," recorded by Mark 5:41 in the episode of the raising of Jairus's daughter.

Tamar (TAY-mahr). Canaanite woman who bore Perez and Zerah to her father-in-law Judah and became an ancestor of Jesus (Mt 1:3).

Tarshish (TAHR-shish). Phoenician colony in southern Spain, whose name denotes a center of smelting metallic ore (1 Kgs 10:22; Ps 72:10).

Tarsus (TAHR-suhs). Birthplace and early residence of the apostle Paul (Acts 21:39; see also Acts 9:30). It was the capital of the Roman province of Cilicia, and located at the confluence of East and West.

Temple (TEM-puhl). House of worship that was built by Solomon, destroyed and then rebuilt after the Babylonian exile, and finally destroyed in 70 A.D. by the Romans. The Body of Christ is the new temple built at his resurrection. The Church is the spiritual temple made up of living bricks who are the baptized Christians.

Terebinth (TER-uh-binth). A tree, possibly an oak. Trees, especially ancient trees, were highly visible in a desert area and served as landmarks and shrine sites.

Tetrarch (TE-trahrk). Originally, a ruler of the fourth of a country. In Roman times it was employed merely as a title for a ruler over part of a divided kingdom or a prince below the rank of a king (Mt 14:1).

Thaddeus (THAD-ee-uhs). One of the twelve apostles. In certain texts he is called Lebbaeus. He is identified with Judas (Jude), brother of James "the less" (Mt 10:3).

Theophilus (thee-OF-uh-luhs). The personage to whom Luke addressed both his gospel and the Acts of the Apostles (Lk 1:3; Acts 1:1).

Thessalonians (thes-uh-LOH-nee-uhnz). Two of Paul's earliest Letters written to the people of Thessalonica, capital of the province of Macedonia (Acts 17:1-9).

Thomas (TOM-uhs). One of the twelve apostles, surnamed in Greek Didymus, which means "twin" (Jn 11:16; 20:24).

Tiberius Caesar (tai-BIHR-ee-uhs SEE-zuhr). The successor of Augustus Caesar from 14 to 37 A.D. as emperor of the Roman Empire (Lk 3:1).

Timaeus (tai-MEE-uhs). Father of Bartimaeus (Mk 10:46).

Timon (TAI-muhn). One of the seven deacons of the Church at Jerusalem (Acts 6:5).

Timothy (TIM-uh-thee). Son of a Greek father and a Jewish mother, who was converted by Paul, and became one of his most devoted colleagues. Two of the Letters of the New Testament are addressed to Timothy.

Titus (TAI-tuhs). A Greek convert whom Paul calls his true child in the faith. One of the Letters of the New Testament is addressed to Titus.

Tobit (TOH-bit). Ninth of the 13 Historical Books of the Old Testament.

Trachonitis (trak-uh-NAI-tis). A territory to the east of the Jordan. The eastern portion of Bashan (Lk 3:1).

Tubal (TOO-buhl). This is the name of an individual (Gn 10:2; 1 Chr 1:5) and an area. It was probably a city on the Black Sea.

Twelve, The (twelv, thuh). Proper name used by the evangelists for the twelve apostles (Mt 26:14; Mk 14:10; Lk 22:47; Jn 20:24).

Tyre (TAI-uhr). Phoenician city located on the rocky isle facing the eastern coast of the Mediterranean Sea (Mt 11:21f).

Ur (oor). The ancestral city of Abraham. It is unclear whether it is the city of Ur in Babylon or a city in Turkey (Gn 11:28).

Uriah (yoo-RAI-uh). Bathsheba's husband, whose death David arranged (2 Sm 11:14ff). He is mentioned in the genealogy of Jesus (Mt 1:6).

Uzziah (uh-ZAI-uh). Son and successor of Amaziah as King of Judah (2 Kgs 14:21), and an ancestor of Jesus (Mt 1:8f).

Wadi (WAH-di). An often dry river bed (Gn 26:19). The Wadi of Egypt was one of the boundaries of the Davidic kingdom.

Water Gate (WAW-tuhr gayt). A gate restored by Nehemiah on the east of Jerusalem (Neh 8:1ff).

Wisdom (WIS-duhm). Sixth of the 7 Wisdom Books of the Old Testament.

Yahweh (YAH-weh). The proper personal name of the God of Israel, signifying "I am who am" (Ex 3:14f). It is commonly explained in reference to God as the absolute and necessary Being. It may be understood of God as the Source of all created beings. Out of reverence for this name, the term Adonai, "my Lord," was later used as a substitute. The word LORD in the *New American Bible* version represents this traditional usage. The word "Jehovah" arose from a false reading of this name as it is written in the current Hebrew text.

Yahweh-yireh (YAH-weh-YIR-ee). A Hebrew expression meaning "The LORD will see," which Abraham used to name the site where God had stopped him from killing his son Isaac (Gn 22:14).

Zacchaeus (za-KEE-uhs). A tax collector who entertained Jesus (Lk 19:1ff).

Zadok (ZAY-dok). One of the chief priests during the reigns of David (2 Sm 8:17) and Solomon (1 Kgs 1:8, 32ff) and also an ancestor of Jesus (Mt 1:14).

Zarephath (ZAR-uh-fath). An Old Testament town remembered chiefly because Elijah resided there during the latter half of the famine caused by the drought (1 Kgs 17:9ff), which was specifically mentioned by Jesus (Lk 4:26).

Zealot (ZEL-uht). Member of a fanatical Jewish party, strongest from 6 to 70 A.D. It sought to overthrow the Roman authority and establish a Jewish theocracy over the earth. Its members resorted to violence and assassination and provoked the Roman War, which ended with the destruction of Jerusalem in 70 A.D. It seems to have been headed by Judas of Galilee (Acts 5:37). One of Christ's disciples was a member of this party (Lk 6:15; Acts 1:13).

Zebedee (ZEB-uh-dee). Father of the apostles James "the less" and John (Mt 4:21).

Zebulun (ZEB-yuh-luhn). One of the twelve tribes of Israel springing from Zebulun, the son of Jacob and Leah (Gn 30:19f). Christ later carried on his ministry in its regions and thus fulfilled the ancient prophecy of Isaiah (Is 8:23ff; Mt 4:12-16).

Zechariah (zek-uh-RAI-uh). Name of many people, such as: (1) the son and successor of Jeroboam (2 Kgs 14:29); (2) husband of Elizabeth and father of John the Baptist (Lk 1;5ff); (3) the eleventh of the 12 minor prophets of the Old Testament.

Zedekiah (zed-uh-KAI-uh). Son of King Josiah, brother of King Jehoiakim, and uncle of king Jeroiachin, he was the last king of Judah (597-587 B.C.). After being warned by the prophet Jeremiah about the consequences of his policy (Jer 34:2ff), he was captured while fleeing from Jerusalem when it fell in 587 B.C. The Babylonians blinded him and carried him off into exile (2 Kgs 25:6ff).

Zephaniah (zef-uh-NAI-uh). Tenth of the 12 minor prophets in the Old Testament.

Zerah (ZIR-uh). Son of Judah, who is mentioned in the genealogy of Jesus (Mt 1:3).

Zerubbabel (zuh-RUHB-uh-buhl). Grandson of Jehoiachin (1 Chr 3:19), who returned from Babylon and became governor (Hg 1:1), and an ancestor of Jesus (Mt 1:12).

Zion (ZAI-uhn). Central part of the hill on which the temple of Jerusalem was built. This term is often used to designate Jerusalem as a holy city (Pss 2:6; 132:15; Zec 9:9), the Church of God (Heb 12:22), and the heavenly city (Rv 14:1).

Ziph (zif). A city of Judah, probably in the vicinity of Hebron where David spared Sauls life (1 Sm 26:2ff).

APPENDIX 4: INDEX OF BIBLICAL TEXTS

READINGS

RESPONSORIAL PSALMS

RESPONSORIAL CANTICLES

ALLELUIA VERSES AND VERSES BEFORE THE GOSPEL